The New York Public Intellectuals and Beyond

Shofar Supplements in Jewish Studies

The New York Public Intellectuals and Beyond

Exploring Liberal Humanism, Jewish Identity, and the American Protest Tradition

Edited by Ethan Goffman and Daniel Morris

Purdue University Press / West Lafayette, Indiana

Printed in the United States of America.

Library of Congress Cataloging-in-Publication Data

The New York intellectuals and beyond : exploring liberal humanism, Jewish identity, and the American protest tradition / [edited] by Ethan Goffman & Daniel Morris.

    p. cm. — (Shofar supplements in Jewish studies)

    Includes bibliographical references.

    ISBN 978-1-55753-481-1

    1. Jews—New York (State)—New York—Intellectual life—20th century.
2. Intellectuals—New York (State)—New York—Biography. 3. Jews—New York (State)—New York—Identity. 4. Jews—Cultural assimilation—New York (State)—New York. 5. New York (N.Y.)—Intellectual life—20th century. 6. New York (N.Y.)—Ethnic relations. I. Goffman, Ethan, 1961– II. Morris, Daniel, 1962–

    F128.9.J5N46 2008

    305.892'407471—dc22   2008016086

Dedication

To Marianne, Joy, and the Morris children.

Contents

Beyond

Acknowledgments

Special thanks to Susanne Klingenstein for her many useful suggestions and extensive editing help. It is doubtful that this volume would have been completed without her. Thanks also to Morris Dickstein, Ilan Stavans, and John Rodden for their commitment to and help with this project.

The following essays in this volume were originally printed in a special *Shofar* issue on the New York Intellectuals (21, no. 3 [Spring 2003]), some in shorter form:

Nathan Abrams, "'A Profoundly Hegemonic Moment': Demythologizing the Cold War New York Jewish Intellectuals."

Eugene Goodheart, "Jew d'Esprit."

Michael Kimmage, "Lionel Trilling's *The Middle of the Journey* and the Complicated Origins of the Neoconservative Movement."

Susanne Klingenstein, "Town Whores into Warmongers: The Ascent of the Neoconservatives and the Revival of Anti-Jewish Rhetoric in American Public Discourse, 1986–2006." Klingenstein's essay in particular has been greatly expanded for this volume.

Mark Krupnick, "Lionel Trilling and the Deep Places of the Imagination."

Daniel Schwarz, "Eating Kosher Ivy: Jews as Literary Intellectuals."

Ilan Stavans and Morris Dickstein, "Nostalgia and Recognition: Ilan Stavans and Morris Dickstein in Conversation."

Versions of Mark Krupnick's "Jewish Intellectuals and the Deep Places of the Imagination" appeared in *Shofar: An Interdisciplinary Journal of Jewish Studies* (21, no. 3 [2003], pp. 29–47) and in Krupnick's book *Jewish Writing and the Deep Places of the Imagination*, ed. Jean K. Carney and Mark Shechner (Madison: University of Wisconsin Press, 2005).

A version of Mark Shechner's "Mark Krupnick and Lionel Trilling: Anxiety and Influence" appeared in Krupnick's book *Jewish Writing and the Deep Places of the Imagination*, ed. Jean K. Carney and Mark Shechner (Madison: University of Wisconsin Press, 2005).

John Rodden's "Memorial for a Revolutionist: Dwight Macdonald, 'A Critical American'" was originally published in *Society* (44, no. 5 [September, 2007], pp. 51–61).

John Rodden's "Irving Howe: Triple Thinker" was originally published in *Irving Howe and the Critics: Celebrations and Attacks*, ed. John Rodden, pp. 1–3 (Lincoln: University of Nebraska Press, 2005).

Contributors

Matthew Abraham is an assistant professor of writing, rhetoric, and discourse at DePaul University in Chicago. His work has appeared in *Cultural Critique*, the *Journal of the Midwest Modern Language Association*, the *Journal of Advanced Composition, College Composition and Communication, Logos: A Journal of Modern Society and Culture*, and *Postmodern Culture*. He is currently completing a book titled *Controversial Academic Scholarship and the Question of Palestine*. He was the winner of the 2005 Rachel Corrie Courage in the Teaching of Writing Award.

Nathan Abrams is director of film studies at Bangor University. He is author of four books, *Commentary Magazine, 1945-1959: A Journal of Significant Thought and Opinion* (London and Portland, OR: Vallentine Mitchell, 2006), *Containing America: Cultural Production and Consumption in Fifties America*, coedited with Julie Hughes (Birmingham: Birmingham University Press, 2000; London and New York: Continuum, 2006), *Studying Film*, coauthored with Ian Bell and Jan Udris (London: Arnold, 2001), and *Jews and Sex* (Nottingham: Five Leaves Press, 2008). He has just completed a further manuscript examining Norman Podhoretz, *Commentary* magazine, and the rise and fall of the neoconservatives.

Morris Dickstein is distinguished professor of English at the Graduate Center of the City University of New York, where he is also senior fellow of the Center for the Humanities, which he founded in 1993. He teaches courses in English Romantic poetry, modern fiction, film studies, and American cultural history. His books include *Keats and His Poetry* (1971), *Gates of Eden: American Culture in the Sixties* (1977, 1997), and *Double Agent: The Critic and Society* (1992). He has edited *The Revival of Pragmatism* (1998) and contributed a study of postwar fiction to the *Cambridge History of American Literature* (vol. 7, 1999). His most recent books are *Leopards in the Temple: The Transformation of American Fiction, 1945-1970* (Cambridge: Harvard, 2002) and *A Mirror in the Roadway: Literature and the Real World* (Princeton: Princeton University Press, 2005). In the last few years his essays and reviews have appeared in the *New York Times Book Review, Partisan Review*, the *American Scholar, Raritan*, the *Nation, Literary Imagination, Dissent*, and the *Times Literary Supplement* (London). He was a founder and board member (1983-1989) of the National Book Critics Circle, served as vice chair of the New York Council for the Humanities from 1997 to 2001, and was president of the Association of Literary Scholars and Critics in 2006–2007. He was a contributing editor of *Partisan Review* from 1972 to 2003.

Nathan Glazer is a professor of education and sociology, emeritus, at Harvard University and has also taught at the University of California at Berkeley. He was strongly associated with the New York Intellectuals and with the early neo-conservatives in their criticism of the efficacy of government solutions. An early critic of affirmative action, he later grew to recognize the necessity of such programs and the value of multiculturalism. A long-time editor of the *Public Interest,* he has published in *Commentary,* the *New Republic,* and elsewhere. His many books include *The Lonely Crowd* with David Riesman (1950), *Beyond the Melting Pot: The Negroes, Puerto Ricans, Jews, Italians, and Irish of New York City* with Daniel Patrick Moynihan (1963), *We Are All Multiculturalists Now* (1998), and most recently *From a Cause to a Style: Modernist Architecture's Encounter with the American City* (2007).

Ethan Goffman is senior editor for ProQuest's Discovery Guide series and editorial associate for *Sustainability: Science, Practice, and Policy.* He is the author of *Imagining Each Other: Blacks and Jews in Recent Literature* (Albany: State University of New York Press, 2000) and has published in *Grist, E: The Environmental Magazine, Contemporary Literature, Shofar,* the *Indiana Review, Melus, Neue Germanistik, Dissent,* and elsewhere. From 1987 to 1989 he was editorial assistant at *Dissent* magazine. He is designer of the award-winning board game AmuseAmaze. Currently, he is coediting with John Rodden a book of interviews with Irving Howe.

Meredith Goldsmith is an assistant professor of English at Ursinus College. She has published a number of articles on early twentieth-century American writers, including Edith Wharton, Nella Larsen, F. Scott Fitzgerald, and Dorothy West, and coedited *Middlebrow Moderns: Popular U.S. Women Writers of the 1920s* (Boston: Northeastern University Press, 2003). She is writing a book on Edith Wharton's critique of the rise of consumer culture in the 1920s United States.

Eugene Goodheart is Edytha Macy Gross Professor of Humanities Emeritus at Brandeis University. He is the author of many books of literary and cultural criticism and a memoir, *Confessions of a Secular Jew* (The Overlook Press). His most recent book is *Darwinian Misadventures in the Humanities* (Transaction Publishers, 2007). Other books include *The Reign of Ideology* (Columbia University Press) and *The Skeptic Disposition: Deconstruction, Ideology, and Other Matters* (Princeton University Press).

Michael Kimmage is an assistant professor of history at Catholic University. His first book, *The Conservative Turn: Lionel Trilling, Whittaker Chambers, and the*

Lessons of Anti-Stalinism, will be published by Harvard University Press in the spring of 2009.

Susanne Klingenstein is the author of two books on the integration of Jewish literary scholars into American academe: *Jews in the American Academy, 1900–1940: The Dynamics of Intellectual Assimilation* (1991) and *Enlarging America: The Cultural Work of Jewish Literary Scholars, 1930–1990* (1998). She has published numerous articles on Yiddish and Jewish American literature and culture. She is a lecturer in the Harvard-MIT Division of Health Sciences and Technology and cultural correspondent for *Frankfurter Allgemeine Zeitung*. She is currently working on a book about the best contemporary American illustrated children's books from Maurice Sendak to Mo Willems.

Mark Krupnick (1939–2003) was professor of religion and literature in the Divinity School at the University of Chicago, author of *Jewish Writing and the Deep Places of the Imagination, Lionel Trilling and the Fate of Cultural Criticism*, and more than two hundred essays and reviews. He edited the volume of essays *Displacement: Derrida and After*.

Tobe Levin began teaching for the University of Maryland University College European Division in 1979 and is the winner of a Stanley J. Drazek Teaching Excellence Award in 1999 and the UMUC Presidential Award in 2002. She has published more than 100 articles in scholarly and popular journals, edits an electronic book review journal, *Feminist Europa: Review of Books*, and, as translator and author of the afterword, has brought out Fadumo Korn's *Born in the Big Rains: A Memoir of Somalia and Survival* (New York: The Feminist Press, 2006). In 2004 Dr. Levin was an associate at the Five Colleges Women's Studies Research Center at Mt. Holyoke College, and in 2006 scholar-in-residence at Brandeis University. She is currently a nonresident fellow at the W.E.B. Du Bois Institute, Harvard University.

Daniel Morris is professor of English at Purdue University. He is the author of several volumes of criticism and poetry, including *The Poetry of Louise Gluck: A Thematic Introduction* (Columbia: University of Missouri Press, 2006) and *Bryce Passage* (East Rockaway: Marsh Hawk Press, 2004). He is coeditor of *Shofar*.

Peter Novick is professor emeritus of history at the University of Chicago. His best known works are *That Noble Dream: The "Objectivity Question" and the American Historical Profession* (1988) and *The Holocaust in American Life* (1999).

John Rodden has taught at the University of Virginia and the University of Texas at Austin. As author or editor, he has published seventeen books on American, British, and German intellectuals. Among these are *Lionel Trilling and the Critics* (1999), *The Worlds of Irving Howe* (2004), and *Irving Howe and the Critics* (2005).

Ryan Schneider is an assistant professor of English at Purdue University. He has published articles and essays in the journal *Arizona Quarterly* and the edited collections *No More Separate Spheres: A Next Wave American Studies Reader* (Duke University Press) and *Boys Don't Cry? Rethinking Narratives of Masculinity and Emotion in America* (Columbia University Press). His reviews appear in *Modern Language Quarterly, American Literature, Modern Fiction Studies,* and *American Book Review.* His current book project is titled *Feeling Like a Public Intellectual: Affective Poetics and Racial Politics in the Reform Writings of Ralph Waldo Emerson and W.E.B. Du Bois.*

Daniel R. Schwarz is professor of English and Stephen H. Weiss Presidential Fellow at Cornell University, where he has taught since 1968. He has received Cornell's College of Arts and Sciences Russell Award for distinguished teaching. He is the author of *Broadway Boogie Woogie: Damon Runyon and the Making of New York City Culture* (2004) and the widely read *Imagining the Holocaust* (1999). His prior books include *Reconfiguring Modernism: Explorations in the Relationship between Modern Art and Modern Literature* (1997), *Narrative and Representation in Wallace Stevens* (1993), *The Case for a Humanistic Poetics* (1991), *The Transformation of the English Novel, 1890–1930* (1989; revised 1995), *Reading Joyce's Ulysses* (1987), *The Humanistic Heritage: Critical Theories of the English Novel from James to Hillis Miller* (1986), *Conrad: The Later Fiction* (1982), *Conrad: "Almayer's Folly" through "Under Western Eyes"* (1980), and *Disraeli's Fiction* (1979). He has edited "The Dead" (1994) and "The Secret Sharer" (1997) in the Bedford Case Studies in Contemporary Criticism Series and is coeditor of *Narrative and Culture* (1994). He has directed nine NEH seminars and has lectured widely in the United States and abroad.

Mark Shechner is professor of English at the University of Buffalo. He is author of *Up Society's Ass Copper: Rereading Philip Roth* and coeditor with Jean Carney of *Jewish Writing and the Deep Places of the Imagination: The Selected Essays of Mark Krupnick.*

Ilan Stavans is Lewis-Sebring Professor in Latin American and Latino Culture and Five College–Fortieth Anniversary Professor at Amherst College. His books include *The Hispanic Condition* (1995), *On Borrowed Words* (2001), *Spanglish* (2003), *Dictionary Days* (2005), *The Disappearance* (2006), *Love and Language* (2007), and *Resurrecting Hebrew* (2008). He has edited *The Oxford Book of Jewish Stories* (1998), *The Poetry of Pablo Neruda* (2004), *Isaac Bashevis Singer: Collected Stories* (3 vols., 2004), *The Schocken Book of Sephardic Literature* (2005), and *Cesar Chavez: An Organizer's Tale* (2008). His story "Morirse está en hebreo" was made into the award-winning movie *My Mexican Shivah* (2007), produced by John Sayles. Stavans has received numerous awards, among them a Guggenheim Fellowship, the National Jewish Book Award, the Latino Book Award, Chile's

Presidential Medal, and the Rubén Darío Distinction. His work has been translated into a dozen languages.

Alan Wolfe is professor of political science and director of the Boisi Center for
Religion and American Public Life at Boston College. His most recent books include *Does American Democracy Still Work?* (Yale University Press, 2006), *Return
to Greatness: How America Lost Its Sense of Purpose and What It Needs to Do to
Recover It* (Princeton University Press, 2005), and *The Transformation of American Religion: How We Actually Live Our Faith* (Free Press, 2003). He is the author
or editor of more than ten other books, including *One Nation, After All* (1998)
and *Moral Freedom: The Search for Virtue in a World of Choice* (2001), both of
which were selected as *New York Times* Notable Books of the Year.

Wolfe currently chairs an American Political Science Association task
force on Religion and Democracy in the United States. He serves on the advisory
boards of Humanity in Action and the Future of American Democracy Foundation and on the president's advisory board of the Massachusetts Foundation for
the Humanities. He is also a senior fellow with the World Policy Institute at the
New School University in New York. In the fall of 2004, Professor Wolfe was the
George H.W. Bush Fellow at the American Academy in Berlin.

A contributing editor of the *New Republic*, the *Wilson Quarterly*, *Common-
wealth Magazine*, and *In Character*, Professor Wolfe writes often for those publications as well as for *Commonweal*, the *New York Times, Harper's*, the *Atlantic
Monthly*, the *Washington Post*, and other magazines and newspapers. He served
as an advisor to President Clinton in preparation for his 1995 State of the Union
address and has lectured widely at American and European universities.

Professor Wolfe has been the recipient of grants from the Russell Sage
Foundation, the Templeton Foundation, the Smith Richardson Foundation, the
Carnegie Corporation of New York, and the Lilly Endowment. He has twice conducted programs under the auspices of the U.S. State Department that bring Muslim scholars to the United States to learn about separation of church and state.

Introduction

In 1992, with dictatorships of the left and right crumbling worldwide, Francis Fukuyama suggested the end of history as it had been known. In a unipolar world, with no countervailing ideology, liberal democracy would continue its spread. Contradicting the pessimism derived from hot and cold wars earlier in the century, and contradicting relativist views of history, Fukuyama claimed that "there is a fundamental process at work that dictates a common evolutionary pattern for *all* human societies—in short, something like a Universal History of mankind in the direction of liberal democracy."[1] As the Berlin Wall fell, followed quickly by apartheid, the great debates among public intellectuals to define the best form of human society seemed, to some, to be over.

Five years earlier, Russell Jacoby had declared that the last public intellectuals were aging. He meant by that a generation of "writers and thinkers who address a general and educated audience,"[2] including such notables as Lionel Trilling, Irving Howe, and Irving Kristol. This small group, self-described as "the New York Intellectuals," was able to bridge the gap between small publications, academia, and, to an extent, popular magazines. Strangely, while launching the term *public intellectuals* into wider use, *The Last Intellectuals* also declared their death through a retreat into academia and technical prose, leaving an emptiness in the public sphere. Following from Jacoby, the term *public intellectual*, by its nature far-reaching, is often used to refer to the New York Intellectuals. This may be due to the priority of naming—those who coin a term have some proprietary rights—and to the construction of meaning. More generally, the term refers to those who disseminate specialist ideas to a wider public, and the New York Intellectuals and those who followed in their wake certainly did this. In a broader sense, because what distinguishes human beings from other animals is primarily intellect, it might be said—as it was by Antonio Gramsci—that all of us are intellectuals, and because our species is a social one, it might be said that all of us are public. Indeed, the United States is replete with eddies and hidden currents of amateur intellectualism, of people constructing their belief systems from bits of flotsam here and there, most commonly tied to various versions of individualism, liberty, and American nationalism. Yet the United States has also been called an anti-intellectual nation, and those whose primary life activity is sustained and systematic reading of books—and especially of books in the "great tradition" of philosophy and literature derived from Europe—are considered best confined and tamed in our university system. There they might teach youth but have little to do with the actual workings of society; they may be public but only in a rarified setting where their ideas have little immediate impact.

In the years since Jacoby wrote, the gap in the public sphere seems to have grown larger. The university is now an isolated outpost, often under siege, whereas the major media are dominated by pundits mouthing simplistic solutions from opposite sides of an ideological divide. Any idea of a shared search for truth in the public sphere has been replaced by public-relations driven attempts to make one side look better and to destroy the other. The United States, meanwhile, finds itself discredited, isolated, no longer at the cutting edge of an international movement toward liberal democracy. What has gone wrong? Can a new generation—empowered by the Internet—restore the viability of the public intellectual? What does the journey of the New York Intellectuals tell us about the task facing today's public intellectual?

I.

Perhaps the greatest forebear of the public intellectual is Socrates, who acted as a gadfly, a social critic eventually executed for corrupting youth. Simultaneously, he upheld the individual's duty to society, although not as a blind follower of tradition but as an improver, an idealist seeking social perfection. Socrates embodies what have often been considered opposite poles: the public intellectual as simultaneously organic and oppositional. And the United States has its own great tradition of those who might be called public intellectuals, who have spoken truth to power in an attempt to improve society, to push America toward its stated ideals, from emancipationists and suffragettes to civil rights era leaders to today's proponents of cultural diversity.

The nineteenth-century roots of public intellectual discourse are powerful, as Ryan Schneider's essay in this collection shows. This tradition would fuse with European rationalism and Jewish scholarship to create the voice of the New York Intellectuals. Schneider shows how Ralph Waldo Emerson early began theorizing about various versions of the public intellectual, isolated from American society and intrinsically connected to the ideal of individualism, who fuses the ideals of art and intellect. Schneider suggests an ethical grounding in the Jewish tradition, one similar to the mission implicit in the work of African American orator-intellectuals who, while guiding their people toward freedom, also helped America grapple with the greatest contradiction to its professed ideals. However, Schneider argues, the Christian "universal controlling ideology" behind such activist-thinkers as Frances E.W. Harper contrasts with the quotidian ideals behind Jewish philosophy. If many Jewish public intellectuals broke with their community of origin for the "controlling ideology" of communism, so did W.E.B. Du Bois, perhaps the greatest of black public intellectuals. While illuminating a tension between ethnic status and universal ideology, Schneider's essay shows that practical and technical issues may not be enough for the public intellectual, that the drive for a unifying ideology is compelling.

In creative tension with the ideal of the public intellectual as a learned specialist is the ideal of the outsider. In the United States, this has long been provided by the African American presence, whereas beginning in the twentieth century Jewish intellectuals imported a new conception of exile, one tied to European rationalism as well as the quest for social justice. Yet the New York Intellectuals were themselves a small, exclusive group not necessarily open to outsiders. Meredith Goldsmith interrogates and extends the term *public intellectual*. Using Anzia Yezierska as her exemplar and employing Gramsci's idea of the organic intellectual, Goldsmith argues that it is possible to move from the public sphere into the intellectual sphere rather than the reverse, as is the more common concept of the public intellectual. Indeed, as a woman denied entry into the small coterie of Jewish intellectuals, Yezierska had no other available route to a cultural forum than as a popular author. Her primary means of discussing such issues as class and identity, as Goldsmith points out, could not have been the essay but had to be her fictional and semiautobiographical writing. And although she was appreciative of academic and modernist traditions, Yezierska's organic roots allowed her to speak for the working class and for ethnic enclaves more powerfully than did the rarified voice of the traditional public intellectual.

The New York school, an almost entirely Jewish group who achieved great influence in American society, certainly drew upon protest and ethnic traditions, although Europe was their primal source. Starting from various schools of communism and socialism, from the 1930s to the 1980s the New York Intellectuals embarked on a generally rightward course toward liberalism and neoconservatism. Although Jewish intellectuals today remain spread out along the spectrum, the center remains liberal, with a strong current of support for Israel. Simultaneous with their political shift, American Jews have also moved from a position of quietude regarding their Jewish status toward a stronger acknowledgement of their historic and religious background.

Alongside their political emphasis, the New York Intellectuals early in their history immersed themselves in the seemingly antithetical project of championing modernist literary forms that thrive upon ambiguity, irony, and experimentation. The political and aesthetic realms existed uneasily side-by-side in the same intellectual sphere. Why did these schools of thought, socialism and modernism, appeal so strongly to a group of second-generation Jewish immigrants? In a 1969 essay, Irving Howe characterizes the New York Intellectuals as "the first group of Jewish writers to come out of the immigrant milieu who did not define themselves through a relationship, nostalgic or hostile, to memories of Jewishness."[3] The appeal of socialism is obvious for a people rejecting narrow versions of its heritage and attempting to assimilate into a new land. Socialism offered a form of universal society and an ideology replacing religion. For those isolated from a mainstream society that they aspired to join, it offered a universal humanism that would wipe clean the past.

Modernism, strangely enough, offered benefits parallel to socialism for a diasporic people integrating into a multicultural environment (although the word *multicultural* had not yet come into use, and American society certainly celebrated mainstream European culture). Although one version of modernism— that of T.S. Eliot and Ezra Pound—is both elitist and antisemitic, modernism is also culturally eclectic and individualist, traits fitting the agenda of a people reconstructing their identity in a new world. If all public intellectuals have had strong ideas about the role of the arts in society, and if socialism had its narrow notions of art in direct service to political ideals, in the New York Intellectuals we see a strange ambivalence about the social role of art, including literature. Art is to be created by highly individual personalities subject to aesthetic imperatives unattached to political agendas. Yet art is to be analyzed within a social framework as a product of its time.

Modernism, however, while artistically radical, is not by its nature political radicalism, and many of its key figures were conservative. Modernism's complexity may have served as a medium in the journey of Jewish public intellectuals away from left-wing ideology. Surely the greatest force in this journey was the bloody failure of most (ostensibly) communist regimes. Eugene Goodheart portrays the "religious intensity" of the commitment to communism, and the brutal shock of its being exposed as part of "a corrupt and tyrannical regime, masking its cruelty with the language of justice, equality, and comradeship." With belief in the religion of Judaism weakened and its replacement, communism as a secular religion, dead, what is left? This has many answers. For Goodheart what remains is an unfixed identity, a multitude of choices, a kind of ideological diaspora that, in a way, represents a new freedom: "I became a liberal resistant to the extremes of left and right, suspicious of all dogmatisms and responsive to what was of value (or what I took to be of value) in all the positions of the political spectrum."

If the failure of communism repelled Jewish intellectuals, conversely their acceptance by, and success within, American society pulled them toward acceptance of a liberal, democratic, individualistic, and at times capitalist vision. The university has been a primary site for this integration of Jews in American society. Throughout the 1930s and 1940s, economic and political conditions, the small size of the university system, and the limited number of professorships granted to Jews, had kept the New York Intellectuals in a kind of semiprofessional status, underpaid and often writing as a sideline, a situation conducive to "the intellectual as antispecialist, or as a writer whose speciality was the lack of a speciality: the writer as dilettante-connoisseur."[4] Despite poverty and risk, the public intellectual also possessed the freedom of those with little to lose and an outsider's perspective conducive to social criticism. This changed with the burgeoning university system, which by offering affluence, job security, benefits, and freedom to think, lecture, and write, created an actuality as comfortable as that which socialism had promised only in theory.

Until at least the 1960s, the university was a welcoming place only for Jews who submerged their Jewishness. Lionel Trilling, perhaps the personification of the liberal public intellectual, was a key figure in the Jewish transition from outsiderhood to full participation in American intellectual life. The first Jewish professor of English at Columbia University, Trilling defined an academic liberalism in which enlightenment rationalism trumps all other forms of discourse. Yet this great forefather, this consummate intellectual, was in many ways ambivalent about his achievement. The shame behind this ambivalence is even more evident in Daniel Schwarz's description of Jewish repression in 1950s America, particularly regarding the Holocaust: "Jewish silence during and after the war mirrored the much more striking silence, ineffectuality, and complicity of the American community that . . . chose to repress how they were helpless onlookers." However great Jewish success in the university, the suppression of religious, cultural, and historical expression made for an emotional and intellectual incompleteness.

Mark Krupnick believes that Trilling's ambivalence permeates the entire New York intellectual atmosphere, fathers and sons (as well as a few mothers and daughters). To Krupnick, the New York Intellectuals were unable to transcend a thin, overly politicized sensibility to achieve a dynamic integration of intellect and imagination. This failure, characterized by a distancing of personal life, is largely due to an "absorption in ideological politics [that] may lead an intellectual away from the intimate self-knowledge . . . which is necessary for plumbing the deep parts of imagination." Michael Kimmage further develops this theme, presenting Trilling's *The Middle of the Journey* as driven by a revulsion of the extreme left and an inability to embrace conservatism. What remains is a kind of neverland, a less optimistic version of what for Goodheart may be undefined but is nevertheless replete with possibility. For Kimmage, Trilling's abhorrence of radicalism foreshadows the coming of the neoconservatives because its vague liberalism leaves a gap in beliefs waiting to be filled: "perhaps the answer to the dilemma of heritage and country stood right before the eyes of American Jews; perhaps it was America itself." The Jewishness missing in *The Middle of the Journey* is another element awaiting restoration.

Between Trilling and neoconservatism, in the crucial middle period of their development, the New York Intellectuals defined themselves as anticommunist liberals. The *Partisan Review* moved toward what may now be considered a classical American liberalism, anticommunist but still believing that government can effectively initiate social change. Calling for a new evaluation of the self-mythologizing New York Intellectuals, Nathan Abrams argues that many of them moved from being what Gramsci terms organic intellectuals, born of a community and representing it, to traditional intellectuals, pretending to objectivity but actually speaking for the dominant ideology. Abrams criticizes those who accepted "a range of financial inducements and rewards" provided through

CIA-funded front groups to become ideological tools in the cold war, a group associated with *Partisan Review* and later with *Commentary*. And although Jewish intellectuals were already moving toward an anticommunist liberalism, one cannot discount the influence of money and affluence—particularly over the long run, as small, subtle accommodations add up—in molding ideological beliefs. Beyond the relatively minor influence of CIA funding, one could extend Abrams's analysis to include other sources of money right up to the current day.

Partisan Review is one of only a few magazines that have served as primary organs of Jewish intellectual life, reflecting the varying directions in which it is has traveled. As other journals moved rightward, Irving Howe and the group clustered around *Dissent* magazine maintained their belief in democratic socialism. John Rodden captures Howe's double-edged legacy as a triple thinker, his steadfastness, which his supporters take as a manifestation of strong character and his critics as a foolish inability to adapt to changing social and intellectual currents. Howe did change early in his career from a Trotskyite believing that Stalin had subverted essentially noble communist ideals to a skeptic regarding the roots of the Bolshevik revolution. Yet he stopped there, maintaining to the end a fidelity to the term *socialism*. He also became a more realistic political thinker (his detractors on the left might say an apologist for the powers that be), one who consistently opposed extremism. His attacks on the New Left in the 1960s reflected a fear that the left was being hijacked once again, as it had been by the communist rhetoric of his youth. In his triple refusal to succumb to radicalism, the trends and jargon of the university, and neoconservatism, Howe is best remembered, as Rodden phrases it, as "a model of the humanist intellectual."

Dwight Macdonald was another great iconoclast of the New York Intellectuals. He stood out among them as a non-Jew, a Yale-educated member of America's traditional elite who early found his way to communism as an answer to the world's injustices. Like Howe he became a follower of Leon Trotsky in reaction to the savagery of Soviet-style communism. Yet unlike Howe, Macdonald never felt comfortable with mainstream American liberalism. If Howe used his socialism as a tool to nudge post–New-Deal Democrats toward a better society, Macdonald remained uncomfortable with all political camps. Unwilling to endorse a system he considered compromised, Macdonald continued fighting for an unrealized ideal. In a way, he is an extreme example of the American individualist, for instance in the person of Henry David Thoreau, rebelling against a corrupt society. As Rodden argues, Macdonald was far more effective and influential as a naysayer than as a builder of workable alternatives, fulfilling a traditional role of the public intellectual as a check on social complacency, "an aristocratic radical charged with exposing the ersatz and the overhyped."

In the 1960s *Commentary* magazine, under the stewardship of Norman Podhoretz, briefly flirted with New Left positions; however, Podhoretz and *Commentary* soon moved toward a position celebrating success in the American milieu and even exhorting the virtues of capitalism. So were born the neoconservatives who, while decrying big government and finding unacknowledged strength in the free market, also strongly supported Israel. Their style is closer to Howe's political engagement and, perhaps even more so, to Macdonald's combative iconoclasm than to Trilling's cautious humanism. The neoconservatives, however, employed their rhetoric not as naysayers but as yea-sayers to the possibilities of America, possibilities they saw as undercut by radical dissent.

A moment had arrived when Jews could be both comfortably American and Jewish. As Susanne Klingenstein puts it, their "new rhetorical style—combative, direct, idea-focused . . . has been attributed to their roots in the Old Left." Eventually the ascendance of the neoconservatives would give intellectual moorings to the Reagan administration. In describing this period, Klingenstein focuses on the reaction of older conservatives who, after years out of power, "felt beleaguered by the Jews and ousted from their rightful place," once a clearly conservative president was finally in office. Their diatribes reenact "immigrant history as observed by an old-stock American who in the 1910s would have perceived the arriving Jews as 'herds' of Yiddish-speaking 'refugees' fleeing from the 'offensives' of mob violence in tsarist Russia."

Neoconservatism, however, has never been espoused by more than a small portion of Jewish Americans, including public intellectuals. While strung out along the political spectrum, Jewish Americans currently tend toward a middle-of-the-road liberalism. Support for Israel may be the major issue that remains to unite Jewish intellectuals. Even this support, however, is highly qualified in some circles, for instance in *Tikkun*, a magazine that was begun in opposition to *Commentary*'s increasing conservatism and that considers criticism of Israel's excesses necessary for the future of the Jewish state.

So where do Jewish intellectuals stand today? Mark Schechner maps out one strand of influence, from Lionel Trilling to Mark Krupnick to himself, an intellectual lineage of argumentation, of wrestling with one's heritage under the overarching liberalism of a conception of American society that will be open, inclusive of Jews and others. The forum that concludes the first section solidifies this impression; contemporary Jewish intellectuals stand largely as moderate, secular liberals not too different from those of the 1950s, albeit more frank about their Jewish past. Despite the noise of the neoconservatives, most Jewish intellectuals have resisted that change of direction. Of course the forum is far from a representative sample, yet it does highlight some central points as to where public intellectuals have been and where they are now. All agree—to varying extents—that the Jewish intellectuals were more influential within limited intellectual circles than in mainstream society; that from a position of relative powerlessness they spoke for rationalism and for justice; that they moved from a position of universalism to one of increasing ethnic identification; that they depended upon a relatively small core group that over time has attenuated and lost its coherence. They also seem united in their belief that the public intellectuals as a group are not dead but more diverse than ever and that great challenges for our public intellectual discourse lie ahead. Many of these challenges lie in the areas of globalism, economic inequality, and international strife. To grapple with them requires an awareness of the multitude of cultures and societies that overlap in a tension at times bountifully creative, at times brutally destructive.

II.

Any picture of intellectual life from the 1970s to today would be incomplete without mention of another key movement: multiculturalism. Daniel Schwarz upholds the way ethnic studies has led to new freedom of expression for Jewish intellectuals. Whereas Jewish professors helped open the door to previously excluded groups, the relationship was mutually beneficial; "it is curious how—perhaps as the social price for acceptance—Jewish scholars in English departments only pushed for Jewish studies after the establishment of other ethnic and minority studies." The repressed may have returned, but Jewish studies remains poised in a liminal position, maintaining a strong attachment to enlightenment rationalism and often emotionally distant from most of the multicultural movement.

The term *multiculturalism*, however, means different things to different people, from an updated version of the melting pot that acknowledges the contribution of many peoples while leaving America centered largely in Anglo-Saxon traditions, to a complete upsetting of cultural tradition, especially of the Western classics. Although conservative critics fear that multiculturalism leads to a segregated, tribalist society, in practice this is rarely the case. Most proponents of multiculturalism acknowledge a central role for democracy, for an engagement of multiple perspectives. So, too, is democracy sanctioned by a movement related to, yet strangely divergent from, multiculturalism: globalism. For multiculturalists, democracy tends to mean the right of all groups to make their voices heard; globalists, at least those who favor the current version of globalization, emphasize that free societies, and free markets, need democracy. However, the status and even the basic definition of globalism remain undetermined as activist protests, along with deep concerns about unfettered economic liberalization, spur revised thinking about the relationship between capitalism and free society.

The evolving relationship between older public intellectual approaches in an atmosphere of interlocking globalism and multiculturalism underlies the conversation between Morris Dickstein and Ilan Stavans. The common element may be diaspora. Dickstein is part of an older wave of immigrants moving into an America that defined itself by assimilation, then went on to develop a nostalgia for the old language, the old streets: "Even if the *shtetl* is a mythical creation, it is a creation I think that's a psychological necessity." In an America more accepting of multiculturalism, Stavans feels less nostalgia. Still, his complicated Jewish-Mexico-United States configuration occurs in a country—and a world—of uncertain definition. Comparing their experience of exile and reinstatement in a new land to that of more recent immigrants, Stavans and Dickstein range over issues of cultural displacement and reinvention, illustrating how "a person becomes a hybrid of identities and a hybrid of languages." Assimilation has lost its all-consuming power; immigrants are now assumed to change the society they are changed by. Although growing up Stavans had thought of American Jews as at "the center of culture, they knew who they were," he comes to understand "a different side of what American Jews are all about—fragmented, shrieking at the same time about different things, and fighting about religion and about culture." Social stability is revealed as illusory in a world of eternal change and displacement.

American identity has also been complex, marked by often-conflicting identities. In this discourse the African American role has always been central. My own contribution builds upon the African American protest tradition described by Ryan Schneider to show that recent attempts to place black intellectuals as heirs of the Jewish tradition are somewhat misplaced, that these intellectuals build upon their own strong traditions. After a period of consolidation and recognition in the 1990s, the upheaval of the new century seems to leave African American intellectuals somewhat forgotten. However, in a world newly riven with fundamental nationalist and religious divisions, African American intellectuals have much to contribute; their historical experience and discourse provide a strong basis for calls for unity and justice.

Multiculturalism, identity politics, feminism, and the role of the public intellectual as activist are all joined in Tobe Levin's contribution. If Francis E.W. Harper, W.E.B. Du Bois, and Anzia Yezierska spoke from the margins and were largely ignored among mainstream intellectuals until the culture wars of the late twentieth century, beginning in the 1960s Alice Walker took up the struggle of her foremothers (unacknowledged by the larger intellectual community as they were at that time). In sharp contrast to the New York Intellectuals, Walker begins from the autobiographical and works outward. The overlapping categories of race and gender begin her discourse.

Elfriede Jelinek, too, works from the personal outward; in her (implicitly hyphenated) position as a German Jew, she simultaneously represents the center of enlightenment tradition and the outsider. Levin explains how the Austrian experience with fascism continues to resonate in Jelinek's brutal sexual imagery, wherein hatred is internalized so that the victim inflicts violence on her own body. Centuries and millennia of Jew-hatred and misogyny flow into each other in the image of self-mutilation. In Levin's words, referring to recent scholarship on the feminization of Jews, "the violence needed to, literally, keep women in their place experiences periodic overflow onto groups that only seem to include men." The demeaning imagery of feminization is easily extended onto other marginalized people, as Said has shown regarding the orient. African American males, interestingly, may be simultaneously hypermasculinized and feminized in regard to actual power. As with Yezierska, Jelinek's protagonists enact society's sexual conflicts in their personal struggles, although in a more sexually explicit way that employs brooding interiorization. Indeed, in celebrating moments of triumph, Yezierska's early stories are more akin to Walker than to Jelinek.

By stark contrast with the New York Intellectuals, then, Jelinek and Walker start from a very personal identity and work outward to a strong political stance, one that resembles the nineteenth-century public activist-orator, albeit in a global context. Although economic status is of great concern to such activist intellectuals, it is not the single center of analysis. What both New York and activist intellectuals do have in common is a telling of "truth to power" (that is, writing and speaking uncomfortable facts to the privileged, who may be surrounded by sycophants or otherwise oblivious), a brave political stance that often advocates for the disenfranchised.

From a politically engaged perspective, the work of Jelinek and Walker is useful in pointing to the commonalities of certain marginalized groups, in rallying the oppressed. This analysis, though, risks reductionism. The danger is of succumbing to brittle ideology, subsuming all conflicts to a simplistic rubric, losing subtlety and complexity. Indeed, narratives of oppression often contradict each other. In writing about female genital mutilation (FGM), Walker runs smack into this phenomenon, patriarchal oppression on the one side, postcolonial oppression on the other. What to do when people who have long been oppressed themselves have deeply ingrained traditions that (at least from a modern, Western perspective) oppress women? Levin shows how badly Walker has been hurt by criticism from African intellectuals and asks, "is multiculturalism good for women? Cultural relativism? In the case of Walker as an activist against FGM, clearly not." The reaction turns toward a universal human rights, an internationalism that would likely please many of the original New York Intellectuals, although the context would have been strange to them.

In one of today's central arenas for public intellectual discourse, it is all too easy to reduce complexity to a simple narrative of the oppressed against the oppressors. Are the long-oppressed Jews struggling once again for their survival against a bloodthirsty enemy that wants them eradicated? Are the oppressed Palestinians victims of the Zionist imperialist aggressors? Identity politics has its dangers. These simplistic narratives seem almost like Plato's ideal forms, prehuman tales of good versus evil tantalizingly easy to accept uncritically.

Identity politics, the politics of oppression, is central then, in horrific form, in the Israeli-Palestinian conflict where one displaced people creates another. Questions of exile and identity clash in a paradoxical conflict; the Palestinians fight against the Jewish presence that brought into being their existence as a people separate from the larger Arab polity. Matthew Abraham's "Simply Said: Edward Said and the New York Intellectual Tradition" raises vexing questions about a man who was in many ways a prototypical public intellectual while standing in bold opposition to the vast majority of Jewish American intellectuals. In a New York far more diasporic to him than to the original New York Intellectuals, Said echoed Irving Howe, blending literary and high European cultural studies and oppositional politics. Like earlier Jewish intellectuals, his diasporic status spurred a search for social justice: "Recognizing the connections between the Palestinian struggle and the liberatory struggles of other oppressed peoples (the Vietnamese and African Americans) Said began to lay the theoretical ground for an expansive study of how the Western culture represents and subjugates difference through the prism of culture." Said, then, is a kind of ironic mirror image of the New York Intellectuals. His existence raises questions about the role of ideology—a necessary yet compromising element—in public intellectual life.

Reading Abraham's article, it is easy to dismiss his claim that Said "enacts a brand of public intellectualism that recaptures the spirit of speaking the untrammeled truth to power." As a passionate spokesman for the Palestinian people, Said seems to have compromised his role as a speaker of the "untrammeled truth" (if one believes that such a thing as the untrammeled truth is available to human beings). This critique, however, is easily turned upon numerous Jewish intellectuals whose neutrality is also compromised in their role as spokespeople for Israel. In promulgating his Just War theory, then, Michael Walzer can be accused of twisting his arguments to conform to his feelings for Israel. The process is a painful one in which a desperate search for moral truth collides with a desperate loyalty toward a damaged people. The wounds of Palestinians and Israelis, even more than those of black and white Americans, are continuously reopened, rather like Prometheus, whose liver was destined to be ripped from his body time and again. Surely one of the great tasks for the public intellectuals of the twenty-first century is to find ways to mitigate the recurring crises caused by this painful gap in understanding that, through the multiplying power of horrendous weapons and terrorist tactics, threatens a widening swath of destruction.

Ethan Goffman
Rockville, Maryland
August 2007

Notes

1. Francis Fukuyama, *The End of History and the Last Man* (1992; repr., New York: Perennial, 2002), p. 48.
2. Russell Jacoby, *The Last Intellectuals: American Culture in the Age of Academe* (New York: Basic Books, 1987), p. 5.
3. Irving Howe, "The New York Intellectuals," in *Selected Writings, 1950–1990*, pp. 240–280 (San Diego: Harcourt, Brace, Jovanovich, 1969), p. 241.
4. Howe, p. 262.

A Note on Organization

The book is organized into two sections. The first, "The New York Intellectuals," is a reflection upon, and a reconsideration of, many of the core Jewish public intellectuals from the 1920s through the 1950s. Written by intellectuals involved with this group, their students, and major scholars of the New York Intellectuals, this section also includes some discussion of their direct influences.

The far more sprawling second section, "Beyond," includes discussions of thinkers and writers who may be said to have prefigured the New York Intellectuals and those who fell outside the core group, as well as present-day public intellectuals. In some ways these all may be considered outliers or peripheral figures, differing in philosophy; racial, ethnic, and/or national heritage; and sex. Like the core New York Intellectuals, these figures are notable for fulfilling the public intellectual mission of bringing the clash of ideas into the wider public sphere, of in some way mixing academic thought with activism. All are understood better in light of the influence and achievements of the New York Intellectuals.

The order in which the essays are discussed in the introduction is different from their placement in the book. The introduction is largely chronological and, to a lesser extent topical, in organization, lacking the bifurcated structure of the larger volume.

The New York Intellectuals

"A Profoundly Hegemonic Moment"

Demythologizing the Cold War
New York Jewish Intellectuals

Nathan Abrams

Introduction

Historians of intellectual life in twentieth-century America have largely been content to write within the constraints imposed by the New York Jewish intellectuals' memories of their own lives. In recent decades, most notably the 1980s, autobiographies and memoirs proliferated, forming what Richard King called a "flood," as those Jewish intellectuals who came to prominence during the forties and fifties began to recollect their lives.[1] These texts constructed and reconstructed their histories in a form of "discursive self-fashioning."[2] As Morris Dickstein pointed out, "the early New York intellectuals have written so much about themselves"[3] that these memories have deeply inscribed the writing of twentieth-century U.S. intellectual history. This inscription has been so profound that historians of this era are often prisoners of their very subjects' constructed histories. Richard King observed how "most people who write about them are still working with the terms of political, literary and cultural discourse that the New Yorkers themselves have laid down."[4] Indeed, as Norman F. Cantor has written, "The *Partisan Review* group and their affiliates—'the New York Intellectuals' as they are now called—have developed their own mythology."[5] This mythology has grown to such an extent that it must be reevaluated.

Although there has been much recent discussion of Richard Posner's book *Public Intellectuals: A Study of Decline*, surprisingly the historiography of the New York Intellectuals has never been extensively subjected to a theoretical analysis

17

utilizing different models of the intellectual.[6] I will attempt here to reevaluate the changing function of the New York Intellectuals as public intellectuals beginning in the 1930s, using the work of, in particular, Antonio Gramsci and Michel Foucault, and paying specific attention to the 1950s and the cultural cold war.

The New York Jewish community of intellectuals was broad, embracing writers, academics, professionals, journalists, poets, artists, critics, politicians, and so on. They were intellectuals in the expansive sense that Antonio Gramsci suggests goes beyond the "traditional and vulgarised type of intellectual" such as "the man of letters, the philosopher, the artist" to include every individual engaged in "some form of intellectual activity" or, as Edward Said has put it, "everyone who works in any field connected either with the production or distribution of knowledge."[7] They are "public intellectuals" in the sense that Russell Jacoby described: "writers and thinkers who address a general and educated audience. Obviously, this excludes intellectuals whose works are too technical or difficult to engage a public."[8]

Organic Intellectuals

The Italian Marxist philosopher Antonio Gramsci observed that every community produces its own intellectuals, characterizing them as "organic intellectuals."[9] According to Gramsci, in a process that, unfortunately, he did not fully describe, each community spontaneously produces a layer of individuals who perform the function of intellectuals in that society. It is the task of these organic intellectuals to raise the self-awareness of their own social group. Furthermore, as Said has put it, they "are actively involved in society, that is, they constantly struggle to change minds."[10] During the 1920s and 1930s in America, precisely this type of organic intellectual began to emerge out of the Jewish community. Rejecting the orthodoxy and observance of their parents and exploiting the new spaces opened up to them, these intellectuals sought to accommodate themselves within the mainstream of American culture. Many of them had attended American public schools as youngsters, confronted with what John Murray Cuddihy called a "civilizing" process aimed at transforming them into Americans.[11] This process of Americanization began to overcome their organic Jewishness and communal attachments. Allied to this Americanizing impulse was the powerful appeal of secular American culture. Russell Jacoby observed how poverty and distance from the ascendant culture produced, in many cases, "an identification, and overidentification" with its values. Jewish intellectuals, many of whom spoke Yiddish as their first language, "fell in love" with English and American literature.[12] Arthur Miller spoke for many when he wrote, "in my most private reveries I was no sallow Talmud reader but Frank Merriwell or Tom Swift."[13] This, in turn, was undoubtedly strengthened by its promise of the full active participation of Jews as *citizens* in society rather than as the "mere parasites" they had been considered in the Old World.[14] One Jewish intellectual, Alfred Kazin, expressed this feeling of opportunity: "Never before had so numerous a mass of Jews been free citizens of the country in which they lived, and so close to the national life."[15] Young Jewish intellectuals, therefore, sought to take advantage of this new and unprecedented freedom that America seemed to promise.

As they sought to move into the American mainstream, however, many young Jewish intellectuals found that antisemitism blocked their path. Antisemitism had long existed in the United States, but it greatly increased during the 1920s and 1930s, continuing into World War II.[16] Due to an increasing perception of a "Jewish problem," the major Ivy League schools introduced quota systems designed to bar Jews. This had a direct effect on the second generation of organic intellectuals, most of whom, as a consequence, went to City College, New York. The answer to antisemitism for many Jews who wanted to move into the American mainstream during the 1930s lay outside of their communities of origin. They had learned that their Jewishness restricted their opportunities and that their communities could not provide outlets for their creative impulses. Instead, they began to look outside the Jewish communities and found solutions within those communities that stressed universalism rather than ethnic particularism. In their search for "place," young Jewish intellectuals overtly rejected particularistic ethnic characteristics and embraced the new communities of cosmopolitanism and the universalism promised by Marxism and its variant forms. Marxism, wrote Paul R. Gorman, "offered a needed middle ground between the influences of the immigrant neighborhood and the national mainstream."[17] Not only did it explain the roots of the economic system that had destroyed their aspirations, but it was also perceived to be the solution to the problem of "homelessness" or "alienation" for which Jews were considered to be the central symbol. This led to a marked shift away from the Jewish community on the part of many intellectuals, even if milder forms of radicalism had been a typical social strain among East European Jews. Where many had contributed to the overtly Jewish *Menorah Journal*, they now wrote for Marxist organs. Irving Howe recalled how many young Jews arrived at articulateness "at a moment when there was a strong drive to both break out of the ghetto and leave the bonds of Jewishness entirely." These young Jews wanted to "declare themselves citizens of the world and, if that succeeded, might then become writers of this country."[18] At this point, then, these young intellectuals' self-fashioning corresponded to that type of intellectual that Michel Foucault called "universal." As cosmopolitan individuals they positioned themselves as the spokespersons of the "universal"; they sought to bear universal values; and they "aspired to be the bearer of this universality in its conscious elaborated form."[19]

The problem of Jewish identity, it was felt, could be solved not through particularistic communal identification as Jews but as universal citizens. Membership in the Communist Party and fellow-traveling organizations offered those concrete advantages that were otherwise denied to them, as well as access to the wider world. The embrace of Marxism was a search for a community to replace the Jewish one they denied and the American one denied to them. Rejecting their organic origins and rejected by America, young Jewish intellectuals discovered a new community in which they were accepted, it seems, without prejudice. Marxism offered a "sense of belonging." They were welcomed as equals and comforted by the promise of egalitarianism. This was nourished by the Soviet experiment, which during the 1930s appeared to be the very model of an egalitarian society that spurned antisemitism and discrimination. More importantly, according to Terry Cooney, Marxism promised "acceptance, belonging, opportunity—a home and a career."[20] Thus, these young organic Jewish intellectuals had fashioned themselves into Foucault's "universal" intellectuals, and the universal intellectual "*par excellence*," according to Foucault, was the writer who valued his/her autonomy.[21]

Many Jewish intellectuals, however, began to find Marxism unacceptable just as they had found the Jewish community before. Although distaste for the Communist Party was felt throughout the thirties, for many it provided the only significant force for organization; hence, their continued allegiance. This distaste, however, soon began to develop into desertion. As Stalin's denouncements of the Bolshevik old guard progressed, he manifested increasingly anti-Jewish impulses, compounded by his persecution of Leon Trotsky. Thus, communism seemed to exacerbate antisemitism rather than offer solutions to it, and following news of the Moscow Trials in 1933–1934, intellectuals began to convert to anti-Stalinism and away from the party. Other defections followed as a result of the second round of the Moscow Trials reported in America during 1936 and 1937, the experience of the Spanish Civil War, and finally the Nazi-Soviet pact of 1939, all of which convinced many others, who had not yet left the party, to do so. Not only had communism not destroyed antisemitism, it had allied itself to those who most actively and openly advocated it. Having abandoned the Communist Party, many young Jewish intellectuals regrouped around the newly reformulated *Partisan Review* journal begun in 1937. The magazine became an independent publication of Trotskyist, anti-Stalinist, and modernist opinion. It contrived to construct its own peculiar discourse based around notions of marginalization, detachment, separation, and independence, as well as cosmopolitanism. The abandonment of Marxism had led to a subsequent investment in modernism because it privileged the outsider, autonomy, and the critique of bourgeois society.[22] So, although Marxism had been forsaken, the intellectuals still retained their organic and universal functions, not least because, in the words of Said, "organic intellectuals are always on the move."[23]

Specific Intellectuals

With the onset of World War II, the function of these organic-universal intellectuals began to change. The impact of the war and the extermination of European Jewry persuaded many Jewish intellectuals to reconsider their Jewishness and Americanness. The attempted solutions of Marxism, cosmopolitanism, and modernism had all failed and misled them because none of them had prevented Hitler. In their place, the war had increased identification with both the American and the Jewish communities. Through service in the United States Army or in federal wartime agencies, universal-organic Jewish intellectuals identified more strongly with the national community than ever before. The Holocaust also prompted Jewish intellectuals to reembrace their Jewishness. Midge Decter summed up the change for many young Jewish intellectuals when she said, "To put it much too crudely, Hitler taught them that they were Jews."[24] To which Irving Howe added, "We knew but for an accident of geography we might also now be bars of soap."[25] It came to be realized, therefore, that Jewishness was ineluctable, what Norman Podhoretz referred to as "Hitler's altogether irrefutable demonstration of the inescapability of Jewishness."[26] Jewish intellectuals, convinced of their inescapable Jewishness, began to use it as the material for a renewed self-fashioning.

When the then cultural center of the world—Paris—fell to the Nazis in June 1940, many intellectuals began to contribute directly to the war effort. They enlisted in intelligence and propaganda agencies like the Office of Strategic Services, the Office of War Information, and other branches of military intelligence. Others joined the armed forces either as soldiers or journalists.[27] Following the end of the war, this development continued when these skills were transferred to other institutions, in particular, the university campuses. Hugh Wilford accurately described a process of institutionalization[28] whereby the shift to a postindustrial economy, an increased demand for trained technicians, suburban migration, the decay of public utilities, and the rising costs of living in New York City all combined to make the intellectuals' position of the 1930s untenable by the 1940s and 1950s. Requiring some form of institutional attachment to subsist, those Jewish intellectuals, who had memories of being denied access to the American mainstream in the past, exploited the unparalleled opportunities offered in both academia and publishing during the postwar period as a result of the decline in academic antisemitism and of the expansion in higher education. Exclusion and antisemitism help to explain the great willingness of Jews to move into the mainstream in the 1940s and 1950s, when given the opportunity to do so without having to hide or reject their Jewish heritage as they had felt compelled to do during the 1930s.

In becoming institutionalized, however, the function of these Jewish intellectuals was redefined. During the postwar period, Foucault noted that the universal intellectual had become obsolete because s/he was no longer required to function as a marginalized, autonomous, and alienated spokesperson. He had observed the growth of a new type of intellectual—the "specific" one—that had supplanted the universal intellectual. According to Foucault, the specific intellectual was precisely situated "within specific sectors," and his or her function was to deploy a particular knowledge within a precise field.[29] Looking at his contemporary U.S. intellectual counterparts, H. Stuart Hughes wrote an article whose title asked, "Is the Intellectual Obsolete?" He warned his peers:

American intellectuals would do well to recall that in their government service they did not function as intellectuals but as "mental technicians." They had assigned jobs to do: they were not free to speculate as their fancy directed. Or, if they did choose to speculate in academic fashion, they ran the danger of going astray and of saying or doing something that in retrospect would look rather foolish. In short, by serving their country they lost some of their independence. Again, as intellectuals, their position was diminished rather than enhanced. And the same is true of those who in the postwar period have accepted the favors of government or of business.

In the future, Hughes warned ominously, intellectuals would have to make "a sharp choice between intellectual independence and government service."[30] Some of the Jewish intellectuals did not heed his warning, and this process of becoming "specific" was completed during the cold war as intellectuals began to move away from their organic-universal role to function as mediators for the emergent anticommunist hegemony.

Hegemony

Andrew Ross remarked that the cold war was a "profoundly hegemonic moment" in American history.[31] The onset of the struggle between the United States and the Soviet Union from March 1947 onward produced an "anticommunist hegemony." According to Antonio Gramsci, the key feature of hegemony is the process whereby a group or a "historical bloc" forms alliances with other interested groups to construct a dominant ruling group. Hegemony is not the exclusive domain of any single group but of a number of groups that act as mediators for the dominant group within a particular alliance. Thus, specific auxiliaries and allies assist the dominant group. Consequently, in order to maintain itself, *mediation* is vitally important for hegemony.[32] A successful hegemony is composed of a network of alliances and relies upon a multiplicity of intricate institutional interdependencies that must be constantly sustained in order to survive. In order to achieve this, hegemony either co-opts individuals or blocs through a potent combination of ideology and financial rewards or enlists the cooperation of those who already share its worldview and discourses. The ideological element of hegemony consists of convincing the other groups of the rightness of the dominant group's worldview; that is, the naturalizing and privileging of its particular discourses. This almost all-encompassing, pervasive form of political power may be described in the words of Foucault as "employed and exercised through a net-like organization."[33]

The anticommunist hegemony in America was constructed around discourses of anticommunism and freedom. The Truman administration initiated a campaign to inform the American public of the external and internal threats posed by the Soviet Union and the communist movement. The concept of freedom was then inserted as a key pillar of anticommunist discourse in what became known as the cultural cold war.[34] Ideas became weapons that, it was believed, needed to be put to organized use. As an expression of the anticommunist hegemony's discourses, the Truman Doctrine of 1947 insisted that the United States had a positive role actively to defend freedom and spread it throughout the world. This was crystallized in the National Security Council directive number 68, which emphasized an activist and interventionist role for the U.S. government. It repeatedly called for a projection of U.S. moral and material strength into the wider world, proclaiming the necessity of the practical affirmation and demonstration abroad of its values. As a part of this campaign, the concept of freedom itself was used as ideological ammunition against the Soviet Union in a discursive war of position. Freedom was promoted as propaganda producing a discursive conflict whereby the rhetoric of freedom was pitched against the rhetoric of peace. The administration did not so much want to foster greater freedom in the United States as to promote freedom as it already existed; it desired that America would become automatically synonymous with freedom in the public mind. Freedom, according to Thomas Bender, became the "masterword in the critical discourse of the era."[35]

Specific intellectuals were vital to this process. According to Paul Bové, intellectuals possessed a "unique" role in the extension, development, and maintenance of the hegemony.[36] Their privileged position was due to their precise situation within modes of cultural production. They had access to the vehicles of mass dissemination of information (television, cinema, magazines, books, newspapers, and radio) and thus were able to function as opinion-shapers. To this end, the administration sought the cooperation of contemporary and prominent opinion-makers and intellectuals in the fight for freedom and anticommunism. As producers and disseminators of information, intellectuals, it was felt, could radiate and incite such speech among the wider public. Intellectuals were favored because, as *private* agencies/individuals, they would mask official administration efforts. Their operation, autonomous both self-consciously and in the public eye, made them appear to be free; their previously and apparently organic and universal nature would endow them with an authenticity that overt governmental patronage denied. As we have seen, some Jewish intellectuals had already begun the process of shifting from the role of universal to specific intellectual through their enlistment in the wartime administration, where they were required to utilize their specific skills. With the inception of the cold war and the establishment of an anticommunist hegemony, many other Jewish intellectuals began to be co-opted by that hegemony. Their support for the anticommunist hegemony, however, altered their function as intellectuals.

Traditional Intellectuals

In either supporting the hegemony or being co-opted by it, Jewish intellectuals became what Gramsci defined as traditional intellectuals. They were the "dominant group's 'deputies,'" who "put themselves forward as autonomous and independent of the dominant social group" but nonetheless seemed to "represent a historical continuity uninterrupted by even the most complicated and radical changes."[37] In becoming traditional, the organic intellectual disappeared. As the cold war shifted the focus from fascism to communism, intellectual efforts switched with them. By 1947 Jewish intellectuals were arguing that they should perform the same tasks against the Soviet Union as they had against Nazi Germany. Sidney Hook called for precisely this mobilization of the intellectual in the service of "truth" because the intellectual was beyond any "national or party interest." He stated:

> This cannot be accomplished by governmental agencies because they are naturally suspect. . . . This campaign should be undertaken abroad primarily by American and English private organizations and professional associations. . . . And, most important of all, a personnel can be recruited from among those educators and publicists who consider themselves not only as Englishmen and Americans but as members of an international community.[38]

Clement Greenberg, managing editor of the highly influential New York Intellectual publication *Commentary*, added in 1948 that, "the writer ought indeed to involve himself in the struggle against Stalinism to the point of commitment."[39] Following the lead of Hook and Greenberg, many of those involved with the anti-Stalinist journals *Partisan Review, New Leader,* and *Commentary* formed the core of a new "international community" dedicated to fighting communism. This community cooperated in the mobilization and promotion of freedom.

Maurice Goldbloom, the executive secretary of the American Association for a Democratic Germany, argued that the United States

> must take a firm position against further encroachment by the Soviet Union on the freedom of those territories which it has not yet absorbed. Such resistance must be carried through on the economic and *ideological* fronts. . . . Today, such a victory can be won without war—but only if the United States adopts a policy far more adequate to the needs of the world.

This was predicated upon the "removal of the abuses of our society," which could then be mobilized as "a weapon in the struggle for the world" because "it is the one indispensable weapon."[40] Underlying this assertion was the premise that Americanism was both ideal and exportable because it was inherently attractive to others. Sidney Hook also favored such an initiative: "though an indigenous part of our tradition, they [the values of democracy] can under certain favorable conditions be broadened so as to become an integral part of world culture." These values can be extended by "an educational, not ideological campaign [that] should be organized throughout the world on the relative merits and achievements of democracy and totalitarianism."[41]

On the Soviet side, in an attempt to spearhead a worldwide campaign against American nuclear capability, a "peace offensive" was launched in 1948. The first move toward the promotion of "peace" as propaganda by the Soviets occurred in August of that year when the World Congress of Intellectuals for Peace was convened at Wroclaw, Poland. Although organized by Polish communists, the conference was not a purely communist affair because it attracted diverse individuals such as the former U.S. assistant attorney general O. John Rogge. The congress elected an international committee assigned the task of attracting European intellectuals to back the "peace offensive."[42] This was followed by similar congresses in Prague and Paris and the awarding of Stalin Prizes to those individuals who had publicly condemned the Marshall Plan, the creation of NATO, or the establishment of the republic in West Germany. In response the U.S. administration acknowledged that abstract notions about the organized use of ideas in the cold war had to be translated into effective weapons. The result was the promotion of freedom to counter the Soviet emphasis on peace. In the following years, the ideological conflict became a confrontation of discourses couched in terms of peace versus freedom. The Soviet Union's discourse of peace was denigrated as empty rhetoric, but more sinisterly, all subsequent calls for peace in America became associated with communism, which was most clearly demonstrated in the reaction to the Waldorf Conference of March 1949 held by the fellow-traveling National Council for the Arts, Sciences, and Professions.

Although the State Department opposed the peace conference, it recognized that to ban it outright would be a massive propaganda coup for the Soviet Union, proving that America was opposed to intellectual freedom. Nonetheless, a procommunist conference to be held in the heart of America had to be counteracted. The conference was allowed to proceed, but the State Department sought to undermine it by subtler means and, at the same time, to reverse its effects in order to benefit the United States. To this end, it recommended that it "discreetly get in touch with reliable noncommunist participants in New York to urge them to do what they can to . . . expose Communist efforts at controlling the conference."[43] It contacted Sidney Hook, setting the trend for other Jewish intellectuals to become involved in the cultural cold war.

The State Department's failure to counteract the conference successfully led Jewish intellectuals to call for more effective action on their own part. William Phillips argued that American intellectuals could no longer afford the "luxury" of "exemption from the practical struggle against Stalinism." The position of intellectuals was dependent upon American military and material strength and consequently the desperation of the situation destroyed the "old liberal and socialist panaceas."[44] Phillips thus suggested nothing less than the mobilization of American intellectuals in support of freedom. Reporting on the conference for *Commentary* magazine, William Barrett asserted that the administration required its intellectuals to assist in its cultural cold war effort: "The United States is not going to get anywhere in this war of ideas unless it succeeds in obtaining some better intellectual grasp of the basis of its propaganda." He observed, "Even in its mortal struggle with Stalinism, America does not have much use for its intellectuals. This may prove its great mistake."[45] Hook hammered the point home: "More literary men and scientists must be drawn into the struggle for freedom."[46] Elsewhere, he wrote: "We face grim years ahead. The democratic West will require the critical support, the dedicated energy and above all, the intelligence, of its intellectuals if it is to survive as a free culture."[47] Bogdan Raditsa called for the deployment of those "American writers, thinkers, historians, and journalists who have the most thorough knowledge and understanding of Communism and its methods, and the deepest commitment to the struggle against totalitarianism."[48] Francois Bondy wrote, "In the face of propaganda, which is the   pon of the totalitarians, our side can afford the truth, and has it as an ally." H added that "truth needs active propaganda just as much as falsehood does."[49]

Led by Hook and mustered by the dismal efforts and short-sightedness of the State Department, many Jewish anticommunist intellectuals created their own counterforce to the Waldorf Conference: the Americans for Intellect l Freedom (AIF), an independent organization of intellectuals devoted to defend-ing and extending cultural freedom. They primarily represented the three key anti-communist journals: the *New Leader*, *Commentary*, and *Partisan Review*. The e intellectuals met at the behest of Hook without any governmental prompting, representing a voluntary effort on their part. Indeed, the intellectual-sponsored initiative of the AIF occurred prior to the formulation of any coherent respor e by the CIA. Intellectual cooperation with the hegemony in the propagation of the cultural cold war began to occur more frequently. Realizing that intellectuals could and should be mobilized in the counterattack, the administration explicitly sought their services by organizing a U.S.-sponsored counterconference known as the International Day of Resistance to Dictatorship and War (April 30, 1949) in Paris. The assistance of intellectuals meant that propaganda attacks against the Soviet Union could be achieved under the guise of freedom, voluntarism, and autonomy. Out of this initiative, the AIF developed into the Congress for Cultural Freedom (CCF), which was actively promoted and secretly funded by the CIA. Hook himself was an unwitting beneficiary of this covert support. The CIA devised the CCF as an intellectual gathering of an international group of writers, artists, and thinkers to defend intellectual and cultural freedom against the forces of totalitarianism both at home and abroad. From its very conception, therefore, the congress represented that type of measure of "practical application" for which NSC 68 repeatedly called. Even its location in West Berlin was an ideological demonstration of the concept of freedom. The congress developed the "core" of a community of "traditional" intellectuals committed to struggling for cultural freedom and against communism.[50]

The international congress spawned a domestic American version. On January 5, 1951, the American Committee for Cultural Freedom (ACCF) was set up as an affiliate of the European congress. The committee called itself a nonpartisan community of "writers, teachers, scientists, and artists of various political preferences" whose purpose was to "take appropriate steps against whatever forces in the present-day world threaten our free culture." The ACCF constituted a new community focused around discourses of freedom and anticommunism: "We expose the Communist conspiracy and its totalitarian threat to America and other free countries" by giving "practical and intellectual support" to other anticommunists and by advising and assisting those involved in loyalty and security difficulties.[51] Many Jewish intellectuals were active in these initiatives, thus agreeing that the "defense of intellectual liberty today imposes a positive obligation"[52] to assist in the propagation of the cultural cold war "with the weapons of the intellect."[53]

The ACCF and the CCF became two of the administration's major hegemonic allies. Through them many Jewish intellectuals participated in the administration's prosecution of the cultural cold war. These agencies were key allies in providing both personnel and material in the U.S. counterattack against the peace campaign. In order to maintain these alliances, the CIA covertly sponsored both organizations, channeling funds through a series of front foundations and conduits, as well as providing a range of financial inducements and rewards to their co-opted specific-traditional intellectuals, such as conferences, editorships, subsidized publishing, and foreign travel. Arthur Koestler lampooned it as the "international academic call-girl circuit" of intellectual conferences and symposia. Frances Saunders describes an "umbilical cord of gold"—a seemingly unlimited source of largesse distributed by the CIA that appeared to have had a great effect in mobilizing Jewish intellectuals. Saunders mentions the attractive fees, the lecture tours, the conferences, the foreign trips, even the villas provided by the CIA. The editor of *Partisan Review*, William Phillips, observed "the nouveau riche look of the whole operation . . . the posh apartments of the Congress officials, the seemingly inexhaustible funds for travel, the big-time expenses accounts, and all the other perks usually associated with the executives of large corporations." To reinforce the point, Saunders quotes V.S. Pritchett's observation, "Expenses, the most beautiful word in modern English. If we sell our souls, we ought to sell them dear." One CIA operative understood this whole process all too well when he stated, "The main concern for most scholars and writers really is how you get paid for doing what you want to do. I think that, by and large, they would take money from whatever source they could get it."[54] In 1952, Louis Kronenberger observed, "our intellectuals are not just more respected, they are better fed." He continued, "Talent is well paid for nowadays, though oftener at the back door than the front."[55] This backdoor was not revealed to be the CIA until the 1960s, and many of those in receipt of its monies denied any knowledge of the source.

Were these intellectuals simply motivated by money? Many of those intellectuals who composed the membership of both organizations *already* believed in the rightness of the administration's discourses because their sentiments were shared. They had preemptively offered their services as intellectuals *prior to* any official approach by the administration. As Sidney Hook recalled, "Their activities on behalf of the Congress were a burden and a sacrifice, *cheerfully assumed* because of the gravity of the issues at stake."[56] As mentioned earlier, many Jewish intellectuals were fierce anti-Stalinists who had been warning of the danger posed by the Soviet Union since the early 1930s, although, surely, some were swayed by the large financial and other inducements offered to them once the CIA became involved.

As is to be expected, those intellectuals involved explicitly deny this. Saunders outlines and documents the rejections of these claims by those who she has shown were recipients of CIA patronage. Most claimed little knowledge of who was paying their expenses, or perhaps they chose not to question the source. Thus the problems of truth and memory rise once again. Saunders ends with a quote from Primo Levi: "There are . . . those who lie consciously, coldly falsifying reality itself but more numerous are those who weigh anchor, move off, momentarily or forever, from genuine memories, and fabricate for themselves a convenient reality. . . . The silent transition from falsehood to sly deception is useful: anyone who lies in good faith is better off, he recites his part better, he is more easily believed."[57] In denying any links to the anticommunist hegemony, Jewish intellectuals exactly fulfilled the role of traditional intellectuals, as outlined by Gramsci. They had clearly "put themselves forward as autonomous and independent of the dominant social group."[58] Edward Shils, for example, insisted that the CCF and the ACCF retained their autonomy and "took no instructions from anyone outside their respective organisations,"[59] while Hook asserted that the "intellectual independence of the Congress [and the committee were] not affected in the slightest."[60] They still claimed a critical distance and autonomy and did not feel that their critical function had been in any way diminished by their deployment by the anticommunist hegemony within the cultural cold war. Terms such as *intellectual freedom, autonomy*, and *dissent* were still used with a distinct lack of irony. Consequently, these intellectuals disputed their labeling as "traditional." Unlike the state-sponsored intellectuals of the Soviet Union, they would argue, they remained free to operate as autonomous and independent thinkers.

Yet not all Jewish intellectuals were co-opted by the anticommunist hegemony, nor were they willing to cooperate with it so enthusiastically. In 1954, a journal designed "to dissent from the bleak atmosphere of conformism that pervades the political and intellectual life of the United States; to dissent from the support of the *status quo* now so noticeable on the part of many former radicals and socialists" was established.[61] Called *Dissent*, it was explicitly designed to provide an oppositional, if not fully counterhegemonic, intellectual and political viewpoint. In particular, it was intended to rival *Commentary*, which had become so affirmative that, in the eyes of Irving Howe and Lewis Coser (the new editors of *Dissent*), it had lost its critical perspective and had become simply an official organ of the anticommunist hegemony. Howe complained of the magazine's "zealousness"; of its anticommunism, which was "indiscriminate and unscholarly" with "its air of rude certainty, its readiness to indulge in the most sweeping generalizations."[62] He was annoyed that *Commentary* had simply become an apologist for the American status quo.[63] In contrast, *Dissent* rejected the prevailing mood of American liberalism among Jewish intellectuals, intending to establish a temper of opposition. *Dissent* became the focus for those who rejected "hard" anticommunism, directing considerable flak at those who acquiesced in the anticommunist witch-hunts, and it was a magnet for those who refused to accept the blandishments and financial rewards offered by the anticommunist hegemony. One of its circle, Meyer Shapiro, a professor of art history at Columbia, snubbed the ACCF because it appeared to be a "front organization" whose purposes were concealed "behind an appeal to other (and less obviously political) ends."[64] Indeed, *Dissent* had been a considerable thorn in the side of *Encounter*—the London-based and CIA-funded journal—and it was *Dissent* that publicly hinted at the problem earlier than most when Paul Goodman wrote in 1962, "Cultural Freedom and the Encounter of ideas are instruments of the CIA."[65] Thus, those Jewish intellectuals who associated themselves with *Dissent* provide a marked contrast to those other Jewish intellectuals; the attempt of the former to remain organic brought up short those who had become traditional during the cultural cold war.

Conclusion

Through their alliance with the anticommunist hegemony, many of the New York Jewish Intellectuals became a stratum of traditional intellectuals. Through the production of anticommunist discourses they represented an interested mediating agency in a network of alliances that formed the cold war anticommunist hegemony. They were the specific auxiliaries and allies, the aides and deputies, who assisted the dominant group, fashioning themselves as autonomous and independent of that group but representing a historical continuity with the past nonetheless. They did not struggle against the forms of power that transformed them into its instruments. Neither did they aim to reveal it, to sap it, or to take it. Instead, because "their urge was for place and role" they "associated" with it. These intellectuals did not fight against their hegemonic cooperation, nor did they resist becoming the hegemony's deputies. Rather they proactively offered their skills in its service, reflecting their willingness to dismiss their original functions as organic and universal intellectuals in the service of the anticommunist hegemony during the cultural cold war. Leslie Fiedler observed that the intellectual now had a "use."[66] Or as Lionel Trilling put it, "Our many bureaus and authorities were created not only as a response to the social needs which they serve, *but also as a response to the social desires of their personnel.*" He added: "Intellect has associated itself with power as perhaps never before in history."[67] Intellectuals, therefore, were not engaged in a local struggle by attacking the hegemony at its weakest points. On the contrary, they were overtly involved in the global battle against communism. Thus, in their failure to struggle against power, these intellectuals extended it.

Such hegemonic cooperation produced major effects within the intellectual community. Discourses were refocused around cold war concepts of anticommunism and freedom, and Jewish intellectuals had to position themselves in relation to them during the cultural cold war. Many Jewish intellectuals functioned as important sites in the radiation of these discourses insofar as they cooperated in a war of position against the Soviet Union, communism, and peace. In doing so, they moved farther away from their organic roots, and hegemonic cooperation meant that they had become traditional and specific. They spoke more for the institutions of the anticommunist hegemony than for the community from which they sprang, becoming the spokespersons for a new Jewish and intellectual anticommunist liberalism. Through an alliance with the dominant discourses of the anticommunist hegemony, they asserted a hegemonic position within American intellectual life. It is perhaps for this reason that Norman Podhoretz, newly appointed and recently radicalized editor of *Commentary* magazine, lamented in 1960, "The intellectuals have failed us by abdicating their traditional role as fanatical devotees of the dream of a good society."[68]

Many of those employed and sponsored by the government and the CIA during the cultural cold war are reluctant to admit their co-optation. They wallow in disingenuousness, lies, half-truths, and obfuscation. The dilemma becomes: who can we trust? Who carries greater weight, authority, and ultimately, authenticity? Do such questions apply to all forms of outside funding; can they or can they not alter critique and make its effect difficult to pin down? Or is an indeterminable self-censorship the result? As Richard King observed, "it is difficult in reading these volumes to work out just how we are to take them or what purpose, beyond self-justification, they are meant to serve."[69] If new research shows the New York Jewish Intellectuals' memoirs and biographies to be of doubtful value, then perhaps it is time for their history to be rewritten anew from a perspective that has not been shaped by theirs.

Notes

The author would like to thank Hugh Wilford and Ethan Goffman for their useful comments on earlier drafts of this article.

1. Examples of these are Norman Podhoretz, *Making It* (New York: Random House, 1967); *Breaking Ranks: A Political Memoir* (New York: Harper & Row, 1979); *Ex-Friends: Falling Out with Allen Ginsberg, Lionel and Diana Trilling, Lillian Hellman, Hannah Arendt, and Norman Mailer* (New York: The Free Press, 1999); *My Love Affair with America: The Cautionary Tale of a Cheerful Conservative* (New York: The Free Press, 2000); Diana Trilling, *The Beginning of the Journey: The Marriage of Diana and Lionel Trilling* (New York and London: Harcourt Brace & Co., 1993); William Phillips, *A Partisan View: Five Decades of the Literary Life* (New York: Stein and Day, 1983); Irving Howe, *A Margin of Hope: An Intellectual Biography* (London:

Secker & Warburg, 1982); Irving Kristol, *Reflections of a Neoconservative: Looking Back, Looking Ahead* (New York: Basic Books, 1983); William Barrett, *The Truants: Adventures among the Intellectuals* (New York: Doubleday, 1982); Ted Solotaroff, *Truth Comes in Blows: A Memoir* (New York and London: W.W. Norton & Co., 1998); Midge Decter, *An Old Wife's Tale: My Seven Decades in Love and War* (New York: Regan Books, 2001).

2.   I have taken this phrase from David Savran, *Communists, Cowboys, and Queers: The Politics of Masculinity in the Work of Arthur Miller and Tennessee Williams* (Minneapolis and London: University of Minnesota Press, 1992), p. 9.

3.   Morris Dickstein, "The New York Intellectuals: Some Personal History," *Dissent* 44 (1997), p. 83.

4.   Richard H. King, "Up from Radicalism," *American Jewish History* 75 (1985), p. 77.

5.   Norman F. Cantor, *The American Century: Varieties of Culture in Modern Times* (New York: HarperCollins, 1997), p. 268.

6.   Richard A. Posner, *Public Intellectuals: A Study of Decline* (Cambridge, MA: Harvard University Press, 2002). However, having said that, the most important example of a more theoretical interpretation is still Christopher Lasch, "The Cultural Cold War: A Short History of the Congress for Cultural Freedom," in his *The Agony of the American Left* (New York: Alfred Knopf, 1969) and also the slightly different original version, "The Cultural Cold War," in the *Nation*, September 11, 1967. Giles Scott-Smith has attempted to build on and expand Lasch's approach in his *The Politics of Apolitical Culture: The Congress for Cultural Freedom, the CIA, and Post-War American Hegemony* (London: Routledge, 2002).

7.   Antonio Gramsci, *Selections from the Prison Notebooks*, ed. and trans. Quentin Hoare and Geoffrey Nowell Smith (London: Lawrence and Wishart, 1971), p. 9; Edward W. Said, *Representations of the Intellectual* (London: Vintage, 1994), p. 7.

8.   Russell Jacoby, *The Last Intellectuals: American Culture in the Age of Academe* (New York: Basic Books, 2000), p. 5.

9.   Gramsci, *Selections from the Prison Notebooks*, pp. 5–6.

10. Said, *Representations of the Intellectual*, p. 4.

11. John Murray Cuddihy, *The Ordeal of Civility: Freud, Marx, Lévi-Strauss, and the Jewish Struggle with Modernity* (Boston: Beacon Press, 1974).

12. Jacoby, *The Last Intellectuals*, p. 90.

13. Arthur Miller, *Timebends: A Life* (London: Methuen, 1987), p. 62.

14. Peter I. Rose, "The Ghetto and Beyond," in *The Ghetto and Beyond: Essays on Jewish Life in America*, ed. Peter I. Rose (New York: Random House, 1969), p. 5.

15. Alfred Kazin, "The Jew as Modern Writer," in *The Ghetto and Beyond*, ed. Rose, p. 423.

16. Leonard Dinnerstein, *Antisemitism in America* (New York and Oxford: Oxford University Press, 1994), pp. 79, 105, 127, 107, 108–109.

17. Paul R. Gorman, *Left Intellectuals and Popular Culture in Twentieth-Century America* (Chapel Hill & London: University of North Carolina Press, 1996), p. 141.

18. Irving Howe, *A Margin of Hope: An Intellectual Autobiography* (London: Secker & Warburg, 1982), p. 137.

19. Michel Foucault, *Power/Knowledge: Selected Interviews and Other Writings, 1972–1977*, ed. Colin Gordon, Leo Marshall, John Mepham, and Kate Soper (Brighton: Harvester Press, 1980), p. 126.

20. Terry Cooney, *The Rise of the New York Intellectuals: Partisan Review and its Circle* (Madison: University of Wisconsin Press, 1986), pp. 43, 50.

21. Foucault, *Power/Knowledge*, pp. 126–127.

22. See Stephen A. Longstaff, "The New York Intellectuals: A Study of Particularism and Universalism in American High Culture" (Ph.D. dissertation, University of California, 1978), pp. 4, 117–122, 124–132; Hugh Wilford, *The New York Intelle   : From Vanguard to Institution* (Manchester and New York: Manchester University Press, 1995), pp. 32–36, 60; Cooney, *The Rise of the New York Intellectuals*, pp. 232–234, 227.

23. Said, *Representations of the Intellectual*, p. 4.

24. Midge Decter, "An Activist Critic on the Upper West Side," in *Creators and Disturbers: Reminiscences by Jewish Intellectuals of New York*, ed. Bernard Rosenberg and Ernest Goldstein (New York: Columbia University Press, 1982), p. 358.

25. Irving Howe, "The New York Intellectuals: A Chronicle and a Critique," *Commentary* 46 (1968), p. 43.

26. Podhoretz, p. 92.

27. See Richard Pells, *The Liberal Mind in a Conservative Age: American Intellectuals in the 1940s and 1950s* (New York: Harper & Row, 1985), pp. 8–9; Wilford, *The New York Intellectuals*, p. 13; Henry Pacter, "The Radical Émigré in the Metropolis," i 1 *Creators and Disturbers*, ed. Rosenberg and Goldstein, p. 122.

28. Hugh Wilford, "The Agony of the Avant-Garde: Philip Rahv and the New York Intellectuals," in *American Cultural Critics*, ed. David Murray (Exeter: University of Exeter Press, 1995), p. 8. For a longer description of this process see Jacoby, *The Last Intellectuals*, in particular the chapter "New York, Jewish, and Other Intellectuals," pp. 72–111.

29. Foucault, *Power/Knowledge*, pp. 126–127.

30. H. Stuart Hughes, "Is the Intellectual Obsolete? The Freely Speculating Mind in America," *Commentary* 22 (1956), pp. 313, 316, 318.

31. Andrew Ross, *No Respect: Intellectuals and Popular Culture* (London and New York: Routledge, 1989), p. 56.

32. Gramsci, *Selections from the Prison Notebooks*, pp. 56–57, 12, 53. The following have also been very useful in developing my understanding of Gramsci's formulation: T.J. Jackson Lears, "The Concept of Cultural Hegemony: Problems and Possibilities," *American Historical Review* 90 (1985), pp. 567–593; Raymond Williams, "Hegemony," in his *Marxism and Literature* (Oxford: Oxford University Press, 1977), pp. 108–114; Michael Denning, "The End of Mass Culture," *International Labor and Working-Class History* 37 (1990), pp. 4–18; Jerome Karabel, "Revolutionary Contradictions: Antonio Gramsci and the Problem of Intellectuals," *Politics and Society* 6 (1976), pp. 123–172; George Lipsitz, "The Struggle for Hegemony," *Journal of American History* 75 (1988), pp. 146–150.

33. Foucault, *Power/Knowledge*, p. 98.

34. The term *cultural cold war* has been relatively undertheorized and thus has not been systematically defined. Possibly the first use of the term was in Christopher Lasch's essay, "The Cultural Cold War: A Short History of the Congress for Cultural Freedom," in his *The Agony of the American Left: One Hundred Years of Radicalism* (London: Pelican, 1973), pp. 64–111. Lasch, however, did not provide a definition of the term. Hugh Wilford, on the other hand, suggested that it was "an ideological conflict" instigated by the United States that began in the late 1940s in response to the Soviet "peace" campaign launched in 1947. It aimed to win "the hearts and minds of the citizens of non-aligned countries around the world," with a special focus on foreign intellectuals and "extended as well into the realm of culture." See his "'Win-

— content

ning Hearts and Minds': American Cultural Strategies in the Cold War," *Borderlines* 1 (1994), pp. 315–326, esp. pp. 315–316. I will use the term here to refer to the ideological, cultural, and intellectual offensive launched by the United States around the term *freedom* in the late 1940s and early 1950s.

35. Thomas Bender, *New York Intellect: A History of the Intellectual Life in New York from 1750 to the Beginnings of Our Own Time* (Baltimore: The Johns Hopkins University Press, 1987), p. 339.
36. Paul A. Bové, *Intellectuals in Power: A Genealogy of Critical Humanism* (New York: Columbia University Press, 1986), p. 24.
37. Gramsci, *Selections from the Prison Notebooks*, pp. 6, 7, 12.
38. Sidney Hook, "Why Democracy is Better," *Commentary* 5 (1947), pp. 195, 204.
39. Clement Greenberg, "The State of American Writing, 1948: A Symposium," *Partisan Review* 15 (1948), p. 878.
40. Maurice Goldbloom, letter to the editors, *Commentary* 4 (1947), p. 97.
41. Sidney Hook, "Why Democracy Is Better," pp. 196, 204.
42. See Robbie Lieberman, "'Does That Make Peace a Bad Word?': American Responses to the Communist Peace Offensive, 1949–1950," *Peace & Change* 17 (1992), pp. 198–228. See also William Barrett, "Culture Conference at the Waldorf: The Artful Dove," *Commentary* 7 (1949), pp. 487–494; Robbie Lieberman, "Communism, Peace Activism, and Civil Liberties: From the Waldorf Conference to the Peekskill Riot," *Journal of American Culture* 18 (1995), pp. 59–65; and John P. Rossi, "Farewell to Fellow Traveling: The Waldorf Peace Conference of March 1949," *Continuity* 10 (1985), pp. 1–31.
43. Quoted in Frank A. Ninkovich, *The Diplomacy of Ideas: U.S. Foreign Policy and Cultural Relations, 1938–1950* (Cambridge: Cambridge University Press, 1981), p. 163.
44. William Phillips, "The Politics of Desperation," *Partisan Review* 15 (1948), pp. 451, 452.
45. William Barrett, "World War III: Ideological Conflict," *Partisan Review* 17 (1950), p. 653.
46. Sidney Hook, "The Berlin Congress for Cultural Freedom," *Partisan Review* 17 (1950), p. 722.
47. Sidney Hook, in the symposium "Our Country, Our Culture," *Partisan Review* 19 (1952), p. 574.
48. Bogdan Raditsa, "Beyond Containment to Liberation: A Political Émigré Challenges Our 'Machiavellian Liberalism,'" *Commentary* 12 (1951), pp. 226–231.
49. Francois Bondy, "Berlin Congress for Freedom: A New Resistance in the Making," *Commentary* 10 (1950), pp. 250, 246.
50. For a detailed account of the whole congress see Sidney Hook, *Out of Step* (New York: Carroll & Graf, 1987), pp. 432–456; Irving Howe, "The Culture Conference," *Partisan Review* 16 (1949), p. 509; Michael Warner, "Origins of the Congress for Cultural Freedom, 1949–50," *Studies in Intelligence*, http://www.odci.gov/csi/studies/95unclas/war.html (accessed March 2, 1997).
51. ACCF advertisement in *Commentary* 19 (1955), p. 25.
52. "Manifesto of the Congress for Cultural Freedom" (1950), reprinted in Peter Coleman, *The Liberal Conspiracy: The Congress for Cultural Freedom and the Struggle for the Mind of Postwar Europe* (New York: Free Press, 1989), p. 251.
53. Hook, *Out of Step*, p. 453.
54. Frances Stonor Saunders, *Who Paid the Piper? The CIA and the Cultural Cold War* (London: Granta Books, 1999), pp. 5, 345, 339, 332, 345.

55. Louis Kronenberger, "Our Country, Our Culture," p. 440.

56. Hook, *Out of Step*, p. 451, emphasis added.

57. Saunders, *Who Paid the Piper?* p. 415.

58.   Gramsci, *Selections from the Prison Notebooks*, p. 12.

59. Edward Shils, "Remembering the Congress for Cultural Freedom," *Encounter* 75 (1990), p. 57.

60. Hook, *Out of Step*, p. 453. I have also discussed this in "The CIA 'Call-Girl Circuit,'" *The Jewish Quarterly* 46 (1999), pp. 80–82.

61. "A Word to Our Readers," editorial, *Dissent* 1 (1954), p. 3.

62. Irving Howe, letter to the editor, *Commentary* 12 (October 1951), pp. 388–389.

63. Irving Howe, "Does It Hurt when You Laugh?" *Dissent* 1 (1954), pp. 5, 6, 7; Irving Howe, "This Age of Conformity," *Partisan Review* 21 (1954), pp. 18–19; Irving Howe, *A World More Attractive* (New York: Horizon, 1963), p. 265.

64. Meyer Schapiro, cited in Wilford, *The New York Intellectuals*, p. 205.

65. Paul Goodman, quoted in Saunders, *Who Paid the Piper?* p. 356.

66. Leslie Fiedler, "Our Country: Our Culture," p. 298.

67. Lionel Trilling, "Our Country: Our Culture," p. 320.

68. Norman Podhoretz, "The Issue," *Commentary* 29 (1960), p. a.

69. King, "Up from Radicalism," p. 71.

Jew d'Esprit

Eugene Goodheart

This essay is an offshoot of a memoir I recently published with the title *Confessions of a Secular Jew*. Here is a confession that I did not make in the memoir: the title was an afterthought. I did not set out to write about being a secular Jew—as if it were a phenomenon as definable as being an Orthodox or Conservative or even Reform Jew. We know what a secular Jew is not, a religious Jew. We might rest perhaps with the positive idea that he is a worldly Jew, but is that sufficient to define him? Religious Jews may also be worldly. Hasidim, for instance, are famous as diamond merchants. If worldliness were all that secular Jewishness comes to, it would seem not to come to very much. Notice I refrain from speaking of secular Judaism because of the religious connotations and associations of Judaism. Abstract definition is a fruitless effort. So perhaps I should begin by describing how I came to write the memoir and how after much struggle I arrived at the title—that is, at the meaning of secular Jewishness.

The germ of the memoir is a personal essay I published with the title "I Am a Jew." Enclosed in quotation marks because it is a translation of the title of a Yiddish poem by a once famous Soviet Jewish poet Itzhik Feffer. The poem is a celebration of Jewish struggles for liberation from the time of Moses through the Maccabean uprisings against the Syrian-Greeks, Bar Kochbah's revolt against the Romans to the struggle against Nazism. Here are two of the many stanzas of the poem (my translation).

> The forty years in ancient times
> I suffered in the desert sand
> Gave me strength.
> I heard Bar Kochba's rebel cry
> At every turn through my ordeal

And more than gold did I possess
The stubborn pride of my grandfather
I am a Jew.

I am a Jew who drank
From Stalin's magical cup of happiness.
To those who wish to destroy Moscow
And turn us out of our land
To them I shout, "Down with you!"
I march together with the peoples of the east.
The Russians are my brothers.
I am a Jew.

As a kid, I attended a Yiddish shuleh where I learned to recite—better, to declaim—Yiddish poems in public. One of the poems I learned was "Ich bin a Yid." When Feffer came to America during World War II to raise money for the Russian War Relief, he visited Camp Kinderland, a summer camp in upstate New York where I was a camper. One of my gifts was the possession of a Yiddish diction that one hears on the Yiddish stage. How I acquired this precocity I cannot say, but I had an extraordinary ear for the words and cadences of Yiddish poetry and was in demand by Yiddish-speaking clubs to recite Yiddish poems. When Feffer arrived at Camp Kinderland, I was asked to recite the poem to a large audience in his presence. As you can imagine, it was one of the great events of my childhood. I have a photo of myself age twelve reciting the poem with clenched fist in the air on a stage draped with Soviet and American flags. "Ich bin a Yid" is not a good poem, filled as it is with banal sentiments, but it has an impressive and stirring sound in Yiddish. Its most memorable line is the unfortunate, "I am a Jew who drank from Stalin's magical cup of happiness." What a terrible irony! Feffer was an apparatchik and a wordsmith. He knew more than he spoke. He certainly knew enough or thought he knew enough to survive in Stalin's Russia. Despots love to be celebrated in poetry. While Feffer focuses his bravado on the grave the Nazis are preparing for him and his fellow Jews, without his knowledge a grave is being prepared for him by his own god, the being from whose hand he has received, so he tells us, the cup of happiness. Some time after he wrote the poem, Feffer was denounced *under the red flag*.

Joshua Rubinstein of Amnesty International has recently published a book, *Stalin's Secret Pogrom*, about the persecution and prosecution of fifteen Soviet Jewish writers on trumped up charges of treason. All were executed, among them Itzhik Feffer. I did not expect to be surprised by the book. I thought it would merely confirm what I already believed about the regime. But I was surprised by the disparity between the innocuousness of the charge against the defendants and the enormity of the punishment. The crime was little more than nationalist sentiment that itself constituted treason. There was no evidence that the expression of pride in one's Jewish identity and sorrow at the price paid for being Jews at the hands of the Nazis was at the expense of loyalty to the Soviet Union. What also surprised me was the effect of the trial (indeed, of the Soviet system) on the integrity of the defendants. Each defendant protested his loyalty to the regime at the same time that the regime's attitude toward him or her (there was one female defendant) was execrable. Fear undoubtedly was a motive, but there was also an inextinguishable devotion to a cause that had gone awry. One writer, Leib Kvitko, testified that the October revolution had brought him to life. Though the defendants had confessed under torture, a number of them displayed courage at the trial in defending their innocence and exposing the injustice of the proceedings. The format of the trial was diabolical. The judge was the prosecuting attorney and refused to believe any statement in court that contradicted the confessions. Even more diabolical was the permission given to each defendant to challenge the veracity of another defendant. Despite the prosecutorial strategy of divide and conquer, many of the defendants behaved admirably. The most craven of the defendants was my childhood hero, Itzhik Feffer.

I grew up indoctrinated in a cause that combined a particular kind of Jewishness and a particular kind of politics. The Jewishness was Yiddish and secular rather than Hebraic and religious; the politics called itself progressive. It connected the struggles of the Jews against oppression with those of the working class against exploitation. The vanguard of the working class was the Soviet Union, and its leader and hero (our hero) was Joseph Stalin. We were secular Jews hostile to religion, but our devotion to the cause had a religious intensity. It was a faith with its own dogmas, and because it was a faith we didn't need evidence to support it.

The organization that sponsored the shulehs that I attended, the International Workers Order (IWO), no longer exists. The IWO mirrored the Soviet Union in its apparent hospitality to diverse ethnic groups. (In theory, the Soviet Union was a confederation of semiautonomous republics or territories. In practice, all power resided in the Russian republic.) The IWO contained Italians, Hungarians, Slovaks, Russians, Finns, Poles, Ukrainians, Rumanians, Croatians, Greeks, Czechs, Spaniards, Cubans, Puerto Ricans, Mexicans, and English, and Blacks as well as Jews, but each ethnic or national group had its separate organization. The Jewish People's Fraternal Order was by far the largest of the organizations and the driving force of the IWO. During the McCarthy period, the IWO was put on the attorney general's list of subversive organizations because of its sympathies with the Communist Party and the Soviet Union. Among the correspondence that I received after the publication of my memoir was a book by a lawyer who had shared my experience growing up; it was about the prosecution and destruction of the IWO. The IWO posed no threat to American democracy. The prosecution did. I suspect that if the Communist Party had come to power in America many of the goodhearted and naïve members of the organization, including some of the leadership, would have found themselves in trouble. All of which does not excuse the fellow-traveling politics of the organization. The immediate enemy of the IWO within the Jewish world was the *Arbeiter Ring*, the Workmen's Circle, which was social democratic and anti-Stalinist. It says something about the temper of the times that we referred to members of the Workmen's Circle as social fascists. Our newspaper was the *Morning Freiheit*, which like the IWO no longer exists; the enemy paper, the *Jewish Daily Forward*, now thrives as an English newspaper.

In the memoir I provide an account of my disillusionment with the "move-ment." I outgrew its false progressivism, false because of its association with a corrupt and tyrannical regime, masking its cruelty with the language of justice, equality, and comradeship. My education at Columbia College in the early fifties and the influence of anti-Stalinist New York Jewish Intellectuals such as Lionel Trilling and his *Partisan Review* colleagues made a significant contribution to the changes I underwent. I became a liberal resistant to the extremes of left and right, suspicious of all dogmatisms and responsive to what was of value (or what I took to be of value) in all the positions of the political spectrum, left, right, and center. But what about the Jewishness linked to it? The poet Wordsworth said, "the child is father of the man." You may outgrow your early formation or think that you have outgrown it, but you don't abandon it entirely; or if you do, you do so at a cost. And yet—here's the rub—my Jewishness was so bound up with the "progressive" cause that after having rejected the cause I couldn't say, when asked, what my Jewishness amounted to. What does it mean to be Jewish without religion, without its rituals and ceremonies? What in other words, does it mean to be a secular Jew? To compound the difficulty of the question, I did not have the advantage of being a Zionist or of even having Zionist sympathies.

Zionism implies that all Jews who live outside of Israel are in diaspora. I have a hard time thinking of myself as a Jew in diaspora because America, not Israel, is my homeland. Religious Jews dream of a return to the Garden of Eden, Zionists of a return to Israel. My early Jewish education was anathema to this idea of return. Our Golden Age was the time when Arabs and Jews lived together in relative peace in Spain before the advent of Ferdinand and Isabella and the Inqui-sition. Translated in modern terms, we advocated a binational state of Arabs and Jews—an ideal hardly realizable in the present circumstances in the Middle East. "The Final Solution of the Jewish Problem" made the quarrels that I might have had with the Zionists irrelevant. The existence of a Jewish state became a neces-sity, its disappearance unthinkable. And yet what is thinkable and problematic is the paradox of a Jewish democracy. What if the Arabs become a majority within Israel, a distinct demographic possibility? Could its democracy survive the test of electing an Arab prime minister? If not, then the Arabs remain permanent sec-ond-class citizens and Israel a democracy that imposes unacceptable limits on the rights of non-Jews. Here is an instance of the unsurmounted legacy of my youth.

What else remains of the Jewishness of my early formation, and how has it evolved? Well, for one thing that Jewish formation instilled in me a sensitivity to social injustice, which survived its contamination with Stalinism. If the Jews were a persecuted people, we had to be alert to the persecution of other peoples. And here I part from a powerful theme in the Jewish tradition. A religious Jew grows up with the conviction that the Jews are a chosen people, meaning that they are morally and spiritually superior, a beacon of light to the rest of the world. This is not simply the view of Orthodox religious Jews. In his book *The Jews*, Arthur Hertzberg, conservative in religion and liberal in politics, insists that the idea of chosenness is essential to Jewish experience. He of course understands that the risk is separation from others, and as the Bible shows, it can become arrogance and cruelty to people who are not chosen. And yet Hertzberg believes that the Jewish people were chosen to bring light to the world. As it turns out, in their historical experience, the Jews after their dispersion from Eretz Israel *were* chosen to suffer persecution at the hands of the rest of the world. So that chosenness in that sense is an empirical fact of Jewish existence. But what of chosenness as an ideal, as a desirable concept? Is it necessary to the definition of the Jew?

The writer George Steiner created something of a scandal when in a novel he provocatively suggested that Hitler derived his idea of Aryan superiority from the Jews. Steiner's point is that the idea of a chosen people is a dangerous, potentially racist idea. My secular Jewish education never spoke of chosenness. The great lesson we learned over and over again was the need for the Jewish people to identify themselves with the suffering of other peoples, to insist on our common humanity. "In the diaspora," I write in the memoir, "the [secular] Jew is a rebuke to xenophobic barbarism. Jewishness, not as chosenness and self-congratulation, but as the gesture outward, the embrace of the other, common ground, a universalism that does not erase Jewish identity." If we want to redeem the word *chosenness*, we might think of it as a product not of biblical times, but of the experience of Jews in diaspora. In exile from ancient Israel, they learned to mix their lives with other peoples even in the face of persecution and became a caution, a sort of warning against religious and ethnic bigotry. Jews because of their experience are chosen, if that's the right word, to affirm our common humanity. Universalism is a relatively recent phenomenon in the history of the Jewish people. It has its origins in the Enlightenment, and it is often translated as assimilation, an impoverishing translation because it leaves out the Jewish inflection that I have just described.

A voice of doubt: a nice sentiment Jewish universalism, but what happens when the outward gesture, the embrace of the other encounters hatred and rejection. There is no turning of the other cheek in our tradition. James Joyce's *Ulysses* contains a powerful scene in a Dublin pub in which the hero, Leopold Bloom, the offspring of a converted Jew, but a Jew nonetheless (in the eyes of the goyim a Jew remains a Jew, no matter what) affirms love in response to the antisemite's hatred. And in the process he evokes the Jewish heroes of the Enlightenment: Spinoza, Moses Mendelssohn, Karl Marx (yes Karl Marx), and even Jesus, whom the Enlightenment remembered as a Jewish prophet and not as a God. Bloom's response does not shame the antisemite, makes no impression on him. His hatred remains incorrigible. But in the eyes of the reader (Jew and gentile) Bloom's noble response rises above the reciprocity of anger.

There is another response to Jew hatred, which is neither love nor hate, and it is embodied in the word *pariah*. *Pariah* is a word bestowed by the antisemite, but it may also be appropriated by the Jew who converts his pariah condition into a power. To be a pariah, or an outsider, may not altogether be a misfortune. When possessed of intellectual power and imagination, the outsider sees the world with critical understanding. He dissents from conventional pieties, from limited worldviews, from oppressive ideologies, from parochial outlooks. So the Jew as pariah, or outsider, may become a critic of the Jewish community as well. Hannah Arendt performed the role, particularly in her book on Eichmann. Among modern writers Kafka is the great exemplar of the artist as pariah. It is the very discomfort of the pariah condition that makes it the fitting habitation for the critic. I am a critic, and though it would be a bit pretentious to call myself a pariah, I have always been attracted to the role of outsider. Between the universalist and the outsider there is a paradoxical affinity. The person who stands alone may become a kind of everyman in his alienation.

Alienation, however, is not the whole story. In a remarkable essay, "The Intellectual Pre-Eminence of Jews," Thorstein Veblen makes a powerful case for the Jewish diaspora's benign consequences for the world. The secular Jew in diaspora is a hybrid who brings the mental energy of the Jewish tradition to modern life. "It is by loss of allegiances, or at best by force of a divided allegiance to the people of his origin, that he finds himself in the vanguard of modern inquiry." He transfers his skepticism about his faith to the modern sciences and the field of scholarship at large. Skepticism is an attitude shared in different ways by religious and secular Jews. Having suffered the slings and arrows of outrageous fortune, even a religious Jew may develop a contentious and skeptical attitude toward God. The Jew has a freedom of expression in his relationship to God that one doesn't normally find among gentiles. Sholem Aleichim has Tevye say what no gentile would dare to utter: "Apparently, if He wants it that way, that's the way it ought to be. Can't you see? If it should have been different, it would have been. And yet what would have been wrong to have it different?"

Speaking of chosenness, I began by saying that I parted ways with the Jewish tradition only to find myself trying to redefine it according to my vision of things. Alain Finkielkraut is right to speak of Judaism's lack of definition as precious because it provides an opportunity to find one's own way into the tradition. Such freedom has its risks, even its dangers. Not everything is permitted. And yet there is a spaciousness and generosity within Jewish tradition and experience that allow for a wide variety of interpretation and self-understanding.

What of the messiah, which Hertzberg reminds us performs a central role in Jewish consciousness? Religious Jews expect the messiah to come and redeem the Jewish people. It's a curious fact, however, that whenever someone has presented himself as a messiah, most notably Jesus and in more recent times Sabbatai Zevi, he is seen as a false messiah. So questions arise: is it because those who have presented themselves are demented or corrupt or both and when the true messiah will reveal himself we will know and accept him? Or is it because there is something treacherous and dangerous in the messianic idea itself? Here's a theory. The messiah is hope that is never realized, that we should never want to see realized, for it is the time of the apocalypse, which is the end of days and brings disaster and death. This is Isaac Bashevis Singer's great theme from the beginning of his career. You will find it in his superb short novel *Satan in Goray*, which deals with the time of Sabbatai Zevi. In his first novel, *The Family Moskat*, Singer concludes with the sentence, "Death is the messiah." (Even the Christian tradition is leery about the coming of the messiah. In the Grand Inquisitor episode in *The Brothers Karamazov*, the Grand Inquisitor tells the returning Jesus to go back where he came from because his promise of freedom would only bring anarchy and chaos.) Messianism has special relevance to me and to many other modern Jews, who lacking a religious faith embraced a secular one. It is no accident that Jews, a persecuted people in a messianic tradition, even if no longer religious, would identify themselves with a revolutionary movement. Communism is a secular version of messianism in its promise of the end of history (a phrase for the end of days) and a glorious new world of absolute harmony—on earth instead of heaven. In unlearning the secular messianic expectations of my childhood and youth, I had no desire to transfer them to religion. And yet here again the openness of the Jewish tradition provides a place for my own thoughts and sentiments, for there is in that tradition (Singer is an example) an antiapocalyptic strain that allows a place for the messiah as a symbol of hope that can never be fully realized. It makes it possible to desire and realize a better, though always imperfect, world without turning it upside down. (Singer has a darker view of the messianic idea than I do.)

Heterodoxy from beginning to end. During a question and answer period after I had given a reading from my memoir, a member of the audience accused me of contributing to the decline of Jewry. I had not transmitted my Jewish education to my children. They had grown up without a religious or cultural heritage and had married out, my daughter to a Protestant, my son to a Catholic. How could I respond to this accusation? I replied with a deflection. I had tried, I said, to provide an honest account of my life and experience. I lacked religious faith, and it would be not only an act of self-betrayal but also a desecration of religion to pretend to a faith I didn't genuinely experience. I had already explained in the memoir how compromised my Yiddish education had been and how both the circumstances of my life and the times made a Yiddish education for my children difficult, if not impossible. But my accuser was not appeased. Like the ultra-Orthodox Jews in Israel who blame Reform and secular Jews for the prospective demise of Jewish identity, he persisted in his criticism. In an accommodating country like America, Jews without belief may spell the end of Jewish identity. Notice I say "may" because there is no certainty in historical outcomes. I could have answered by asking how my accuser could maintain faith in a God who showed Himself to be impotent to protect Jews from the Holocaust. But it

would not be a fair response because the motive of my secularism does not lie
in a disillusionment with God as an omnipotent and benevolent being. Without
illusions of that kind, I never experienced disillusionment. It is not God but human beings who are responsible for the atrocities they inflict upon one another.
The fact is that I experience a certain envy of those who have the consolations
of religion. I did not say what I felt, namely, that I find the temperament of the
Orthodox believer anathema: it is a despotic temperament in its contempt for the
beliefs and unbeliefs of others. I do not want Jewish identity to disappear, but I
am willing to take my chances by allowing my children (as I wanted my parents
to allow me) to choose their own destinies. Of course, no one has absolute control over one's destiny or that of others, but I at least did not want to control my
children's choices.

My memoir is not a guide to the perplexed; it is rather about the perplexity
of being a secular Jew. More than one reader of my book has noted my ambivalences, my anxiety about the attenuation of Jewishness in me and its disappearance in my children. And yet I find in recalling my past and telling stories about
myself and others I experience an inextinguishable sentiment of being Jewish.
Sentiments are notoriously hard to define, but they are nonetheless real. Here is
what I say in my memoir.

Maybe my Jewishness persists in a certain reflectiveness, an inability to
take things for granted, a continuously nagging sense of difficulty and problem,
anxiety, guilt. Christians have historically tried to make Jews feel guilty for the
death of Christ; they have succeeded only in making them aggrieved victims. As
the pope has recently acknowledged, it is the Christians who are guilty of making the accusation and for all the consequences that have ensued. We should at
least be grateful that he has transferred the burden of guilt to his own tradition.
If we are not and do not feel guilty for the death of Christ, of what are we guilty?
Jewish guilt! This, for me, is the crux of the matter. Jewish guilt is the motive for
moral passion, the constant worrying about whether we have done right, done
enough, done too much. How should we react to provocation, injustice, indifference, neglect? In matters large and small, mostly small, but not less significant,
we find ourselves preoccupied with concern about conduct, about how to speak
and act in all situations.

In the centuries of wandering, Jews have learned to shift for themselves, to
adapt, to accommodate, to disappear and reappear, and to invent and reinvent
themselves. They have been experts in living on air, *luftmentschen*. This is what it
has meant historically to be in diaspora. But as Americans, can we say that we are
in diaspora if we have no nostalgia for a home we have never known; indeed, that
our parents and grandparents had never known? My experience of Jewishness is
a residuum of feelings, attitudes, attachments, and knowledge. Alain Finkielkraut
speaks to me when he writes, "Our relationship with Mother is Jewish, and it's
Jewish insomnia that we suffer, replete with feelings of guilt that attack in the
night. Our vital need for books is Jewish, so too our need for Jewish concepts and

for living and breathing the written word. And of course it almost goes without saying: there's our Jewish sense of humor, full of tenderness or despair." And I would add indignation at injustice and patience in the face of adversity. Which is not to say that only Jews have guilt or trouble sleeping or have the need for books or a sense of humor or indignation or patience. But there is a distinctive inflection in the way Jews combine these qualities. The great Russian poet Osip Mandelstam had the poet's instinct for the right simile when he wrote, "As a little musk fills an entire house, so the influence of Judaism overflows all of one's life."

It might be said that secular Jewishness has overflowed into American culture. As I have already remarked, conventional wisdom about the fate of Jewish identity in America is often conveyed by the word *assimilation*, which means the attenuation and ultimate disappearance of Jewish identity. What it ignores is the contribution Jewish writers and artists have made in the shaping and re-shaping of American culture. The musical theater, for example, is in large part the creation of Jewish composers and librettists: Irving Berlin, George and Ira Gershwin, Rodgers, Hart and Hammerstein, Jerome Kern, Stephen Sondheim, among others: secular Jews mostly, if not all. One can hear in both the lyrics and the music of *Oklahoma*, *South Pacific*, and *The King and I*, as examples, a valida-tion of difference and diversity in American life. In "breaking through," writers such as Saul Bellow, Bernard Malamud, and Philip Roth have introduced into mainstream American literature an idiom that contains within it the wit and ca-dences of the Yiddish language. When Bellow's Augie March speaks of himself as American-born, he does not mention the fact that he is a Jew, but in the course of the novel there is no mistaking that he is and that he means to take possession of American life as an American Jew. "Assimilation" does not characterize his swag-ger: I "go at things as I have taught myself, free-style, and will make the record in my own way: first to knock, first admitted, sometimes an innocent knock, some-times a not so innocent." Unlike his European or North African counterpart, the American Jew does not fear antisemitism, which is not say that it doesn't exist in America. The myth and to an extent the reality of America is that it provides its citizens with a space for a variety of self-definition. To be a secular Jew in America is to be a protagonist in any one of a number of stories, including the story that I have just told.

Eating Kosher Ivy

Jews as Literary Intellectuals

Daniel R. Schwarz

In this essay I shall consider the place of the Jewish literary intellectual, the diaspora of Jewish public intellectuals from New York urban culture to the American universities, and the consequent transformation of public intellectuals into literary intellectuals. Writing from a personal perspective and suspecting that some of my memories—like the memories of all of us—are distorted by time and by the demands of narrative teleology that require a coherent story, I write about my own diaspora from a suburban enclave into the world of literary scholars.

I. Situating Myself

In the 1940s and early 1950s when I was growing up in a Long Island community that was one-third Jewish, the Holocaust was a repressed subject among Jews who were often quite assimilated but, with the long shadow cast by events in Europe, wary of the gentile world—sometimes even more so than their parents. I was bar mitzvahed in a synagogue in Rockville Centre, a Long Island suburb; it was the first temple there, and my maternal grandparents were instrumental in establishing it. I remember that much was made of my maternal grandfather and grandmother not only as Jewish elders but as community elders. For they played a role in the suburb's community affairs before moving back to Manhattan after the war. My grandfather knew not a word of Hebrew or Yiddish and, as were all my grandparents, was born in this country. If my memory is correct, the Holocaust was barely mentioned in the Conservative religious school I attended three times a week until my bar mitzvah at age thirteen.

Why was the Holocaust a suppressed subject? Did assimilated American Jews feel they had something to be ashamed of because they did not prevent the destruction of their European counterparts? Did they fear provoking American antisemitism by special pleading? Was it that my parents' generation thought that children's sensibilities could not deal with the horrors of genocide?

Jewish silence during and after the war mirrored the much more striking silence, ineffectuality, and complicity of the American community that, despite the Nuremberg trials and the gruesome images in *Life* magazine and newsreels, chose to repress how they were helpless onlookers or even tacit if unwilling accomplices. We now know how much the American political leadership knew and how little they did about it. The atrocities committed on blacks in these years, particularly in the South, rightfully focused attention on civil rights, but there was surprisingly little linkage to the wartime persecution of Jews, notwithstanding the prominence of Jews in the Civil Rights movement in the fifties and sixties.

My mother's family was quite comfortable. They had moved to Long Island in the early years of the twentieth century. My father's family, once reasonably comfortable in the luggage business, got by after the Depression. They moved to Rockville Centre to open a dry cleaning business, one of many not very successful enterprises, and my mother's parents brought them clothes. My father was (I suspect, barely) acceptable as an eligible Jewish male. Awkward family pictures show my mother's parents and my father's mother—my father's father died before I was born—looking as if the two families belonged to different communities. Bar mitzvahed but not really educated in Jewish religious practices, my father became a certified public accountant, a temple member, and did reasonably well economically, but never had the elegance of my mother's parents. He was, and is, a frugal and prudent man.

Both of my grandfathers were German Jews. One grandmother, who was born in St. Louis in 1888, was a Polish Jew, but her family, like all my grandparents, emigrated to the U.S. at a time close to the Civil War. My mother's mother descended from Hungarian Jews. As I am reminded when I visit Vienna and Budapest, some of my mother's cooking reflects her Austrian-Hungarian heritage. My mother learned it from her grandmother—my great-grandmother whom I never met; she lived with my mother's parents and managed the house while my grandmother went to work with my grandfather in their jewelry business. About five years ago I saw photographs of my mother's forebears that were never before shown to me. They were German Jews born as far back as 1800, including some in German military uniforms, born around that time; there were my relatives, many of whom must have been left behind and whose children or children's children may have died in the Holocaust. My maternal grandfather was a formal man. Until I was ten I thought he took a shower with his tie on. My father's father, born in this country but deceased before I was born, insisted that his children learn German. My father spoke of an uncle who sympathized with the Germans during World War I. I always imagine how German these people must have felt even here. What an irony!

While I had some sense of Jewish identity, my childhood and adolescence were insulated from flagrant antisemitism, and my friends were just as likely, if not more likely, to be non-Jewish as Jewish. I confronted my Jewish identity when in 1961–1962 I did my junior year in what was still postwar Europe. I saw the Anne Frank house, was approached by Jews with numbers on their arms who wanted to meet American Jews, and saw the shards of the Warsaw ghetto. As I drove through Germany a number of times, I slept in inexpensive small guest houses only to awaken and see pictures of SS officers on the walls.

I married a woman who converted to Judaism; we were married by the Reform Jewish rabbi who presided over the process and ceremony of conversion. My sons were bar mitzvahed in a Conservative temple, the only temple in Ithaca until recently, and I still am a dues-paying member of the congregation. I was remarried to a Jewish woman in the same synagogue. Of the small number of Jews in my English Department at Cornell, I am the only member of the local temple, although I only go on the high holy days, and never for more than part of the long Conservative services.

I remain an agnostic but with deep spiritual—if I may I use that term—ties to my Jewish heritage. Passover and Hanukkah mean a great deal as family holidays, and my wife and I light the candles on Friday night if we are home—if we remember. My visit to Israel in 1985–1986, built around a lecture at Hebrew University in Jerusalem, accentuated my moderate Zionist sympathies. More and more, when I travel in Europe, I visit synagogues and Jewish sites and learn about Jewish history.

I have become more interested in my Jewish heritage as I became aware of how my Jewishness defines me as a scholar. Had I written *Imagining the Holocaust*, my book on Holocaust narratives, in the early 1970s when I was trying to make tenure, it would have been a passport to obscurity.

II. The Jew as (Not Always Comfortable) Guest in the House of English Literature

Many of the teachers who most influenced me were, by the standards of the day, outsiders and oddities: the first black teacher in my Long Island school district passionately taught me ninth- and eleventh-grade English; Barbara Lewalski, the only woman in the English Department at Brown from 1963 to 1968, when I did my graduate work there, was one of my paradigmatic figures; in college, two closeted gay professors influenced my thinking at a time when lifelong bachelors were suspect, and one became a lifelong influence and friend.

One found no tenured Jews on the rolls of Ivy League English departments before World War II; indeed, there were not many Irish or Italians. In part because of the importance of Einstein and in part because of the involvement of Jews in the Manhattan project, Jews were welcome in the more egalitarian and meritocratic world of the hard sciences before they were welcomed in the more elitist world of the humanities. But Jews did make inroads in English departments of public universities before they were welcomed in the Ivy League. For example, Berkeley had a considerable number of Jews on its English faculty by the late 1960s, the time when I began my teaching career at Cornell.

Jewish graduate students were expected to pursue the authorized subjects, to submerge their identity, and to find a common pursuit with other graduate students in studying Anglo-Catholic and Puritan writers. Raised in a Jewish home in New York, one distinguished female academic wrote on Flannery O'Connor at Berkeley and "identified," as she puts it, with O'Connor's southern Catholicism, rather than with her own marginal situation as a Jew in a gentile universe.

As a graduate student at Brown, I did my share of cultural cross-dressing when writing my master's thesis on Christian imagery in Browning's *The Ring and the Book* or working on a seminar paper on Spenser's *Shepherdes Calendar*. The department chair and a few of the faculty were Jews.

We need to remember that the dominant ideology, New Criticism, not only sought to eliminate the biography of the author but to focus on the ideal reader; homogenized the ethnic differences of the audience; and assumed that all readers brought similar experience—a keen sensibility and knowledge of literary tradition—to a text. The New Criticism and the other major Anglo-American formalism—neo-Aristotelian criticism— emphasized aesthetic values at the expense of representation of an anterior world. Erich Auerbach's influential study *Mimesis* discussed representation as a formal matter, not one involving messy social issues. Written after he escaped from Nazi Germany, the book never situates its author as a Jew.

Major English departments in the sixties and seventies were dominated by Anglophiles. With few exceptions, the antisemitic ravings of Pound, as well as the equally objectionable if less strident antisemitism of Eliot, were either excused as the eccentricities of men of genius or dismissed as unsuitable matters for discussion. In "Circumscriptions: Assimilating T.S. Eliot's Sweeneys" in *People of the Book*, Rachel Duplessis compellingly asks, "Were New Criticism and our carefully received reading strategies in some way complicit with the ravishing loss of Jewish particularity?"[1] In graduate school many of us, trained on the formalist rubric of organic form, read without noticing, or pretended not to notice, antisemitic passages. (While my dissertation director was a Jew with ambiguous feelings about his Jewishness, he was cognizant of the antisemitism in these paradigmatic modern writers). After all, were we not part of that imaginary audience of ideal readers on which New Criticism and Aristotelian criticism depended—even as we ignored the reality that the imagined audience of ideal readers were WASPs? We immersed ourselves in elaborate and arcane Christian theological debate to understand Milton or Hawthorne without reflecting that we were part of a different tradition, but perhaps we took secret satisfaction in learning that Milton knew Hebrew. Perhaps, too, we took pleasure in knowing that the exegetical tradition of literary criticism resembled the conversational

and inquisitive mode of Talmudic studies, or what we—as assimilated Jews—
imagined Talmudic study to be.

Figures like M.H. Abrams, Harry Levin, Lionel Trilling—those who found
a place with the Ivy League—as well as Irving Howe and Alfred Kazin—New York
Intellectuals who made their mark—became spiritual fathers to those of us who
took up English and American studies in the 1960s.[2] To them I would add Meyer
Shapiro, the great Columbia art historian. Kazin and Howe embraced their Jewishness far more dramatically than my friend who called himself Mike Abrams
and wrote under the name M.H. Abrams rather than use his actual name, Meyer.
Abrams eschewed being too Jewish, and rarely—at least in my presence—talked
about his Jewishness until after he retired. Quietly he contributed generously to
the United Jewish Appeal (UJA), but he created an identity as the archetypal
Harvard-educated English professor: art connoisseur, pipe smoking gourmet,
lover of classical music and dilettante recorder player, dedicated Cornell sports
fan. In conversation, he eschewed unpleasant topics from the shortcomings of
colleagues to the Holocaust.

When I arrived at Cornell in 1968 I encountered in the English Department a few older Jewish colleagues. Wary of being too Jewish, most had experienced antisemitism, which they spoke of to younger Jewish scholars only after
they knew them well and even then in hush-hush tones. My generation, too,
was taught that it was best not to be too Jewish; as another colleague put it, "As
a graduate student, I was taught not to walk around with a Hebrew National
salami hanging out of my pocket." Some disguised their Jewish heritage by name
changes or a refusal to acknowledge their Jewish ancestry. Virtually none of my
Jewish colleagues had temple affiliations; some gave almost surreptitiously to the
UJA, whereas others of Jewish parentage denied their Jewishness. One colleague,
whose father had been at CCNY with my father and came from a distinguished
Jewish family, responded tartly to a UJA solicitation, "You mustn't assume from
my name that I have Jewish origins."

I confess to having always felt uncomfortable within the mostly WASPish
world of Ivy League English departments. Except for one woman who very much
played down her Jewish identity, I have here for forty years dealt with non-Jewish
chairs, at least some of whom seemed to be uncomfortable dealing with Jews.
Was it that discomfort that draws me to outsiders for my subjects? For my college honors thesis and Ph.D. dissertation I chose as my subject Joseph Conrad,
a Polish émigré who felt himself an outsider in England. For my first book, I
chose Benjamin Disraeli, the Jew who became prime minister and always—even
though he had been converted as a boy, thanks to his father—thought of himself as a Jew and maintained a strong if eccentric sense of Jewish identity. After
writing my two literary studies on Conrad, I turned to James Joyce, who left his
homeland dominated by the Catholic Church and the British Crown to wander
in exile and who identified with Jews. Teaching and writing on Joyce required a

knowledge of what to me were exotic Catholic rituals and legends, but I did focus a fair amount in my *Reading Joyce's "Ulysses"* on Bloom as a Jew.

Certainly the dominant style for Jews in my department has been to mimic WASPish customs and behavior. The person who was chair during most of my assistant professor years had a preferred way of saying "no" that at first sounded like "yes." He would say, "I agree with you on principle," before saying, sometimes two conversations or weeks later, why he couldn't or wouldn't do something. To my ethnic heritage, with its emphasis on frankly confronting opposing views, this mode of discourse seemed incredibly odd. Even though I had done my graduate work at Brown—where Jews did not hide their Jewishness quite as much as at Cornell—I was not familiar with the professorial locutions in the form of innuendo, litotes, and euphemism.

Have I experienced covert or overt antisemitism in my professional career? I could cite scattered anecdotes, but the truth is I don't know. For example, I was at a party in 1973 after the Arab-Israeli conflict that year when I overheard a senior and esteemed member of my department declaiming to his listeners, "The Jews on campus get uppity whenever Israel batters the Arabs." On one hand, I did get tenure at a time and in a department when many didn't. On the other, the only self-identified Jews—other than one creative writer who taught half-time and never mentioned her Jewish heritage in my company—who ever held endowed chairs were M.H. Abrams and Joel Porte, and neither has had a religious affiliation.

Certainly it was made clear to me that my New York accent and direct if not brash manner were odd. That I didn't go to Harvard for any of my degrees was another minus in some eyes in a department that has had only Harvard Ph.D.s as department chairs for twenty-five years. I made a point of being who I was and not pretending I was someone else. I spoke my mind at meetings, disagreed when I thought it was a matter of principle to do so, and probably didn't always do myself good in the process.

Among the Jews I have known at Cornell, the subject of what it is like to be a Jew and teach English and American literature has never been, so far as I know, the subject of a public or private discussion in my forty years here. And yet for those of us Jewish professors, and for our Jewish students as well, it is surely a more compelling subject than so many that we address. Why do Jews act as if this issue didn't matter? Even in *People of the Book: Thirty Scholars Reflect on Their Jewish Identity*—the collection edited by Jeffrey Rubin-Dorsky and Shelley Fisher Fishkin—one finds a fair amount of evasion of what makes literary studies appealing to Jews, what defines the Jewish contribution, and what is the nature of Jewish relationships among multicultural colleagues. Why do contemporary Jews in literature departments—much like the first group of Jews who were on these faculties—often accept without resistance being grouped by minorities as part of a Caucasian hegemony when their experience has much in common with those very minorities? Indeed, it is curious how—perhaps as the social price for acceptance—Jewish scholars in English departments only pushed for Jewish studies after the establishment of other ethnic and minority studies.

III. Leslie Fiedler's Challenge to the New Criticism

In the 1960s every Jewish graduate student knew the fairy tale of Leslie Fiedler: exiled in Missoula, Montana, where he wrote and taught before returning to the East to SUNY, Buffalo; in his life and work he thumbed his nose at the academic establishment and parochial historical criticism and what he saw as the narrow formalism of New Criticism while making a very substantial reputation based primarily on one important and subversive book, *Love and Death in the American Novel* (1960). Published when he was in his forties, Fiedler's book was embraced by younger academics and graduate students as relevant to overlooked themes and issues.

At a time when the relevance of literary study was being increasingly called into question by rampant McCarthyism and, later, the Vietnam War, the anti-war protest movement, and the resulting fissures between university and society, Fiedler's book argued that literary study was central to our lives. Fiedler's bold discussion of psychosexual and political issues fulfilled the desire of younger academics for a more lively and engaged critical discourse. For Fiedler, literary criticism is, as he writes in an encomium to his mentor, William Ellory Leonard, "an act of total moral engagement, in which tact, patience, insolence, and piety consort strangely but satisfactorily together; nor can anyone who once listened to [Leonard] believe that the truth one tries to tell about literature is finally different from the truth one tries to tell about the indignities and rewards of being the kind of man one is—an American, let's say, in the second half of the twentieth century, learning to read his country's books."[3]

Retrospectively we can see that Fiedler enacts the ambiguity of Jews in English studies who, on the one hand, study a majority culture, accommodate to it, and are shaped by it, but on the other not only arrogate that culture for our own understanding and professional ends but often bring to the subject an outsider's perspective and to the profession's customs and manners a somewhat different set of values. We make English studies our instrument, even as it makes us the instrument of English studies, its voice, and its spokespeople. Put another way: like other conquerors we become the conquered.

In Fiedler's work on Joyce, we see not only his kinship with Leopold Bloom but feel he is writing about his own experience in the academy: "Anti-Semitism is everywhere in *Ulysses* the chief, almost the sole mode of relating to Jews available to gentiles; and indeed it is only in response to it that Bloom can feel himself a Jew at all since ritually and ethnically he scarcely qualifies."[4] Yet he also acknowledges that as an oddity—"a literary Fiedler on the roof of academe"—he has benefited at times from philo-Semitism.[5] I doubt I can say the same. Fiedler, like many Jews of his generation, writes as a Jew responding to a gentile world that defines him as a Jew *and* a representative of his people to outsiders.

IV. Finding a Home in a Restricted Neighborhood

How does being a secular Jew with an emphasis on this life in this world shape my sensibility? In answering that question, let us remember that each Jew has his own particular background and story to tell. Jewishness taught me that the fabric of everyday life matters more than one controlling ideology. That I am a humanistic critic who has insisted that literature is by humans, about humans, and for humans is related to my concept of being Jewish. So, too, is my interest in the novel. It taught me that each reader, like each character in the novel, needs to be taken seriously. For me each reader also means each student I teach.

Because Jews have historically lived on the margin—in ghettoes and shtetls, never sure of what pogroms tomorrow will bring—Jews have tended to be skeptical of sweeping universals and to dwell in particulars. Traditionally, Jews accept a world of fragments and enjoy small pleasures. The weekly routines focusing on the Sabbath and, for religious Jews, daily prayers in morning and evening paradoxically focus on the temporal dimension even while providing temporary escape from that dimension. Jewish theology is more concerned with relations between humans and God and humans among themselves than a specific vision of the hereafter. Even Orthodox Jews stress the gap between man and God and hence turn their attention to the world in which they live.

For most Jews other than the ultraorthodox, reading and interpreting biblical texts is an open and exegetical process. When one looks at the Talmud, one sees an unresolved dialogue among diverse commentators. In Judaism there are no ex cathedra statements, no Nicene creed, no attempt to resolve interpretive questions with single statements. In the Passover Haggadah the various rabbis comment dialogically upon the meaning of the Exodus story and specifically the meaning of the Passover customs, but the discussion is not resolved. The very term *Haggadah* means "the telling," and it is an open and evolving text that responds to changing historical circumstances. Before the founding of the state of Israel, it often took on a Zionist coloration to encourage the emigration of Eastern European Jews who were victims of pogroms and the Holocaust. The focus became more and more upon the captivity in Egypt as a metaphor not only for the Diaspora in general but for state-sponsored pogroms, most notably what Lucy Davidowicz has called "The War against the Jews," or what we know as the Holocaust.

Thus the Talmudic exegetical tradition—a tradition of commentary—encouraged debate and dissent. I regard discussions of texts I teach and in particular professional literary criticism as a kind of continuing midrash or commentary on literary texts. The tradition of studying the Torah and endlessly debating its meaning, of allowing dissent in its codification, gave space for specific and diverse readings that resisted universals, for elegant arguments for different positions, and for pluralism without dogmatism (the imposition of one position) or relativism (the notion that all views are equal). Openness to diverse perspectives is not at odds in making choices and judgments or in understanding that in some situations we cannot give equal weight to various interests. Just as I reject measuring life on a vertical dimension that assumes that we are poised between heaven and hell and that this life is a prelude to another life, I am skeptical of readings of the texts that see them in only one coordinate, whether Marxist, gay, feminist, or poststructural. All of the aforementioned are important ways of perceiving but need to be conceived as part of a pluralistic and dialogic epistemology.

Finally, my work has focused on ethical issues. Jews derived a strong sense of ethics from this Talmudic tradition of extracting from the Bible its moral implications and applicability for living today. Thus Jewish thinking derives much more from practice than theology. As Susanne Klingenstein writes, "The absence of a single work outlining Jewish ethics, the moral theory behind ritual observance or orthopractice, has to do with the fact that ethical insights are regarded as an outgrowth of a specific discretionary form of behavior, which requires you to examine every act and action, to do nothing carelessly and thoughtlessly: Jewish moral thought emerged as a consequence of moral conduct."[6] Jewish tradition is ethically based—isn't the Talmud a discussion about law and ethics?—with an emphasis on what Aristotle called the "ineluctable modality of the visible" (and Joyce redefined into "What you damn well have to see"). Moreover, in Eastern Europe, the hereafter was less a concern than eking out a living in the face often of arbitrary changes in the political winds. Unlike the Christian or Greek tradition, Jewish tradition eschewed universal explanations and sought to explore the human dilemma in a complex antagonistic world where Jews were marginalized, isolated, and persecuted. Jews by necessity lived in time and looked for partial solutions.

V. Jews as Public Intellectuals

While Jews were still having a difficult time finding a place in prestigious universities, especially those in the Ivy League, many of the public intellectuals of the 1930s, 1940s, and 1950s were Jews and were associated with the *Partisan Review. Partisan Review,* as well as *Commentary,* had many but by no means all Jewish writers. Except for Trilling and art historian Meyer Shapiro at Columbia, the Jewish New York Intellectuals were considered academic outsiders by many Ivy League Anglo-Saxon elitists in the 1950s and 1960s. Jewish figures like Kazin, Howe, and Leslie Fiedler all worked mostly on American literature rather than the more validated English tradition. *Partisan Review* as well as *Commentary* helped establish the prominence of Saul Bellow, Bernard Malamud, and Philip Roth. Writing about second-generation Jews who became immersed in the broad tradition of Western culture, Terry A. Cooney observes: "What attracted a certain group of young intellectuals was a cultural promise, a literary tradition, and a pattern of social protest that together provided a basis for rejecting middle-class culture, though its sources lay embedded within that culture. . . . The sense of universal significance associated with their educational commitments seemed the opposite of the narrow concern young intellectuals saw in the Jewish community."[7] Jewish intellectuals existed on a kind of borderland between Jewish and gentile culture. Abandoning the security of their own communities without finding full acceptance in the communities of which they strove to be part, they became at once cosmopolitan and marginal. Within New York, especially with the second generation of Jewish intellectuals like Howe and Norman Podhoretz, however, their Jewishness created a common bond, a community that could not exist elsewhere, and a sense of belonging to an urban Jewish culture. Paradoxically, Jews within the New York intellectual community felt a common bond even while eschewing being too culturally Jewish.

Although a shared sense of Jewishness formed a common bond among many of the contributors to *Partisan Review*, the plight of Jews in Europe was, somewhat surprisingly, not a focus of the magazine in the later 1930s and early 1940s. Trilling surely disassociated himself from self-conscious American Jewish culture and denied its intellectual viability.[8] The aforementioned Jews preferred to see Jews as marginal, outsider, cosmopolitan, and wanderer, as representative of the modern condition in that each American—and especially those not part of the WASP establishment—had to create their own cultural tradition. Cooney observes how Jews embraced secularism and the here-and-now world as an alternative to mysticism and Platonism: "[F]or many in the *Partisan Review* circle, rational and secular values were not just necessary to a sophisticated culture; they were also intimately tied up with resistance to anti-Semitism."[9]

What are public intellectuals? Knowledgeable in philosophy, history, public issues, and psychology, they are figures who speak to a wider audience than would a specialist and who speak in lucid and comprehensible terms. They place their insights in a broad cultural context. Gradually, like Trilling, Howe, Clement Greenberg, and Harold Rosenberg—and gentiles like Edmund Wilson and Mary McCarthy—they earn the confidence of their readers that their wide intellectual experience has earned their attention. They have *gravitas*.

Public intellectuals also need an audience concerned with similar issues. In our diversified if not divided and divisive culture—where there is so much to be known and where special interest groups insist on focusing on their own segment—what matters to some is of no interest to others. I grew up in a world where a film by Truffaut or Fellini—or in New York a major exhibit at the Met on Picasso, Egypt, or China—needed to be seen and discussed as soon as possible. Now we are overwhelmed with information, books, films, and exhibits; although we always had to make choices, we now do so more often in terms of our cultural enclaves.

In the heyday of *Partisan Review*, literary criticism was more accessible to a literate audience than it is now. In the humanities and social sciences, there has been a schism between academic culture and an intellectual audience. While the university world has become the center of intellectual activity and we find Jews occupying prominent places as literary intellectuals at major universities, including the Ivy League, the retreat into private enclaves and jargon has been responsible for the decline of the literary critic as public intellectual. It may be now that our most influential public intellectuals are scientists like the late Carl Sagan and Stephen Jay Gould, both not so incidentally Jews. If public intellectuals depend on finding an apt audience, it isn't surprising that discussion of environmental issues such as global warming and public health issues such as the AIDS epidemic have become the focus of public discourse. In sociology figures like Daniel Bell, Daniel Moynihan, or David Reisman affected the way we thought about social and moral issues. Now academic disciplines adopt a special vocabulary that excludes all but the cognoscenti. It may be that Jews took the lead in providing explanations and exegesis, but as they became comfortably absorbed within the academy, they often abandoned that role as cultural mediator and middleman.

For a time the *New York Review of Books*, coedited by Robert Silvers and Jason Epstein, was essential reading for American intellectuals, but it now displays its own kind of parochialism, often printing twice-told tales of writers whose work it has published for decades. Today, the *New York Times*—now a national newspaper printed in a number of cities and distributed throughout the entire country—performs that role for many, especially in Tuesday's *Science Times*, Friday's movie and art reviews, Saturday's *Arts and Ideas*, and occasionally on Sunday in articles in *Arts and Leisure*, *News of the Week*, the *Sunday Magazine*, and the *Book Review*. Yet the *New York Times* is patronized by academics for its middle-of-the-road political views or its reduction of complex research into lucid terms.

VI. Jews as Literary Intellectuals: Shared Qualities and Contributions

Jews as literary intellectuals played as varied a role as their gentile counterparts, ranging from Morton Bloomfield's medieval scholarship to Marjorie Garber's challenging of accepted notions about the nature of literary studies. Yet based on my forty years of living in the world of literary intellectuals, I would like to make a few bold—and rough—generalizations about Jews in English departments and other departments of literature.

1. Jews have tended to be less committed to univocal explanations of thematic and aesthetic patterns and more to pluralistic ones. For one thing, the Jewish intellectual tradition values the process of inquiry as much as the goal. For another, few Jewish literary intellectuals have embraced the dogmatism of ultraorthodox Jews—and even within that tradition the interpretation of every biblical passage is a matter of commentary and exegesis.

2. Jews have had an interest in multidisciplinary approaches and have been more likely than their non-Jewish counterparts to import historical and philo-

sophical and psychoanalytic contexts into their work. In some ways this moved them to a detached view of the Christian cosmology that dominated the tradition of English and American literature. Because intellectuals often write to explain things to ourselves, we shouldn't be surprised that, beginning with Abrams's explanation of how Christianity informed Romanticism in *Natural Supernaturalism*, Jews—including Harold Bloom and Geoffrey Hartman—took the leading role in explaining the oddities of Romanticism. Among the later generations of Jewish literary intellectuals, luminaries from Geoffrey Hartman to Stanley Fish, Sandra Gilbert, and Steven Greenblatt have made great contributions to literary studies in the past few decades, including promulgating major synthesizing overviews and theoretical formulations—but formulations grounded in the experience of reading. Fish may have been a tad more "Surprised by Sin"—to cite the title of his reader response study of Milton—than those immersed from childhood in Christian theology.

Jewish sensibility tends to reject unilateral explanations, and the New Critical concept of an ideal reading repressed that sensibility. The appeal of poststructuralism for Jews might be in its very focus on indeterminacies, gaps, and fissures in traditional explanations. That Jacques Derrida and his mentor Emmanuel Levinas were Jews who examined complex issues in prolix, complex, and erudite ways may have influenced poststructuralism's appeal.

3. In the scholarship of Jews, formal issues have taken a backseat to content, and Jews have tended to eschew the purely aesthetic and to insist on considering how humans are represented—in recent years with a more inclusive focus on Jews, blacks, women, gays, and middle and lower classes. Jews in the academy are more likely to be public intellectuals like Trilling and Morris Dickstein relating literature to larger cultural issues. They have been interested in investigating the interplay among individual achievement, artistic tradition, and historical context. This originally may have been because many of them have eastern urban backgrounds, where reading the *New York Times* if not the *New Yorker* and *New York Review of Books* is part of being an educated adult.

4. Interested in representation, Jews have tended to study human life in particular cultural contexts through interpretative analysis of individual behavior, discourse, and social practice. Beginning with Auerbach and Abrams, they have often focused on interpreting artistic continuities and changes—and relating them to political, social, economic, religious, and intellectual developments—as they evolve through time. Jews are more likely to be informed about current political issues and related cultural phenomena and are more likely to do synthesizing work. Jews have been more interested than their gentile counterparts in examining ethical questions inherent in literary texts, questions that concern the nature of justice, the good life, or human values in general.

5. Jews not only homogenized the academy in terms of ethnic background but in terms of social classes. Many came from second-generation immigrant families. Many Jews came from the New York area with New York speech. The

otherness of Jews not only paved the way for women, self-identified (as opposed to closeted) gays, blacks, Hispanics, and other ethnic minorities into formerly gentile enclaves but also lent necessary political support and tolerance to opening doors and windows to a diverse population of faculty and students.

If the first generation of Ivy League professors were anglicized, some of the second and third generation resisted this kind of assimilation, refused to be "clubable," modified some exclusionary practices, insisted on tolerance for otherness and difference, and thus opened the door for women, blacks, and other minorities. Jews were more likely to be outspoken about the accepted rituals of academic life.

In my experience, Jews and ethnics were in the vanguard of welcoming women, African Americans, and gays into the academy. (Certainly in the 1970s and 1980s I taught a far greater percentage of graduate students in these categories than did most of my colleagues.)

Jews have been more likely to be politically active, usually on the side of leftist politics. They were often campus leaders of the anti–Vietnam War movement. They opposed Joseph McCarthy and the House Un-American Activities Committee in the 1950s and were activists in the Civil Rights and ban-the-bomb movements. Today Jews debate Middle Eastern politics.

6. Coming almost exclusively from a tradition that emphasized life in this world rather than as a prelude to a better world, Jews have been more likely to have a humanistic bent and to realize texts are by humans, about humans, and for humans. They have been interested in how humans behave, whether as authors or characters or readers, and less interested in purely scholarly matters such as editing or philology. Surely there is a comparative dearth of Jews in English medieval studies, where those issues along with hagiography and Christian typology dominate.

7. Whether they acknowledge it or not, Jews are often guests in American and English traditions that have been driven by primary writings and criticism that were driven in turn by different religious and cultural assumptions. There is something paradoxical about Jews teaching texts written by believing Christians who think that the Jews are at best apostates and heretics and at worst Christ murderers and about Jews reading critics who did little to separate themselves from these views and who socially looked upon Jews from a steep and icy peak. At elite universities some Jews accommodated themselves to these traditions and even cross-dressed as gentiles, and in my experience, all too few struggled to understand the aforementioned paradoxes. Those that did were, like Alfred Kazin and Irving Howe, more likely to teach in urban public universities such as CUNY—the City University of New York.

At times Jewish academics of the second and third generation have become the insiders. Of course, given how cultures replicate themselves as they assimilate newcomers, there is no reason that Jews in the humanities should not be ambitious or that they should disguise ambition behind an ironic facade as did prior generations of WASPs. We know that the drive for recognition and reward always has an element of narcissistic careerism. The difference between the later generations of Jewish literary intellectual scholars and the first one is that we can acknowledge this. Thus while one can praise the prominence of Jews, one can also note sardonically that Jews are not immune to the kind of careerism that David Lodge addresses in *Small Worlds*—Stanley Fish is rather proud that he is the model for Morris Zapp—and that Israel has been in the forefront of the kind of flamboyant academic conferencing he satirizes.

VII. Conclusion: The Return of the Repressed

Let us think about how some Jewish literary intellectuals have once again taken the role of public intellectuals. For several decades, Jewish scholars passionately taught and still teach Anglo-American literature, but in recent years many have been rethinking whether these professional interests have repressed ethnic concerns. Why do assimilated Jewish scholars of different theoretical persuasions who used to discuss Wordsworth and Hardy in the halls now passionately discuss their Jewish pasts and their common interest in Holocaust studies even if they have different theoretical perspectives? How do we account for the return of the repressed and the sublimated? Is it because these Jews became tired of cross-dressing to gain acceptance in Anglophile English departments within prestigious universities?

For Jews in the literary departments, the subject of the Holocaust may be one way to deal with the Diaspora and may, indeed, be a way of returning to our intellectual homeland. We have come a long way since Jews in American English departments were told that their Jewishness would be a negative factor in their careers or when non-Jews of lesser ability were encouraged to go into academics because they seemed to have the correct social graces. One notes that a kind of Anglo-Saxon cosmopolitanism and reserve still are important factors in the manners and mores of major English departments. There can be no doubt that various Jewish academics from Greenblatt—a recent president of MLA—to Fish occupy a large place in the intellectual landscape of the humanities, but they often do so in subjects remote or at an oblique angle from their ethnic heritage. Yet now the Holocaust has become a fashionable subject. Quite a number of Jewish scholars who decades ago had made their careers in English or language studies have returned to their origins. Jewish members of other university departments pride themselves on being part of Jewish studies programs.

When and why did cross-dressing abate for some Jews in prestigious English departments? For one thing, as I have already mentioned, ethnic studies made it permissible to own one's past; for another, cultural and ethnic studies expanded dramatically the range of what one could address in one's courses and research. In the wake of African American, Asian American, and Native American ethnic consciousness, it became permissible for Jews to discuss their past. That Jewish students wanted courses in their history was demonstrated by the numerical success of Holocaust courses and other Jewish studies courses. I had each year many more students who wanted to be members of my seminar on Holocaust memoirs and fiction than the fifteen students that the seminar accommodates.

As they reach midcareer and perhaps are realizing that their professional lives have not so many years to go, many Jewish scholars begin to go back to their own heritage and history. Some, like Hartman and Harold Bloom, began in traditional English studies and turned more to their Jewish heritage. In some ways, *our*—for am I not speaking of myself?—collective cultural silence in the Anglophiliac world has poignantly (and maybe, we should say, pathetically) mirrored that of some Holocaust survivors who tried to bury the past. I am thinking of survivors who seem to have successfully put behind them the concentration camp universe, only to find out that the experience cannot be repressed or sublimated. Now some of us want to use our skills to reconnect to our European antecedents, whether they be emigrants generations ago or Holocaust survivors. Jews realize that the discontinuity in their history created by mass destruction left not only an absence of specific people, a human loss, but also a generational gap—indeed, an epistemological gap—in their actual and metaphorical lineage. We want to close the gaps in the vertical relations not only with our parents but with our children as well. Realizing perhaps that our own survival depended on a geographic accident, we want to understand the plot that might have been. In Anne Frank's pictures we see our children, our nieces and nephews. We try to build bridges in our memory from our world to the Holocaust's inexplicable *erasure* of history as well as from our world to what might have been had European Jewry continued to flourish—and we inevitably fail in both endeavors.

Holocaust studies has not only developed in the wake of ethnic studies but has become a centerpiece, an essential field. In short, the study of "the war against the Jews" has become an industry. One can almost say it has the cachet that women's studies had a decade ago. Indeed, Jewish women, who had obliterated that part of their identity when becoming active in the women's movement, are now often in the forefront of those reexamining their Jewish roots and the Holocaust. The *Times Literary Supplement*, which barely mentioned Jewish studies for decades and patronized Jews when not ignoring them, overflows with reviews and discussion. More than Marcel Ophul's *The Sorrow and the Pity* (1969) and Claude Lanzmann's *Shoah* (1985), Green's teleplay series *Holocaust* (1978) and Spielberg's *Schindler's List* (1993) have put the Holocaust in the popular conscience. Generous donors underwrite Jewish studies the way they once underwrote yeshivahs in Israel. Book publishers compete for Holocaust studies because they sell. Museums, photography, books, and films feed upon one another and whet the very appetite they are meant to sate. Psychoanalytic critics have focused on the effect of trauma upon the memory of survivors and how it affects the children of survivors.

If the public literary intellectual has been subsumed into the university star system with a corresponding loss of influence that characterizes ivory-tower intellectuals who have retreated into specialized discourse and small book sales, the Holocaust as subject—along with questions of Jewish identity, assimilation, and the moral implications of Zionism, especially as they are rendered in the arts—may be the bridge to participation in cultural debate and engaging a larger audience. Put another way, Jews as literary intellectuals are discovering a way to be not only public intellectuals but also self-identified and proud Jews.

Notes

1   Rachel Duplessis, "Circumscriptions: Assimilating T.S. Eliot's Sweeneys," in *People of the Book: Thirty Scholars Reflect on Their Jewish Identity*, ed. Jeffrey Rubin-Dorsky and Shelley Fisher Fishkin (Madison: University of Wisconsin Press, 1996), p. 139.

2.   I have neither the space nor inclination to add to Susanne Klingenstein's overview on Jews in the academy in her two fine studies *Jews in the American Academy: The Dynamics of Intellectual Assimilation, 1900–1940* (New Haven: Yale, 1991) and *Enlarging America: The Cultural Work of Jewish Literary Scholars, 1930–1990* (Syracuse: Syracuse University Press, 1998). Perhaps I should say that I don't always agree with her programmatic division of Jews into various academic generations.

3.   Leslie Fiedler, preface to *Love and Death in the American Novel* (New York: Criterion, 1960), n.p.

4.   Leslie Fiedler, *Fiedler on the Roof: Essays on Literature and Jewish Identity* (Boston: David R. Godfine, 1991), p. 55.

5.   Ibid., p. 104.

6.   Susanne Klingenstein, "Stranger in Paradise: Encounters with American Jews," in *People of the Book: Thirty Scholars Reflect on Their Jewish Identity*, ed. Jeffrey Rubin-Dorsky and Shelley Fisher Fishkin, pp. 197–202 (Madison: University of Wisconsin Press, 1996), p. 193.

7.   Terry A. Cooney, *The Rise of the New York Intellectual: Partisan Review and Its Circle, 1934–1945* (Madison: University of Wisconsin Press, 1986), pp. 14–15.

8.   See Cooney, p. 237; Cooney includes Kazin in the above sentence.

9.   Cooney, p. 243.

Jewish Intellectuals and the "Deep Places of the Imagination"

Mark Krupnick

Have American Jewish intellectuals penetrated to the "deep places of imagination"? What? What kind of question is that? What are these "deep places," and why should intellectuals, Jewish or otherwise, wish to get to them? The terms I use are in quotation marks. Who first used them and in what connection? Why deep places rather than high places? After all, Shelley, a great intellectual as well as man of imagination, wrote of being "pinnacled in the intense inane." And what kind of intellectuals, apart from their being Jewish, are we talking about?

These are some of the questions that I explore in the pages that follow. It was Lionel Trilling, in his most influential book, *The Liberal Imagination*, who first talked of deep places of the imagination in connection with the socially oriented American writers of the 1930s and 1940s. Trilling thought that these writers, and precursors like Theodore Dreiser and Sherwood Anderson, had failed of greatness because they had not penetrated the deep places of imagination as had the pioneering figures of European literary modernism.

Because Trilling first raised the issue, I have taken him as my guide, but I have also asked to what extent Trilling was able to improve on the writers he found wanting by himself acceding in his own writing to the deep places. I have added comments on two of Trilling's near-contemporaries to suggest a general slant on the Depression–World War II generation of Jewish intellectuals in America.

1. Trilling was the most distinguished in his generation of American Jewish public intellectuals. A reader today might reasonably expect that critics who came of age during the Depression would have been far more attentive to socioeconomic issues and to clearly political ideology than were the public intellectuals of the closing years of the past century. Our own contemporaries focused on

issues that are primarily cultural: Derridean deconstruction versus the possibility of stable knowledge, the question of the canon, topics canvassed in feminist and queer studies, and the role of African American studies in the curriculum.

These have been mainly academic affairs, different in their urgency from the crisis of capitalism and rise of fascism in the 1930s. The Jewish intellectuals of New York City were preoccupied above all by one political issue: the fate of socialism. The debate over communism, or more precisely Stalinism, provided the background for the essays included in *The Liberal Imagination*.

It is remarkable in this light that Trilling defined his own vocation as a public intellectual in broadly cultural terms. In the memorable preface to *The Liberal Imagination,* he wrote not of communism as such but of Enlightenment liberalism and its degeneration in his own time. He defined liberalism as "a large tendency rather than a concise body of doctrine," and he cited Goethe's opinion that liberalism consists not of ideas but of "sentiments." At this point Trilling made clear that he had in mind a "natural connection," perhaps even a "kind of identity," between literature and culture on the one hand and politics on the other.[1]

Here Trilling carved out his personal conceptions of politics and culture, conceptions that are very different from the densely materialist conceptions of most of his intellectual contemporaries and our own. He said that his sense of the connection between literature and politics would seem especially valid "if we do not intend the narrow but the wide sense of the word politics . . . for clearly it is no longer possible to think of politics except as the politics of culture, the organization of human life toward some end or other, toward the modification of sentiments, which is to say the quality of human life."[2]

The breadth, albeit the vagueness, of Trilling's concerns marks him off from the anticommunists of the *Partisan Review* circle as much as from the politically correct Stalinists. Still, he insisted that he remained a political man, a man of the left, and of his moment. He was above all an intellectual foe of Stalinism, and it is useful to keep in mind that in New York City in the 1940s many more Jewish intellectuals were devoted to Stalinism, if only in the form of fellow traveling, than to the anti-Stalinist leftism of *Partisan Review* and *Commentary*.

It was certainly, in the context of the Depression–World War II years, an unusual political intellectual who spoke up, as Trilling did, for "the gratuitous" and celebrated the imagination of "variousness, possibility, complexity, and difficulty." At bottom, even Trilling was not devoted to an aesthetic approach to art, and even if he did not characteristically proceed by way of the close examination of individual literary texts, he remained more a literary than a political man. He argued throughout the 1940s and into the 1950s that the characteristic mark of the American "liberal imagination" was precisely its *lack* of imagination. He consistently favored the literary imagination as opposed to the literal-minded liberal imagination.

2. This argument appears most concisely in Trilling's essay "The Function of the Little Magazine," which he reprinted in *The Liberal Imagination.* That essay

initially appeared as the introduction to a collection of essays honoring *Partisan Review*, the particular little magazine that first published many of his own best essays of the 1940s. The collection is *The Partisan Reader: Ten Years of Partisan Review, 1933–1944: An Anthology.* The book was edited by William Phillips and Philip Rahv, who had founded the journal with the support of the Communist Party and, after nine issues, reemerged as editors of the still-Marxist but now anti-Stalinist periodical.

This essay is brief and mainly consists of one central idea that Trilling repeats several times but does not much develop. Moreover, like his model, Matthew Arnold, Trilling invokes a number of key terms but does not define them with precision. Still, it is, I think, one of the most important of Trilling's essays in helping us think about his career and about Jewish writing in America in his time and since.

For my purposes here, his most important assertion is that "There is no connection between the political ideas of our educated class and the deep places of the imagination." Trilling offers three chief elements in that crucial formulation: "political ideas," "our educated class," and "the deep places of the imagination," and he suggests there ought to be a connection among them.

The deep places of the imagination are the most important element, but I will come to them last. Let me look first at our educated class. Sometimes Trilling calls it the "educated middle class." The people he has in mind were mainly Jews of New York: professors and schoolteachers, attorneys and doctors, editors and others engaged in what we nowadays call the "media," and politically engaged readers of magazines of civic opinion like the *Nation* and the *New Republic*.

Trilling derived his idea of the educated middle class from Arnold's *Culture and Anarchy*, in which the latter distinguishes between the large British commercial middle class, which he denounced for its "philistinism," and the relatively small but culturally vital wing of that class. In both Arnold's and Trilling's times, the educated middle class was politically liberal, but clearly the progressive, even Marxist, tinge that term had acquired in the 1940s was absent in Victorian England.

So we come here to the political ideas that are said to have so little connection with the deep places of the imagination. Trilling emphasized the discrepancy that seemed to him to have existed from the mid-1920s to the mid-1940s "between the political beliefs of our educated class and the literature that, by its merit, should properly belong to that class." Elsewhere, he puts it that "no connection exists between our liberal educated readers and the best of the literary minds of our time."

These statements seem strange inasmuch as they imply that the educated middle class espoused political sentiments and convictions with which Trilling identified. How, in view of his impatience with the views of that class, can he here speak of its deserving a better literature than it got? As I have observed, a substantial part of the progressive middle class in New York was made up of Stalinist fellow travelers, and Trilling's opposition to the broad political-cultural influence of Stalinism is the grand motive behind his work in the 1940s. Outside of New York, liberalism at a minimum—this is Trilling's summing up—stood for "suspiciousness of the profit motive, a belief in progress, science, social legislation, planning, and international cooperation, especially where Russia is in question."

Like others in the *Partisan Review* circle, Trilling was immensely distrustful of Soviet motives; as a temperamental and philosophical pessimist, he had little faith in human progress; and as he made clear in his brilliant demolition of the Kinsey Reports, he might not be hostile to science, but he was certainly hostile to the scientism that had wormed its way into American social science. And he made clear in the preface to *The Liberal Imagination* how he felt about a culture that pinned all its hopes on social engineering. The political process—involving organization, rationalization, bureaucratization—could only dull the emotions. Above all, it was fated to be disconnected from "the deep places of the imagination."

Midcentury American progressivism failed, in Trilling's view, because it "produced a large literature of social and political protest" but no writers of the first quality. This was a large-public rather than a little-magazine literature because readers responded eagerly to the flattery of having their own convictions confirmed. "At its best," Trilling says, this literature "has the charm of a literature of piety. It has neither imagination nor mind." Moreover, readers' pleasant experience of having their political virtue confirmed had nothing to do with "the real emotions of literature." Only when a writer penetrated to the deep places of the imagination had the reader the possibility of experiencing "real emotions."

So we see Trilling writing about literature in terms of "imagination," "mind," and "emotions" without defining any of these terms or their interrelations. He did not speak of the "symbolic" imagination, the favored term of Ernst Cassirer and the American philosopher Suzanne Langer, or of the "mythopoeic" imagination, as would Northrop Frye, the dominant critic of the cohort that came to prominence in the American fifties.

To understand Trilling's argument without adequate detail and precision on his own part, we have to follow his dialectical thinking. If the liberal beliefs of America's middle class had no connection to the deep places of the imagination, what political beliefs were associated with the greatest literature? And if the progressive "literature of piety" failed of depth, where was that depth to be found? At this point Arnold would have proffered his "touchstones," those passages from Chaucer, Shakespeare, Milton, and other English classics that set the standard against which the literature of the present could be judged. Trilling, on the other hand, offers as his criterion the literature of European modernism. Specifically he cited Proust, Joyce, Lawrence, Eliot, Yeats, Mann (in his creative work), Kafka, Rilke, and Gide.

It does not require great critical intuition to see that Eliot's "The Wasteland" is the product of an imagination marked by a profound sense of complexity. In "The Function of the Little Magazine,"[3] Trilling, without naming the titles of the liberal-minded books he detests, is leading his reader to compare a work like Eliot's with a novel like John Steinbeck's *The Grapes of Wrath* (1939), which became a best-seller in its time because it confirmed its liberal readers in their *bien-pensant* convictions. Trilling was taking particular aim at the fiction, like that of Steinbeck and Sherwood Anderson, that was so much admired during the years of the Popular Front for its celebration of "the people."

Of the modernists he mentions, Trilling makes the point that "all have their own love of justice and the good, but in not one of them does it take the form of the ideas and emotions that liberal democracy, as known by our educated class, has declared respectable."[4] Trilling might have gone further, as he did in other essays. Many of the great modernists were not merely indifferent to modern liberalism; they actively despised it and embraced views that were authoritarian and even reactionary. Eliot and Wyndham Lewis, whom Trilling does not mention, flirted at times with fascism. And, of course, Ezra Pound did more than flirt; he barely avoided being imprisoned after World War II for acts of treason on behalf of Mussolini's fascist government. So Trilling might in this essay have elaborated on the question of the seeming affinity between literature at its imaginative best and the glories of monarchy and empire. But he wanted, instead, to press home the imaginative poverty of middle-class liberalism as it expressed itself in literature.

3. To avoid that poverty, literature had to show the evidence of "mind" and "real emotions." But that was not all. Literature had to accede to the "deep" places of the imagination. Trilling only mentions in passing what was to be found in his deep places. He writes that "the same fatal separation" that exists "between the political ideas of our educated class and the deep places of the imagination" also exists in "the tendency of our educated liberal class to reject the tough, complex psychology of Freud for the easy rationalistic optimism of Horney and Fromm."[5]

What is to be found in Freud, and what his liberal-minded revisionists played down, is the power of instinctual life. For Freud, as for Trilling after him, unconscious fantasies and the instincts and their vicissitudes could not easily be managed by social engineering and adaptation to the environment. It is clear, looking at the work of Erich Fromm and other psychologists of the 1940s and 1950s, that the rationalistic, antitragic left-wing politics of the 1930s had been exchanged, with the discrediting of socialism, for a new, seemingly apolitical psychology that in fact perpetuated the same basic assumptions but with an emphasis now on the self rather than on the collectivity.

In 1965 Susan Sontag published her first and arguably most influential book. That book's title, *Against Interpretation*, alerted its readers to its polemical intention. Sontag's patriarchal precursors, the mainly Jewish intellectuals of *Partisan Review*, had always looked for the truth in the depths. Following Marx, they exposed a society's false consciousness in order to expose its material, economic foundation; following Freud, they sought to penetrate a dream's manifest content to interpret its latent content. In either case, with the Marxists or Freudians, the truth was below, in the depths, and had to be interpreted. With the title of her book and its emphasis on film and discussions of Camp and the "new sensibility," Sontag was declaring her new emphasis on arts of the surface. Following Roland Barthes and Sausurrean linguistics, she followed the trace of the signifier rather than digging for the signified. We can think of Trilling as representative of the energizing quest for the deep places that Sontag repudiated.

Moreover, I asked in my introduction why Trilling refers to the sacred precincts of imagination as deep rather than, say, high. After all, the most imaginative literature of the British nineteenth century, Trilling's academic specialty, was that of the High Romantics. And for the Romantic poets the greatest achievement of the imagination, the Sublime, was literally a high place, not only "beyond culture," as Trilling would put it, but beyond this world altogether.

Trilling had a different notion of the Sublime as occurring not on Alpine peaks or higher but in "the foul rag and bone shop of the heart." We might speak of a desubliminated idea of the Sublime. The deep places, then, had to do with the instinctual life, which was quite as integral to the life of the imagination as mind and real emotions. Trilling was interested not in the instinctual life as seen in soccer-game brawls, but in the Unconscious, chiefly of the repressed, "civilized middle class." Trilling had great respect for the mysterious life of the affects and instincts, though he appears to have been mainly baffled in his attempt to understand and to channel the workings of that unconscious life in himself.

His personal longing for greater freedom from the Jewish superego and the obligations of the public intellectual that he imposed on himself emerges in his inventive 1955 essay on the Russian-Jewish writer Isaac Babel. Whatever its accuracy as an interpretation of Babel, this essay is revelatory as testimony of one exemplary Jewish intellectual's relationship to European literary modernism.

Babel made his earliest fictions from his experience riding horse with a regiment of Cossacks enlisted in the Soviet cause in the period of bloody civil war following the Russian Revolution. Trilling based his essay on the anomalousness of a Jew "with spectacles on his nose and autumn in his heart,"[6] as Babel said of himself, riding into battle with his own people's traditional enemies, who had murdered and raped them in successive pogroms.

A salient indication of Trilling's identification with his subject is his claim that Babel was a divided man, as Trilling saw himself. This was not a reason for devaluing either Babel or himself. It was the characteristic mode of the artist and the way to avoid falling for the simplifications of ideology. *Complexity, variousness,* even *ambiguity*—these were all positive terms for Trilling. Babel's "heart," he writes, was "a battleground for two conflicting tendencies of culture."

On the one hand, Babel was a Jew who "conceived his ideal character to consist in his being intellectual, pacific, humane." On the other, he was powerfully drawn to the Cossacks, even though to the Jews the "Cossack was physical, violent, without mind or manners." In the Jewish imagination, the Cossack stood for "animal violence," "aimless destructiveness."[7]

But in his later fiction Tolstoy had depicted the Cossack quite differently, as the man of instinct incarnate. As Trilling sums up that view, Tolstoy "represented the Cossack as having a primitive energy, passion, and virtue. He was the man yet untrammeled by civilization, direct, immediate, fierce. He was the man of enviable simplicity, the man of the body—and of the horse, the man who moved with speed and grace."[8] The Cossack was the noble savage, characterized by everything that was lacking in the literature and lives of Trilling's educated middle class, not that the poor Jews of the *shtetln* were middle class.

Trilling seems to me to achieve in his own comments on the Cossack a passion and directness that are seldom present in his characteristically modulated and sinuous writing. He seems to me to figure forth a desire of his own for a saving wildness, for access to the deep places of the imagination where sexual and aggressive instincts exist in unmodified form to be tapped. "Our fantasy of the noble savage," he says, "stands for our sense of something unhappily surrendered, the truth of the body, the truth of full sexuality, the truth of open aggressiveness."[9] Trilling reveals a certain wistfulness as well.

His terms derive from Freud and from the literature of modernism, which celebrated the principle of amoral energy, whatever might subvert the passionless life of bourgeois civilization. So "Babel's view of the Cossack was more consonant with that of Tolstoi than with the traditional view of his own people."[10] And Babel's response to the fierceness of the Cossack accounts for what Trilling calls the "lyric joy" of the short stories in his collection *Red Cavalry*.

Tolstoy was hardly a modernist, but his celebration of the Cossack reveals the broad tendency around the end of the nineteenth century to see Western civilization as depleted and in need of emotional-instinctual rejuvenation. But, as Trilling argues, it was not the Cossacks' violence as such that recommended itself to Tolstoy and Babel. "Rather [Babel] was drawn by what the violence goes along with, the boldness, the passionateness, the simplicity and directness—and the grace." Yeats and D.H. Lawrence were similarly drawn to "archaic cultures and personalities" for the sake of the spiritual grace they made possible. Trilling sometimes does have an Arnoldian touchstone to nail down a point. He produces one here in saying that this grace was what "Yeats had in mind in his love of 'the old disturbed exalted life, the old splendor.'"[11]

I have to qualify what I may be seeming to argue. Trilling was not looking chiefly for a model of conduct. The grace and the joy he celebrates are aesthetic attributes, and his praise is not for archaic peoples in their historical actuality but as they served an aesthetic idea, as they fed into the deep places of the imagination. The point has to be made because in the 1960s the youth culture, as Trilling saw it, was a deplorable example of "modernism in the streets."[12] He reacted strongly against the transformation of modernism from an imaginative idea into a basis for social action. He himself would have put it in Freudian terms, attacking the counterculture as an instance of "acting out." But how well did Trilling himself do in reaching down into the deep places of the imagination? The question seems worth asking because, in my own view, it was central to his writing, and the clue to the conflicts, ambivalence, and ultimately the pessimism that marked his image of himself.

4. It is hard to see, because Trilling is so identified with the critique of the communism of the 1930s and 1940s, how much he remained a man of the 1920s. He was an undergraduate at Columbia from 1921 to 1925, the years R.P. Blackmur called the "anni mirabiles." During those years some of the greatest works of the modernist writers appeared, and the young Trilling himself aspired to become a writer of fiction rather than a politically engaged intellectual. In the five years after graduation from college, Trilling wrote and published several promising short stories of his own, as well as reviews of Jewish-oriented books, in the *Menorah Journal*. That journal was edited then by Elliot Cohen, who two decades later became the first editor of *Commentary*.

Trilling's creative phase temporarily ended with the Depression years, when on the small salary of a Columbia instructor he was obliged to support his parents, who had been victims of the 1929 crash, and to look after an ailing wife. He also revised over and over his Columbia University doctoral dissertation on Matthew Arnold and struggled to launch his academic career despite senior colleagues in Columbia's English department who distrusted him "as a Marxist, a Freudian, and a Jew." But by the end of the decade the university's president, Nicholas Murray Butler, had read and admired the young instructor's dissertation-turned-into-a-book on Arnold and let his desire be known that nothing should stand in the way of Trilling's chances for tenure.

The 1940s became his decade of greatest literary creativity. He wrote the essays that established him as one of this country's most eminent literary critics and public intellectuals, and in the middle years of that decade he published short stories and an ambitious novel, *The Middle of the Journey*. Perhaps the most successful of the stories is "Of This Time, of That Place," a tale of a professor's relationship with a troubled student, a Romantic visionary of a Blakeian type. Although this story is often thought to have been based on Trilling's experience as a teacher with Allen Ginsberg, Trilling did not actually meet Ginsberg until after the story appeared in 1943. But it is prophetic also in taking up an issue that would long preoccupy him: the relation between a capacity to penetrate the deep places of the imagination, on the one hand, and emotional instability on the other. About the time he was writing "Of This Time," Trilling also published his well-known essay "Art and Neurosis."

The work that was decisive for his future as a writer of fiction was *The Middle of the Journey*. Trilling had worked at it off and on all through the 1940s. Its themes are such that, to give them their due, he would have had to draw on imaginative resources not conspicuous in American writing of that or any other time. Trilling approached the question of the relationship between communism and the intellectual class from the point of view of conversion and deconversion, death and resurrection.

The novel is set in the late thirties and is based on Trilling's actual acquaintance with Whittaker Chambers, the Communist Party spy who recanted and became the famous accuser of Alger Hiss and, during the early cold-war years, a fierce right-wing ideologue. The problem is that Trilling lifted the ground-experience, in which Jewish intellectuals figured centrally, into the realm of abstraction. He set his novel in summertime Connecticut, as if a drama of de-conversion from communism might believably take place in what we now think of as John Cheever country. Also, all the characters have gentile names, and the novel as a whole reads like an extension of Great Books at Columbia with its echoes of Dante, Mann, E.M. Forster, and Lawrence. Trilling's hero, himself a former communist, becomes ill and suffers a near-death experience, has a Dantean vision of a rose, and emerges purged of the political and religious extremism that were alternative temptations in this age of -isms. The *Middle of the Journey* has an intellectual suavity that was rare in its time, as Edmund Wilson characterized it, of books that were either recycled classics or written to be commercial successes. But that urbanity was part of the problem: Trilling's novel is undermined by what another critic, John Bayley, sniffed at as its genteel "Episcopalian aroma."

Reviewers were either indifferent or hostile. Wounded by that critical response, Trilling never published a story again; nor did he, as far we know, write fiction even if only for his own desk drawer. But his failure with the critics can hardly be said to have ended his concern with the deep places of the imagination. The moral imagination he exhibits in some of his best essays has plainly tapped into deep places, even if in different parts of the pool from those he explored in writing his fiction. Critical interpretation and commentary always have the possibility of penetrating the deep places of the imagination. Just think, for example, of Joseph Brodsky on Rilke or Derrida on Paul Celan.

The sympathetic imagination can allow a great critic to penetrate to the creative springs of his own being. We see that in Trilling's essay on Babel and in a separate essay, his reading of Babel's startling short story "Di Grasso: A Tale of Odessa." That reading appears with a multitude of other readings of individual texts, mainly by modernist authors, in *The Experience of Literature*. That anthology, with its brief essays on stories like "Di Grasso" and Kafka's "The Hunter Gracchus," helps us to see how penetrating was the exegetical imagination of this public intellectual who was torn between his pleasure in reading and the felt obligation to exercise his cultural authority. Trilling's enthusiasm for the life of the imagination did seem to plummet in the early 1950s. R.P. Blackmur wrote of this second Trilling, the cultural authority, as "an administrator of the affairs of the mind." It is not an attractive designation, but it does fit the Trilling of essays like "Freud: Within and Beyond Culture," which was originally presented in 1955 as the Freud Annual Lecture at the New York Psychoanalytic Institute. He wanted here to correct the tendency of American social science and revisionist, post-Freudian psychology to endorse the "over-socialized view of man" that was pervasive in the fifties.

That essay and most of the others he wrote in that decade on individual authors and texts suggest a coming to terms with his own failure of genius, of inspiration. Indeed, essays in *The Opposing Self* on George Orwell and William Dean Howells, on Jane Austen's *Mansfield Park* and "Wordsworth and the Rabbis," all seem to recommend a retreat from the vitalism, the apocalypticism, and the moral extremism of some of the revered figures of modernism. Trilling seemed fatigued. Of course, this tendency was part of a retreat in the fifties from politics, in Trilling's case not only from left-wing politics but from politics altogether.

The Freud he came to praise was the pessimistic author of *Civilization and Its Discontents,* who seemed to him to provide a rationale for his stoic acceptance of his own self-created public burden. But sometimes, it seems, he did have doubts as to whether the road he had taken had been the right road for him. The marvelous essay he published in 1951 on the childhood origins of Keats's sensuousness is an example, if rather a wistful one. And when the editor Stanley Burnshaw,[13] an old friend, urged Trilling in the early 1960s to take up fiction again, he seemed to be seriously considering the possibility. But then there arose the debate in England on science versus the humanities as the proper foundation of a university education, and Trilling decided to intervene in yet another "cultural episode." His contribution to that debate is reprinted in his 1965 collection, *Beyond Culture,* as "The Leavis-Snow Controversy." It is a good essay, but I would have preferred a new story by him.

5. Trilling's critical contemporaries were no more successful in penetrating to the deep places. Like most of the older Jewish intellectuals, the two I have chosen as examples did not start out as academics and did not hold doctorates. Trilling was exceptional—in a group that included Lionel Abel, Clement Greenberg, Harold Rosenberg, and Philip Rahv—in belonging both to the world of public intellectuals and that of university professors.

If Trilling attended more to abstract ideas than to imagination, Alfred Kazin failed to achieve the distinction of the finest critics-theorists of his time precisely because he had few compelling general ideas. But if I had written about Kazin in the years when I myself was starting out, I would not have judged him as having failed in any respect. On the contrary, it was Kazin, more than any other critic, who in my teenage years guided me in thinking about American literature and showed me by his own example how one might write about books. At my college library in the late fifties I used to slink away from my solitary carrel and course assignments to the magazine reading room, where there were people around and I could read magazines like *Commentary,* the British periodical *Encounter,* and the *Reporter,* a glossy liberal anticommunist magazine in which Kazin's evocative reviews frequently appeared.

I was not to be as enthusiastic about Kazin's later writing in the *New York Review of Books* as I had been about his pieces in the *Reporter* and the Sunday *New York Times Book Review.* As I grew older, Kazin's influence paled in relation to later critic-heroes of mine like Frank Kermode. I came upon Kermode early in the 1960s in an early collection of his own reviews, *Puzzles and Epiphanies,* a James-Joycean title that suggests a formalist commitment to literary modernism absent in Kazin. As with many members of his New York generation, Kazin's influence waned in the sixties with the surge in new (French) approaches to reading. Indeed, it is hard to believe that Kermode was born only four years later than Kazin (b. 1915), who himself was ten years younger than Trilling.

Apart from modernism, the other commitment Kazin never made, and here he followed Trilling, was to literary theory. Trilling was able, during his life, to escape the oblivion that is the fate of the critic who does not hew to the fashion of his day because in his last book, *Sincerity and Authenticity,* he kicked out against the cultural currents that seemed to him the negative side of the insurgent culture. For his effort he received the critical applause of faculty conservatives, especially in England, who were grateful because he summarized in cogent terms the frustration they had mainly expressed in rants. And then Trilling died, rather suddenly, in 1975, when theory was at its peak.

Kazin, for his part, lived for two more decades and continued to write at a furious pace. As the title of one of his best books put it, for him "writing was everything." But no single one of his subsequent books earned for him the prestige of his very first book, *On Native Grounds.* This was as an extraordinary achievement, the product of repeated days and years of full-time research and writing at the New York Public Library. Kazin was twenty-seven when it came out.

But even this early triumph reveals the one great flaw that has deprived Kazin of a following such as Trilling and others have had. Kazin briefly studied with Trilling at Columbia after receiving his bachelor's degree from City College. That is a curious detail because *On Native Grounds* is a celebration of the liberal-minded movement of American letters from the forepart of the twentieth century that Trilling repeatedly attacked from the late thirties on. For Kazin, American writing from Howells to Dreiser to Sinclair Lewis and into the thirties marked a salutary declaration of independence from European, especially British, models. Kazin wrote as a celebrant of American progress. Nothing could have been less Trillingesque.

Kazin's pageant manifested a generous spirit of enthusiasm, and of emotion generally, but less in the way of analysis and argument, what Trilling called "mind." Many years later Kazin published another substantial work of literary history: *The American Procession.* Pageants and processions: again, hardly the kind of metaphor Trilling favored. And Kazin's sketchy portraits of the writers he included, without close, focused readings of particular texts, suggest that from his earliest days as a reviewer in the *Times* and the *New Republic* Kazin was above all a popularizer, a reviewer rather than a critic, who differed from the critics more closely associated with *Partisan Review* in being—horror of horrors—a middlebrow.

If Kazin was not truly an intellectual, although he was certainly a public voice, what constitutes his interest? The answer, for me, has to do with the succulent emotional element in his writing. And this, in Trilling's conception, must always be an element of the great creative imagination.

But then another question raises itself. Were these real emotions? Kazin certainly made the books he reviewed more accessible by conveying to the reader the feelings that these books evoked in him. But in search of emotion in Kazin, one finds that the best place to look is his large body of autobiographical writing. One sees that he was as much a memoirist as a literary critic, although it is hard to make a sharp distinction between the two functions inasmuch as many of his finest critical observations appear as one-liners in his memoirs and journals.

Kazin's emotionalism turns out to be an uneven affair. His first memoir, *A Walker in the City,* is about the prevailing sense of wonder in a boy growing up in a poor Jewish immigrant family in the Williamsburg section of Brooklyn. Kazin plainly strove for a lyric effect. But his lyricism does not typically make for joy, as in Babel, because it frequently spills over into sentimentality, as when he describes the passionate frustrated yearning of an unmarried female relative who lived in the family's small apartment. A later memoir, *New York Jew,* offers profiles of some of the famous people Kazin met during his own years of relative fame. The latter memoir has the opposite flaw from that of *A Walker in the City.* The author himself is more an absence than a presence in his own story.

Notwithstanding my cavils, Kazin's trilogy of memoirs (also *Starting Out in the Thirties*) includes some of his best work. But he did not fully come into his own as an autobiographer until the last decade of his long life, when his true subject, a religious yearning for faith, made itself explicit for the first time.

Writing Was Everything is more about Kazin's reading than his writing. It is organized around Kazin's search for grace in the books he was reading during the years of the Holocaust and directly after. He had been dispatched to Europe as a journalist after the war and found himself hailed by writers in Paris and Rome for his pioneering work on the new American fiction that was now attracting European writers. But he himself "wanted fiercely to learn Europe," which he proceeded to do in contemplating the writing of metaphysical and mystical writers like Simone Weil, the French Jewess who had turned against Judaism and had been claimed by many Catholics who found inspiration in her writing. But the quarrel over whether Weil truly became a Catholic was less important to Kazin than his sense of her as an unchurched clairvoyant who intuited the "urgent connection between the death of Europe in the Second World War and the eclipse of a God embodying the absolute good."[14]

Kazin's own unchurched, but Jewish-inflected, spirituality consisted in an agonized allegiance to his own "inability to believe." That inability and the will to overcome it pervade the pages of Kazin's last book, *A Lifetime Burning in Every Moment,* which seems to me also the author's best. *A Lifetime Burning* does not suffer, as does Kazin's literary criticism, from a deficiency of general ideas because it is a selection of snippets—cultural observations, prayers, outbursts of feelings—that were culled from personal journals he kept from 1938 to 1995. The reporter's sharp eye is as much in evidence as the religious yearning, but it is the latter that I want to emphasize because it is the basis of his intensity.

This is a writer painfully sensitive to the divine silence but also open to the possibility of ecstasy. Ultimately he is not as concerned with "mind" as is Trilling because he is placing his bets elsewhere. In one of the many prayerlike reflections that dot the pages of his last two books, Kazin appeals to a very great mythopoeic writer, William Blake, and asks, "But where—how—is the writer to be found who will have the inner certainty to see our life with the eyes of faith, and so make the world shine again?"[15]

6. My other near-contemporary of Trilling, Irving Howe, had in common with Kazin that for at least two decades they dominated the Sunday *New York Times Book Review* when it came to writing on new American and European fiction and Jewish-related books. They were both immensely lucid, and their thinking was consistently accessible. I must confess they were objects of resentment to younger reviewers like myself. By the time they finally vacated their privileged places at the *Book Review* and other popular periodicals, we had years before given up on our old ambition to succeed them as regulars.

Howe did not figure as importantly as Kazin in my own education as a critic. I had missed him by a year at Brandeis, where I wound up with Philip Rahv, another New York old-timer, as my dissertation adviser. Howe was like Rahv in aspiring to an overall perspective on literature and society and in being absorbed in practical politics in a way that neither Trilling nor Kazin was. His life, as he recorded it in his "intellectual autobiography," *A Margin of Hope*, consisted of a series of public controversies in which opinion was everything.

Howe was the anti-Kazin in that he seldom registered feelings and appears to have experienced few shining moments. In his polemical writing, the range of affect is narrow; he manifests mainly what he describes as "corrosion and distrust."[16] Those feelings owed much to his particular family background, but they were reinforced by the sorry fate of socialism, to which he had pinned his hopes from the beginning. Despite Howe's spirit of exasperation, however, his idealism inspired the loyalty of gifted younger intellectuals with whom he came into contact. At his political quarterly, *Dissent*, he fostered the work of younger colleagues like the political theorist Michael Walzer, the literary academic David Bromwich, and the novelist Brian Morton.

Since my observations about Howe and the imagination will be mainly negative, I want also to pay homage to another special quality of his. No one of the Old Left intellectuals was more sheerly competent. He wrote valuable full-length critical studies of Sherwood Anderson, William Faulkner, and Thomas Hardy; other books on the history of the Communist Party and Walter Reuther; collections of his own essays in political and cultural criticism; and he edited innumerable volumes, including a selection of Trotsky's writings and works of translation from Yiddish poetry and fiction. A full Howe bibliography would probably come to more than a hundred titles, and these books are ably done, at least the many I have read through or of which I have read parts. Unlike Kazin, Howe was like Trilling in leaving an important intellectual legacy. But it is not, I think, as a critic who was able to guide readers to the imaginative and emotional depths of the literary works he discussed. And it is not, I think, as a public intellectual, although he was certainly that as much as any one of the New York Intellectuals. Rather, Howe's gift to future readers and scholars consists in having introduced them to the riches of Yiddishkeit in the books of translations he edited and in his most famous work, *World of Our Fathers*.

The latter book is full of fascinating information, but it suffers from nostalgia like Kazin's when it idealizes the lost world of union-organizing, socialist-inclined Yiddishkeit on New York's Lower East Side. The idealization is all the greater because the middle-aged Howe was expiating his youthful rebellion against his parents. To the extent that as a youth he had fled the parochial world of the Jewish immigrants in favor of cosmopolitan Marxism, in his later years he returned in a rush. His profound disillusionment with the New Left in the 1960s added greater urgency to his effort at retrieval of his Jewish past.

Howe failed in another respect that seems the reverse of his Yiddish sentimentality but is actually its complement. His affectless intellectual memoir, *A Margin of Hope*, illustrates Trilling's point about the political consciousness's being antithetical to imaginative depth. Howe's kind of absorption in ideological politics may lead an intellectual away from the intimate self-knowledge that Trilling had to such a high degree and that is necessary for plumbing the deep parts of imagination.

I was struck by the three pages near the end of this 350-page book that Howe devotes to his father, a garment sweatshop worker. Howe's avoidance of the personal elsewhere in his life story contrasts with Kazin's candor in registering his hurt about his father's muteness. The Kazin family muteness was a function of the uncrossable gap between many uneducated and emotionally stricken immigrant fathers and their American-born intellectual sons. Although frequently confused about his emotional life, Kazin was aware of the origins of his yearning for "You the Everlasting" in his traumatic experience of silence when he was very young: "Speak, Father, speak!"[17]

It happens that I visited New York some time after Lionel Trilling's death in the mid-1970s because I had been thinking, even before he died, of writing a book about him and wanted to hear the recollections and opinions of his contemporaries. I met with Jacques Barzun, Clement Greenberg, Will Barrett, Kazin, Howe, and a few others. In general, Howe commented appreciatively about Trilling, but at a certain distance, as he did in *A Margin of Hope* and at various other places during his career. It was a complicated relationship but plainly not an adversarial one, as in the case of Kazin. Then, toward the end of our time together, Howe mentioned in passing that his own father was sick and that he would be going up to the Bronx to see him later that day. It was hard to identify Howe's attitude or emotion in relation to his planned visit. He simply seemed slightly depressed. But I would not have guessed that his father was dying and that this was causing a moral-psychological crisis for the son.

This I learned from the few pages in *A Margin of Hope.* Here the relevant passage begins, "The day my father died I felt almost nothing." But that blankness itself points to emotional crisis. If Howe had felt more at the time, no doubt he would have devoted more pages to his lifelong ambivalence toward his father than, as he did, to his quarrels in the 1960s with the SDS leader Tom Hayden.

The fact that Howe "felt almost nothing" does not mean he was not present at his father's end. It is the relationship between the son's frozen affect and the father's inveterately disapproving attitude toward him that Howe's profile both exposes and half-conceals. These are unusual pages amid Howe's huge body of work and make a reader wonder what this autobiography might have been like had the author not insisted, in the rest of it, on being so intellectual and remote.

The consequences for Howe of his father's lifelong disdain for him were complex. He understands and clearly identifies with the old man's "gift for discrimination" while at the same time he is crippled by the internalized conviction that he is not a good and loving person. And the son's ambivalence causes him to be evasive at the end: he takes three hours to get to and from his father's hospital but spends only twenty minutes there. He "could not look at his [father's] wasted body, for I knew myself to be unworthy, a son with a chilled heart."[18]

That a person of Howe's integrity and selfless loyalty to the lost cause in America of democratic socialism, that such a person should feel himself at root unworthy may shock the reader. But just maybe his internalized sense of self-disdain was itself a major element in his later attachment to so pure and ideal a political goal. But that is impossible to know because Howe makes no connections between his utopian politics and his most intimate emotions. He says, "Even before my father died, I had made him into a myth." And "myth for him is hardly a positive term, a conduit for imaginative expression." Rather, "Myths are wonderfully convenient for blocking the passage between yourself and your feelings."[19]

His father might have become a symbol of the evil progenitor had Howe been in touch with the hatred and rage that were inevitably a consequence of the pain his father had visited on him. His father spent fruitless years as a presser in a garment factory. In *World of Our Fathers,* the wounded son turned this weak, abrasive father into the myth of a vital community united by shared values. Howe expiated his largely repressed anger toward that father by way of an idealized portrait of a world he once sought only to repudiate. *World of Our Fathers* is a valuable introduction, however uncritical, to that world and proved to be Howe's commercially most successful book. But that is because it became a coffee-table icon for assimilated, middle-class Jews, who, like Howe himself, were forever removed from that world. That is, notwithstanding the author's intention, *World of Our Fathers* was greeted as a work of cultural piety.

In *A Margin of Hope,* Howe's habit of emotional repression continues to muffle his account of his relationship with his father even though, as he says, it is "the only story I had to tell." Still, the few pages that he gives to this tragic parent-child misunderstanding make me wish he had opened himself more to personal emotion and self-reflection. Instead, as autobiographer he offers us a life in which he rehearses stale opinions about once-controversial, now largely forgotten figures like Kate Millett.

Had I time and space, I might take up selected public intellectuals from more recent cohorts. Examples who come to mind are two former students of Trilling who became editors at magazines of opinion, especially opinion about issues of Jewish concern: Norman Podhoretz, ultimately the editor-in-chief of *Commentary*, who came upon the intellectual scene in the early 1950s, and Leon Wieseltier, a baby boomer and long-time literary editor of the *New Republic*. I will limit myself to some reflections on Podhoretz, who has been far more prolific as a writer.

Podhoretz, who started out as a literary-cultural critic in Trilling's own mode, later gave up on the life of letters to become a publicist for neoconservatism. In my view Podhoretz failed to penetrate the deep places of the imagination because he sacrificed disinterested "mind" for partisan advantage and gave up on the possibility of imaginative grace, joy, and surprise for the sake of right-thinking virtue in the neoconservative battle against communism.

Podhoretz is the now-retired editor of *Commentary*, the monthly periodical that he directed for four decades. When he started out during the early years of the cold war, he seemed destined to become Trilling's successor, a penetrating interpreter of modern American literature and culture as Trilling had been of the English nineteenth century and the ruling assumptions of intellectuals in his own time. *Doings and Undoings*, Podhoretz's first book, was one of the most promising works of literary and cultural criticism of the early sixties. As in Trilling's case, Podhoretz did not write linked chapters that formed themselves into a book-length study. On the contrary, his book was made up of separate reviews and essays, most of which had previously appeared in *Commentary*.

This book had one major flaw. That was its impatience with literature itself and the author's compelling drive to translate literary texts and careers into ideological terms. Podhoretz was a prodigy when it came to instant history, simplifying the texts before him so as to expose their *Tendenz*. So it should not have been surprising when only a few years later in a precocious autobiography titled *Making It* Podhoretz for all practical purposes bade farewell to literary criticism. He insisted in *Making It* that his New York literary mentors were all, like himself, less interested in art and culture than in vulgar success. If that were so, it followed logically that Podhoretz ought to be grabbing for the golden ring.

Podhoretz saw as the 1970s got under way that the nation was moving still farther to the right, and he seized the occasion to move the magazine in the same direction. From that point on, he transformed *Commentary*, which had been a magazine of literature and culture, into an organ of right-wing political polemic. Gradually Podhoretz became a leader of the new neoconservatism.

Of the Jewish ex-leftists who became neoconservatives during the 1970s and 1980s Podhoretz became best known for his presence at White House social events. During that time the quality of his thought declined as his prestige increased. Most notable in terms of my interests in this essay, the habits of attention he had learned from Trilling gave way to the simplifications and compromises of practical political debate. Podhoretz had been a protégé of Trilling, but his writing deteriorated. Ultimately he became an example of the political lack of imagination that his former mentor had warned against in the forties.

One has only to consult Podhoretz's successive reviews of novels by Philip Roth. From the first, Podhoretz tracked Roth, his contemporary, as if the future of American Jews depended on which of them prevailed. In the 1990s he praised Roth's *American Pastoral,* which attacks the lunatic fringe of the sixties antiwar movement (represented by the hero's mad daughter) and offers a complementary appreciation of the uneducated Jewish generation of the 1940s (the hero's parents), which was passionately pro-American during its war. Podhoretz read that novel as ideology pure and simple, evidence that Roth, the Prodigal Son, had finally seen the light. That light was Podhoretz's long-held official creed, a central pillar of which was defense of ordinary Jewish-American manners and morals. But then in Roth's next novel, *I Married a Communist,* the author deviated from *Commentary* orthodoxy. Podhoretz, not having any idea by this time in his career how to deal with a novel except in terms of its political implications, was dumbfounded.

More could be said about Podhoretz's elaborate summing-up in three post-*Commentary* books. One, *Ex-Friends,* is a characteristically self-aggrandizing performance in which the author tries to boost himself in the order of posterity by recalling intellectual quarrels which led to his being dropped by better-known, more truly talented "friends" such as Trilling, Norman Mailer, and Hannah Arendt. The will to be associated with the powerful and famous, even after breaking with them, will remain to the end with this never-quite-arrived example of the cultural *arriviste.*

Podhoretz's two most recent books have been testaments. The first was a panegyric to America that might have been composed by Ronald Reagan's speech writers. The other was a hymn to orthodox Judaism that has less to do with religion than with a search for absolutes that confirm the author's social prejudices, like that against homosexuality. The moral of the Podhoretz story: it is possible to become more intellectually barren than even Trilling conceived when you abandon the literary imagination in favor of simplified political polemic and hypocritical piety. It seems a shame to conclude with Podhoretz inasmuch as so many of his Jewish contemporaries and successors were and are more flexible, more intelligent, more imaginative. But I have wanted to limit myself here to public intellectuals who once belonged in some way to the line of Lionel.

So I have offered phenomenological if highly judgmental descriptions of how various Jewish intellectuals have or have not achieved access in their writing to the deep places of the imagination. The next major question would be the *why*. What accounts for the relative failure of Jewish public intellectuals with regard to the imagination?

How have the Jews managed in this respect in comparison with other groups such as African Americans or feminists or queer theorists or postcolonialists? Is the performance of Jewish intellectuals a function of the larger social history of Jews in America? No doubt it is, but exploring the relationship between the social history of America's Jews and the imagination of Jewish writers would require at least as much space as the present essay. I shall leave it to another observer.

Notes

1. Lionel Trilling, preface to *The Liberal Imagination: Essays on Literature and Society* (New York: Doubleday Anchor Books, 1950).
2. Ibid., p. 7.
3. Lionel Trilling, "The Function of the Little Magazine," in *The Liberal Imagination*, pp. 97–106.
4. Ibid., p. 102.
5. Ibid., p. 102.
6. Lionel Trilling, *Beyond Culture: Essays on Literature and Learning* (New York: Viking Press, 1965), p. 129.
7. Ibid., p. 127.
8. Ibid., p. 128.
9. Ibid., p. 128.
10. Ibid., p. 128.
11. Ibid., p. 137.
12. Trilling may or may not have coined the phrase "modernism in the streets," but as much as any commentator he spelled out its cultural implications.
13. Burnshaw was a well-known figure for decades on the New York literary scene. As a book editor, he proposed and provided constant encouragement for Trilling's anthology *The Experience of Literature*. Burnshaw was also a talented poet, radio playwright, and memoirist. I exchanged several letters with him in the course of researching my book on Trilling, *Lionel Trilling and the Fate of Cultural Criticism* (Evanston: Northwestern University Press, 1986).
14. Alfred Kazin, *Writing Was Everything* (Cambridge, MA: Harvard University Press, 1995), p. 92.
15. Ibid., p. 152.
16. Irving Howe, *A Margin of Hope: An Intellectual Biography* (New York: Harcourt Brace Jovanovich, 1982).
17. Alfred Kazin, *A Lifetime Burning in Every Moment*, p. 195.
18. Howe, p. 339.
19. Ibid., p. 338.

Lionel Trilling's *The Middle of the Journey* and the Complicated Origins of the Neoconservative Movement

Michael Kimmage

> And did the countenance divine
> Shine forth upon our clouded hills?
> And was Jerusalem builded here
> Among these dark satanic mills?
> —William Blake, "A New Jerusalem"

Elliot Cohen's mission statement for *Commentary*, published in the magazine's first issue, was titled "An Act of Affirmation." Writing in November 1945, Cohen betrayed an acute consciousness of the Holocaust and an attendant optimism about America, the best hope for a Jewish people devastated by European carnage. He betrayed as well a longing for an end to diaspora. Cohen celebrated the "faith that, out of the opportunities of our experience here, there will evolve new patterns of living, new modes of thought, which will harmonize heritage and country into a true sense of at-home-ness in the modern world."[1] In 1945, *Commentary* was not the neoconservative magazine it would become in the late 1960s; there was, of course, no such movement for it to oppose or affirm in 1945. Still, it was affirming America in words that must have given radical readers pause: heritage and country, at-home-ness in the modern world, and all of this under the auspices of a capitalist superpower. Cohen's mission statement contained elements of what would become the neoconservative movement: an insistence upon religious heritage as well as proud participation in the American polity. The opportunities of the American experience might dissolve the polarities that diaspora had imposed: tradition versus modernity; assimilation versus Jewishness; diaspora versus at-home-ness. Implicit to Cohen's statement was the failure of the left, of the Soviet Union, to meet the needs of American Jews, or of any Jews for that matter. Communism was simply not the answer. Perhaps the answer to the dilemma of heritage and country stood right before the eyes of American Jews; perhaps it was America itself.

Lionel Trilling was a friend of Cohen's, a contributor to *Commentary* from its early days onward, and a subtle critic of the American left; his ideas would inspire such neoconservatives as Irving Kristol, Gertrude Himmelfarb, and Norman Podhoretz. Trilling was both a diagnostician of the left's failure with regard to communism and the proponent of a liberal alternative to radicalism. His 1947 novel, *The Middle of the Journey*, was his most personal reckoning with the ideas of his generation, and it was oddly prescient.[2] Unlike many of his intellectual contemporaries, Trilling saw that the demise of the Soviet alternative would foster new kinds of conservatism, intermingling conservative and liberal ideas and forcing liberals to meet the intellectual challenge of conservatism. Trilling never became a neoconservative himself, but his refashioning of liberalism offered a foundation on which neoconservatives would later build their own ideological edifice. He took a step to the right, whereas the neoconservatives took three or four. In *The Middle of the Journey*, Trilling presumed a bond between the American intelligentsia and radicalism, and in this, too, he was prescient. His vision of the 1930s shed light on the origins of 1960s radicalism. The communist intelligentsia of the 1930s was creating an adversary culture that would grow into the counterculture of the 1960s. The title of the novel evokes an uncompleted journey. Read in retrospect, it sheds light on the origins of the New Left and the neoconservative movement that took root in the 1970s. Trilling's novel was historically inaccurate in only one respect. Its characters were not Jewish.

Understood as a Jewish novel that refuses to be Jewish, *The Middle of the Journey* exposes the tensions behind Cohen's optimism, behind his faith in the potential for Jews' at-home-ness in modern America. By extension, *The Middle of the Journey* suggests a troubled point of origin for the neoconservative movement insofar as it was a Jewish movement. These tensions and troubles could, more modestly, be construed as a matter of Lionel Trilling's character. By the time he published *The Middle of the Journey*, he was a successful professor at Columbia University as well as the first Jew to gain tenure in the English department of an elite university. Born in 1905, Trilling was an atypical New York Intellectual because he did not begin life in the working class or as an immigrant. His parents had immigrated to the United States by way of England. They were middle-class and, in his mother's case, well versed in English literature. His parents raised him in an Orthodox home, but they wanted him to succeed as a middle-class American. His mother dreamed that her son would one day become an Oxford don (which for a year he did). Trilling was destined, in other words, to assimilate, and he repeatedly chastised his literary nemesis, Ludwig Lewisohn, a Jewish-American writer who wrote self-consciously Jewish novels, for failing to assimilate and for retaining too sentimental an attachment to Judaism.[3] The absence of Jewish characters in *The Middle of the Journey* was a conscious choice on Trilling's part, one that indicated an urge to blend in, to replace particularity with normalcy. In response to David Kleinstein, a reader of the novel who wrote to Trilling about its striking lack of Jewish characters, Trilling posed a rhetorical question: "don't you think it might be very useful to have Jews just walking around in fiction, not certified as good or suffering or significant, but just like everybody else?"[4]

Trilling's letter to Kleinstein is so unpersuasive that it only restates the question. Why did a critic who consistently praised sociological verisimilitude in fiction violate this quality in his own novel? And why did Trilling sidestep the American-Jewish symbiosis Cohen hoped to encourage with *Commentary*? Reviewing *The Middle of the Journey* in *Commentary*, the cultural critic Robert Warshow asked why Trilling ignored "the fact that the middle-class which experienced Stalinism was in large part a Jewish middle class, driven by the special insecurities of Jews in addition to the insecurities of the middle-class in general."[5] If the answer does not lie in Trilling's character alone or in his impetus to grant Jews their overdue normalcy in literature it must lie in the ideological content of the novel. Trilling counterposed an extreme conservatism to a liberalism that is postethnic and postreligious, leaving no place for the modern, assimilable Judaism that Cohen was calling for. In *The Middle of the Journey*, conservatism and religion are synonymous, as are liberalism and secularism. Liberalism is founded on reason and high culture. In the language of Matthew Arnold, the subject of Trilling's first book, liberalism is Hellenic and conservatism Hebraic.[6] *The Middle of the Journey* illuminates Trilling's distance from Cohen. Perhaps heritage and country were not so easy to harmonize. Perhaps the heritage of diaspora, of apart-ness rather than at-home-ness, had to be sacrificed for the liberalism of the United States.

Ideology explains the absence of Jewishness, and ideology in *The Middle of the Journey* is the triad of liberalism, radicalism, and conservatism. Conservatism entails a negation of the Enlightenment, a religious absolutism that is tantamount to the negation of the modern world. It is very much a paleoconservatism. Liberalism in the novel is the embodiment of the Enlightenment: it is secular, rational, skeptical, impervious to excess, even an excessive faith in its own tenets. To translate these ideologies into Jewish terms, one would get something like Orthodox Judaism on the one hand and a secular liberalism anchored in Western culture on the other. The liberal might long for moral laws unsullied by self-doubt and equivocation. The liberal protagonist, John Laskell, longs for the sincerity and ritual of a presecular era. His liberalism is, however, not to be combined with the religious dogma of true conservatism. To have made the characters Jewish would have exposed the distance between the novel's liberal hero and the religious Jew, between the assimilated American and the expositor of religious heritage. The hard choices of diaspora would have remained: tradition versus modernity, heritage versus assimilation. Was it not easier to deal with the conflict between liberalism and religious conservatism on the more mainstream terrain of Protestant America? Was it not simpler to write a novel that achieves, in the words of John Bayley, "almost too conspicuously at times an Anglican or Episcopalian fragrance"?[7]

* * *

Ideology is not disembodied in *The Middle of the Journey*; it is made manifest in characters. Each of the main characters was at one time a communist, but only the Crooms remain radical. They are a young, educated couple with one foot in the radical circles of Manhattan and the other in the pragmatic (and careerist) mentality of the New Deal. Two characters follow the path of the ex-radical, and neither becomes anything like a neoconservative. Gifford Maxim, whom Trilling modeled on his college classmate Whittaker Chambers, had been the most radical of them all, a member of the Soviet underground, as Chambers had been in reality.[8] Maxim's break with the party sets the novel in motion. *The Middle of the Journey* begins with Maxim fleeing the Communist Party, which he believes is bent on killing him. Maxim argues that the party is evil, that communism, too, is evil. His ethical categories make clear his new perspective, that of a Christian and a conservative. He foresees a Manichean battle between communism and its antithesis, a Christian conservatism, and has no reservations about enlisting on the side of the conservative right. To the novel's protagonist, John Laskell, Maxim symbolizes an immanent shift from left to right, a pendular swing that will bypass liberalism altogether. To some degree, he follows Maxim in making this swing, at least to the extent of accepting Maxim's reports of Communist Party perfidy. Laskell's acceptance is momentous, coming as it does in the late 1930s (when the novel is set), the moment of maximum liberal enthusiasm for Moscow. Nevertheless, it does not make Laskell a conservative. He must distance himself from the Crooms, for they are still tied ideologically to the Soviet Union, but he must distance himself as well from Maxim. He must defend his liberalism against threats from the left and the right. In this way, the abstractions of ideology collide with the immediacy of individual lives.

The collapse of communism as an ideal is the set-piece event of *The Middle of the Journey*, and it is not merely ideological. *The Middle of the Journey* may be excessively cerebral. The novel lacks a certain liveliness, and it is tempting to say that Trilling was too much of a literary critic to be a first-rate novelist. Trilling may have arrived at this conclusion himself after writing *The Middle of the Journey*, especially after reading the less-than-glowing verdicts of his critics. After 1947, Trilling never published anything other than literary criticism. Whatever his shortcomings as a novelist, though, Trilling had one exceptional skill. He could connect the whole being of his characters to their convictions. Only rarely do the ideological fissures that order the novel find expression directly; they find expression mostly in disagreements over literature, over assessments of people, and over the minutia of cultural style.[9] When Maxim breaks with the party on the most acrimonious possible grounds, Laskell must choose between Maxim and the radical Crooms. Though Laskell would at first prefer to side with the Crooms and remain a radical, he ends up on Maxim's side. He is not convinced by Maxim's political arguments but by the Crooms as people; they gradually appear to Laskell as disturbing exemplars of the radical spirit. The culture of the Crooms begins to disgust him, not because it is philistine: to the contrary, the Crooms are sophisticated, urban people. Their culture disgusts Laskell for its disingenuous idealism and for the poverty of its imagination, disassociated as it is from the profundity of religion and tradition. They are at once naïve and arrogant. Culture and ideology condition each other in Trilling's literary world, and in both areas the left has lost its way.

In *The Middle of the Journey*, the Crooms and the left are one. The reader learns this through Laskell's eyes. The novel develops along his deepening insight into the Crooms, an insight that ultimately destroys his friendship with them. They are an impeccably modern couple, a couple for the twentieth century. It is hardly a compliment when the narrative voice informs us that "Henry Adams would have understood Arthur Croom and envied his chances."[10] Arthur's relationship to communism is convenient. It is not too radical for a professor of economics; it is almost a private commitment, an "agreement with the Party [that] began where theory left off and where moral and will began."[11] The reference to Henry Adams's envy underscores Arthur's opportunism. The novel portrays a world in which ambitious intellectuals are on the left, in which intellectuals are on the left almost by definition. The Crooms' culture is a secular religion that guarantees virtue to those who hold the right opinions about politics, and for the Crooms, the culture of the left obscures any relation between their leftist convictions and their ambition. This culture allows the Crooms to live in Manhattan and summer in Connecticut without actually considering themselves middle class. After all, they have oriented their sympathy toward the proletariat. This is sufficient for political rectitude, if more tepid than membership in the Communist Party. It puts them on the side of the righteous, although they are at the same time upwardly mobile within the middle class. Laskell slowly intuits this moral corruption and is repulsed by it.

Arthur is ambitious within the context of bourgeois America without accepting the tension between his ambition and his leftist principles. His wife, Nancy, is troubling to Laskell in other, more serious ways. For one thing, she stands closer to the Communist Party than Arthur does. When Maxim was still in the underground, he had asked Nancy to receive letters for him, a small but essential contribution to the practice of espionage. She granted his request without telling her husband. She possesses a militancy that Laskell had not even noticed when they were all within the radical orbit. As Laskell slowly breaks away from the movement, this militancy frightens him. Maxim has told Laskell that the Communist Party wishes to kill him. For a while, Laskell does not believe Maxim. The evidence that convinces him, crucially, is not the transcript of the Moscow trials or Stalin's manipulation of the left in the Spanish Civil War. It is the conduct of Nancy in rural Connecticut, as far away as one could possibly be from the killing fields of the Old World. Unwittingly, she confirms Maxim's reports of terror in the party: "the summer had shown him [Laskell] a kind of passion in Nancy Croom . . . the ultimate consequence of which might logically be just such an act as Maxim feared for himself."[12] The act Maxim feared is murder.

The Crooms' pathology expresses itself most cogently in their attitude toward their handyman, Duck Caldwell. Though Duck is the impoverished son of a senator, for the Crooms he is the proletariat incarnate. He is a type rather than an individual for them. As Nancy puts it to Laskell, "He's a very important kind of person . . . even if you don't consider him just personally."[13] They praise his authenticity, his reality, and in doing so they miss the deep-seated malice of his character. This analysis of the Crooms belongs to Laskell, who starts by noticing "a brooding solicitude for Duck which seemed to him inappropriate."[14] Inappropriateness is the least of it. Duck is cruel and irresponsible. He is, in a word, evil, but for Arthur he is more or less a social statistic, deprived of agency by society, by the inequalities of the capitalist system. For Nancy, Duck is a more romantic figure, sullen because of his awareness that America is unjust. He is the carrier of political reality. This misjudgment of Duck shows Laskell the myopia of the Crooms, a myopia that points to a larger dishonesty, as "the final reality that the Crooms wanted was one of application and hard work and responsibility. And all they reported of Duck, apart from his manual skill, suggested only anarchy or evasion."[15] As the example of Duck makes clear to Laskell, the progressivism of the Crooms has led them away from accurate moral judgment into complicity with evil. They do not see the "emptiness masking itself as mind and desire" in Duck, nor do they see it in their own communist selves.[16]

Over time, Laskell must face "his fresh full knowledge of what he has to escape in Nancy."[17] This is at the same time a knowledge of what he has to escape in the left. Laskell's moral transformation is at the heart of the novel, and it goes back into his past. Prior to his radical self was a mildly romantic self. He had tried to escape a bourgeois destiny with art: "until he was twenty-four he had planned a literary career. He wrote quite well and he had been in revolt against the culture of his affectionate and comfortable Larchmont family."[18] Though context implies that Laskell is a WASP, the religious designation is insignificant, for he "had been brought up without religion."[19] Religious influence is lacking, and the influence of art yields to the claims of radical politics. As a radical, Laskell dedicated himself to the study of urban planning, writing a socialist book (*Theories of Housing*). He falls in love with a woman who had settled in New York for its artistic and intellectual life, as had Laskell himself, but she dies before they can marry. Laskell is older than the Crooms, has a penchant for art that they lack, and has suffered from loss in a way that they have not. Finally, Laskell contracts scarlet fever and almost dies shortly before he visits the Crooms at their summer home. He cannot quite understand "what a strange and illuminating experience" his illness and brush with death have been.[20] He cannot understand why the nearness of death should have restored to him his youthful hunger for beauty.

Three factors converge to detach Laskell from the Communist Party. The first is the wisdom his illness has conferred. Compared with the intensity of facing death, radical politics seem dreary and worthless. The second factor is his disgust with the Crooms' progressivism, and the third is the candor and force of Gifford Maxim, the anticommunist conservative. The first two factors are joined when Laskell realizes that Nancy cannot discuss his illness. He wants to communicate its beauty, the deepening of character it instilled in him, and she wants to pretend that it never happened. The subject of death, Laskell comes to feel, is reactionary for people like the Crooms, life's most grievous challenge to progressive fantasies of growth and improvement.[21] These two factors in turn encourage Laskell to believe Maxim, who wants to convince him of the party's willingness to commit murder. In a curious way, Nancy's nervousness regarding the subject of death makes Maxim a credible anticommunist witness. Laskell makes this connection himself: "had he [Laskell] not, in some way, wanted to tell her just what Maxim had wanted to tell him, that people really do die?"[22] In believing Maxim, Laskell separates himself forever from the Communist Party; in believing Maxim by observing Nancy, Laskell alienates himself from the culture of the left, communist or otherwise. What is left is "a large vacancy in his thought—it was the place where the Party and Movement had been."[23]

The vacancy is not filled in the course of the novel. Nor, given the title, would one expect finality in this regard, but the focus of tension shifts midway, the moment Laskell accepts Maxim's view of the party, from Laskell's dispute with the Crooms to his dialogue with Maxim. The focus shifts, that is, from left to right. Laskell uncovers conservative leanings in himself and an affinity with Maxim that surprises him. At least as important, though, is the barrier Laskell erects between himself and Maxim. In this respect, the novel bears directly on the neoconservative movement that began some twenty-five years after its publication. Laskell has broken ranks, and Maxim has done so even more dramatically. Yet they do not join arms and walk off into the political sunset. That would be to enact a synthesis in which Trilling did not believe. There is an unbridgeable gap between the Hebraic conservatism of Maxim and the Hellenic liberalism of Laskell: Maxim appears to be walking off to Jerusalem and Laskell to Athens, even if both are equally eager to run away from Moscow. One might add a footnote to these metaphors of civilization: Washington shows no promise of rivaling Jerusalem or Athens (though it is certainly preferable to Moscow). In *The Middle of the Journey*, the wealthy liberal Kermit Simpson bankrolls "a rather sad liberal monthly . . . run on what he called Jeffersonian principles."[24] Neither the liberal Laskell nor the conservative Maxim has much interest in Jeffersonian liberalism; for them, it is either moribund or inadequate. The enthusiasm for America, explicit in both Cohen's mission statement for *Commentary* and in the later neoconservative movement, could not be attributed to either Laskell or

Maxim. They may discover Washington later on in their journeys, but this is not at all inevitable.

Maxim's conservatism follows from his involvement with the Communist Party. As an anticommunist, he is not simply afraid of the Communist Party. He considers himself guilty for the service he had rendered to the party. As Stalin's servant, Maxim had participated in the expansion of Stalin's power. "My hands are bloody," he explains to Laskell, "because of what I was, because of what I consented to, because of my associations."[25] He had assisted in the career of a vicious tyrant and in the spread of a vicious ideology. More tangibly, Maxim cannot forget that he helped Theron Walker, a poet, to go fight in the Spanish Civil War, in which Walker died. Maxim had committed crimes, bloodying his hands, for the sake of a criminal empire and ideology, and his search for forgiveness takes him to Christianity. Christian piety defines for him the moral categories that he needs as an ex-communist: good, evil, sin, and redemption. Toward the end of the novel, he confronts the Crooms about their communism. He clarifies the value Christianity has for him, which he claims is its superiority to the system of radical ethics. The radical places responsibility for injustice on social structure, whereas Christianity places this responsibility on the individual soul. This responsibility is softened by Christ's mercy. "In my system," Maxim tells the Crooms, "although there is never-ending responsibility, there is such a thing as mercy."[26] In the radical system, derived from the thought of Karl Marx, only history can sweep away the debris of crime and injustice, and history might well prove merciless. In Maxim's case it already has.

Maxim puts his views in writing with a review of "Billy Budd," penned "quite in the Anglican manner of Matthew Arnold."[27] His review is both an exposé of the radical mind and a formulation of his conservative philosophy. To allude once again to Matthew Arnold, one might term Maxim's review a Hebraic reading of Melville's short story. It is Hebraic in the sense that Maxim's concerns are primarily moral and, more importantly, in the way the story is used to defend an immutable moral law. However charming or naïve or beautiful Billy Budd may be, he is guilty of murdering Claggart. Billy Budd represents "Spirit," Maxim argues in his review, but he appeals to the radical sensibility less for his spiritual beauty than for his position in the class structure. He is Claggart's subordinate. From the radical perspective, his killing of Claggart has a revolutionary aura about it, reinforced by the emancipation denied Billy Budd when Captain Vere puts him to death. From Melville's story, Maxim extracts a conclusion that is the opposite of the radical one. Vere was right to execute Billy Budd, though justice in this case is full of tension. Hence, "it is the tragedy of Law in the world of Necessity" that the story outlines, but tragedy cannot mitigate the moral essence of the story. The moral law is required to defend against evil. To license murder in the case of Billy Budd is to invite disaster, precisely what communists had done by substituting history and politics for good and evil. They had given up the sanction against evil by loosening the moral law, by allowing the party to constitute this law, and by allowing spurious means in the name of glorious ends. Maxim emphasizes the Calvinism of Melville and the sinfulness of human nature, for "as long as Evil exists in the world, law must exist, and it—not Spirit—must have the rule."[28]

Maxim's review foreshadows the novel's denouement. Duck Caldwell—in the role of Billy Budd—inadvertently kills his sick daughter. She has a weak heart, and he strikes her fatally in a fit of drunken rage. Duck's crime has an intricate moral resonance. Laskell has had a romantic liaison with Duck's wife, Emily. He has coached the Caldwells' daughter, Susan, to recite Blake's poem, "A New Jerusalem," and when she stumbles on a line in public performance, Duck lashes out at her.[29] Duck may or may not know about his wife's infidelity; his daughter may or may not have stumbled because of Laskell's intrusion into her family circle. The crime, then, has several layers. Primarily, it is the consequence of Duck's evil character, but it is also connected to the affair between Emily and Laskell. The guilt that obsesses Maxim descends onto the character of Laskell as well. Laskell seeks in vain for solace from the progressive verities of his own recent past, realizing that "educated people more and more accounted for human action by the influence of environment and the necessities and habits imposed by society. Yet innocence and guilt were more earnestly spoken of than ever before."[30] The Crooms have lost the ability to speak incisively about guilt, as they have about illness and death. Though they are full of moral passion, full of earnestness, they lack a sense of individual agency or an appreciation for the limits set by nature. By the time Duck kills his daughter, Laskell is no longer a progressive.

Laskell's guilt takes him to the side of Maxim, who "wanted company in his own guilt."[31] Even when they had been radicals, they had shared an interest in conservative questions—such as the "social considerations which he [Laskell] had often discussed with Maxim, the nature of modern society, the individual and his relation to the social whole, the breaking of the communal bonds."[32] Exactly what Laskell shares with Maxim after he, too, breaks with communism and the Communist Party is unclear, though whatever it is that they share makes them both enemies of the Crooms (and the Crooms enemies of them). They share something like a moral vocabulary, in which the individual is the basic unit and to which belong words like *conscience, sin, guilt,* and *forgiveness.* The Anglican tones of Maxim's Arnoldian review are not gratuitous. They are counterposed to the angular, hard qualities of the modern Crooms. In *The Middle of the Journey,* Laskell and Maxim come to seem old-fashioned in their moral leanings, Maxim a plausible contemporary of Matthew Arnold or Cardinal Newman and Laskell a sensitive Bohemian of the 1920s. As Jewish characters, Laskell and Maxim might have found common ground in the fact of their Jewishness. They might have recognized their Jewishness as the source of their common moral vocabulary. Had they been Jewish, though, they could not have traveled backward in cultural time without brushing up against Jewish history and without pondering their place within it. Nor could their journeys have been exempt from reflection on European Jewry and possibly on Zionism as well. The political dilemmas of twentieth-century Jewish history would have been unavoidable, and we know from his letter to David Kleinman that Trilling wished to avoid exactly these dilemmas. As Americans of vaguely Protestant background, Trilling's characters have the entire field of Anglo-American culture on which to draw and no crisis other than that of their own conscience on which they must reflect.

Maxim and Laskell do not both move forward as Protestant Americans. Laskell grants religion its power. He even criticizes himself with religious ritual in mind, regretting that he had forgone the sacrament of marriage with his first love. He laments "his comfortable willingness not to be married to her, not to have that responsibility, which, in turn, meant that when she died there had been no way to realize and to express his grief, for he had not realized his relation to her."[33] Formally, however, Laskell eschews religion. He embraces instead the Hellenic qualities of beauty and pleasure and art, which for him are associated with Emily Caldwell. Emily's character can be glimpsed through Nancy Croom's condemnation of it: "She's cheap Village, cheap Provincetown, quaint tearoom . . . she was born in 1912—spiritually, I mean—and she died in 1930, and she doesn't know it yet."[34] An insult for Nancy is praise to Laskell. His first sight of Emily, walking uphill with her daughter, could be an image from a Greek vase. She possesses "the quality that, vague and no doubt pointlessly, people have a desire to call Greek."[35] Laskell and Emily conduct their tryst by a river on a summer's afternoon, and it seems the very realization of nature's imperative, an episode more in the manner of Ernest Hemingway than Matthew Arnold. Emily has no trouble speaking about death or love or beauty; in this sense, her "death" in 1930 is her greatest virtue. She is radical in her own right, but her radicalism has all of the 1920s aestheticism that the Crooms and the Communist Party alike are conspiring to crush. Emily recalls the title of Max Eastman's memoirs, *Love and Revolution*, with the accent on love.

Laskell handles his guilt in a way that touches on his liberalism, just as Nancy's guilt toward her husband touches on her radicalism, and Maxim's guilt about his past touches on his conservatism. Maxim demands the intercession of God for forgiveness. His violation of the law was absolute, in his view, and it remains so after his conversion to Christianity. He lives very much in the presence of his guilt. Nancy simply remains silent about her guilt. When she realizes that Maxim will not expose her complicity in his espionage operations—her serving as a letter drop for him, without informing her husband—she says nothing either to him or to her husband. She has served the cause and committed an indiscretion in the process, but the cause of communism is greater than such indiscretions; to achieve its ends it may even depend on them. Laskell is guilty of two things, of not marrying his first love and of his role in the death of Susan, Emily's daughter. He has not killed, but neither has he upheld the highest moral standard in his romantic life. His models of forgiveness (which he desperately seeks) derive not from religion but from art, the art of Mozart and Shakespeare.

He revels in the final scene of *The Marriage of Figaro*, when the count finally asks forgiveness of the countess, that "magical last scene where farce moves to regions higher than tragedy can reach."[36] It is an example of nobility of character, not of submission to God's judgment and mercy, an example repeated in *Hamlet*. Nothing Hamlet "says rings with a greater and graver note of masculinity than his 'God give me your pardon, sir. I have done you wrong.'"[37] These are the literary precedents for the forgiveness Emily bestows on Laskell by kissing him toward the end of the novel. Without a word, with only this gesture, she frees him from culpability for Susan's death. Laskell's moral world has a graciousness and ease that neither Maxim's nor Nancy's could match.

With his liberalism, his antiquated sentiments, and his moderation, Laskell is a foreigner to the world of the 1930s, which is to say a foreigner to the modern world. This world will belong either to Maxim or to the Crooms, to one or the other of their moral absolutes. The Crooms own the 1930s, the Red Decade, but to Maxim belongs "the future," and the future is no cause for optimism in *The Middle of the Journey*. "If Arthur Croom was the man of the near future," the narrative intelligence informs us, "Gifford Maxim was a man of the far future, the bloody, moral, apocalyptic future that was said to come."[38] Maxim's access to the future is an indictment of his character. His extremism will expedite the apocalypse, and his potential for success suggests opportunism. Realizing this, Laskell knows that his sympathy for Maxim is finite. Maxim is a threat to the liberal graces that Laskell cherishes, just as the Crooms had once been allies but on closer inspection proved to be enemies. The Crooms, however, are the vehicles of a dying ideology: "Laskell saw that the intellectual power had gone from that [the radical] system of idealism, and much of its power and drama had gone. And it would be brought by the swing of the pendulum, not by the motion of growth. Maxim was riding the pendulum."[39] Right and left are locked in mortal combat. The terrible vigor of the right and the corruption of the left describe the illiberal contours of the future. Laskell's liberalism is neither terrible nor corrupt, but it lacks strength and self-confidence; its civilized mildness leaves it vulnerable to more ruthless ideologies.

* * *

In 1984, Ronald Reagan posthumously awarded Whittaker Chambers a Medal of Freedom. Reagan's reference to the Soviet Union as an evil empire hearkened back to the language that Chambers (and his likeness Gifford Maxim) had employed as an anticommunist, the passion for which came from an understanding of Soviet communism as evil. Could one say that the Christian Right and the renewed Republican Party of the 1980s were the future Laskell foresaw? Had the intellectual power gone from left to right? Was Reagan's presidency evidence for the bloody, moral, apocalyptic future alluded to in *The Middle of the Journey*? The acute historical sense Trilling demonstrated in *The Middle of the Journey* had its limits. It suited the quandaries of intellectuals and the connection between these quandaries and the movement of political culture, but the American state took its own, unpredictable course. Whatever the rhetoric of Reagan, the reality of his presidency was not dictated by the religious extremism of a Gifford Maxim. The Reagan Revolution did not reject the modern world, as Maxim does. It was altogether too bourgeois to entertain apocalyptic solutions to political problems. It was moral but, once again, not in the sense that Maxim wanted politics to become moral. William Bennett was not the leader of a latter-day Inquisition. Talk of an evil empire receded when the orthodox Leninist, Mikhail Gorbachev, began to speak of *glasnost'* and *perestroika*, regardless of the fact that Gorbachev had coined these words for the sake of preserving the Soviet empire. The right had its victories in the 1980s, but it was not the right of Gifford Maxim.

It was, rather, the right of the neoconservatives. Emerging in the 1970s, neoconservative intellectuals opposed themselves to the New Left that was born in the 1960s. Against the New Left's criticism of the cold war, the neoconservatives mounted a defense of American power. Against the New Left's critique of capitalism, the neoconservatives declared their support for free enterprise. Against the New Left's championing of Third World liberation movements, the neoconservatives anchored themselves in Western civilization. To the radical ethos embraced by the New Left, the neoconservatives preferred the bourgeois family and the Judeo-Christian moral heritage. Not all neoconservative intellectuals were Jewish. Nor was Judaism necessarily the primary concern of those who were, but for the many Jewish neoconservatives, Judaism and Jewishness were a source of inspiration. Judaism was one aspect of a tradition that made them conservative. When Elliot Cohen described his faith in the "new patterns of living and new modes of thought" that would create a home for American Jews in the modern world, he could not have imagined the culture wars of the 1970s and 1980s. The arguments of the Jewish neoconservatives might well have been more American and more partisan than those that Cohen had in mind. He was calling for a renewal of Jewish culture in America, and however much neoconservatism had a Jewish inflection, it was emphatically a movement within American culture and politics. To the extent that Cohen was concerned with harmonizing "heritage and country," however, the Jewish neoconservatives offered one example of how this could be done. It was hardly an accident that one of the main magazines of the neoconservative movement was *Commentary* and that one of the main neoconservative intellectuals was Norman Podhoretz, a former student of Trilling's, who took over Elliot Cohen's job as editor of *Commentary* in 1960.

The neoconservative harmonization of heritage and country did not garner Trilling's support. He died in 1975, when the neoconservative movement was only beginning to coalesce, and he was never able to put his reservations into his own words. Shortly before he died, he began work on an autobiography, and if he had lived to complete it, he might have engaged directly with his political sympathies and antipathies. One might be able to say with greater clarity where his attack on the Old Left of the 1930s ended and where his doubts about the incipient neoconservatism of the 1970s began. Two explanations have since been offered, one by Trilling's widow, Diana, and the other by Norman Podhoretz. Diana argued that Lionel Trilling was a nineteenth-century liberal like Laskell, forced to navigate between left and right, though this is an explanation that explains too little.[40] Neoconservatives have drawn extensively on the thought of nineteenth-century liberals like Matthew Arnold. Gertrude Himmelfarb, for example, has used her scholarship on Victorian liberals like John Stuart Mill to inform her writing as a neoconservative intellectual. The other explanation is that Trilling was unwilling to fight the New Left as he had the Old Left because he was tired by the 1960s.[41] This also explains too little vis à vis Trilling and the neoconservative movement. A negative fraternity is not quite a fraternity. Much as Trilling disliked the New Left, he simply would not accept a formal allegiance to conservatism, even a conservatism so imbued with liberal premises that it merited the name of neoconservatism. Accused periodically of having a "conservative imagination," Trilling never understood himself to be a conservative.[42]

Clues to Trilling's rejection of the neoconservative label lie in *The Middle of the Journey*. One can be either a Gifford Maxim or a John Laskell. Laskell learns a great deal from Maxim and gives Maxim the gift of his respect, but most of all Laskell learns that he and Maxim are not comrades in their anticommunism. Their ideological commitments are incompatible. It may be that Laskell thirsts for a liberal imagination as opposed to a fixed ideological position, but even this freedom is a quality that inheres to liberalism, that makes liberalism the most attractive of ideologies to Laskell. Similarly, Maxim cannot make common cause with the liberalism of his friend. "You are proud of that flexibility of mind," he tells Laskell. "But it won't last, John, it's diminishing now. It's too late for that—the Renaissance is dead."[43] The moral relativism of the liberal persuasion appalls Maxim. It stems, he is sure, from liberal secularism, for it is only God who gives life meaning, in Maxim's view, and only this meaning that ensures the validity of law. All else is either nihilism or anarchy. In addition, Maxim sees the Crooms as liberals whose sliding scale of moral value has exposed them to the corruptions of Stalinism. Laskell might be a humane liberal, but his liberalism is too weak to fight the evil of communism. In the hands of people less decent than Laskell, liberalism will invite evil, for it is blind to what evil is, just as the Crooms are blind to the evil of Duck. In the ideological world of *The Middle of the Journey*, neoconservatism is not a conceivable harmonization of country and culture but an unholy alliance of Laskell's liberalism and Maxim's conservatism. It is an impossibility.

Laskell is therefore a poor role model for the neoconservative. As a post-Christian in America, he can slip easily into the liberal mode. Had he been made a Jewish character, he might have caused either himself or his creator, Lionel Trilling, the embarrassment that Sidney Hook felt after publishing an article about Jewish social philosophy. In his article, Hook attempted to harmonize his rationalist liberalism with his Jewish heritage. He argued for "emphasizing the principles of actual pluralism, political democracy, privatization of religion a democratic socialist welfare state, and the supremacy of the rational or scientific method."[44] Surely with this social philosophy Jews could make their way in the modern world. Hook, it seemed, had met Elliot Cohen's challenge. A problem arose when Hook's mentor, John Dewey, read the article. Dewey "with an amused look in his eyes mildly inquired why I had left him out. He subscribed to all the criteria I listed. What I preferred as a social philosophy for Jews seemed to him good enough for everyone."[45] Trilling might have characterized Hook's anecdote with a favorite adjective of his. Its lesson is *complicated*.[46] For Trilling, this adjective tokened an acceptance of paradox and difficulty, to which he contrasted the ideological simplicities of communism, represented in *The Middle of the Journey* by the Crooms. The task of the anticommunist intellectual was to recognize exactly how complicated the world is when seen without an all-explaining ideology. This complexity runs throughout Trilling's criticism. In his only novel, he could have made Laskell's liberalism more complicated by making Laskell Jewish, but then he would have faced the problem behind Hook's anecdote, to which Trilling had no more of an answer than Hook did. The Jewish neoconservatives proved more assertively Jewish and less assertively liberal than either Hook or Trilling; they carved their position out of the space between Laskell and Maxim. To the extent that the origins of neoconservatism are in Lionel Trilling's anticommunism, these origins are complicated indeed.

Notes

1. Elliot Cohen, "An Act of Affirmation: Editorial Statement," *Commentary* (November 1945), p. 2.
2. *The Middle of the Journey* has been recently rereleased: *The Middle of the Journey* (New York: New York Review of Books Classics Series, 2002).
3. See, for example, "Of Sophistication," *Menorah Journal* 14 (January 1928), pp. 106–109, and "Flawed Instruments," *Menorah Journal* 18 (April 1930), pp. 380–384. Both are highly critical reviews of novels by Lewissohn.
4. Lionel Trilling to David M. Kleinstein, March 20, 1948, Lionel Trilling Papers, Baker Library, Columbia University, Box 10.
5. Robert Warshow, "The Legacy of the '30's: Middle-Class Culture and the Intellectual's Problem," *Commentary* 4 (December 1947), p. 543. Emphasizing the themes of death and evil in *The Middle of the Journey*, Ruth Wisse notes that "there could hardly be a more Jewish set of themes, especially in the aftermath of the Holocaust, when the book was written. Trilling's novel was a blueprint for the cultural reversal that became known as neoconservatism, but he removes his characters from the Jewish milieu where this movement actually ripened, thereby depriving the book of its social substantiveness." *The Modern Jewish Canon: A Journey through Language and Culture* (New York: The Free Press, 2000), p. 17.
6. Matthew Arnold's most succinct discussion of these terms is in chapter four of *Culture and Anarchy*, "Hebraism and Hellenism." Arnold understood Hebraism to be moral and legal and Hellenism to be intellectual and aesthetic. Trilling's book on Matthew Arnold is *Matthew Arnold* (New York: Norton, 1939).
7. John Bayley, "Middle-Class Futures," *Times Literary Supplement*, April 11, 1975, p. 398.

8. Trilling discussed the relationship between Gifford Maxim and Whittaker Chambers in "Whittaker Chambers and *The Middle of the Journey*," *New York Review of Books*, April 17, 1975.

9. Trilling's sense of politics and culture may explain his talent for intermingling the two in his novel. As he wrote in the preface to *The Liberal Imagination*, "it is no longer possible to think of politics except as the politics of culture, the organization of human life toward some end or other, toward the modification of sentiments, which is to say the quality of human life." *The Liberal Imagination: Essays on Literature and Society* (New York: Viking, 1950), p. ix.

10. Lionel Trilling, *The Middle of the Journey* (New York: Viking Press, 1947), p. 49.

11. Ibid., p. 151.

12. Ibid., p. 233.

13. Ibid., p. 106.

14. Ibid., p. 10.

15. Ibid., p. 96.

16. Ibid., p. 193.

17. Ibid., p. 186.

18. Ibid., p. 32.

19. Ibid., p. 285.

20. Ibid., p. 186.

21. In *The Liberal Imagination*, Trilling describes such emotional chill as a problem of liberalism in general, which "somehow tends to deny them [emotions] in their full possibility" because of liberalism's "drift towards a denial of the emotions and imagination." *The Liberal Imagination*, pp. x, xi.

22. Trilling, *Middle of the Journey*, p. 110.

23. Ibid., p. 234.

24. Ibid., pp. 118–119.

25. Ibid., p. 270.

26. Ibid., p. 299.

27. Ibid., p. 154.

28. Ibid., p. 156.

29. The poem is no less thematically pertinent to *The Middle of the Journey* than "Billy Budd." Susan stumbles on the poem's final stanza:

> I will not cease from mental fight
> Nor shall my sword sleep in my hand
> Til we have built Jerusalem
> In England's green and pleasant land.

Blake's longing for Jerusalem while he laments industrial England (with its "dark satanic mills") evokes the utopian drives of communism. The poem is suggestive with regard to questions of Jewishness in the novel. Blake is appropriating Jerusalem for purposes that lie between Christianity and the radical sensibility. The metaphoric quality of Jerusalem in "A New Jerusalem" deprives it of any specifically Jewish significance, so that one might ponder building Jerusalem in England. The line, "I will not cease from mental fight," which Laskell had forced Susan to repeat when coaching her, is a kind of liberal mantra for Laskell, who refuses to succumb to the certainties of the left or the right.

30. Ibid., p. 145.

31. Ibid., p. 268.
32. Ibid., p. 135.
33. Ibid., p. 267.
34. Ibid., p. 78.
35. Ibid., p. 16.
36. Ibid., p. 68.
37. Ibid., p. 187.
38. Ibid., p. 55.
39. Ibid., p. 300.
40. "His own stand is in the traditional liberalism of the nineteenth century," Diana Trilling wrote, "and, complicate the situation though he does, he remained a traditional liberal until his death. Nothing in his thought supports the sectarianism of the neo-conservative movement." *The Beginning of the Journey: The Marriage of Diana and Lionel Trilling* (New York: Harcourt, Brace, 1999), p. 404. For a recent history of neoconservatism see Jacob Heilbrunn, *The Knew They Were Right: The Rise of the Neocons* (New York: Doubleday, 2008).
41. Norman Podhoretz has written that "to me it seemed clear that Lionel had lost his appetite for another fight against the Left." *Ex-Friends: Falling out with Allen Ginsberg, Lionel and Diana Trilling, Lillian Hellman, Hannah Arendt, and Norman Mailer* (New York: Free Press, 1999), p. 90.
42. The phrase comes from an essay by Joseph Frank, "Lionel Trilling and the Conservative Imagination," *Sewanee Review* 64 (Spring 1956), pp. 296–309. Trilling's low estimation of American conservatism as an intellectual endeavor may begin to explain his rejection of the label. "It is a plain fact that nowadays there are no conservative or reactionary ideas in general circulation," he wrote in what are perhaps his most quoted words. "This does not mean, of course, that there is no impulse to conservatism or to reaction. Such impulses are certainly very strong, perhaps even stronger than most of us know. But the conservative impulse and the reactionary impulse do not, with some isolated and some ecclesiastical exceptions, express themselves in ideas but only in action or in irritable mental gestures which seek to resemble ideas." *The Liberal Imagination*, p. vii.
43. Trilling, *The Middle of the Journey*, p. 304. The reference to the Renaissance resonates with Matthew Arnold's chapter "Hebraism and Hellenism." "As the great movement of Christianity was a triumph of Hebraism and man's moral impulses," Arnold writes, "so the great movement which goes by the name of the Renascence was an uprising and re-instatement of man's intellectual impulses and of Hellenism." *Culture and Anarchy*, J. Dover Wilson, ed. (Cambridge: Cambridge University Press, 1932), p. 139.
44. Sidney Hook, *Out of Step: An Unquiet Life in the Twentieth Century* (New York: Harper & Row, 1987), p. 352.
45. Ibid., p. 353.
46. Trilling's love of the word *complicated* haunted Norman Podhoretz: "I can hear him even now [twenty-four years after Trilling's death] pronouncing the word, perhaps his favorite in the whole English lexicon, with his rather thin voice lovingly lingering over the first syllable." *Ex-Friends*, p. 101.

Memorial for a Revolutionist

Dwight Macdonald, "A Critical American"

John Rodden

Portrait of the (New York) Intellectual as a Yale Man

Unlike his friend and intellectual contemporary Lionel Trilling, whose centenary in 2005 was commemorated widely in the U.S.—via national academic conferences as well as articles in the *New York Times* and the leading intellectual magazines—Dwight Macdonald's centennial went largely unnoticed.[1] Nonetheless, Macdonald was during the middle decades of the twentieth century "Our Best Journalist," in Paul Goodman's characterization in *Dissent* in 1958.[2] That same year the historian John Lukacs speculated in the Jesuit magazine *America* that Macdonald might become "the American Orwell," noting that Macdonald's "lonely and courageous positions coincide with the often lonely positions taken by George Orwell amidst the leftist intelligentsia in Britain."[3] Indeed, from the 1940s to the early 1970s, Macdonald was the best-known political and cultural critic to the general American public. His finest work makes him a worthy descendant of H.L. Mencken and Edmund Wilson, and like them "an American, an American in the individualist tradition," in Lukacs' words.

Dwight Macdonald had the (perhaps questionable) distinction of being cast—along with several other leading members of the *Partisan Review* circle[4]—as the "typical New York intellectual."[5] Yet he is probably the most unusual candidate within their group for that dubious honor.

Educated at Phillips Exeter and Yale University, Macdonald was an upper-middle-class suburban WASP—unlike the other leading figures of the New York Intellectuals, a mostly urban Jewish group. Another notable exception in this regard—indeed, even more so as a female member of their circle—was Mary Mc-

94

Carthy, who became one of Macdonald's closest friends.[6] Macdonald served as the model for McCarthy's essay "Portrait of the Intellectual as a Yale Man" and also for her character Macdougal Macdermott in her early postwar satirical novel, *The Oasis*.[7] (Macdonald was also the object of Saul Bellow's biting satire in *Humboldt's Gift*, appearing in the figure of Orlando Higgins, the lightweight nudist intellectual.)

The Political Pilgrim—Stage Left

After graduating from Yale University in 1927, Macdonald soon joined the fledgling publishing enterprise of his fellow Yale alumnus Henry Luce as a staff writer for *Fortune* in 1929. Macdonald stayed with the magazine for seven years. He finally resigned when he felt that he was being politically stifled as he began to move leftward and embrace Marxism, a journey catalyzed by his 1933 marriage to Nancy Rodman and the influence of her wide circle of radical friends.[8] Macdonald became a self-declared Trotskyist in 1936.

Yet it was also true that, like many intellectuals, he became associated in the mid-1930s with the Communist Party because it seemed to represent the only decent alternative to what he judged the inexorable outcome of capitalism: imperialism, fascism, and economic depression. The Soviet purges of 1935–1938 deepened Macdonald's commitment to Trotskyism and induced him to join the Socialist Workers Party (SWP) in 1939, the main political sect of American followers. Macdonald did so with the fervor of a new convert—but with the retained critical faculties of someone who was no communist stooge.

Inevitably, Macdonald's falling-out with the SWP was just a matter of time: it finally occurred when Trotsky decided that regardless of the Soviet Union's actions, such as the German-Soviet Nonaggression Pact of 1939 or the Soviet attack on Finland in the fall of that same year, Stalin's Russia had to be supported—because it was a "worker's state," albeit a deformed one. This decision appalled Macdonald, who immediately and publicly began to criticize Trotsky's views, both in SWP-sponsored organs and in the non-Trotskyist press. As a result, the SWP began to demand that Macdonald submit all his writings to the party leadership before publishing them. That was too much for Macdonald, who concluded that Trotskyism "was merely a variant of Stalinism." Macdonald's recalcitrance and skepticism toward the SWP leaders and even Trotsky himself did not please the "Old Man": "Everyone has the right to be stupid, but Comrade Macdonald abuses the privilege!" groused Trotsky.[9]

This zinger has been much quoted, though Macdonald's biographer Michael Wreszin speculates that it may be apocryphal (and Macdonald's clever invention).[10] But what is clearly established is that one of Trotsky's last acts before he was assassinated in 1940 was a reply to Macdonald. Macdonald had castigated Trotsky for his suppression of the Kronstadt uprising, which he never repudiated, let alone issue an apology for the executions of the defeated rebels. (Even today, orthodox Trotskyists tend to downplay the whole brutal incident in much the same dismissive tones as orthodox communists do for later Soviet atrocities.)

Certainly Macdonald was temperamentally and socially unsuited to the SWP. For instance, in full conspiratorial mode, most members took secret party names. But in his inveterately puckish, nose-tweaking spirit of bemused defiance, Macdonald adopted "James Joyce." Could anyone have been more antithetical to the passionately committed ideological stances of Lenin and Trotsky than the ingenious ludic artist who authored *Finnegans Wake*?

Already by this time Macdonald had affiliated with a group of radical intellectuals who also exhibited the audacity to buck party discipline and think for themselves. In May 1937, Macdonald became one of the editors who refounded *Partisan Review* (*PR*), working with editors Philip Rahv and William Phillips to shift it from a Communist Party organ to an independent left-wing quarterly.[11] Here he found his niche.

During this brief interval of a year or two, Macdonald was jubilant: he felt at home among this group of predominantly Jewish Trotskyists. He had momentarily discovered a hospitable milieu that slaked his thirst for informed debate about politics and avant-garde sophistication in culture—the *PR* "herd of independent minds," in Harold Rosenberg's memorable phrase. And despite his subsequent dissatisfactions with most of his *PR* colleagues over their positions on World War II, McCarthyism, and the New Left, Macdonald's encounter with this like-minded literary species also furnished him with his vocation: for the rest of his life he would be a journalist, critic, editor, and commentator for various magazines, a list that would include the *New Yorker*, the *New Republic*, *Esquire*, and *Encounter*, to mention just a few.

Macdonald's years with *PR* (1937–1943) were formative ones. He completed much of his political education at this time, though Rahv and Phillips always regarded him as naïve and lacking a coherent political philosophy. Macdonald flirted with various left-wing factions besides the SWP during the late 1930s and early 1940s, remaining a Trotskyist until the middle of World War II; he was in fact enamored of Trotsky personally throughout this period and considered him an exemplary instance of the man of action and the man of reflection combined for a worthy radical purpose. Because of the dizzying divagations of his political course occasioned by his numerous, abrupt ideological about-faces, Macdonald frequently was taken to have a frivolous political mind and was regarded as something of a jokester. As we shall see, however, the simple truth is that such matters as "coherence" or even consistency were of secondary concern to Macdonald: in essence he was a counterpuncher, a member of the (sometimes) loyal opposition, a thinker who exemplified the classic conception of the modern intellectual as a critic of the powers-that-be—and indeed also as a critic-from-within, a critic of the intelligentsia and of his own side, however temporary his alliance with that side might be.

Like most of his colleagues among the New York Intellectuals, Macdonald was highly critical of the liberalism of the New Dealers and of the illiberal liberalism of the Stalinists. He considered the nineteenth-century liberal mind to be outdated in the modern world. Liberal philosophers such as John Dewey and William James, along with contemporary liberals such as Lewis Mumford and Arthur Schlesinger, according to Macdonald, were ill-equipped to understand the threats posed by mass man and the highly unstable economic conditions of the mid-twentieth century. During his Trotskyist phase, Macdonald saw them as blind to the fact that an authoritarian system such as communism or fascism would be needed to achieve an egalitarian, ordered, law-abiding society.[12] The independent liberal-left positions advocated by socialists such as his wife Nancy's brother, Selden Rodman, editor of *Common Sense*, seemed to Macdonald utterly naïve because they blithely assumed that "sweet reason alone" could transform monopoly capitalism into a decent socialism. For all his hatred of dictators such as Hitler, Stalin, and Mussolini, Macdonald harbored a veiled admiration of them as men of power who did not shrink from the exercise of ruthless force to achieve their ends.

For a short time, Macdonald was able to reconcile his SWP allegiance with his freethinking *PR* affiliation. As we have seen, when Macdonald joined *Partisan Review*, it was being transformed by editors Rahv and Phillips from a Communist Party tract into an independent Marxist organ sympathetic to Trotsky, then in exile in Mexico. *Partisan Review* was designed to blend Marxist theory with serious commentary on art and culture. Macdonald fit in well—at least intellectually. He had read Marx and admired Trotskyism because, in his words, it "was the most revolutionary of the sizeable leftwing groups . . . and, above all . . . it was led by Trotsky, whose career showed that intellectuals, too, could make history."[13]

In the September–October 1940 issue of *PR*, Macdonald published an extended obituary of Trotsky: "Trotsky is Dead." Here he argued that in his last years Trotsky "had understood so much and yet did not understand enough; he probed boldly and deeply and yet did not go deep enough." Echoing the intraparty critique of Trotsky by ex-SWP member Max Shachtman, who had recently broken with the SWP to form his own dissident Trotskyist sect, Macdonald insisted that Trotsky had failed to understand the full significance of developments in Stalin's Russia and Hitler's Germany in the 1930s. Although Stalin was certainly not taking Russia in a socialist direction, neither was he restoring capitalism. Instead, he "has created a new form of class exploitation—call it 'bureaucratic collectivism' for lack of a better term [the Italian Bruno Rizzi is usually credited with this coinage]—and only on this basis can the development of the USSR in the last ten years be understood."[14] Similarly, although Trotsky had provided a marvelous commentary on the Nazis' rise to power in Germany, he had failed to see that Hitler's regime had also set about building a new type of exploitative class society that was converging with Stalin's Russia.

Always Against the Grain

But Macdonald always chafed at orthodoxy, sooner or later becoming a rebel within any group that he joined, as he noted in his two essay collections recounting the early postwar era, *Memoirs of a Revolutionist* (1957) and *Against the American Grain* (1962).[15] He resigned from the SWP in October 1940 after only fifteen months as a member because the leadership demanded strict adherence to its party line[16]; soon he would also break with his *PR* associates over their support for the Allies in World War II. Macdonald possessed a temperament quite allergic to groupthink, and he bristled at toeing any party line for long, Marxist or otherwise. (Like the other Marx whom he admired, Groucho, Macdonald was never comfortable with any group that would have him.)

The outbreak of World War II posed a problem for Macdonald. Always "against the American grain"—as well as virtually any other—he refused to take sides in a struggle that he regarded as a clash between two forms of imperialism. Macdonald believed the ultimate victor in such a conflict would be a mongrel form of fascism, and he argued that the only hope for democracy in the United States or Great Britain was a genuine social revolution. In 1941, with the war now a world conflict, Rahv and Phillips argued that the left should actively support the Allies despite their flawed political views, but Macdonald disagreed. He remained a pacifist and saw nothing of value emerging from the war.

Macdonald's pacifist-isolationist stance toward the war rankled most of his fellow *PR* editors and led to acrimonious debates that divided him from them. Macdonald had to fight to get his fellow editors to agree to publish his pacifist rejoinders to George Orwell, *PR*'s London correspondent, which appeared in the autumn of 1942. Indeed, his Marxist and secular Jewish colleagues at *PR* considered him hopelessly confused as a political thinker and much more of a moralist than a socialist, suggesting in one published editorial dispute that Macdonald's ethical impulse was (in his phrase mocking them) "leading to . . . horror of horrors, the Church!"[17] Macdonald readily admitted that moral and ethical considerations governed his ideological outlook—though he never exhibited, as he also noted, the slightest interest in religion or God.

In 1943 he cowrote in *PR*, with art critic and junior editor Clement Greenberg, a long essay, "Ten Propositions on the War," which opposed the war in uncompromising terms. Arthur Koestler pointed to a flaw in Macdonald's conception of the war as a struggle between Nazism and capitalism, claiming that even if "we are fighting against a total lie in the name of a half-truth," the half-truth still merited qualified support. Macdonald rejected Koestler's criticism as shallow justification for supporting an evil capitalist system.[18] The situation came to a head in mid-1943 when Macdonald attempted to take control of the magazine with the intention of changing it from a literary to a political review with a strong antiwar stance. Finally, under pressure from Rahv and Phillips, Macdonald resigned from the editorial board of *PR* in July 1943. Soon he set about founding his own magazine, which he launched with his wealthy wife Nancy's family inheritance.

Macdonald named his journal *politics*. (He always preferred to lower-case its title.) He wanted the new journal to be more political than *PR*, which steered away from controversial positions during the war out of fear of censorship. For five years (1944–1949), largely as a one-man labor of love, *politics* voiced a radical contrarian view toward the most popular war in American history. Often wrong-headed, it nonetheless demonstrated a side of Macdonald that still holds up: his bold outspokenness, even when crying in the wilderness, and his fundamental human decency in the face of unrestrained patriotism (and often nationalism).

The intellectual historian Gregory D. Sumner has noted that Macdonald's *politics* "occupies a special, almost legendary place in the history of American radicalism" because it offered "a communitarian alternative to both Marxian socialism and cold war liberalism."[19] Macdonald's *politics* denounced the bombing of civilians by both the Allies and the Axis, stood among the first to call attention to the Nazi death camps,[20] and railed against the hypocrisy of fighting a war for democracy with a segregated military. Its contributors included numerous leading European intellectuals such as George Orwell, Nicola Chiaromonte, Victor Serge, Simone Weil, and Albert Camus, along with expatriate intellectuals such as Bruno Bettelheim, Lewis Coser, and Hannah Arendt.[21] Sumner adds that Macdonald and the *politics* circle advanced ideas in the 1940s that foreshadowed "the experiments in 'participatory democracy' associated with the New Left two decades later, and they also anticipated current debates about the need for an independent sphere of civil society initiated by dissidents from the former Soviet bloc."[22]

I agree. Macdonald insisted that the greatest danger facing the intellectual left in America was becoming little more than the voice of the Roosevelt administration and the liblabs,[23] a jab at the probusiness liberals and moderate Labourites who eschewed socialism. He still believed, although with diminishing conviction as the war progressed, that the best outcome would be a social revolution that would overthrow the capitalist system and create a genuine proletarian society. His finest work for *politics*, however, was not his political theorizing, which has dated badly. It was rather his caustic essays that upbraided, in his trademark blistering prose, various misguided supporters of the war.

One essay in particular gained Macdonald notoriety: "My Favorite General," a report of a bloodthirsty late-wartime speech by General George S. Patton, Jr., praising American soldiers for killing the "goddamn Germans" and "purple-pissing Japs." Appearing in the October 1945 issue (and republished in *Memoirs of a Revolutionist*), this essay serves as an interesting commentary on how time transforms values. Macdonald's Patton speech opens the enormously successful film *Patton* (1970). Delivered brilliantly by actor George C. Scott, it serves to humanize Patton and even enshrine him—hardly what Macdonald had in mind when he first published the speech. Here is part of it in Macdonald's rendition:

> All through your army career, you've bitched about what you call "this chicken-shit drilling." That drilling was for a purpose: instant obedience to orders and to create alertness. If not, some sonofabitch of a German will sneak up behind you and beat you to death with a sock full of shit. . . .

Remember, men! You don't know I'm here. . . . Let the first bastards to find out be the goddamn Germans. I want them German bastards to raise up on their hind legs and howl: "JESUS CHRIST! IT'S THE GOD-DAMNED THIRD ARMY AND THAT SONOFABITCH PATTON AGAIN!" We want to get the hell over there and clean the goddamn thing up. And then we'll have to take a little jaunt against the purple-pissing Japs and clean them out before the Marines get all the credit. There's one great thing you men will be able to say when you go home. You may all thank God that thirty years from now, when you are sitting at the fire with your grandson on your knee and he asks you what you did in the Great World War II, you won't have to say: "I shoveled shit in Louisiana."

Full of verve and wit, *politics* showcased Macdonald's remarkable ability— which he had honed at *PR*—to go against not just the American grain (like most progressives), but also against the ideological consensus of his intellectual cohort and immediate ideological reference group as well (like today's neoconservatives). Another case in point was Macdonald's hilarious critique of Stalin sympathizer Henry Wallace and his torturous speechifying on behalf of the USSR. Here Macdonald lashed out at former Vice President Wallace, who had been dumped from the Democratic Party ticket as FDR's running mate in 1944. Appearing in the May–June 1947 issue of the magazine and later collected in *Memoirs of a Revolutionist*, the piece was titled "A Note on Wallese":

Wallaceland is the mental habitat of Henry Wallace plus a few hundred thousand regular readers of the *New Republic*, the *Nation*, and *PM*. It is a region of perpetual fogs, caused by the warm winds of the liberal Gulf Stream coming in contact with the Soviet glacier. Its natives speak "Wallese," a debased provincial dialect.

Wallese is as rigidly formalized as Mandarin Chinese. The Good People are described by ritualistic adjectives: "forward-looking," "freedom-loving," "clear-thinking," and of course, "democratic" and "progressive." The Bad People are always "reactionaries" or "red-baiters."[24]

This feisty, punchy style characterized *politics* from the start. In the inaugural issue in February 1944, Macdonald announced that although his journal had no party line, it did have an editorial policy: "The magazine's political tendency will be democratic socialist. Its predominant intellectual approach will be Marxist, in the sense of a method of analysis, not a body of dogma . . . It will be partisan to those at the bottom of society—the Negroes, the colonial peoples, and the vast majority of common people everywhere, including the Soviet Union."[25] (Here we see how *politics* anticipated both the black civil rights campaign of the 1950s and the dissident, anti-Soviet protest movement in Eastern Europe of the 1980s.) As for the USSR, Macdonald reaffirmed his revolutionary opposition to the war and reiterated his outraged conviction that the USSR had degenerated into a model of "bureaucratic collectivism": "Russia is a new form of class society based on collective ownership of the means of production by the ruling bureaucracy."[26]

The Anarchist Turn

Macdonald's position was, at the time of *politics'* inauguration in 1944, still that of a heretical Trotskyist. But he soon embraced a stance that can best be described as anarcho-pacifism. During the last months of World War II, *politics* was unambiguously pacifist-anarchist, an unpopular stance in the midst of what became known as the "Good War."

But Macdonald never saw it as "good"—or even as a necessary evil. Indeed, the closing weeks of the war profoundly depressed Macdonald. He was appalled by the massive Allied bombings with their terrible civilian causalities, a disgust that reached sickening levels when the United States used atomic bombs against Japan. Macdonald rushed out a special article for the August 1945 issue of *politics*, which trumpeted (in capital letters) that "the concepts of war and progress are now obsolete" and that "atomic bombs are the natural product of the kind of society we have created."[27] The latter point reflected the fact that Macdonald was rapidly losing his residual faith in the political sense and decency of the American people. Macdonald was also nauseated by the Allied betrayal of the Poles in the Warsaw Uprising, by the Allied intervention in the Greek civil war on the side of the rightists, and by the discovery of the Nazi extermination camps.

Convinced that mass movements in the modern world ineluctably lead in the direction of violence and ultimately totalitarianism, Macdonald formally abandoned Marxism in early 1946. He gave up all hope of socialist revolution in favor of the notion of individual witness. His break with Marxism was announced with the publication of "The Root Is Man," an ambitious essay that appeared in two parts in the March and April 1946 issues of *politics*. Finally despairing of political activity altogether and trusting only the integrity of the single individual, Macdonald insisted that political responsibility ultimately rested with the single individual: "the root is man."[28]

Why did this sharp turn in his politics occur? The reality is that it was actually much less abrupt and sudden than Macdonald's harshest critics have allowed. It had in fact been developing for more than a decade. Macdonald always had an interest in the behemoth of the modern state. During his honeymoon with Nancy in Majorca in 1934, he spent most of his time studying the rise of dictators and the dangers posed by the excessive concentration of centralized power. Macdonald's belligerent antiwar stance fed both his deepening hatred of statism and his idealistic insistence on an ethical approach to political life. Moreover, his growing pacifism was compatible with the anti-imperialist war position of the SWP. All of these developments contributed in the mid-1940s to his embrace of a full-blown anarcho-pacifism.

Macdonald attempted to explain how the modern state practiced terror against its own people. In "The Responsibilities of Peoples," which appeared in March 1945, Macdonald rejected the concept of the collective guilt of the Germans, noting that the Allies had perpetrated their own terrible atrocities during the war, especially the mass bombing of cities. As a good anarchist, he worried that the autonomous person was losing control to the growing power of the state. He was pessimistic about the future. In particular he was gradually losing his conviction that political activity could solve the world's problems.[29] During the early cold war era, his biographer Michael Wreszin has observed, "as the fear of another war approached, Macdonald became obsessed with the power of the state to lead people into war."[30]

Thus Macdonald's sharp turn away from Trotskyism and toward anarchism, pacifism, and individualism reflected and fit well with his anathema toward Stalinism and the Soviet state. But Macdonald's embrace of anarcho-pacifism was not merely a response to historical and political developments; there were also personal and intellectual influences at work. Chief among them were the roles that two religious women played as exemplars of the committed intellectual for Macdonald: Simone Weil and Dorothy Day, about both of whom he later wrote flattering *New Yorker* profiles in the 1950s. Weil wrote for *politics* as Macdonald was formulating the basic ideas of "The Root Is Man," and she became for him, in the words of his biographer Michael Wreszin, "a saint of individual activism." In particular her *politics* essay on Homer's *Iliad* in November 1945 convinced Macdonald that the exercise of force or coercion eventually enslaves those who employ it.[31]

As for Dorothy Day, Macdonald occasionally spoke at her invitation at the regular Friday night forums of the Catholic Worker groups in New York, and he once told William Shawn, editor of the *New Yorker*, that he was "greatly impressed by Dorothy Day and her colleagues," who are "absolute pacifists, ardent pro-unionists, politically extreme radicals, distinguishable from Trotskyists only by their anarchistic bent, and they live lives of voluntary poverty. Helping the poor and the underdog is their main activity."[32] It is significant that Macdonald's profiles of Weil and Day form the two closing chapters of *Memoirs of a Revolutionist*. Unlike Weil or Day, however, Macdonald never moved toward a religious foundation for his radical values. The basis for his outlook always remained an individualistic secular morality. It is also true that this stance fit best with his own temperamental bent toward individualism and rebelliousness, as his decision to launch *politics* as a one-man operation also testified.[33]

Macdonald's linkage of mass art and cultural forms of totalitarianism also reinforced his belief in anarchic individualism: all forms of centralized authority and bureaucracy seemed to him evil. Although his critics derided him as having succumbed to the depoliticization of American intellectuals and the turn toward quietism in the 1950s, Macdonald viewed his anarcho-pacifist stance as an example of authentic critical dissent and the assumption of full individual responsibility for revolutionary change or reform. Throughout the 1950s he continued to call for a revival of the American anarchistic tradition—he often wore a button endorsing Emma Goldman—and it was revealing that he was asked to speak on "the relevance of anarchism" at the first national SDS convention in New York in June 1960.[34]

Macdonald termed his form of pacifism "friendly resistance," and in the mid-1940s he became an active member of the War Resisters League and the Militant Peacemakers. Macdonald defended resistance to the draft and the public burning of draft cards. He corresponded with militant pacifists and with jailed conscientious objectors, and he also commissioned articles from anarchists and pacifists living in communes. His biographer Michael Wreszin concludes, "He was drawn to [anarcho-pacifism] for ways to live his own life, to find more personal fulfillment, to escape the pressures, the lack of time for reflection in the rat race of urban existence."

Macdonald's last great campaign in *politics* was a frontal attack on the candidacy of Henry Wallace for president in 1948. Once again, Macdonald didn't so much support an actual candidate or party, either liberals or the socialist alternative, but rather defined himself in opposition. He viewed Wallace's Progressive Party as little more than a cover for the Communists and their fellow travelers. Macdonald wrote a number of sharp-tongued articles in *politics*—similar to "A Note on Wallese," from which we have already quoted—on that nightmare state that he dubbed "Wallaceland," a realm of utopian dreams and political illusions. He expanded these essays into a book, *Henry Wallace: Man or Myth* (1948), arguing that Wallace demonstrated how debased American liberalism had become: it had degenerated into fuzzy political thinking while parroting the Communist Party line.

Although Macdonald sometimes liked to believe that he contributed to Wallace's poor electoral performance in the 1948 presidential election, he ultimately derived scant comfort from Wallace's humiliating defeat. Indeed, Macdonald wrote in 1948 that he had lost his faith "in any general and radical improvement in modern society, whether by Marxian socialist or pacifist persuasion and ethical example." Socialism and pacifism, he claimed, "were quite bad for the people" because they underestimated the threat from Stalin's perversion of communism. By this time Macdonald had completely shed his Marxist past. Marx had been his Baedeker to the radical world, he said, but he was no longer interested in the Marxist approach to political questions.

What in fact remained constant throughout the early postwar era was Macdonald's hostility to communism. The communist *coup d'état* in Czechoslovakia in March 1948, followed by the Berlin blockade, turned Macdonald into a cold warrior. With the outbreak of the Korean War in June 1950, his liberal anticommunism deepened and led to his temporarily becoming a fierce anti-Stalinist rallying to the defense of America against Soviet aggression. (Fifteen years later, he was to return to the radical camp by publicly opposing the Vietnam War.)

So Macdonald, once a disciple of Trotsky, was an antiwar Marxist until the war's end and then gravitated toward anarchism. He remained a pacifist until the time of the Berlin Blockade in 1947–1948, when he reluctantly accepted that the U.S. was the "lesser evil." His critical support for the U.S. against the rising threat of Soviet imperialism culminated in his controversial declaration of "I Choose the West," voiced during a 1952 debate at Mount Holyoke with Norman Mailer, which Macdonald published as an essay of that title a few years later (also collected in *Memoirs of a Revolutionist*).

As I have already suggested, these dramatic shifts in his political positions resulted in Macdonald's being dismissed by many of his New York Intellectual colleagues as a political knave, a lightweight thinker more in love with a good quip than with serious analysis. To Irving Howe, Macdonald possessed a "table-hopping mind." Daniel Bell mocked him as "the floating kidney of the Left." Admittedly, Macdonald could decimate intellectual fashions, but his own mercurial political enthusiasms rivaled the rise and fall of women's hemlines.[35]

If Macdonald indeed espoused any consistent politics, he belonged to the radical tradition, always insisting that one should "go to the root"—whether that meant a program of revolutionary justice in the 1930s or whether it signified a decade later that "the root is man." But consistency was never Macdonald's strong suit. Yet it is also true that he was not taken seriously—especially by pure political types such as Sidney Hook and Philip Rahv—because his acrid sense of humor and crusty satirical persona were unusual in the rarified cerebral atmosphere of the *PR* crowd, where comedy was considered something for the borscht belt. By the late 1940s he was in danger of being marginalized. His fellow *PR* editor William Barrett issued the ultimate verdict of their intellectual community when he later wrote, "For him every venture into politics was a leap toward the Absolute. . . . He was a kind of Don Quixote or Galahad, alternately tilting at windmills in quest of the Holy Grail."[36]

"A Critical American"

From 1944 until 1947 Macdonald published *politics* first as a monthly, then sporadically. When his enthusiasm for *politics* and Nancy's funds both exhausted themselves in early 1949, Macdonald closed down the magazine. He then fell into his deepest despair about the fate of humanity, losing any positive political vision and even faith in his own ability to influence the direction of political affairs, which now seemed to him beyond the control of men in the wake of the bomb and the division of the world between the two superstates, America and the Soviet Union. Instead Macdonald channeled his full energies into literary and cultural criticism, which he had largely neglected during the 1940s in favor of politics and *politics*.

During the 1950s, Macdonald never fully lost his interest in political topics relating to domestic and foreign policy. But his best work now addressed cultural politics and the arts. While he thought of himself as a defender of the traditional canon, he concentrated his efforts on a critique of the middlebrow literature that thrived at midcentury—and that he despised. Although he continued to contribute political pieces occasionally to the little magazines and the literary-intellectual quarterlies, Macdonald wrote increasingly for mass circulation magazines such as *Esquire* and the *New Yorker*, whose staff he joined in early 1952. His feisty criticism in their pages amounted to a running commentary on what he regarded as the shabby "midcult" of postwar America.

The decade and a half following the disbanding of *politics* in 1949 marks Macdonald's most creative period. These years would also see him rise from a fringe political journalist to the status of America's most influential cultural arbiter. However consciously, Macdonald in the 1950s and early 1960s sought in many ways to emulate the role that Orwell had played in England as the unpredictable, sometimes cantankerous, brutally honest observer of the national cultural scene. Purposefully or not, Macdonald in the 1950s did indeed aspire to become the "American Orwell."

What distinguished Macdonald in these years was an almost uncanny ability to expose the cultural fads and intellectual frauds of the day. It was a role perfectly suited to the withering *ad hominem* prose style that he had mastered in the 1930s and 1940s from his battles within the *Partisan Review* circle, where he had become a specialist in literary abuse. Once he turned to cultural criticism, Macdonald's judgments took on a new sense of self-confidence. His positions on culture and art were firm and witnessed no sharp reversals. His cultural criticism never succumbed to the tendency that entered his political writings due to his contrarian's anathema toward party groupthink and any ideological "line," a penchant that had led to his being dismissed by his New York Intellectual colleagues as "the Peter Pan of the Left."

Characteristically written with passion, authority, and certitude, Macdonald's cultural criticism reveals his conservative side. It also shows his mistrust in the judgment of the American public. A streak of elitist pessimism about American society and its preference for midcult and lowcult runs through Macdonald's criticism of the 1950s and early 1960s, a pessimism that diverged sharply from the Marxist-induced revolutionary idealism and optimism of his Trotskyist phase.

In the 1950s Macdonald was preoccupied with cultural politics, especially the widening gap between high culture and mass culture. The major result of this interest was his landmark essay "Masscult and Midcult," published in *PR* in 1960. This essay was "high concept," a challenging "think" piece, and it argued that high culture was being dumbed down by the insidious forces of mass taste into coffee-table midcult, which inevitably catered to the lowest common denominator. It was the most important cultural essay that Macdonald ever penned. (Today, in an age of academic literary criticism dominated by technical theories such as deconstruction and multiculturalism, "Masscult and Midcult" is largely unread.)

For all his negativity about the corrupting influence of midcult and how it dumbed down high culture, Macdonald's cultural criticism of the 1950s was the finest work of his lifetime. Once again, just as he had shown in his political commentary in *PR* and *politics* a decade earlier, he was always at his best writing against the grain of contemporary tastes. Typical was Macdonald's proud, sharp letter of protest to the editor of *Twentieth Century* in December 1958. Macdonald contested the editorial introduction to his essay "America! America!" that had appeared in the previous issue. The editors of this British magazine had written that they "would not publish Dwight Macdonald's spirited and witty comment on American life" if Macdonald himself were not "a good American." Macdonald wrote in reply that "patriotism has never been my strong point." He continued: "I don't know as I'd call myself A Good American. I'm certainly A Critical American, and I prefer your country, morally and culturally, to my own."

Macdonald's keenest cultural essays in the 1950s and 1960s invariably fulminate against the tawdry artifacts of midcult and mass culture. Part of the reason Macdonald took pleasure in assaulting them—such as Mortimer Adler's pretentious Syntopicon (the governing midcult concept in his Great Ideas series) or Webster's New Third International Dictionary—was his belief that the lowcult indulgences of the American *demos* had undermined the nation's taste. "Democracy" in the Eisenhower era had come to mean dumbing down. Here is an excerpt from his caustic mockery of the "Revisers" who modernized language in the Revised Standard Bible:

> Reading their work is like walking through an old city that has just been given, if not a saturation bombing, a thorough going-over. One looks about anxiously. Is this gone? Does that still survive? Surely they might have spared *that!* And even though many of the big landmarks are left—their fabric weakened by the Revisers' policy of modernizing the grammatical usage—so many of the lesser structures have been razed that the whole feel of the place is different. In Cologne, in 1950, the cathedral still stood, alone and strange, in the midst of miles of rubble.[37]

Serious essays on Ernest Hemingway, Mark Twain, and James Agee show Macdonald becoming more and more disenchanted as the 1950s advanced. His pessimism deepened because he could find no repository for his hope: political affairs had turned sour for him and seemed futile and boring, and he found little to cheer in the world of literature. Macdonald's clever, if merciless, parody of Hemingway shows the characteristic tone of his literary criticism during the decade:

> He wrote a novel called *Across the River and Into the Trees*. It was not a good novel. It was a bad novel. It was so bad that all the critics were against it. Even the ones who had liked everything else. The trouble with critics is that you can't depend on them in a tight place and this was a very tight place

indeed. They scare easy because their brains are where their *cojones* should be and because they have no loyalty and because they have never stopped a charging lion with a Mannlicher double-action or did any of the other important things. The hell with them. Jack Dempsey thought *Across the River* was OK. So did Joe Di Maggio. The Kraut thought it was terrific. So did Toots Shor. But it was not OK and he knew it and there was absolutely nothing he could do about it.[38]

Curmudgeon or Antisemite?

Radical by conviction, Macdonald was conservative in temperament and taste, and this made him a traditionalist and even a curmudgeonly elitist in his later years. He came to hate avant-garde art and lashed out at both the action painting of Jackson Pollack and Beat poets such as Allen Ginsberg and Jack Kerouac. Macdonald took special pleasure in puncturing what he considered critically inflated works such as Colin Wilson's much-hyped pseudophilosophical treatise of 1950s existentialism, *The Outsider*. (Macdonald's savaging of Wilson in 1957 was unusual in one sense. As his aforementioned letter to the editor of *Twentieth Century* attests, he was otherwise an Anglophile who believed that the English literary and critical scene was superior to the American.) His last significant literary-political accomplishment was his championing of Michael Harrington's *The Other America* in the *New Yorker* in January 1963. Harrington's book had appeared nine months earlier and sold poorly; Macdonald's feature story brought it to President Kennedy's attention and thus helped launch the War on Poverty in the 1960s.

Macdonald also gave vent to his curmudgeonly side throughout these years in his expression of a mild antisemitism quite common among his classmates at Philips Exeter and Yale. Macdonald had in fact harbored a WASPish condescension and even antipathy toward Jews during his teens, once writing to a Jewish girl that he "disliked rather violently the Jews as a race." His early antisemitic attitudes had much to do with his rearing, especially with his mother's negative social attitudes toward minorities and immigrants. By his late twenties, when he participated in the predominantly Jewish community of New York Intellectuals associated with *Partisan Review*, he outgrew most of these early attitudes.[39] Nonetheless, Macdonald was suspected by some Jewish colleagues of being antisemitic, though most of them concluded that he simply relished argument and meant no personal offense in his highly critical attitudes about Israel, Palestine, Zionism, and his interpretation of the circumstances of the Holocaust.[40]

Although Macdonald's antisemitic rearing was reinforced at Philips Exeter and Yale University, both of which embraced a genteel racism that was common during that time, his biographer Michael Wreszin notes, "Macdonald's entry in the 1930s to the *Partisan Review* circle soon led him to conclude that an intellectual's identity had to be grounded in a cosmopolitanism that repudiated national chauvinism." Macdonald sometimes called himself "a non-Jewish Jew," even proclaiming himself on occasion "an honorary Jew"; he declared proudly that "Red Rosa [Luxemburg] has long been my favorite revolutionist." Nonetheless, of course, he recognized that he was not Jewish, and as a result he often felt "alienated" (a signature term of the New York Intellectuals) as an outsider among the New York Jews. He condemned explicit displays of antisemitism, but he also castigated what he perceived in the early postwar era to be Israel's mistreatment of Arab refugees. Macdonald's exuberant intellectual jousting in defense of such positions, conducted in an impersonal yet aggressively charged tone, could easily be mistaken for antisemitic remarks by those not well acquainted with him.[41]

Macdonald thus adopted the values and culture of a group of secular intellectuals who had largely disavowed their Judaism and embraced socialism. The New York Intellectuals were cosmopolitan, broadly assimilate, and only marginally ethnic. They were proud to defend modernist literature and to deride cultural philistinism. Preferring the European cultural tradition emerging from the Enlightenment to their own Jewish cultural heritage, they did not return to their Jewishness until the 1950s, in the aftermath of the Holocaust. By the late 1950s and the early 1960s the theme of Jewishness began to be of greater importance to many members of the group—and to American Jews generally—than liberal anticommunism.

Unlike most of the New York Intellectuals, Macdonald supported the awarding of the Bollingen Prize for Poetry to Ezra Pound for his *Pisan Cantos* in 1948. Macdonald condemned the poetry for its antisemitism, but he praised the judging panel for having made the award on the basis of their estimate of the literary quality of Pound's poetry, leaving aside all political considerations, including the fact that Pound was accused of treason for his participation in Italian fascist propaganda against the Allies during World War II. Macdonald noted approvingly that no such state-supported award that honored the autonomy of art could possibly be given in a fascist or communist country.

Fifteen years later, adopting a stance that both set him farther apart from his *PR* colleagues and once again demonstrated his inveterate inclination to go against the grain of his reference group, Macdonald also joined the minority among the New York Intellectuals. He defended Hannah Arendt's book *Eichmann in Jerusalem: A Report on the Banality of Evil* (1963), which described how European Jews collaborated in their own destruction during the Holocaust. The book triggered fierce exchanges and mutual recrimination from its critics and advocates within the New York Jewish community. Macdonald was a close friend of Arendt, and he defended her as a fellow cosmopolitan who disavowed the ethnic partisanship of her Jewish intellectual critics. Echoing his position on the Pound controversy, Macdonald admired Arendt for maintaining an allegiance to independent, internationalist values that were opposed to patriotism and jingoism of all types.[42] (Macdonald was an anti-Zionist because of his antistatist, anarchistic convictions.)

Back to the Barricades

Having largely abandoned political commentary after *politics* folded and immersed himself during the 1950s in cultural criticism that he published in the *New Yorker* and other magazines, Macdonald began to write film reviews for *Esquire* in 1960. Soon he also rediscovered his left-wing political convictions and enthusiastically supported the new radical movements. He was atypical of his generation of intellectuals in his embrace during the 1960s of the counterculture, the New Left, and the antiwar movement. Most of his left contemporaries from the 1930s went in exactly the opposite political direction, and not only those who had turned rightward. For instance, Irving Howe remained a radical yet wrote numerous scathing attacks on the New Left. So this new political turn by Macdonald witnessed him not only moving against the grain of his own drift away from political engagement but also cutting against the grain of his generation's attitude toward the New Left and the antiwar movement.

Yet other factors also governed Macdonald's political radicalization at this time, issues associated with his complex personal psychology. In 1967 he participated in the March on the Pentagon, lamenting only that he couldn't get arrested (as did his friends Robert Lowell and Norman Mailer). But he was in fact "arrested" in another, tragic sense: his once prolific pen was frozen. The sad fact is that, though Macdonald was living out a second youth in the 1960s, he really marched in the streets because he could not sit still in his study. He became permanently depressed and morose, burdened by a severe writer's block that lasted the rest of his life and was exacerbated by heavy drinking.

Drawn back into political action in the mid-1960s by the Vietnam antiwar movement and by the student protests against the universities, Macdonald recaptured the radical self of his Trotskyist and *politics* years—walking picket lines, protesting against military recruitment, and denouncing the Johnson administration's conduct of the war. Unlike many aging, born-again leftists of the 1960s—Sartre is the most notable example—he was not seeking to live out a romantic radical experience that he had missed out on during his youth: Macdonald was always a proto-New Leftist. Other New Left enthusiasts of his generation—such as Philip Rahv—became at times virtual parodies of the old 1930s selves whom they wished they had been. But the continuity of Macdonald's outlook and behavior in the 1960s with his core values during his Trotskyist and anarcho-pacifist periods, which ranged from his late twenties to his mid-forties, is striking: the connection between Macdonald's attitudes of the 1960s and during the *politics* years is especially apparent: the unwavering stance of *politics* was moralistic, independent, and anti-institutional—in essence, very much like the New Left.

Nonetheless, what Macdonald could not recapture was his fluid pen—and he tortured himself for this failure with endless self-recriminations. By the early 1970s, Macdonald found it impossible to compose even an essay or book review.

He spent his last decade distracting himself from his misery. Macdonald led a peripatetic existence as an intellectual gypsy, lecturing at various colleges and universities throughout the U.S., trying vainly to recharge his intellectual batteries by becoming an academic circuit rider and playing the role of the radical elder. Urged by friends to write his autobiography, which might have represented a history of American intellectual life in the mid-twentieth century, his literary impotence and drinking bouts stopped him. Macdonald died in December 1982 at the age of seventy-six, one of the last of the great critics of his generation.

"He's All Dwight"

"Dwight" (strangers, in fact even enemies, called him that and did so affectionately) was an inspired visionary and a creative, offbeat thinker with many friends and few enemies—despite his acid pen. Mary McCarthy's line about Macdougal Macdermott in *The Oasis* applied fully to Dwight too: "The targets of his satire could never truly dislike Macdermott, for they found themselves endowed by it with a larger and more fabulous life."[43]

Indeed, Dwight was a brilliant mind and a gifted writer. He certainly had the talent to be the American Orwell. Why did he fail to realize his potential? Why did he waste his prodigious energies on editing, on occasional journalism, and on peripatetic culture chat in his numerous rounds of college gigs?

In hindsight, Macdonald's abrupt turns, sudden manias, and intellectual "table-hopping" gave his work brio and color at the cost of significance and enduring impact. Orwell was a much steadier figure, both temperamentally and artistically, and he evolved politically and culturally, whereas Macdonald lurched from Luce to Lenin on his way to Lennon and popcult—in the process depleting his prodigious energies (and genuine enthusiasm) for both political and cultural criticism and ultimately leaving him without any commitments or vision to affirm. In the face of his terminal case of writer's block and numerous incomplete projects, Dwight berated himself mercilessly. As his addictions filled the vacuum left by his retreating talent, his only (quite inadequate) "out" was the bottle.

The fact is that Dwight suffered from what could be called a gluttony for life experience. He could be a charming fellow, indeed a raconteur. ("He's All Dwight," Hannah Arendt once fittingly titled an affectionate portrait of Macdonald.)[44] Dwight loved the whole fabulous whirlwind of life—in fact, he loved to talk and always treated people, including his college students, as intellectual peers (even when he ripped apart their ideas).[45] Dwight's calendar was usually full, and he liked it that way. Excitement and variety were important to him rather than comfort and playing it safe. At his best he was playful and positive, imaginative and inventive. Yet he was also easily bored and tended to overvalue spontaneity and thus new beginnings. When it came to meeting people, designing projects, and immersing himself in the nitty-gritty of passing political and cultural events, he could have benefited from a large dose of sobriety.

Dwight also found it excruciatingly difficult to remain steadfast during what felt like confining, painful phases of commitment. To limit himself often seemed like a form of death—but moderation and concentrated effort were precisely what he needed. When he was healthy, he was focused and purposeful and fully gratified to contribute something valuable to American criticism and culture. At his worst he became unproductive and stymied, preoccupied with ways of entertaining and distracting himself. His creativity became supplanted by anxiety, impatience, and a passion to consume—and the fatal outcome was a myriad of partially completed projects and protracted periods of ennui and frustration. Many of his excellent ideas—such as his long-announced major critique of Big Steel, his analysis of the political economy of fascism, his historical study of the labor movement, his manifesto for anarcho-pacifism, his book-length treatise on mass culture, his critical appreciation of Edgar Allan Poe—never got off the drawing board, which became an additional source of frustration for him.[46] He strenuously avoided dealing with his frustration, but he was too alert to repress his awareness of it. Ashamed that he was squandering his great potential, both his frequent expression of exasperation and his cutting, often condescending attitude toward rival opinions masked his own disgust with himself.

Dwight was thus, as it were, an intellectual thrill-seeker, reckless in pursuit of charged encounters, looking for highly stimulating sources of cultural entertainment yet quickly jaded by them. It was in this more subtle sense, beyond the alcoholic binges, that he burned out and damaged himself from his excesses. These tendencies wearied him and proved wearing on others as well. Although he was indeed already a proto-New Leftist two decades earlier, it is also true that the playful energy of the counterculture powerfully attracted the *puer* in Dwight. In other words, one of the reasons that the New Left and the student movement captured his interest is that he couldn't stand being bored—and both the antiwar protests and the counterculture felt refreshingly new and different to him, an adventure for which he had longed. (Part of the reason Dwight turned to movies was also that they were a new form of "serious" art for young intellectuals of the sixties whose passion for them also gave Dwight the feeling of recapturing his youth.)

Yet his vain attempts to force himself to concentrate only exacerbated his cerebral circus; he really needed to quiet his mind and embrace the work of writing as a mundane, often laborious task of sentence-by-sentence composition— and also to accept the anxiety that inevitably surfaces when the words will not come.[47] By the late 1970s, Dwight lacked the concentration to write at all. It was primarily the damming up of his literary energies that led him to take a string of one-year appointments at several universities. When the teaching stints ceased to come, he fell into a deep depression, which is precisely what his frenetic pace of activity had been staving off. Deprived of his manic-depressive defense as a university instructor, he deteriorated from dilettante to escapist, and his form of escape was the bottle. Dwight had maintained a hungry anticipation of the future

until his old age, but now he turned negative and wallowed in his misery as his
health deteriorated and his writer's block paralyzed him.

Final Discriminations

Macdonald once remarked about himself, "When I say 'no' I'm always right and
when I say 'yes' I'm almost always wrong." He was correct. His most lasting accomplishment was not his political essays, which have dated, but the cultural
criticism he perfected in the 1950s. The best of it, however, was negative. His
eye for a phony (to use a 1950s word) was quick, and his unrivaled talent was
for spotting shams and demolishing the work of the intellectually pretentious.
Unfortunately, most of his positive criticism, such as "Masscult and Midcult," is
obsolete. His onetime fellow *Partisan Review* editor, the poet Delmore Schwartz,
once summed him up: "Yes, antagonism for its own sake is his appetite and neurosis, and none of his political predictions come true, but he is a master of expository prose."

True enough, but Macdonald's enthusiasms for a cause blunted his skeptical edge, first as a Trotskyist hack for the Socialist Workers Party and then again
in the 1960s. The man who had been famous for unmasking the intellectually
shoddy was taken in by the kinds of frauds and poseurs that he had exposed
in the past: Eldridge Cleaver, the Black Panthers, Norman Mailer's overhyped
Armies of the Night, and the vulgarities of Abbie Hoffman, the Yippies, and the
youth movement. Barbara Garson's tendentious play *MacBird!* (1967), which cast
President Johnson as a Macbeth who murders John F. Kennedy, was puffed up by
Macdonald into a great work of art. Where left-wing fashions were concerned,
his normally clear-eyed judgment now failed him.

Macdonald grew ashamed of not just his literary impotence generally but
of his incapacity to write a large work that might have had lasting value. Today
Macdonald is seldom quoted, though he is occasionally cited as a significant literary figure of the past. One must especially lament his failure to write his own
full-scale Life-and-Times autobiography, a project that his friend John Lukacs
urged him to pursue in numerous letters and conversations. No one was better
equipped to write an intellectual portrait of America at midcentury than Dwight
Macdonald. He had the prowess to do so, but he allowed himself to be diverted
to other projects usually unworthy of him. This was ultimately his own verdict
on himself; he judged himself by a book standard, indeed by the standard of a
magnum opus. He could not fully accept that he had excelled in the form of the
topical and occasional essay like the other New York Intellectuals of his generation, most of whom had become skilled in intellectual journalism and critical
polemic from their early Marxist training in dialectics and disputation.

And this severe judgment on himself finally did come to bear much truth:
unlike the achievements of Trilling, Howe, Mary McCarthy, Harold Rosenberg,
and others—all of whom wrote books still read today—the wretched truth is that

Macdonald squandered his brilliant literary gifts and authentic political passions in polemics, in ephemeral reportage and book reviews, in political fashions, and ultimately in alcohol. That is why he is largely forgotten.

Yes, all this was tragic. And yet: the tragedy of Dwight Macdonald's final years ought not to receive undue weight. Above all, it must not be permitted to overshadow his record of notable achievement during the prime of his life: his three decades of both distinguished commentary and impassioned engagement in the leading political and cultural events of his age.

What legacy does Macdonald leave us today? Just a quarter-century after his death, Macdonald is a forgotten man—unjustly so. True, he was wrong about many of the biggest events and issues of his lifetime, ranging from his positions on the New Deal and World War II to his ill-considered ardors for the Black Panthers and the Yippies.[48] But Macdonald's genius was to "go to the root" and work through such wrongheaded positions to emerge with an original vision that reflected deeply held values and spoke to the main issues of his time, whether it was his quintessential American reformulation of anarchism in the 1940s or his stellar cultural criticism of the 1950s. As I indicated earlier, despite his reputation as the Peter Pan of the New York Intellectuals, as an unserious thinker who caromed from ideology to ideology, Macdonald was actually quite consistent in his political and cultural outlook after breaking with the SWP and *Partisan Review* around the beginning of World War II. He remained during his last three decades a firm egalitarian and libertarian in politics, a fervent antistatist and antiwar activist, and an elitist and traditionalist in art and culture—and he remained a radical humanist from beginning to end.

Macdonald sought to live a life of intellectual integrity, and despite his many mistakes and failures, I would insist that he did so. As he once wrote of Orwell in a 1958 essay reprinted in his last collection, *Discriminations* (1974), he was "tougher on himself and his own side."[49] Czeslaw Milosz spoke about the pertinence of "Macdonaldism," not just for Eastern Europeans but for the future of humankind. "They are surely able to appreciate his betting on slow processes in the human mass, and his belief that one man counts, or if we are lucky, three or four men linked by friendship. Macdonald seems to have pinned his hopes on the fermentation sealed beneath the surface, which is not automatic and to which everyone can contribute."[50]

Dwight did indeed pin his ultimate hopes on a trust in the prospect of human maturation, a faith that he sustained across the decades through an old-fashioned communitarian vision of mutual aid in the anarchist spirit. And that is a political legacy worth not only honoring but also reinvigorating. A renewed appreciation of Dwight Macdonald's work, especially his trenchant critiques in *politics* of both liberalism and totalitarianism, is crucial to the task of revitalizing both political liberalism and radicalism in the twenty-first century.

The relevance of Macdonald's heritage for the renewal of the mainstream American tradition of liberal thought warrants further mention. Like Lionel

Trilling, Macdonald was a fierce critic of the "liberal imagination"; unlike Trilling, he maintained no vision of an ideal liberalism against which he measured the shortcomings of the liberal imagination. Like Trilling, Macdonald lamented that liberalism was the dominant, if not the sole, intellectual tradition   midcentury in the United States. Unlike Trilling, he did not believe that liberalism needed to be recalled "to its first essential imagination of variousness and possibility, which implies the awareness of difficulty and complexity," but rather that intellectuals needed to "go to the root," which meant embrace an authentic radical tradition. Macdonald rejected any notion of liberalism as advanced by most rationalists a belief in human perfectibility, an optimistic faith in progress, and the correction of wrong by human reason. To Macdonald, these were shibboleths. In reality, according to Macdonald, twentieth-century liberalism consisted of progressive clichés, imprisoning systems of political machination, and systematic if benevolent discrimination based on complacent acceptance of social conditions. Stalinist fellow-traveling was his most glaring example of misguided liberalism during the 1930s, but Macdonald insisted that a debased Marxism alone was not responsible for the deficiencies of liberalism.

And yet in another sense, again like Trilling, Macdonald was a liberal critic of liberalism, the critic of the left from within its own ranks. He would have agreed with Trilling's praise in *The Liberal Imagination* of Hawthorne's "dissent from the orthodoxies of dissent." And as the orthodoxies of dissent rapidly changed in the mid-twentieth century, Macdonald's positions changed with them. His radical, anticapitalist stance never altered, but his specific positions often seemed, as one sympathetic critic expressed it, "more numerous than the *Kama Sutra*."[51] Macdonald shifted course as the cultural and political winds demanded, though he was throughout his career a passionate political skeptic and a defender of high cultural standards.

Dwight did indeed always go "against the grain." As he himself once put it, he certainly was "A Critical American." Milosz once called him "a totally American phenomenon" in the tradition of Thoreau, Whitman, and Melville—"the completely free man, capable of making decisions at all times and about all things, strictly on the basis of his personal moral judgment."[52]

I believe that "Macdonaldism" can help not only to revivify American liberalism but also to keep radical discourse alive in this country. One man does count—and he (or she), if inspired with a sufficiently compelling vision, can draw together three or four or many more. Macdonald himself did that, not just in forming a community around *politics* but also through his voluminous writings over the course of a long and productive career. If much of his political journalism has become rather dated, his example is nonetheless worth remembering and indeed has lost none of its relevance.

Sadly, whether he was an American Orwell—manqué or not—there is nobody like him on the current intellectual scene. There are many anarchists, pacifists, and cultural mandarins today, but no intellectual has forged a political and cultural vision to compare with the comprehensiveness of Macdonald's perspectives during his prime. One can point to various writers and intellectuals who resemble him in different respects: Christopher Hitchens, the British expatriate writer and a vocal Macdonald admirer, is certainly the most prominent, and he shares both Macdonald's contrarian and even Trotskyist orientation as well as his cultural elitism.[53]

So Macdonald casts a long shadow; his absence leaves a large hole in American intellectual life. Indeed, for those willing to read Macdonald, it is above all his insouciant prose style and no-holds-barred crusading criticism—and particularly his self-appointed role as an aristocratic radical charged with exposing the ersatz and the overhyped—that can still exert a claim on our interest and attention today.

And that is why he is worth remembering.

Notes

1. See, for instance, Gertrude Himmelfarb, "The Trilling Imagination," *Weekly Standard*, February 21, 2005. An academic conference devoted to Trilling was also hosted by the University of Louisiana at Lafayette in November 2005.
2. Paul Goodman, "Our Best Journalist," *Dissent* 5 (Winter 1958), pp. 82–86.
3. John Lukacs, "Dwight Macdonald: Another Orwell?" *America,* May 17, 1958.

    Dwight Macdonald has often been compared to George Orwell as a nondoctrinaire radical. The two shared much in common—a hatred of communism, an appreciation of good literature, and sympathy for the downtrodden. Unlike Orwell, however, Macdonald and his work have fallen into undeserved neglect since his death because so much of his energy was directed at topical issues of his time that mean little to most people today. His virtual invisibility on the current national scene testifies that reputations do not last in time unless one produces one or two major works—and makes them sufficiently interesting and challenging to scholars that they are taken up within an academic field and enshrined as landmarks or curricular touchstones.

    Here again, one notices the vast difference with George Orwell, who wrote at least two classics—*Animal Farm* and *Nineteen Eighty-Four*—which have been given canonical status not only by scholars of British literature but also by leading political and literary intellectuals of both the left and the right. But what if one does not work within an identifiable intellectual or political tradition, or at least in clear dialogue with a tradition? (Consider: Marx, Engels, Lenin, Trotsky, Gramsci. Or Freud, Jung, Klein, Erikson, Lacan.) Orwell was an unpredictable figure, but he conducted an impassioned dialogue with the socialist tradition—and indeed with the tradition of English literature. By contrast, Macdonald jumped from Marxism to anarchism and pacifism and back again, and he wrote mostly about passing political issues or about the artifacts of midcult that quickly disappeared. Both Orwell and Macdonald were gadflies who refused to toe a political or cultural line, but Orwell added to the tradition by writing classic works, whereas Macdonald did not.

4. Among the other nominees for the role of the representative figure of the group have been Lionel Trilling, Philip Rahv, and Delmore Schwartz. See William Barrett, *The Truants* (New York: Anchor Press/Doubleday, 1982).

5. Robert Lowell even enshrined his nominee, Irving Howe, in a poem titled "The New York Intellectuals." See Robert Lowell, "The New York Intellectuals," in *Notebooks, 1967–1968* (Boston: Farrar, Straus & Cudahy, 1968).

6. Perhaps McCarthy was not, however, so much an outsider as Macdonald. Late in life, she revealed in her autobiography that she had a Jewish grandmother. See her *Intellectual Memoirs: New York, 1936–1938* (New York: Harcourt Brace Jovanovich, 1992).

7. See Mary McCarthy, "Portrait of the Intellectual as a Yale Man," in *The Company She Keeps* (New York: Harcourt Brace, 1942). For Macdonald's opinion of *The Oasis*, see *A Moral Temper: The Letters of Dwight Macdonald* (New York: Ivan R. Dee, 2001). Macdonald was not the only friend of McCarthy, or the only model upon whom the male protagonist of "Portrait of the Intellectual as a Yale Man" was based. John Chamberlain, another Yale graduate and the book critic for the *Wall Street Journal* and contributor to several Luce publications, was the physical model for Jim Barnett, the naïve, guileless Stalinist intellectual. Other facets of Jim Barnett were based on Robert Cantwell and Malcolm Cowley, who were Yale men too.

   Macdonald was also the model for Mike, the bewhiskered intellectual whom children mistake for Uncle Sam in McCarthy's story "The Hounds of Summer," originally published in the *New Yorker* in 1962. See *The Hounds of Summer and Other Stories* (New York: Avon, 1981).

   For more on McCarthy's portraits of Macdonald in her fiction, see Carol Brightman, *Writing Dangerously: Mary McCarthy and Her World* (New York: C. Potter, 1992) and Frances Kiernan, *Seeing Mary Plain* (New York: W.W. Norton, 2000).

8. As the Depression deepened its hold in the United States, Macdonald began a rapid intellectual evolution toward the far left, growing angrier year after year at the failings of American capitalism. And so it was not surprising that in June 1936, after the editors of *Fortune* scrapped one of his articles, a highly critical study of United States Steel Corporation, that Macdonald resigned. This was no minor gesture. At the time, Macdonald was making $10,000, an almost princely sum in the depths of the Depression.

   Macdonald's resignation impressed Mary McCarthy, who wrote in *The Oasis* about Macdougal Macdermott, the editor of a radical libertarian magazine much like Macdonald's *politics*: "[T]en years before, he had made the leap into faith and sacrificed $20,000 a year and a secure career as a paid journalist for the intangible values that eluded his empirical grasp." Mary McCarthy, *The Oasis* (New York: Random House, 1949). See also Carol Gelderman, *Mary McCarthy: A Life* (New York: St. Martin's, 1988).

9. Michael Wreszin, *A Rebel in Defense of Tradition: The Life and Politics of Dwight Macdonald* (New York: Basic Books, 1994).

10. Ibid.

11. *PR* was originally founded in 1934 as a magazine of the John Reed Clubs, which placed it under the auspices of the American Communist Party. For the early history of *PR*, see Terry Cooney, *The Rise of the New York Intellectuals: "Partisan Review" and Its Circle* (Madison: University of Wisconsin Press, 1986). See also Alexander Bloom, *Prodigal Sons: The New York Intellectuals and Their World* (Oxford: Oxford Univer-

sity Press, 1986); Alan Wald, *The New York Intellectuals: The Rise and Decline of the Anti-Stalinist Left from the 1930s to the 1980s* (Ann Arbor: University of Michigan Press, 1987); and Neil Jumonville, *Critical Crossings: The New York Intellectuals in Postwar America* (Berkeley: University of California Press, 1991).

12. The anticommunist "vital center liberalism" of the New Deal, promoted by centrist liberals such as Arthur Schlesinger, Macdonald insisted, was ineffective in confronting the great danger represented by postwar Stalinism. Macdonald's attacks on liberals, labor, and the New Dealers were relentless; he referred to them as the "liblabs," a term of sneering ridicule meant to impugn the wishy-washy complacency of postwar liberal democracy. On "liblabs," see also note 23.

    During World War II and after, he maintained a steady barrage of invective against the liblabs for their view that the war and its aftermath would redeem the Wilsonian dream of a rationalized and peaceful world order, indeed that the war was a democratic crusade that would globalize the New Deal. By contrast, Macdonald saw the war as an old-style power struggle between the Western democracies and the totalitarians.

13. Wreszin, *Rebel*, p. 193.

14. Dwight Macdonald, "Trotsky Is Dead," *Partisan Review* 7 (September–October 1940), quoted in Wreszin, *Rebel*, p. 206.

15. Dwight Macdonald, *Memoirs of a Revolutionist: Essays in Political Criticism* (Cleveland: Farrar, Straus & Cudahy, 1957) and *Against the American Grain* (New York: Random House, 1962).

16. He remained with the Socialist Workers Party for two years, writing a number of articles for their journal, *New International*, mostly labored pieces of Marxist exegesis—which, in the words of Macdonald biographer Stephen Whitfield, "have sunk of their own weight into oblivion." See Stephen Whitfield, *A Critical American: The Politics of Dwight Macdonald* (Hamden, CT: Archon Books, 1984).

17. See Wreszin, *Rebel*.

18. Wreszin, *Rebel*, p. 146.

19. Gregory D. Sumner, *Dwight Macdonald and the Politics Circle: The Challenge of Cosmopolitan Democracy* (Ithaca: Cornell University Press, 1996).

20. Among the most influential material he published in *politics* was an essay by the German Jewish émigré Bettelheim, "Behavior in Extreme Situations," an investigation of the Nazi concentration camps and one of the first attempts to grasp the totality of the Holocaust. Macdonald had been skeptical of stories of Nazi atrocities, but Bettelheim changed his thinking about the barbarities to which people in wartime were susceptible. Probably *politics* was the first journal to discuss in full detail the horrors of the Holocaust when Macdonald published the then-unknown Bettelheim in 1944 on the behavior of prisoners in the concentration camps.

21. Macdonald enlisted a distinguished international group of writers on the left to contribute to his new magazine (including a number of Americans such as Paul Goodman and C. Wright Mills). Macdonald wanted *politics* to become the vehicle for an intellectual exchange between America and Europe. (Nicola Chiaromonte became Macdonald's close friend and tutor on European political and cultural affairs.) Possessing a clearly defined internationalist as well as radical stance, *politics* would become (in Macdonald's words) a "transplanted spore of European culture" in the American body politic. Macdonald was something of a snob about European intellectuals, believing them more politically and culturally sophisticated than their

American counterparts. The role of *politics* was in effect to europeanize provincial American culture.

22. See Sumner.

23. Although Macdonald was one of those who popularized the term in its denigrating connotation, *liblab* (liberal-labor) was in general usage in the postwar 1940s. As the welfare statists and the New Dealers began to split into imperial, anti-imperial, and modified imperial segments, liblabs continued to insist on domestic progress and equality, on the value of an American model (which meant something other than brute power), and on closeness to European social democracy. Macdonald's derisory usage imputed that liblabs were stereotyped in thought and hopelessly anachronistic.

24. "A Note on Wallese," *politics*, March–April 1947. See also Dwight Macdonald, *Henry Wallace: The Man and the Myth* (New York: Vanguard, 1948), p. 24.

25. "Why Politics?" *politics* 1 (February 1944).

26. Ibid.

27. *politics* 2 (August 1945).

28. "The Root Is Man," *politics*, 3 and 4 (April and July 1946), pp. 194–197. Deepening Macdonald's political disillusionment were personal problems: his marriage was falling apart, and the work of putting out *politics* had lost its appeal. He drifted into a passionate affair with the novelist Joan Colebrook that left him alternately exhilarated and depressed. He eventually divorced Nancy, with whom he had two sons, and married Gloria Lanier, the wife of an old friend, in 1952. This second marriage was a qualified success, though Gloria was never an intellectual comrade-in-arms as Nancy had been.

29. "The Responsibility of Peoples," *politics* 2 (March 1945).

30. Wreszin, *Rebel*.

31. See Dwight Macdonald, "Comment on Simone Weil's, 'Factory Work,'" *politics* 3 (December 1946).

32. Wreszin, *Rebel*, p. 302.

33. Another personal relationship that influenced Macdonald's turn to anarchism in the mid-1940s was with Paul Goodman, whose sexual libertarianism and anarchic sensibility ultimately contributed to the breakup of Macdonald's marriage to Nancy. Like Goodman, Macdonald became a vociferous defender of individualism and personal freedom, including the sexual. In that connection, a related formative influence on Macdonald's anarchism was Wilhelm Reich. Macdonald gave Reich space in *politics* to explain his controversial Organotherapy, which also fit with Macdonald's anarcho-pacifist, communal interests and his emergent bohemian radicalism. Macdonald accepted Reich's critique of the connection between sexual repression and totalitarianism. See Wreszin, *Rebel*, pp. 286, 351.

34. Wreszin, *Rebel*, p. 366.

35. Wreszin, *Rebel*, pp. 88, 452.

36. William Barrett, *The Truants: Adventures among the Intellectuals* (New York: Anchor Press and Doubleday, 1982), p. 221.

37. *Against the American Grain*, p. 273.

38. *Against the American Grain*, p. 169.

39. A few other members of the New York Intellectuals—Fred Dupee, Mary McCarthy, and James Burnham among them—were not Jewish. But as in the case of the New York Trotskyists of the 1930s and 1940s, most of the *Partisan Review* circle was overwhelmingly Jewish. They referred to Dwight and the other non-Jews as "our distinguished *goyim*."

40. Wreszin, *Rebel*, pp. 310–312.
41. For example, writing for *Esquire* in August 1960, Macdonald triggered a firestorm of criticism from the Jewish community when he wrote in his negative essay-review of *Ben Hur, King of Kings,* and *The Greatest Story Ever Told* that the Jewish community's financing of these movies was aimed at assuring that the Romans would be "the fall guys" for the crucifixion of Jesus, for there were "no ancient Romans around and there are many Jews and fifteen million dollars is fifteen million dollars." Similar to the recent controversies about Mel Gibson's movie *The Passion of the Christ,* Macdonald was charged with antisemitism for branding the Jews as "Christ-killers"—though his defenders argue that he was just being contrarian, going against the grain as always. On this episode, see Wreszin, p. 410.
42. For a glimpse of Macdonald's close personal relationship with Arendt, see their correspondence in *A Moral Temper: The Letters of Dwight Macdonald,* ed. Michael Wreszin (New York: Ivan R. Dee, 2001).
43. McCarthy, *The Oasis.*
44. Hannah Arendt, "He's All Dwight," *New York Review of Books* (August 1, 1968).
45. Dwight identified strongly with his college students. He dwelt in a nonhierarchical psychological environment, and the student culture easily enabled him to show his modesty by refusing to be an authority figure for the youth—while at the same time resting assured that the students would be flattered by his modest insistence on their treating him as an equal.

    He was in fact a true democrat who treated others as equals. But his democratic ethos was often driven by an inveterate tendency to equalize authority and by an unwillingness to accept that any hierarchical structure could have a reasonable purpose. Equalizing authority reflected his desire for unlimited freedom. He didn't want to be the boss, and he didn't want to be under a boss, so he equalized authority to avoid being told or avoid telling others what to do. (He was therefore attracted by the security of belonging to a group of like-minded thinking people, but the only time when he truly experienced this without diverse conflicts was when he gathered them around himself as the hub of *politics.*)

    Under such circumstances, *politics* could only be a one-man operation; the Macdonald organization had to be an "ad-hocracy" that functioned on an egalitarian, first-name basis. Individuality, experimentation, and creativity were the order of the day. The editorial, marketing, sales, and finance departments were Dwight and his wife Nancy, whose inheritance bankrolled the venture.
46. Dwight was the *puer,* the eternal child who never quite landed on the planet because he never fully accepted the value of sticking it out, the necessity of persistent, focused effort to actualize his dreams. Although he would have been grounded by a commitment to a major long-term project as his ultimate life work, his intellectual promiscuity would not permit that. He needed a tether to complete a project worthy of his talent, that is, a daily routine that would have developed a firm habit of self-discipline.
47. He was both gifted and burdened by a habit of splitting attention among different interests—a great strength for an imaginative editor or a prolific journalist but a crippling hardship for an author of book-length manuscripts. It was as if his capacity to endure the painstaking writing process exhausted itself at the length of an essay and thus rendered the goal of writing a book unthinkable. He was a marvelous editor and teacher of expository writing; yet like many editors, he seems to have dealt with his

frequent writing blocks by channeling his energy into the literary activities of others as a close reader of their work. James Atlas credits Macdonald with having practically coauthored large sections of Atlas's biography of Delmore Schwartz; Irving Howe credits Macdonald with nothing less than having "taught me how to write."

48. The difference with Orwell is here again notable—and the consequences for Macdonald's reputation significant. Unlike Orwell, Macdonald was wrong a great deal. Orwell was indisputably right on the three big issues that he confronted in his lifetime—imperialism, fascism, and Stalinism—whereas Macdonald was wrong about many things in politics and culture, ranging from 1930s Marxism to 1960s Maoism. If one is wrong and also has no classic works that stake a claim on the interest of intellectual successors and the academic mind, one's legacy is jeopardized. Clearly, people linked to political power get cited in the media frequently, but their influence declines steeply over time. This is even more so the case for someone without political power—someone like Macdonald, who gained prominence because he had access to cultural organs with political power, such as *Partisan Review* or the *New Yorker*.

Moreover, Macdonald founded an intellectual journal that lasted only five years—and only the first two or three of those years were vibrant. On the other hand, Irving Howe inaugurated a journal, *Dissent*, that recently entered its sixth decade of publication and has become a landmark in the intellectual and political tradition of American radicalism. For this reason, it is more likely that the legacy that Irving Howe represents will endure, at least until *Dissent* expires—whereas Macdonald has had no direct successors to continue his heritage or champion him. Whereas numerous contributors affiliated with *Dissent*, or even those writing against its positions, continue to cite Irving Howe, professors of cultural studies and media studies do not cite Macdonald's work on mass culture or his critiques of midcult. Unlike the case of Theodor Adorno, no scholars have had an interest in taking Macdonald's work into the academic sphere and giving it a chance of canonical endurance. So when the issues that directly inspired Macdonald to write his mass cultural critiques exited the scene, his work vanished from public discussion along with it.

In *Public Intellectuals*, Richard Posner raises the question of why intellectuals are so often wrong, especially when they write outside their narrow subfield of academic expertise. He argues that one reason is that they are not "penalized" for being wrong by a loss of any kind. Posner wants such public intellectuals to pay at least a reputational price for being wrong. He believes that more responsible public intellectual discourse will emerge if intellectuals are held accountable for their predictions and claims and not given a "free pass" on sundry topics just because they happen to be expert in an unrelated field—he cites the fact that many people consider the work in linguistics of Noam Chomsky to somehow justify his political arguments about topics ranging from the Vietnam War to politics in the Mideast. Posner argues that, however valid and compelling Chomsky's scholarly work in linguistics, it ultimately bears no relation to his political discourse and should not influence the reader's opinion of it.

Whatever one's view of Posner's argument, it is indisputable that Macdonald has paid a steep price for "being wrong"—his loss of reputation, even within radical intellectual circles. See Richard Posner, *Public Intellectuals: A Study of Decline* (Cambridge: Harvard University Press, 2001).

49. *Discriminations: Essays and Afterthoughts, 1938–1974* (New York: Grossman, 1974), p. 336.

50. Milosz expressed this observation in his review of the 1953 edition of *The Root Is Man,* which Macdonald arranged to have printed as a pamphlet. Czeslaw Milosz, *Beginning with My Streets: Essays and Reflections,* quoted in Sumner, p. 6.

51. Sumner, p. 5.

52. Ibid.

53. See Christopher Hitchens, *Letters to a Contrarian* (London: Basic Books, 2000), p. 123.

Irving Howe

Triple Thinker

John Rodden

Irving Howe (1920–1993) was a vocal radical humanist and the most influential American socialist intellectual of his generation. Howe was also, in my view, the last major American public intellectual—certainly the last of the Old Left. Not only was he prolific—he wrote eighteen books, edited twenty-five more, penned dozens of articles and reviews, and edited *Dissent* for forty years—but he was proficient and more often brilliant in virtually every literary endeavor of his mature years. Although some readers may find his work on the relationship between politics and literature to be most valuable, I believe that his contributions to the study of Yiddish literature and Jewish immigrant history are most likely to last.[1]

Indeed, it is quite possible that Howe's work will endure longer than that of the elder generation of New York Intellectuals in whose shadow he sometimes found himself.[2] Not only is much of his rich *oeuvre* of literary and political criticism still in print, but *Dissent*, which Howe faithfully edited for four decades, celebrated its fiftieth year of publication in 2004. Woody Allen's joke two decades ago in *Annie Hall* that the magazine should merge with the neoconservative journal *Commentary* and be renamed *Dysentery* elicits today no more than a smile from serious readers. Allen's movie has become a period piece, whereas *Dissent* continues to represent the distinctive voice of American social democracy and radical humanism.

Of Celebrations and Attacks

Yes, Irving Howe had his admirers—and his detractors.

"Irving made a lot of enemies in his lifetime," recalled Robert Boyers, an intellectual and friend on the left. Indeed Howe was fond of the remark of William Dean Howells that anyone could make enemies but the real test was to keep them. By that criterion, he succeeded well. Though he occasionally reconciled after falling out (with a few writer-intellectuals, such as Lionel Trilling and Ralph Ellison, and a few New Leftists, such as Jack Newfield, Carl Oglesby, and Todd Gitlin), Howe made and kept an impressive number of enemies.

Howe's chief enemies and most severe critics included onetime friends and colleagues in his New York circle who had moved to the right in the late 1960s and 1970s: Hilton Kramer, Norman Podhoretz, Saul Bellow, Midge Decter, Joseph Epstein, and Sidney Hook. But other harsh critics stayed on the political or cultural left—and disapproved of Howe's moderate socialism—or moved even farther leftward, such as Alexander Cockburn, Philip Rahv, and the majority of those New Left leaders whom Howe had excoriated in *Dissent*'s pages.

Still other opponents, such as Richard Kostelanetz and Philip Roth, were literary or aesthetic rather than explicitly political adversaries. For instance, Bellow dismissed Howe as "an old-fashioned lady."[3] Roth, upset over Howe's attack on *Portnoy's Complaint* as reinforcing Jewish stereotypes, parodied him as Milton Appel, a "sententious bastard. . . . A head wasn't enough for Appel; he tore you limb from limb."[4]

Other foes attacked Howe as a critic-shark who patrolled New York's cultural currents. During the late 1960s, when acrimonious differences over the Vietnam War and the counterculture split American intellectuals into rival camps, the poet Robert Lowell lambasted Howe as the archetypal "New York Intellectual,"[5] an elitist radical looking down on humankind. Lowell wrote in his sardonic poem, "The New York Intellectual" (1967):

> Did Irving really want three hundred words? . . .
> How often one would choose the poorman's provincial
> out of town West Side intellectual
> for the great brazen rhetorical serpent
> swimming the current with his iron smile![6]

In the early 1970s, Philip Nobile mocked Howe as "the Lou Gehrig of the Old Left, . . . who is always there when you need him with a clutch position paper on the Cold War, Vietnam, Eugene McCarthy, confrontation or sexual politics." Nobile added that Howe often assumed a gatekeeping or policeman's role, "serv[ing] as the Left's chief of protocol, correcting the manners of apocalypticians and calling for coalitions always and everywhere."[7] To Lowell and Nobile, Howe was an American commissar imbued with the joy of sects, an intellectual iron man whose pen never ran dry. Or, as Nobile once remarked of Howe's circle: "They must be New York intellectuals. See how they loathe one another."[8]

By contrast, some of Howe's neoconservative critics—such as his first biographer, Edward Alexander—value his literary criticism and his work on Yiddish literature; they confine their ire largely to his political writing, which they consider naïve or ideologically blinkered and unable to change with the times.[9] Alexander and other Jewish neoconservative critics have been especially hard on Howe for his positions on Israel, particularly his support of the Israeli Labor Party and left-oriented organizations associated with the peace camp, such as American Friends for Peace Now. [10] Neoconservative opponents have also castigated Howe's articles for the Trotskyist sectarian group to which he belonged in the early 1940s, pieces that Howe wrote in his early to midtwenties and never reprinted—and for which he felt rather apologetic in later years. [11] A few neoconservative critics seem determined to haunt him with them.

But the celebrations of Howe's political acumen, intellectual range, and particularly his Jewish cultural criticism and collections of Yiddish literature vastly outnumber the attacks. Already by the mid-1960s, recalled Kenneth Libo, Howe's graduate student at Hunter College and later his research assistant and collaborator on *World of Our Fathers*, Howe "had become a hero of sorts to many liberal-minded academics of my generation." Upon publication of *World of Our Fathers* in 1976, notes one literary historian, Howe "was greeted as a cultural hero" within the American Jewish community. [12] Reviewing *World of Our Fathers* that year, the Catholic priest-sociologist Andrew Greeley exclaimed that "us Irish, we should be so lucky to have an Irving Howe." In 1977, the editors of *Moment* published a poll in which ten prominent American Jews listed the ten "most formative books of the Judaic world, representing all times, all places." *World of Our Fathers* was the only book on American Jewish history to make any of the lists—alongside the Bible, the Talmud, the Passover Haggadah, and the daily prayer book. [13]

Frustrated by what he regarded as the universal hallucination bedeviling the New York literary community, such praise of Howe drove Nathan Zuckerman (aka Philip Roth) to exclaim about "Milton Appel" in *The Anatomy Lesson*, "When literary Manhattan spoke of Appel, it seemed to Zuckerman that the name Milton was intoned with unusual warmth and respect. He couldn't turn up anyone who had it in for the bastard. He fished and found nothing. In Manhattan. Incredible." [14]

If anything, the celebrations have only intensified since Howe's death. "A kind of moral hero," wrote Mitchell Cohen in *Dissent*. "One of the steadiest minds in modern American life, and one of the most steadying, . . . the splendid voice of social democracy," eulogized the *New Republic*, alluding to Howe's essay collection of the mid-1960s, *Steady Work*. "A monument to a range and a depth almost impossible to imagine in one human being, combined with a quiet decency," Robert Kuttner rhapsodized. Leon Wieseltier went, if anything, even further. "A great-souled man," Wieseltier called Howe in the *New York Times Book Review*, "the man who, more than any American intellectual of his generation, by his work and by his example, conferred greatness upon the homeliest of qualities, . . . the quality that mattered most to Orwell and Silone: the quality of decency." [15]

More recently, Richard Rorty lauded "Howe's incredible energy and his exceptional honesty," making him virtually "a warrior-saint" who "came to play the role in many people's lives that Orwell did in his." [16] "*World of Our Fathers* WAS my ethnic revival," recalled Matthew Frye Jacobson. "There is no doubting that Howe was among the spiritual authors of my most deeply held scholarly and civic convictions."[17]

Indeed the intense admiration continues to the present. In 2003, Joseph Dorman called Howe "a true intellectual hero of the Left."[18] Even Ronald Radosh—a former adversary within the New Left who had moved far to Howe's right—pronounced him "undoubtedly one of our country's most eminent intellectuals, a man of passion and intelligence."[19]

Such paeans strike most neoconservatives as deplorable. (Alexander is a notable exception.)[20] "Preparations are apparently under way to make [Howe] into the American Orwell," lamented Joseph Epstein, who dismissed Howe's radicalism as evidence of a politically immature and insecure thinker, indeed of a card-carrying lifetime member of "the Old People's Socialist League." Hilton Kramer has agreed, castigating Howe's principled refusal to renounce socialism as fashionable leftism and hopelessly maudlin utopianism. Indeed Kramer has pronounced all of Howe's political writings, including his work on politics and the novel and other literary essays written from an explicitly left-oriented perspective "worthless."[21]

Neoconservatives are not alone in refusing to canonize Howe as "St. Irving."[22] In a memorial column on Howe in the *Nation*, Alexander Cockburn derided Howe as "an assiduous foot soldier" in the campaign to "discredit vibrant political currents electrifying America and supporting liberation movements in the Third World," a lapsed radical whose "prime function in the last thirty years of his life was that of policing the Left on behalf of the powers that be."[23]

The Writer as Culture Hero

However much Howe's "enemies" may ridicule comparisons portraying him as "the American Orwell,"[24] one cannot deny that the ongoing controversy about Howe's heritage does indeed resemble the cultural politics of Orwell's reputation.[25] Indeed, with the exception of Noam Chomsky, probably no American left-wing thinker in the post–World War II era has provoked more disagreement within the left and aroused more vitriol on the right than Irving Howe. And I would argue further that Howe, like Orwell before him, became the "conscience" of his generation and ultimately even of our nation's intelligentsia. As a result, the stakes involved in disputes about Howe's legacy are high. For to elevate or denigrate Howe—as has long been similarly the case with Orwell in Britain—is to affirm or assault nothing less than the recent history of the American liberal-left, the status of the radical dissenting tradition, and the relevance of social democracy or democratic socialism to the American polity.

To understand how Irving Howe has come to occupy such a cultural role—and how he himself understood that role—let us recall the literary-political legacy that Howe embraced as his own. And let us do so by way of a quartet of intellectuals

dear to Howe's heart, those who formed the intellectual-moral center of his critical outlook. For a leitmotif of this essay, which is quite evident in the critical responses already quoted, is the (contested) perception of Howe as a literary-political
hero. I believe that he aspired to a kind of intellectual heroism[26]—very much like
the writers with whom he identified, the figures who came to figure prominently
in his imaginative and emotional life. Indeed, Howe's choice of literary-political
models furnishes insight into his much-disputed legacy as well as his impressive
achievement.

Howe exalted four near-contemporary figures who inspired him from his
youth onward: Trotsky, Orwell, Ignazio Silone, and Edmund Wilson. Frequently
Howe's identifications with this quartet ran so deep and intense that his depiction of them amounts to self-portraiture.

Howe's first great hero was Leon Trotsky, the man whose political orientation Howe embraced as a teen when he entered the Trotskyist youth organization, the Young People's Socialist League. Howe's enduring fascination with
Trotsky's leadership skills—and indeed his high regard for Trotsky the man and
writer as a "figure of heroic magnitude"—is well-known.[27] Trotsky's personal
example and writings helped draw Howe into and sustain him in the Trotskyist movement. Howe remained a committed Trotskyist for more than a dozen
years, from the age of fourteen to his late twenties. Even after officially with-
drawing from his Trotskyist sect, the Shachtmanites (led by Max Shachtman),
in October 1953 at the age of thirty-three, Howe continued to include Trotsky
among his culture heroes, the only explicitly political figure among them (except, perhaps, for Norman Thomas).[28] Howe's biographical study *Leon Trotsky*
(1977) makes clear his youthful veneration of Trotsky: "How intransigent he
remained in defeat! To have come even briefly under his influence during the
1930s was to learn a lesson in moral courage, was to learn the satisfaction of
standing firm by one's convictions, to realize that life offers far worse things than
being in a minority."[29]

On the final page of *Leon Trotsky*, Howe concludes: "A good portion of
the writings of this extraordinary man is likely to survive and the example of his
energy and heroism is likely to grip the imaginations of generations to come. . . .
Trotsky embodied the modern historical crisis with an intensity of consciousness and a gift for heroic response which few of his contemporaries could match.
Leon Trotsky in his power and his fall is one of the Titans of our century."[30]

Indeed Howe retained a passionate, conflicted, yet lifelong identification
with Trotsky for his "moral courage" and ability to stand alone.[31] (Some critics
have argued that Howe whitewashed Trotsky and downplayed his moral as well
as political crimes.)

Howe's great esteem for Orwell, whom he repeatedly acknowledged as his
"intellectual hero," is well known. And this time Howe chose well: Orwell's skepticism toward ideology countered the influence of Trotsky's allegiance to Marxist
abstraction and the god of System.

Moreover, Howe rightly intuited that he and Orwell shared significant literary affinities, above all a similar kind of rhetorical, inventive (rather than creative or purely literary) imagination. Like Orwell, who was the twentieth-century master craftsman of enduring catchwords and neologisms, Howe carved lapidary formulations in powerfully, and sometimes beautifully chiseled prose, whereby he too added phrases to the cultural *Zeitgeist*. Howe especially admired those passages in which an author wrote "clenched" prose—a favorite Howe epithet—and Howe's own best writing possessed a rigorous, taut dynamism. Indeed, one could say that the prose gifts of both writers crossed from the rhetorical to the journalistic. Like Orwell's catch phrases, Howe's coinages were often polemical—and directed at explicitly political targets: "this age of conformity" (his swipe at the intelligentsia's conservative turn in the 1950s), "socialism is the name of our desire" (adapted from Tolstoy's famous assertion about God), "the New York Intellectuals" (a phrase that he gave wide currency, if not invented, to characterize his *Partisan Review* circle), "guerrillas with tenure" (perhaps his sharpest cut at the New Left's guru scholars),[32] "a world more attractive" (a little-known phrase of Trotsky expressing love for art over politics), "confrontation politics" (what Howe characterized as the New Left's negotiating style), and "craft elitism" (how arcane literary theory, exemplified by poststructuralism, exploits jargon to exclude the nonspecialist reader), among other phrases.[33]

Orwell did not hesitate to borrow words and phrases for his own purposes and to reinscribe them—and neither did Howe. This is apparent in Howe's book titles, such as his volume of literary criticism, *A World More Attractive*, which recalls Trotsky's phrase but transmutes a political phrase to foreground aesthetic principles. But it is also evident in his edited volumes, such as *The Radical Imagination* and *The Radical Papers*, which nod to Trilling's celebrated *The Liberal Imagination* and to the Pentagon Papers, respectively.

Ignazio Silone was, for Howe, a literary-political hero much like Orwell, another writer and radical about whom Howe felt no ambivalence. Howe felt a closer fraternal proximity to Silone than to Orwell, as if Silone were merely a slightly elder intellectual big brother. "My favorite living writer," Howe once called Silone.[34] (It is also notable that Silone was the only member of Howe's pantheon who ever published in *Dissent*.)

In his essay on Silone originally published in 1956, Howe acknowledged Silone as an exemplar of the conscientious, responsible, outspoken dissident intellectual who lived on "an intellectual margin."[35] (I believe this phrase served as the germ for the title of Howe's autobiography, *A Margin of Hope*.)[36] Indeed Howe came to see himself as a kind of Jewish-American Silone: "The man who will not conform," Howe wrote, Silone "is a dissenter." Howe elaborated in terms that suggest veiled autobiography: "His own attitude toward socialism was to retain the values, even if he could not retain the doctrine. Silone's demand, at once imperious and relaxed, was that others would share with him a belief in the recurrent possibility of goodness."[37]

Howe calls Silone "a luminous example" of "a patient writer, one who has the most acute sense of the difference between what he is and what he wishes."[38] Howe proceeds in terms that suggest Silone's heroes—and their author himself—represent a level of heroic living that Howe strives to reach in his moments of utopian yearning:

> The hero of Silone's fiction feels that what is now needed is not programs, even the best Marxist programs, but examples, a pilgrimage of good deeds. Men must be healed. They must be stirred to heroism rather than exhorted and converted. Unwilling to stake anything on the future, he insists that the only way to realize the good life, no matter what the circumstances, is to live it. The duality between the two heroes, between the necessity for action and the necessity for contemplation, between the urge to power and the urge to purity is reflected in Silone's own experience as novelist and political leader. In his own practices as an Italian socialist, he is forced to recognize that the vexatious problem of means and ends involves a constant tension between morality and expediency.[39]

Furthermore, Howe agreed with Silone that heroism is "a condition of readiness, a talent for waiting, a gift for stubbornness." Howe admired Silone's resolution and steadfastness despite the fatiguing labor of striving for a more virtuous social order, what Howe called Silone's "heroism of tiredness." Howe aspired to such a heroism himself.[40] Ultimately he realized that patience, alertness, and waiting had to be his way, too, the way of all those who would hold fast to the ideals of socialism. And so, Orwell became for Howe a model of "the intellectual hero," Silone "the hero of tiredness."[41]

Edmund Wilson was the only American member of Howe's heroic quartet. Yet young Howe prized Wilson partly for his mastery of the European literary and political traditions. For the cosmopolitan writer-critic just beginning his career at *Partisan Review*, the American outpost of European culture in the mid-1940s—indeed the premier cultural magazine of the American intellectual world from the 1930s through the 1950s—Wilson represented European intellectual sophistication on native ground. He stood before Howe as an *engagé* intellectual (like Orwell and Trotsky) who had never succumbed to the coarseness of ideology (unlike Trotsky—and indeed unlike the youthful Trotskyist Howe). Of course, Wilson was also the only member on this high stage of Howe's literary pantheon within Howe's intellectual orbit in New York, a fact that obviously rendered him a figure in even closer proximity (physically, if not fraternally or ideologically) to young Howe than Silone. Howe could (and did) get to know Wilson personally.[42] Ultimately he granted Wilson, too, a measure of heroism—and Wilson's literary stamina, indeed superhuman energy, matched Howe's own. Unlike Silone, Wilson was a hero of tirelessness:

> Writers and critics looked up to him, both those for whom he served as a mentor and those ambitious enough to have him as a model. . . . His career took

on a heroic shape, the curve of the writer who attains magisterial lucidity in middle age and then in the years of decline struggles ferociously to keep his powers. One doesn't customarily think of writers as heroes; nor are heroes always likeable. But in Wilson's determination to live out the idea of the man of letters, in his glowing eagerness before the literatures of mankind, and in his stubborn insistence on speaking his own mind, there is a trace of the heroic.[43]

These remarks of Howe on Edmund Wilson came to apply to Irving Howe himself. In *A Margin of Hope*, Howe cited Wilson as his chief literary model (along with Orwell).[44] As with Howe's other literary heroes, one discerns a resemblance to Wilson in Howe's own "magisterial lucidity" and "stubborn insistence on speaking his own mind"—and also a "trace of the heroic."

Irving Howe, Triple Thinker

The animating idea of one of Wilson's critical studies, which Howe much admired, serves as the title for my essay: "the triple thinker." I mean it to apply here both in the sense of Howe's immersion in and mastery of three worlds—literary, political, and Jewish—as well as in Wilson's sense. "The artist should be triply (to the *n*th degree) a thinker," wrote Wilson in *The Triple Thinkers* (1938), which set forth his ideal of the writer's relationship to society and reflected his disillusion with Marxism as a way of reforming society or even adequately describing it.[45]

Wilson's triple thinkers—above all, Pushkin, James, Shaw, and Flaubert, from whom Wilson borrowed the phrase—are unwilling to renounce responsibility either to themselves or to their society.[46] They refuse either to dwell in a private garden of self-cultivation or to turn themselves into political hacks or social do-gooders. Instead, they seek meaning in the tensions between their inner and outer worlds. These tensions stimulate intellectual leaps, indeed imaginative triple jumps. The triple jumper of the mind soars dialectically to the triple thought: art functions as an existential guide. Aestheticism—art for art's sake—is the single thought. Its antithesis, the double thought, arises from the realization that beauty does not exist as a transcendent, eternal abstraction but rather arises from social circumstances. This insight, if it loses dialectical fluidity and ossifies beyond conviction to dogma, becomes the doctrine that art must promote social reform. The triple thought is the recognition that art is all this and much more, indeed that the work of art can enlarge our awareness, ennoble our inner lives, and enrich the human condition. This recognition can also be credited to Trilling—and perhaps can serve as an ethos for the New York Intellectuals in their heyday and the way they blend art and politics while resisting ideology.

I regard Irving Howe as a Flaubertian—or Wilsonian—triple thinker. Although Wilson's exemplary thinkers were nineteenth-century literary men *par excellence*, triple thinking is not associated with a particular epoch, form, genre, or style.[47] It envisions new relationships, connects the real to the ideal, interweaves the social and artistic planes—and generates disturbance.

Irving Howe certainly was a thinker ("to the *n*th degree") who generated a lot of disturbance. And I would argue that he moved far beyond the double thought (and sometimes doublethink) of his youthful Trotskyist dialectics to become a mature "triple thinker," one of our most sophisticated critics, possessed of a rare gift to appreciate art as an existential guide—like his models Orwell, Silone, and Wilson himself.

Indeed, as I have already suggested, Howe's thinking was also triple in another sense: he commanded trilingual fluency in three domains. Howe lived concurrently in three overlapping, interacting worlds: American socialism, humanistic criticism, and Yiddish culture—and he commuted constantly among them. They were his three great loves—and he witnessed all of them grow pale and frail in his own lifetime.[48]

Howe's lifetime of faithful commitment to politics, literature, and Jewish culture formed the center of his mature thought. First came (at least in his public life) Howe's politics: Howe the activist, the editor of *Dissent*, the radical humanist and committed writer. Then there was Howe the literary and cultural critic, especially Howe the prose stylist and lover of language. The last (yet perhaps also first) love concerns Howe the Jew, the East Side boy, the faithful steward of *Yiddishkeit*, the author of *World of Our Fathers*.

Of Life and Letters

Not just Howe the socialist, critic, and Jew—but also Howe the man—is my concern in this essay. So: what kind of man was he?

Howe not only popularized the phrase "New York Intellectual" in his brilliant 1968 essay of that title; he also came to personify, as both his admirers and adversaries have recognized, some distinctive features of the species.[49] The personal memoirs of friends and colleagues invariably address his complex personality and intellectual temperament. Most of Howe's acquaintances speak with affection and gratitude about both his mentoring role in their intellectual lives and his comradely companionship on their political and professional journeys. The colleagues of Irving Howe with whom I've talked invariably also speak of him as intense, an indefatigable worker, a man who strove relentlessly toward his goals, a man capable of single-minded effort, a man of strong moral principles who would not rest until the job was done and done right, a man whose opinions and beliefs on any subject were neither held lightly nor separated from his personal relations.

I spoke with Irving Howe on only two occasions: at an Orwell conference in 1983, when I interviewed him, and during his visit in 1986 to the University of Virginia, when he lectured on the American Renaissance from sections of *The American Newness* (1986).[50] He had just retired from the City University of New York, where he had held the chair of Distinguished Professor of English and was on the verge of receiving a MacArthur Foundation fellowship in 1987.

I noticed Howe's intensity, but I was also impressed by how his work became more reflective (and autobiographical) with the years. When I shared that perception with Howe's friends, they described to me his mellowing, his growing capacity to relax, his increasing ability to transcend partisanship. The mature Howe knew there was also a time for frivolity and lightness—and so he learned in later life to open himself to new pleasures, such as the ballet.[51] He didn't let his purposefulness degenerate into anxiety about achieving a goal. As Daniel Bell put it in his tribute to Howe in *Dissent*, "Irving changed not only his opinions but the way he held them."[52]

For me, it is not just Howe the critic and intellectual but Howe the man, and the man within the writings, who proves compelling. It is a quality of human presence and indeed of presence in the word, especially the modulation and rhythm of his discerning, composed, often poignant literary voice that stays with me. What inspires me above all is the trajectory of his career, Howe's wherewithal to change—less his political outlook than his personal manner. When I met and corresponded with him during his last decade, he had already begun to exhibit a patient trust in the slow work of dialogue, in the slow work of time—that is, he was applying his convictions about the need for "steady work" not just to his political vision but to his personal values—the true mark of a Wilsonian triple thinker.

Howe himself recognized all this. "Looking back at my disillusionment with political ideology," he wrote in 1982, "it would be more correct to say that my politics changed because I became, I like to think, more humane, tolerant, and broadminded. If I'm right in using those adjectives, then it became easier for me to acknowledge things that a rigid ideology would deny."[53] As he grew older, he became more flexible, more open to the alternative views and differing gifts of others—as well as more practical and nuanced in his daily politics.

But if Howe mellowed, he did not become lukewarm. He always ran hot on both justice and equality, the pole stars of his radical humanism; he stayed cool—nay, cold—to neoconservative celebrations of capitalism, far-left diatribes against "Amerika," and academic jargon of all kinds. In short: Irving Howe stuck to his convictions. Opposition only served to fortify his dogged determination. He could be abrupt and flinty when confronted with what he regarded as stupidity. Or when he encountered intellectual complacency or smugness—especially if it rested on academic credentials. (He was proud that he had become a chaired professor without ever bothering to get a Ph.D.) He usually found the most effective way of doing things in the least amount of time and could be irritated by people whom he felt were wasting time by questioning his method or his rationale. He was unusually sensitive to criticism because he subjected himself to very high intellectual standards that included sharp self-criticism, so that further negative feedback rarely seemed to him necessary. All of which is to say: he relaxed his manner; he never relaxed his standards.[54]

Talking to his friends, I also became more aware of Howe's rare capacity to hold together the big picture with the fine points. He always had a mind for facts, categories, and technical detail that nonetheless did not lose sight of larger questions. And in his later years, his great self-discipline seldom deteriorated into grim determination, even though he maintained his impassioned sense of mission that led him to want to improve the world. As Leon Wieseltier observed in his memorial address on Howe: "He saw the end of socialism. He saw literature mauled by second-rate deconstructionists and third-rate socialists of race, class, and gender. And he saw the world of Yiddish disappear. But he never surrendered to nostalgia. He remained almost diabolically engaged with the politics and culture of his time."[55]

Although Howe was astonishingly erudite, he did not disdain the dirty work of politics, the necessary efforts to bring about the reforms he believed in. He was willing to get into the trenches and bring about the changes he advocated. But there were times—such as during the Vietnam War in 1966–1967, when he wrote *Thomas Hardy*—when he also sought to go "far from the madding crowd" and immerse himself in literature in a quiet natural setting.[56] He came to enjoy the give and take of political involvement less and less in his last two decades, though he remained politically active.[57] Most of all, as his friends confided to me, he improved his ability to talk *to* others rather than *at* others.

Howe became more tolerant; he did not become permissive. He never granted that people could just do whatever they liked. Rather, he developed the talent of the tolerant man to respect differences of opinion, never believing that everything was equal and nothing made a difference. He learned to drop debating points—and in doing so he became far more accepting of others without ever simply becoming indifferent. He remained upright while becoming less self-righteous.

Howe's hunger for social justice could go beyond moral seriousness to almost messianic longing. In *World of Our Fathers* Howe exalted *menshlikhkayt* [humaneness], calling it "that root sense of obligation which the mere fact of being human imposes upon us." It is a "persuasion that human existence is a deeply serious matter for which all of us are finally accountable. . . . We cannot be our fathers, we cannot live like our mothers, but we may look to their experience for images of rectitude and purities of devotion."[58]

Again that "seriousness." But also "rectitude" and "purity": these attributes too were central both to Howe's literary sensibility and his commitment to socialism. A man of principle, he maintained a "purity of devotion" to the ethos of socialism—and referred to himself as a radical humanist even after *Dissent* dropped its masthead motto ("a socialist quarterly") that explicitly identified the magazine with socialism in the late 1950s.[59]

The Crumb on His Coat

Howe's son, Nicholas, relates that the phrase "It's like the crumb" became an endearing shorthand joke between Howe and his friends to describe a wonderful, gratuitous detail in a work of fiction—which, as detail evolved into story, assumed the form of an anecdote.[60]

Especially at his memorial service and in the memorial issue of *Dissent* (Fall 1993), his family, friends, and colleagues sprinkled delicious *shtiklakh* (morsels) about Irving Howe's foibles and eccentricities. Everyone spoke about "Irving."

These first-person reminiscences, composed of striking details and revealing anecdotes, vividly evoked the man—and make vivid reading for us today. The crumbs abound: Irving at the baseball game reminiscing with beer-guzzling fans about having seen Babe Ruth play in Yankee Stadium, Irving brusquely ending a phone conversation by hanging up the phone before a friend would say good-bye, Irving leading a *Dissent* editorial meeting with a mixture of benevolence and argumentativeness. Some recollections consist of choice *shtiklakh*, while others are less edible or digestible to his friends. Nonetheless, the crumbs on his coat are there.

One crumb often passed around among his friends was the joke that Irving Howe was the last nineteenth-century Russian writer. Indeed, Howe does seem made in the image of the Russian intellectual of that era: a utopian, an idealist, a radical reformer, an impassioned advocate. Morris Dickstein once called him "a counter-puncher who tended to dissent from the prevailing orthodoxy of the moment, whether left or right, though he himself was certainly a man of the Left. . . . Whatever way the herd was going, he went in the opposite direction." And these attributes were not confined to his political or cultural criticism. They manifested themselves in his prose style. As Nicholas Howe observed, Irving had "a utopian faith in the reader."[61]

Unsurprisingly, Irving Howe also deeply identified—and ever more so as he grew older—with the greatest nineteenth-century Russian writer, utopian, and reformer/revolutionary: Leo Tolstoy.

I have already discussed Howe's four literary-political models from the generation immediately preceding his own. But Howe honored other literary and political figures from other generations too. Let us also attend here briefly to another diverse quartet of inspirational—and cautionary—influences on Irving Howe.

One of them was Tolstoy, who also induced Howe to hold the looking glass up to himself. Howe's comments on Tolstoy are transparently self-reflexive: "I love the old magician in the way that Chekhov and Gorky loved him—for his relentlessness of mind, his unquenchable desires. Of course he succumbs to moral crankiness, to intemperate demands for temperance; but stubborn and even perverse, he remains faithful to the contradictions of his sensibility."[62]

And there is more: "Tolstoy keeps groping for some stable position between the esthetic and the ethical. He never quite finds it, but he can write as if indeed he had found it." All this mirrors Howe—with his love of the ballet and the polemic, his affinity for literary criticism and politics, his tense balance between poetical sensibility and ideological conviction. As if to supplement Tolstoy's *Confessions* by voicing his own, Howe adds this (self-) criticism of his moral passion: "In a few instances, Tolstoy's ethical imperiousness does overwhelm his esthetic pattern."[63]

Yes, Howe's own vulnerability to self-righteousness and godlike Final Judgment must also be conceded—and they never vanished completely. But Howe largely avoided the fate of another epic Russian author, one of the greatest twentieth-century writers, Alexandr Solzhenitsyn: "What has happened to Solzhenitsyn?" Howe asked in 1989. "The answer is that his zealotry has brought about a hardening of spirit."[64] Solzhenitsyn lacked what Howe often referred to as "moral poise," which he defined as a sense of "ease in a world of excess." Instead Howe himself heeded the example of the Yiddish writers whom he cherished for their wondrous balance amid adversity, above all Sholom Aleichem, the "dominant quality" of whose literary imagination

> is his sense of moral poise. I can't resist a few more words on the matter
> of "moral poise" . . . [Y]ou see how balanced, at once stringent and tender,
> severe and loving is his sense of life. [65]

Howe also aspired to such moral poise—and that is why Aleichem was also a literary (and political) model for him. And Howe himself could indeed be a stringent and severe man. That was the form that his tender sense of life sometimes assumed, the means whereby he maintained a poised balance amid all the demands of his triple loves. The balance did indeed sometimes have something of the tenseness—the "intemperate temperance"—of the aged Tolstoy. That was the price that his friends—and above all Howe himself—paid his daimon for his extraordinary intensity, concentration, and passion.

One is reminded that Howe began his career with a study of another intemperately temperate man. In his first book, *The UAW and Walter Reuther* (1949), coauthored with B.J. Widick, the twenty-nine-year-old Howe wrote that Reuther, a left-wing anti-Communist labor leader whom he much admired, was "*an unfinished personality*" battling to reconcile the pursuit of power and the call to a nobler vision. Which would be stronger, mused Howe, the drivenness or the dream? [66]

Howe too remained an unfinished personality. But then—who doesn't?

Irving Howe—skeptical dreamer, chastened revolutionary, driven reformer, and reluctant antiutopian animated by utopian longings—held these oppositions in coiled (or "clenched"), productive tension to the unfinished fin   still yearning, still striving, still steadily working toward his vision of a better orld. [67]

The Ravages of Time

"Should anyone remember?" Howe asked in the closing lines of his posthumously published *A Critic's Notebook* (1994). Ever the devil's advocate against his own positions, Howe was speaking here in the voice of a young skeptic who doubts his elders' experience holds any lessons pertinent to the present—yet who is also sanguine about the future: "And isn't it wonderful that we have survived all these catastrophes?"

After a pause, the senex Howe—the old man of the left—replies. His response echoes today as though Howe were speaking from the grave: "Yes, it's wonderful, but our hearts also sink before the ravages of time."[68]

And many who remember Irving Howe also feel regret about the man's death, which reminds us of the inevitable human fate that we all succumb ultimately to the ravages of time.

But the spirit of a true calling does not succumb; it endures. As Howe declared in his landmark essay "This Age of Conformity," published a half-century ago in 1954:

> What is most alarming is not that a number of intellectuals have abandoned the posture of iconoclasm of the Zeitgeist. Give them a jog and they will again be radical, all too radical. What is most alarming is that the whole idea of intellectual vocation has gradually lost its allure.[69]

It never lost its allure for Irving Howe. He remained a model of the humanist intellectual, and he impresses me as such today. So let Howe himself have the last word:

> The most glorious vision of the intellectual life is still that which is called humanist: the idea of a mind committed, yet dispassionate, ready to stand alone, curious, eager, skeptical. The banner of critical independence, ragged and torn though it may be, is still the best we have.[70]

Notes

1. Indeed, my own view is that Howe's critical legacy will ultimately have more to do with his revival of *Yiddishkeit*, including the American Yiddish poets, than with the politics of the novel or his valiant attempt to salvage and renew American radicalism. Robert Boyers and others have built on the strand of Howe concerned with the politics of the novel, but there has been no systematic attempt as yet to honor and further develop his contributions to Yiddish literature and culture.

2. The New York "elders" sometimes compared with Howe include: Lionel Trilling, Philip Rahv, Sidney Hook, Dwight Macdonald, Harold Rosenberg, and Hannah Arendt. Even after their deaths, Howe was often cast in their shadow via unfavorable comparison. Or he was criticized as "too polemical" or "too prolific." In the 1980s he attained the status of a monument on the liberal-left, but his reputation went into eclipse even before his death. (It was significant that, whereas Trilling's obituary appeared on page one of the *New York Times*, Howe's notice was run on page 22 of Section D.) The appearance of two excellent biographies in the last few years, Edward Alexander's *Irving Howe: Socialist, Critic, Jew* (1998) and Gerald Sorin's *Irving Howe: A Life of Passionate Dissent* (2002), have brought Howe back into the public eye and more than redressed the previous decade of relative neglect.

   The peak of Howe's recognition and broad influence occurred in the late 1970s and early 1980s, between *World of Our Fathers* (1976) and *A Margin of Hope* (1982)—just as the height of Trilling's fame in the 1950s also occurred long before his death. In the wake of the success of *World of Our Fathers*, which received the 1976 National Book

Award, Howe and Kenneth Libo edited a popular illustrated volume of history, *How We Lived: A Documentary History of Immigrant Jews in America, 1880–1930*. Really a coffee-table book, it was selected in 1979 as a main choice of the Book-of-the-Month Club. It was also a selection that year of the History Book Club, the Jewish Book Club, and the Jewish Publication Society. By contrast, *Selected Writings* (1990), a collection of his best essays across more than forty years, received only scattered attention with no effort to sum up Howe's career. By the mid-1980s, the vogue for theoretical academic criticism meant that concerns in the literary-academic world had moved beyond Howe's methodless, "amateur" criticism.

3.   Quoted in Gerald Sorin, *Irving Howe: A Life of Passionate Dissent* (New York: New York University Press, 2002), p. 313 n24. Bellow's remark appears in a letter to their mutual friend Al Glotzer, an erstwhile Trotskyist comrade, written at the time of Howe's death in 1993. Bellow, who had veered rightward into neoconservatism since the 1960s, was criticizing Howe and *Dissent*, which Bellow regarded as a backward-looking, stodgy, behind-the-times relic of socialism. Bellow wrote to Glotzer: "He struck me as rather quaint, like an old-fashioned lady, who still cans her tomatoes in August."

4.   Philip Roth, *The Anatomy Lesson* (New York: Farrar, Straus and Giroux, 1985), p. 474.

5.   Several of the leading figures associated with *Partisan Review* (*PR*), "the house organ of the American intellectual community" in the early post–World War II era—among them Trilling, Rahv, Delmore Schwartz, and Mary McCarthy—have also been nominated by various observers as the archetypal New York Intellectual. See, for instance, William Barrett, *The Truants: Adventures among the Intellectuals* (New York: Doubleday, 1982). (The characterization of *PR* is by Howe's friend, the liberal historian Richard Hofstadter, in his *Anti-Intellectualism in American Life* [New York: Knopf, 1963], p. 394.)

6.   Robert Lowell, *Notebook, 1967–1968*, 3rd ed. rev. and expanded (New York: Farrar, Straus and Giroux, 1970).

7.   Philip Nobile, *Intellectual Skywriting: Literary Politics and the New York Review of Books* (New York: Charterhouse, 1974), pp. 135–136.

8.   Nobile, *Intellectual Skywriting*, p. 13.

9.   They take, as it were, two-thirds of Howe's corpus and approve it: "Two cheers for Irving Howe." Or sometimes less: Edward Alexander in *Irving Howe: Socialist, Critic, Jew* gives one rousing cheer for Howe's work—or at best one and a half cheers: socialist—no; critic—yes; Jew—yes (*Yiddishkeit*) and no (Israel). Alexander's harshest criticism of Howe's politics is for his support of the Israeli left and the peace process—and his castigation of what he regarded as Israeli militarism in the guise of national defense. For Alexander, Irving Howe was critic first, then socialist and Jew. Alexander sees Howe as a great critic, a misguided political thinker—who exhibited a misconceived politics that reflected a refusal to grow up—and a false friend to Israel. Alexander, an English professor, especially identifies with Howe the literary critic and strongly endorses the preservative, traditionalist positions of Howe on the literary canon and his hostility to postmodernism and deconstruction. (The Old Left and neoconservatives are closest on positions with regard to culture and literature. They tend to share a respect for the classics and literary canon—and even for conservative modernist writers such as Pound and Eliot.) In addition to his biography of Howe, see Alexander's *Irving Howe and Secular Jewishness: An Elegy* (Cincinnati: University of Cincinnati Press, 1995).

10. Although Howe was an anti-Zionist before the Six-Day Arab-Israeli war in 1967, he developed strong links and friendships in Israel in the 1970s (and even married an Israeli woman). During his last two decades, Howe was a strong and articulate, if critical, supporter of Israel.

11. See Alexander, chapter 2.

12. Hasia R. Diner, "Embracing *World of Our Fathers*: The Context of Reception," *American Jewish History* 88, no. 4 (December 2000), p. 449. The American Jewish community celebrated *World of Our Fathers* as an act of homage to American Jewish history and as a semitic version of Alex Haley's *Roots*, another bestseller in the bicentennial year. Diner recalls that the Jewish community centers "staged 'Lower East Side' fairs to accompany his presentations, and the strains of Klezmer music wafted from the social halls at the reception afterwards" (p. 450).

13. Quoted in Diner, p. 453.

14. Roth, *The Anatomy Lesson*, p. 482.

15. Mitchell Cohen et al., "Remembering Irving Howe," *Dissent*, Fall 1993, pp. 515–549. "Irving Howe," *New Republic*, May 31, 1993, p. 10. Robert Kuttner, *Dissent*, Fall 1993. Leon Wieseltier, "Remembering Irving Howe (1920–1993)," *New York Times Book Review*, May 20, 1993, p. 31.

16. Richard Rorty, *Achieving Our Country* (Cambridge, MA: Harvard University Press, 1998).

17. Matthew Frye Jacobsen, "A Ghetto to Look Back to *World of Our Fathers*, Ethnic Revival, and the Arc of Multiculturalism," *American Jewish History* 88, no. 4 (December 2000), pp. 473–474.

18. Joseph Dorman, review of *World of Our Fathers*, by Irving Howe, *New York Times Book Review*, March 2, 2003, p. 13.

19. Ronald Radosh, "A Literary Mind, a Political Heart," *Los Angeles Times Book Review*, April 6, 2003, p. 10.

20. "One of the most original, principled, and independent minds of twentieth century America," wrote Edward Alexander of Howe in his biography. Alexander, p. 9.

21. Hilton Kramer, "Socialism Is the Name of Our Desire," *Twilight of the Intellectuals* (Chicago: Ivan R. Dee, 1997).

22. The phrase—intended facetiously as a counter to all "the quasi-religious eulogies"—is Jeremy Larner's in his memoir of Howe, "Remembering Irving Howe," *Dissent* 40, no. 4 (Fall 1993), pp. 539–542.

23. Alexander Cockburn, "A Few Tasteless Words about Irving Howe," *Nation*, May 14, 1993, p. 822.

24. Howe's friends and junior colleagues certainly embrace the analogy. As Josephine Woll wrote in "Remembering Irving Howe," *Dissent* 40, no. 4 (Fall 1993), pp. 515–549: "For Irving, Orwell was the model of a writer. For me, Irving was."

25. See my *George Orwell: The Politics of Literary Reputation* (New York: Oxford University Press, 1989), p. 29.

26. His biographer, Gerald Sorin, calls Howe "a hero of sorts," applying Howe's remarks to Silone's "heroism of tiredness" to Howe himself (p. xiv).

27. Irving Howe, *Leon Trotsky* (New York: Viking Press, 1978), p. 161.

28. On Howe's high regard for Norman Thomas—as a politician and speaker rather than a writer—see *A Margin of Hope: An Intellectual Autobiography*, chapter 5 (New York: Harcourt Brace Jovanovich, 1982).

29. Irving Howe, *Leon Trotsky* (New York: Viking Press, 1978), p. viii.

30. Howe, *Leon Trotsky*, pp. 192–193.
31. Howe wrote in his preface to *Leon Trotsky*: "I have remained a socialist. I have found myself moving farther and farther away from [Trotsky's] ideas yet he remains a figure of heroic magnitude" (p. viii).
32. Howe also used the phrase in the 1980s and 1990s to characterize radical professors who favored multiculturalism and postmodernism over the classical literary canon and the traditional liberal arts curriculum.
33. One measure of the influence of Howe's 1954 essay is that a book appeared later that year under the title: *The Age of Conformity* by Alan Valentine (Chicago: Regnery Press, 1954). Another is the appearance of John W. Aldridge's *In Search of Heresy: American Literature in an Age of Conformity* (New York: McGraw-Hill, 1956).
34. Quoted in Sorin, p. 161.
35. *Decline of the New* (New York: Harcourt, Brace & World, 1970), p. 290. The essay was first published as "Silone and the Radical Conscience," *Dissent* 3 (Winter 1956), pp. 72–75. It was revised and reprinted in *Politics and the Novel* and *Decline of the New*.
36. All this is from the essay "Silone: The Power of Example," *New Republic*, September 22, 1958, pp. 18–19. A further measure of Howe's regard for Silone was that he and Lewis Coser dedicated *The American Communist Party* (1958) to "Ignazio Silone and Milovan Djilas—two men who more than any other stand for the attempt to create a non-Communist radical option in Europe."
37. *Decline of the New*, p. 290.
38. *Decline of the New*, p. 284.
39. *Decline of the New*, pp. 285–287. This tension between the attractions of power and purity was one that Howe also carried throughout his life—as a radical who wrote for Henry Luce and *Time*, as a critic of conformist bourgeois life who became a chaired professor of English, and so on.

    Howe obviously found inspiration in Silone's public example of how to creatively maintain and balance these oppositions. What, then, would he have had to say about recent revelations about Silone's preference for means to ends and his choice of expediency over morality as an Italian socialist? Silone's radical credentials and noble image have been soiled by evidence discovered during the 1990s in the files of the Italian fascist secret police that he was an informant to the fascists in the 1930s. Other documents establish that Silone was knowledgeable about CIA funding of the Congress for Cultural Freedom and other anti-Soviet cultural activities of the Western intelligence services in the cultural cold war—activities that Howe castigated in "This Age of Conformity" and in *Dissent*'s pages throughout the 1950s and 1960s. In light of these findings, Howe's praise of Silone sometimes rings most ironically: "The memory of [Silone's] refusal to accommodate himself to the fascist regime stirred feelings of bad conscience among literary men who had managed to become more flexible. Alas, men of exemplary stature are often hard to accept. They must seem a silent rebuke to those who had been less heroic or more cautious." *Decline of the New*, p. 288.
40. The recurrent theme of Howe's essays in Part Four of *Decline of the New*, which consists of three substantial essays, is heroism. Orwell is his "intellectual hero" (p. 269); Silone is his "hero of tiredness"; and T.E. Lawrence exemplifies the entire "problem of heroism" (pp. 294–325).
41. *Decline of the New*, p. 293.

42. Wilson was one of the senior lecturers invited to teach the Christian Gauss seminars in the spring of 1953. Howe was selected as a junior lecturer, and he attended one of Wilson's sessions. Years later, Howe turned down a submission to *Dissent* from Wilson, who, rather than hold a grudge, "teased him about being turned down by a magazine that didn't even pay." See Sorin, pp. 94, 147.

43. Irving Howe, "A Man of Letters," in *Celebrations and Attacks* (New York: Horizon Press, 1979), p. 221.

44. Irving Howe, *A Margin of Hope*, p. 168.

45. Edmund Wilson, *The Triple Thinkers*, expanded ed. (New York: Oxford University Press, 1948), p. 71. See also Janet Groth, *Edmund Wilson: A Critic for Our Time* (Athens: Ohio University Press, 1989), passim; David Castonovo, *Edmund Wilson* (New York: F. Ungar, 1984), pp. 33–42; and Jeffrey Meyers, *Edmund Wilson: A Biography* (Boston: Houghton Mifflin, 1995).

46. The collection's title derived from Wilson's essay "The Politics of Flaubert," and it was intended to provide Wilson with a unifying theme for his numerous fugitive pieces addressing such disparate figures as Paul Elmer More, A.E. Housman, Christian Gauss, John Jay Chapman, Marx, and Ben Jonson. In addition to the aforementioned quartet of main nineteenth-century figures (Pushkin, James, Shaw, Flaubert), the highlights of *The Triple Thinkers* are the introduction to Pushkin (including Wilson's own prose translation of "The Bronze Horseman"); theoretical studies, "Marxism and Literature" and "The Historical Interpretation of Literature"; and "Morose Ben Jonson," Wilson's interpretations of Jonson's dramas, in which he subjects the Jacobean dramatist to speculative psychobiography.

47. I am well aware that the unpolitical Flaubert would have been unlikely to characterize Howe or even Wilson himself—at least during his Marxist phase in the 1930s when the first edition of *The Triple Thinkers* (1938) was published—as a triple thinker. Flaubert opposed socialism, the ideal of social equality, mass education, universal suffrage, and revolutions in general. Wilson quotes Flaubert's 1853 letter to Louise Colet: "The triple thinker . . . should have neither religion nor fatherland, nor even any social conviction" (pp. 73–74).

48. Howe's triple thinking flowed, therefore, from his involvement in three different worlds, i.e., from the seriousness he brought to politics, literature, and Jewish life. But he was hardly orthodox in any of those worlds. He was political, but his radicalism marginalized him in liberal and conservative America. He loved literature, but his disdain for professionalized "lit crit" made him an outsider in the literary academy. He was Jewish and valued his roots, but he could not accept a rejection of universalism and nationalism at the expense of the Palestinians. His insights and his own outsider status were linked. Howe's boundary crossing helps explain not only his originality and intellectual contributions but also his many conflicts and enemies.

49. See Irving Howe, "The New York Intellectuals," *Commentary*, March 1968, pp. 14–15.

50. During the reception after his 1986 lecture at Virginia, Howe chatted at length with several of us about whether it might be timely to reissue his landmark study *Politics and the Novel* (1957). "There's been nothing like it since then," a few of us agreed. And, in fact, Howe did come to reissue it in 1992—perhaps gently nudged by our enthusiasm for the book.

51. See Irving Howe, "Ballet for the Man Who Enjoys Wallace Stevens," *Harper's*, May 1971, pp. 102–109. See also Sorin, pp. 177–178, 222–223, 270, 286.

52. Daniel Bell, "Remembering Irving Howe," *Dissent* 40 (Fall 1993), p. 517.

53. Irving Howe, "The Range of the New York Intellectuals," in *Creators and Disturb-ers: Reminiscences by Jewish Intellectuals of New York*, Bernard Rosenberg, ed. (New York: Columbia University Press, 1982), p. 287.

54. See Sorin, pp. 146–147.

55. Leon Wieseltier, memorial address on Howe, delivered May 24, 1993.

56. Irving Howe, *Thomas Hardy* (New York: Macmillan, 1967).

57. Howe's supporters on the organized left in the 1970s could best be described as com-ing from the Democratic Socialist Organizing Committee (DSOC), a group that merged with a small New Left group called the New American Movement (NAM) in the early 1980s. It is important to acknowledge Howe's political involvement in this strain of American socialism, even though literary criticism and *Dissent* became more central to his life and work than organized socialism after the late 1940s.

58. *World of Our Fathers*, p. 645.

59. Just a year before his death, in his preface to the 1992 edition of *Politics and the Novel*, Howe wrote that his 1957 study "was written at a moment when I was drifting away from orthodox Marxism. . . . I still hold firmly to the socialist ethos which partly inspired this book, but the ideology to which these essays occasionally return no longer has for me the power it once had" (p. 7).

60. On the genre of the anecdote, see my book, *The Politics of Literary Reputation* (New York: Oxford University Press, 1989).

61. Dickstein is quoted in the *New York Times* obituary on Howe, May 7, 1993. See also Nicholas Howe, introduction to *A Critic's Notebook* (New York: Harcourt Brace, 1994), p. 12.

62. *A Critic's Notebook*, p. 316.

63. *A Critic's Notebook*, pp. 315–316. Occasionally Howe also lost his precarious balance between esthetic and ethical, with the latter overwhelming the former. And indeed, maintaining his much-prized "moral poise" depended chiefly on keeping his literary poise. Howe was blessed with a power rarely given to a critic, a power difficult to control: he had the literary equivalent of "perfect pitch." His ear for good prose style was nearly faultless. He possessed both an exquisitely fine sense for the rhythm and cadence of sentences and a superb judgment about *le mot juste*. These talents proved ideal equipment for a literary critic. But Howe's concentrated energy could become a sharp weapon when it contracted and overfocused on the foibles of an adversary or homed in on isolated details of an ideological dispute. He was marvelous when he related a political element to the big picture, but he could be cutting and wound-ing when he became preoccupied with small concerns. Under such circumstances, he could use morality as a club. Such was arguably the case with Tom Hayden and the young New Leftists whom he blasted when they visited him and *Dissent* in 1965. On that episode, see Todd Gitlin, *The Sixties: Years of Hope, Days of Rage* (New York: Bantam Books, 1987), pp. 171–176.

64. Irving Howe, "The Fate of Solzhenitsyn," in *Selected Writings*, pp. 459, 463.

65. Introduction to *The Best of Sholem Aleichem*, ed. Irving Howe and Ruth R. Wisse (Washington, DC: New Republic Books, 1979), p. xvii.

Aleichem was also a "culture hero" of Howe, but less a personal, intellectual hero (unlike Trotsky, Orwell, Silone, and Wilson) than a nineteenth-century spirit of the age. Howe wrote of Aleichem: "I think of him as a culture hero in the sense that Dickens and Mark Twain were culture heroes. For he embodies the culture of eastern European Jews at a time of heightened consciousness" (p. 12). See also Howe's essay,

"Shalom Aleichem: Voice of Our Past," in *A World More Attractive* and in *Selected Writings*.

66. Irving Howe and B.J. Widick, *The UAW and Walter Reuther* (New York: Random House, 1949), p. 199. Howe's portrait of Reuther resembles a description of Howe's own former commissar self who had been in thrall to Trotskyist sectarian politics—a life that Howe by 1949 had largely ended: "Reuther eats, sleeps, and talks union. He is as close to a political machine as any man alive today. He has forgotten how to relax and how to play. Reuther is characteristic of a generation of radicals that came to feel leftist politics is a dead end but could not throw off the moral compulsions that had led them to such politics" (p. 201). By all accounts of his acquaintances, this passage could also describe Howe's own struggle at midcentury to work through his Trotskyist past.

67. Fittingly enough, in the last article he published in *Dissent* during his lifetime, Howe proposed "two cheers for utopia"—two, not three—yet genuine, heartfelt cheers nonetheless. Irving Howe, "Two Cheers for Utopia," *Dissent* 40 (Spring 1993), pp. 131–133.

68. Irving Howe, "Writing and the Holocaust," *New Republic*, October 27, 1986, p. 34.

69. Irving Howe, "This Age of Conformity," in *Steady Work* (New York: Harcourt, Brace & World, 1966), p. 319. The essay originally appeared in *Partisan Review* (January–February 1954).

70. Ibid., p. 323.

Mark Krupnick and Lionel Trilling

Anxiety and Influence

Mark Shechner

I

Mark Krupnick was sixty-four years old when he died of ALS, amyotrophic lateral sclerosis, in March 2003. Popularly known as Lou Gehrig's Disease, ALS is a neuro-degenerative illness that attacks the voluntary muscles and is always fatal. Mark had known that he was fatally ill for two years, and during that time, under the increasing difficulty of declining physical powers, he had devoted himself to finishing a book that he titled *Jewish Writing and the Deep Places of the Imagination*, after a phrase from Lionel Trilling's essay "On the Teaching of Modern Literature."

I first learned of Mark's illness late in its advance, in October 2002, when I received a brief note from him that said the following: "According to the clinic where I go I have to reckon on only months not years to live. I'd give you my phone number, but an early muscle loss was my ability to speak." As I was to learn, his physical condition was horrible beyond these laconic words. Mark had lost not only the power of speech but also the swallowing reflex, and he spent much of his time on a noninvasive ventilator, a machine that forced air into his lungs. He had limited use of his hands, and could type away, sometimes with a single finger, at his correspondence and to continue to work on the book he was close to finishing. The keyboard had become virtually his last avenue of communication, as it was attached to a speech synthesizer, and e-mail was his lifeline to the world beyond home.

Mark's letter set off five months of urgent correspondence between us, the greater part of it focused narrowly on the book. Chatting, gossip, and personal matters, including his pain, his terror, and his rage, were only intermittent. There was work to be done. Mark began sending me drafts of essays in progress and others from his files that were to go into the book, and while he wrestled with the final text of some essays, I was assembling an archive of his writing. We agreed early on that, should he be unable to get the book into publishable shape before his death, his wife, Jean Carney, and I would see it through publication at the University of Wisconsin Press. The book, published in 2005, is the result of those labors.

Mark and I had known each other for three decades at least; I had read admiringly his earliest essays and reviews, including the incendiary broadsides that appeared in Philip Rahv's ill-fated journal *Modern Occasions* between 1970 and 1972, where Mark served as associate editor. I was certainly aware that he had taken Lionel Trilling to the woodshed in 1971 for the publication of a lackluster anthology of essays in criticism titled *Literary Criticism: An Introductory Reader* and that upon later reflection Mark had felt rueful about it and in 1986 published a full-length critical appraisal of Trilling, *Lionel Trilling and the Fate of Cultural Criticism*. In the 1971 review, it was up against the wall for Trilling, in a style that sounded like an insurrectionary fusion of the "manic-impressive" Philip Rahv (Delmore Schwartz's witty phrase) and notes from the Weather Underground. I don't wish to suggest that in writing the Trilling book Mark was performing an act of atonement; Mark was too tough minded for mea culpas and too self-aware to be driven to exhaustive labors by mere feelings of contrition. Rather, as his career took on its own momentum, he discovered in himself needs for which Lionel Trilling again became important as a model and a teacher, rather than a disappointment and a target. If Harold Bloom's theories about the anxiety of influence needed a modern case history, Mark could have supplied one.

Mark Krupnick's intellectual life was Shakespearean with intrigue, some of it self-generated out of his search for a secure intellectual patrimony and some of it thrust upon him from the bitter arena that E.M. Forster called "the world of telegrams and anger." He had even hired a lawyer at one point to protect him from Diana Trilling's threats to take legal action to prevent *Lionel Trilling and the Fate of Cultural Criticism* from gaining publication. The novelist Harold Brodkey once spoke of "the infinite oral thuggery" of New York literary life, and Mark's particular manner of elbowing his way into that life in the early 1970s and then fielding his share of elbows in return was an apprenticeship in being a New York Intellectual. Mark was all of thirty-one and an assistant professor at Boston University when he leaped feet first from the cruise ship *Academia* into this flaming sea of cultural polemics. The Trilling blowup and its long, turbulent wake was his intellectual bar mitzvah. But Mark was a street kid from Irvington, New Jersey, a largely Catholic working-class suburb of Newark, and he'd learned well how to bluff it out on the street. He held his own.

In 1970 Mark had been recruited by Philip Rahv to be an assistant editor on *Modern Occasions*, Rahv's new venture after leaving *Partisan Review*. The inaugural issue in fall 1970, which headlined the "Salad Days" section of Philip Roth's novel *My Life as a Man*, along with essays by or interviews with Mary McCarthy,

Noam Chomsky, Robert Lowell, and Hilton Kramer, found Mark in the review section taking aim at two of literary postmodernism's favorite sons, John Barth and Donald Barthelme.

The books under review were *City Life*, one of Barthelme's jaunty miscellanies, and Barth's *Lost in the Funhouse*, subtitled *Fiction for Print, Tape, Live Voice*. Though both books had garnered a modicum of critical acclaim and academic buzz—both writers had academic appointments—they were light entertainments at best, fashionable symptoms of a period that was against interpretation and had an affection for the aleatory and the capricious—remember "the happening"?

As I write this thirty-four years later, Mark's brisk dismissal holds up remarkably well as a prescient, if somewhat cantankerous and hortatory, criticism. Mark's review was promising indeed; it had phrasing and bite, and one could imagine Mark, out on a different trail in life's garden of forking paths, becoming an acerbic critic of contemporary fiction: scattering anathemas while rendering sharp judgments, a younger John Aldridge or Randall Jarrell calling writers to account and refusing to be taken in by shoddy goods or facile pyrotechnics.

That didn't happen. The very next review Mark wrote became a cause célèbre that redrew the map of his professional career. It was a review of Lionel Trilling's *Literary Criticism: An Introductory Reader*.[1] Trilling by the late 1960s had been turning his energies in an increasingly professional and institutional direction. The probing and sometimes confessional essays he gathered in *The Liberal Imagination*, *The Opposing Self*, *A Gathering of Fugitives*, and *Beyond Culture* had given way to textbook publication. In 1967, he produced the three-volume anthology of world literature for college freshmen, *The Experience of Literature*, whose prefaces alone, republished in 1979 in the uniform edition of Trilling's writing, came to 302 pages, making it one of his longer books. *The Experience of Literature* was an attempt to outline a great tradition in drama (Sophocles to Brecht); poetry (Wyatt to Lowell); and fiction, largely modern, from Hawthorne to Malamud. It was a labor of summing up, a tour de force of canon formation.

Literary Criticism: An Introductory Reader was a less muscular production. An introduction to criticism for undergraduates featuring forty-five essays in criticism from Plato to Susan Sontag, it was a guided tour to Western thought, to Western *mind* that, coming at the end of the 1960s, loomed above the landscape like one of those forbidding ziggurats of tradition that the sixties themselves were all about bringing down. The book has nothing in it of the intellectual journalism that Trilling himself so successfully practiced, and only Susan Sontag was summoned to speak for the New York Intellectuals, on being "against interpretation." In confronting this particular version of Trilling and finding it remote and donnish, Mark was nothing if not a man of his generation.

Mark's review was a smash-and-grab attack on the master. At a time when a certain decorum still shaped polemics on culture, it was an act of lèse majesté. Mark dealt harshly with Trilling's "reverence for the customary and the established" and his "increasingly priggish distaste for less elevated conditions of being."[2] Trilling, Mark wrote, had come on the scene in *The Liberal Imagination* as a hero of agonistic thought, a dialectician of the spirit, whose favorite image of the critic confronting the great books of modern literature was Jacob wrestling with the angel. "But increasingly the critic as spiritual wrestler seemed eager to come to terms, to renounce the trials of the will and bathe in 'the sentiment of being'—a condition of spirit exemplified, in Trilling's view, by writers as oddly different as Wordsworth and William Dean Howells. Increasingly there was evident in Trilling's criticism the desire for rest, the will to discontinue willing, the impulse to disengagement."

The review sparked an outcry both in and out of the *Modern Occasions* office, and one of the contributing editors, Hilton Kramer, resigned in protest, causing Rahv to sneer something about the "bourgeois fetishists of culture."[3] Diana Trilling would harbor a lifelong resentment against Mark, and in her own memoir of her marriage to Lionel Trilling fumed that Mark had been a lieutenant for Rahv in those days and had in effect accepted a contract to whack her husband.[4] Mark would take the opportunity of reviewing Mrs. Trilling's book, *The Beginning of the Journey,* in 1994, to deny that he had written on assignment and attest rather that he had reacted personally to what he perceived to be Lionel Trilling's failure to address the fevers and tensions of the age as he had in the 1940s, preferring instead to retreat into the cool Doric of tradition.[5]

Mark had earlier confessed in *Lionel Trilling and the Fate of Cultural Criticism* that his initial disappointment went beyond the passions of the moment to something deeper, his need for an intellectual legacy. In a 1981 review essay of Daniel Bell titled "Fathers, Sons, and New York Intellectuals," Mark raised the legacy issue both on Bell's behalf (as a latecomer to New York intellectual life) and on his own.[6] "By the mid-fifties . . . the owl of Minerva had already prepared for flight, and it was possible to begin taking stock. But this ending has taken a long time, and it has only been in the last ten or so years that a consensus has formed that the world of our intellectual fathers has in fact disintegrated. Some of us sons have been trying to determine what remains useable of the inheritance they have left."[7] As one of those sons, restless and fractious though he often was, Mark made of that legacy his perpetual quest, and it is little wonder that one of his favorite books was Philip Roth's memoir of his last year with his father, *Patrimony.* That search is the inner meaning of *Jewish Writing and the Deep Places of the Imagination.*

I cannot think of anyone else among my contemporaries in the profession of letters for whom the mystery of patrimony loomed so large. In a sense, it was Mark's enduring monomyth, his North Star, the secular Torah for which his essays served as commentaries. He may have come of age as the raging Oedipal son, wanting nothing so much as to speed up the dialectic of generational succession, but what son in becoming a father himself has not puzzled over his own inheritance? As a non-Jewish Jew he was on the lookout for a minyan of like-minded non-Jewish Jews and for a non-Jewish Jewish rabbi who would give him now and then a shtick secular toyreh (a bit, that is, of secular torah). Thus the figures he engaged so resolutely throughout his life: Philip Rahv, Alfred Kazin, Irving Howe, Geoffrey Hartman, Clement Greenberg, George Steiner, Cynthia Ozick, Daniel Aaron, Daniel Bell, Saul Bellow, Jacques Derrida (whose late books on mortality were among his bedside reading),[8] Philip Roth, and always—again and again—Lionel Trilling, constituted his imaginary minyan, his personal congregation.

Accordingly, the main line of his career looked like a conversation with his intellectual others, his fathers, each time viewed from a different angle, each time expounding a different Torah portion. Trilling was not Mark's only rabbi, and when in the 1990s Mark came upon the work of Geoffrey Hartman—largely the nontheoretical writing—he found a figure every bit as compelling as Trilling and with deep places that were beyond Trilling's grasp. Besides his early studies of Wordsworth and late writing about the Holocaust and the problematics of intellectual witness, Hartman's life was thick with trauma and loss, having been as a German child one of the last to escape to England with the Kindertransport. Moreover, best of all for Mark, Hartman was personally accessible as Mark got to know him in the 1990s. But it was Trilling to whom Mark returned again and again, writing no less than the book about him and two substantial essays afterward, both of which are included in his final collection of essays.[9] Because Mark kept refining and recomposing his views of Trilling, I'll restrict my remaining remarks to a few central issues in *Lionel Trilling and the Fate of Cultural Criticism*.

II

The self for Trilling is always a conscious, personal achievement,
an expression of free will. We may inherit our genes,
but we make our selves.
—Mark Krupnick

"I missed Trilling's leadership at the time," Mark wrote in *Lionel Trilling and the Fate of Cultural Criticism*, "and wrote about him with some bitterness in 1971. I am not disposed to judge him as harshly now as I did fifteen years ago. Given the uncertainties Trilling had about nearly everything, it was right for him to turn to history for understanding rather than to trumpet opinions about which he was unsure simply because, in his intellectual milieu, everyone was supposed to have a ready opinion about everything."[10]

Mark himself, as his career matured, turned decisively away from polemics as a calling, from the whole notion that thinking creatively about history, culture, and identity required one to have a ready and combative point of view. But then, jettisoning ready opinion, what else was there?

What lay beyond opinion itself, beyond posture, stance, and positioning, and how did Trilling point the way toward an answer? *Lionel Trilling and the Fate of Cultural Criticism* was the opening of that question, which Mark undertook in the spirit of cautious, probing inquiry. The Trilling whom Mark encountered was one who devoted his life to discovering an adequate relation to ideas and, even more critically, an adequate relation to himself.

Mark wrote of Trilling: "He conceives of his personal identity as being intimately involved with his relation to advanced ideas. He wants to be able to 'give the credence of my senses' to these ideas or better ones so that society will seem real to him. But the ultimate goal of his quest for an adequate theory remains personal. If society can be made to seem more intelligible and manageable, he will then feel more anchored and real in relation to that society."[11] It is not at all surprising that the book about Trilling should also be a book about Mark and that the Trilling he discovered was one whose particular steps toward becoming himself were of the greatest personal interest to him. Lionel Trilling comes into focus as a man who had been self-created through his relation to books. "The self for Trilling," he observed, "is always a conscious, personal achievement, an expression of free will. We may inherit our genes, but we make our selves."[12]

Lionel Trilling and the Fate of Cultural Criticism was far from being a one-dimensional study of a literary critic in search of himself by a literary critic in search of himself. It was a full-featured study of Trilling's mind, a mind in evolution, restless and ill at ease with itself. It disclosed, to use a jargon prevalent in the 1980s, a "decentered" Trilling who could say with Kafka, "What have I in common with the Jews? I scarcely have anything in common with myself." But then there was nothing quite so *au courant* about Mark's book; nothing in its critical lexicon suggested that Mark was out to postmodernize Lionel Trilling, to bring his self-confessed ambivalences up to date and repackage him for a new generation of scholars who had cut their teeth on *Tel Quel*. Mark's purposes were simpler and more direct: to model Trilling from the inside, to get behind the masks, the sententiae, the buzzwords and see plain the core of ambivalence that had brought such a tension into Trilling's essays.

Trilling, however, proved to be an elusive guide to Trilling. Though "the self" and its formation was the central preoccupation of his career, it was always abstracted, "*the* self," never *my*self. The first-person singular pronoun remained foreign to him, a ball that was always out of play, visible to the eye but bouncing around in foul territory. As Mark was quick to point out, Trilling presented himself as self-fashioned and yet always at the ready to alter the pattern. Was he a tailor's son for nothing? This sartor was perpetually resartus. Long before deconstruction became a fashion in the academy, Trilling was practicing it on himself, defending positions from one essay to the next that seemed to stand in opposition to each other, suggesting a turn of mind that Mark characterized as exhibiting an "allergy to closure." There was Trilling the Dionysus wannabe and Trilling the archaic torso of Apollo; Trilling who celebrated freedom from the conditioned life and Trilling who bemoaned the lightness of culture; there was Trilling who extolled the historical imagination and Trilling who invoked timeless mythic themes; there was Trilling who celebrated "the opposing self" and Trilling who exalted the middle class and defended William Dean Howells and his American faith in the "more smiling aspects of life"; Trilling who led the charge against the Popular Front in the 1940s and Trilling who confessed two decades later to fatigue before the vulgarities of "the movement." "Not having a fixed, easily summarized position is for Trilling itself a kind of position."[13] And again, "We need to speak not of fixed ideological positions but of alternations and fluctuations of mood. Trilling refines and corrects the culture by performing these operations first on himself."[14] What kind of a father was that? Was this not maddening? Was this the house in which Mark, having left his father's home in Irvington, was going to live? Not at all. What Mark finally responded to in this long immersion in Trilling and which surfaces boldly in *Deep Places* was not the fussiness, the conspicuous ambivalence, the meandering positions and fluctuating moods, the dissolving ego. It was the sturdiness of the writing itself, the lessons in applied psychoanalysis, the depths Trilling could reach in his portraits of artists in "The Poet as Hero: Keats in His Letters," "Freud: Within and Beyond Culture," "Emma and the Legend of Jane Austen," "Isaac Babel," and "Joyce in His Letters." These were durable goods indeed, as the 2001 publication of Trilling's major essays under the title of *The Moral Obligation to Be Intelligent*[15] abundantly testifies. Mark may have written about the polemical Trilling, the Trilling of opinions and their discontents, but what he absorbed through decades of sustained reading was another Trilling, the portraitist, the character analyst, the writer of indelible cameos, the Trilling who without fanfare plumbed the deep places of the imagination by immersing himself in the lives of others. Here Mark found the occluded Trilling, the novelist manqué but also the novelist redux, who was far more adept at creating characters in his critical essays than ever he had been in his stories and his novel. This was also Trilling the psychoanalyst, applying what he had gathered from Freud's theories and from his own years on the couch. And it was also Trilling the rabbi of character, as understood by the nineteenth century, a composite of reason, durability, rectitude, and judgment. In absorbing these lessons, Mark Krupnick became this unlikely rabbi's belated talmid.

Notes

This essay is freely adapted from the author's introduction to the book of Mark Krupnick's essays, *Jewish Writing and the Deep Places of the Imagination*, ed. Jean K. Carney and Mark Shechner (Madison: University of Wisconsin Press, 2005).

1. "Lionel Trilling: Criticism and Illusion," *Modern Occasions* 1, no. 2 (Winter 1971), pp. 282–287.

2. Mark Krupnick, "Lionel Trilling: Criticism and Illusion," *Modern Occasions* 1, no. 2 (Winter 1971), pp. 285, 286.

3. See Mark's essay "He Never Learned to Swim: A Memoir of Philip Rahv," *The New Review* (London) 2 (January 1976), pp. 33–39.

4. Diana Trilling, *The Beginning of the Journey: The Marriage of Diana and Lionel Trilling* (New York: Harcourt Brace & Company, 1993).

5. "A Marriage of True Minds," *Salmagundi* 103 (Summer 1994), pp. 213–224. That review was substantially revised for the *Jewish Writing* volume.

6. "Fathers, Sons, and New York Intellectuals," *Salmagundi* 54 (Fall 1981), pp. 106–120.

7. Mark Krupnick, "Fathers, Sons, and New York Intellectuals," *Salmagundi* 54 (Fall 1981), pp. 106–120.

8. Though Mark did not write about Derrida again after his collection of essays *Displacement: Derrida and After* (Bloomington: Indiana University Press, 1983), he continued to read him, at least his personal books. Among the books he kept at his bedside were Derrida's *The Work of Mourning* and *The Gift of Death*.

9. The long essays are "Lionel Trilling and the Politics of Style," in *American Literary Landscapes: The Fiction and the Fact*, ed. Ian F.A. Bell and D.K. Adams, pp. 152–170 (London: Vision Press and New York: St. Martin's Press, 1988), and "Jewish Intellectuals and 'The Deep Places of the Imagination,'" *Shofar* March 23, 2003, pp. 29–47. Both are reprinted in *Jewish Writing and the Deep Places of the Imagination*.

10. Mark Krupnick, *Lionel Trilling and the Fate of Cultural Criticism* (Evanston, IL: Northwestern University Press, 1986), p.149.

11. Krupnick, *Lionel Trilling and the Fate of Cultural Criticism*, p. 20.

12. Krupnick, *Lionel Trilling and the Fate of Cultural Criticism*, p. 21.

13. Krupnick, *Lionel Trilling and the Fate of Cultural Criticism*, p. 58.

14. Krupnick, *Lionel Trilling and the Fate of Cultural Criticism*, p. 125.

15. Lionel Trilling, *On the Moral Obligation to be Intelligent: Selected Essays*, ed. Leon Wieseltier (New York: Farrar, Straus & Giroux, 2001).

Introduction to the Forum

For this forum, we invited leading public intellectuals to share their answers to four key questions about the history, influence, and current status of Jewish American public intellectuals. We were pleased when Morris Dickstein, Nathan Glazer, Peter Novick, and Alan Wolfe agreed to participate. We gave participants considerable latitude in their answers; they could choose to answer each question sequentially, answer only selected questions, or use the questions as a prompt to write a related essay.

1. What do you think characterizes the tradition of the Jewish American public intellectual? Who, in your mind, are the leading figures?

2. Fifty years ago, the New York Intellectuals played a prominent role in the world of literary and political opinion. What do you think were the most important contributions of the New York Intellectuals to the tradition of the public intellectual in America? Do you think that they are a phenomenon of the past or that the tradition they founded is alive and well today?

3. Who are the public intellectuals of today? What specific groups of Jewish public intellectuals stand out? How important are the neoconservatives as a group of Jewish thinkers, and why are they now so prominent?

4. How do you feel connected to the/a tradition of the Jewish public intellectual? How do you feel connected to the Jews?

Alan Wolfe

1. I guess this is the appropriate place just to remind readers that not all the New York Intellectuals were Jewish. Mary McCarthy, Dwight Macdonald, and others shared with the Jewish intellectuals just about all the characteristics that made them what they were, including their literary sensibility; their ability to write about many subjects; their political passion; their wit; and their on-again, off-again relationship with the left. And without wanting to be too much of a troublemaker, I also have trouble ranking them. Some were leaders in the creative arts, others were scholars, and still others were political thinkers. If we think in

terms of long-term significance, Arendt would probably be the most important, but that is because philosophy usually deals with issues of permanent human interest. In that sense, her work on the human condition will surely outlast the more topical considerations of Macdonald or the textually dependent ones of a Philip Rahv. Her philosophical work will also survive her own more unfortunate comments about Little Rock or Eichmann.

2. I do not believe that they were a once-only phenomenon. The tradition to which they contributed is very much alive today. Although many Jews can be found among today's best public intellectuals, the current group is far more diverse in terms of gender and race than the group of the 1950s. And there are not as many little magazines with great influence in the culture as there were. But more books are read by more people; there are limitless media outlets; and the public still wants to hear from people with interesting things to say. The professionalization of academic life for a while had a negative impact on public intellectuals, but the hunger has returned and purely academic scholarship is increasingly self-referential. The opportunities to be a public intellectual are exciting and numerous.

3. I do not think that neoconservatives are all that important as public intellectuals today. Some of the older generation—Daniel Bell and Nathan Glazer—never really became neoconservatives. Those who chose to identify with the Republican Party are more policy wonks these days than intellectuals because in the interest of defending the president they rarely put aside their partisanship. (Indeed the way conservative intellectuals closed ranks around George W. Bush in 2004 despite the president's disastrous policies serves to remind us that many of them were once involved in the sectarian left.) The so-called Straussians have had little of importance to say since they decided to become players in politics rather than thinkers.

Morris Dickstein

1. There is no single tradition of Jewish intellectuals in America. Apart from the brief career of poet Emma Lazarus, there weren't any Jews among prominent American intellectuals until the First World War, though there was a huge intellectual ferment within the immigrant world itself, as Hutchins Hapgood reported in *The Spirit of the Ghetto* (1902). The children of German Jews were the first to breach the barriers. Ludwig Lewisohn could not secure a teaching job in English after gaining a Ph.D. at Columbia, but Walter Lippmann launched a brilliant career as a journalist soon after graduating from Harvard in 1910; Horace Kallen, who had been William James's teaching assistant at Harvard, wrote pioneering essays on America's nascent multiculturalism; Alfred Stieglitz, Paul Rosenfeld, and Waldo Frank played key roles in promoting the new modernist

culture that followed the war. Except for Kallen, an early Zionist as well as a theorist of cultural pluralism, none of them made much of their Jewish background, and Lippmann remained in virtual denial until the end of his long life.

In the late 1920s, a self-consciously Jewish but not parochial group of intellectuals took shape around Elliot Cohen and the *Menorah Journal*. In the early essays and stories of Lionel Trilling, one of Cohen's young discoveries, we can see these writers reaching for the cultural mainstream while wrestling with issues of Jewish identity, a concern largely buried when the New York intellectuals emerged as political and literary figures in the 1930s and 1940s. Their passage through Marxism made them determined universalists, and their exuberant discovery of the wealth of Western culture encouraged them to turn their backs on the ghetto and reject the material dreams of the Jewish middle class. But their Jewishness was inscribed in the very lilt of their sentences, their aggressive, ironic style of argument, and above all their affinity for the radical perspectives of modernist literature, Marxism, and psychoanalysis, all pioneered by secular Jews. The Holocaust, the Eichmann trial, and the rise of a vigorous Jewish American literature gradually awakened them to the significance of their origins. Once the Jewish world of Europe went under, they tried to recover parts of a Jewish past they had left behind or never known. Irving Howe's anthologies of Yiddish literature and Alfred Kazin's lyrical memoirs were early landmarks of this return.

2. At a time when American culture and politics remained isolated from the world at large, the great contribution of New York Intellectuals was their cosmopolitanism, which came through in their range of reference to art, politics, literature, history, philosophy, and the broad traditions of European culture. While the literary curriculum still favored cozy, middlebrow American authors, they followed one of their role models, Edmund Wilson, in writing about Flaubert and Kafka, Proust and Joyce. They were attuned to new currents of twentieth-century thought, beginning with Marx and Freud, but also to the rise of totalitarian fascism and communism, which did not yet alarm most Americans, who had always felt secure an ocean away from the Old World. But this orientation toward Europe also narrowed their perspective because they were much more preoccupied with the Russian Revolution and the Spanish Civil War than with anything actually happening in the United States. In their heart of hearts they still considered this a provincial country with boring democratic politics and an undeveloped, undemanding culture that scarcely repaid an intellectual's sharp-witted attention.

Their worldliness got a boost from the arrival of so many European emigrés in the thirties and forties, which tremendously enlivened the art and literary scene, the psychoanalytic world, and many academic disciplines, including history, art history, sociology, and political theory. But the lofty disdain of the Europeans sharpened the intellectuals' contempt for popular culture. They remained oblivious to important features of American life. The one development they connected with perhaps too strongly was the cold war, despite their embarrassment with a demagogue like McCarthy. The anti-Soviet mood seemed at once a fulfilment and a travesty of their own earlier anti-Stalinism. Once America became a bulwark against the Soviet Union, the intellectuals lost some of the critical perspective that had been so essential for them. Previously little more than a New York-based fringe group without wide readership or influence, they were now being discovered and acclaimed. From this followed the neoconservative turn that brought erstwhile Trotskyists into the heart of the establishment. Some grew intoxicated with their proximity to power. Pulling back from liberal universalism, they threw in their lot with Jewish and national interests as they saw them. Though they mocked liberal altruism, they remained committed to the welfare state that liberalism had conceived as a safety net in a market economy.

3. For all the laments over the "last intellectuals," not only were intellectuals furiously active in debates over the invasion of Iraq but, in the case of the neoconservatives, exerted real influence over policy. In the debates leading up to the war, Jews on the left were divided between liberal hawks like Paul Berman and editors of the *New Republic*, on one hand, and antiwar voices ranging from moderates like Michael Walzer to ultraleftists such as Noam Chomsky. But the catastrophic aftermath of the invasion and the Bush administration's domestic policies unified the opposition in ways not seen in many a year. A growing sense of crisis made politics an overweening interest. At the same time, there was also a considerable shift among literary intellectuals from arcane theory toward public intellectual activity, so that they too were drawn toward real politics rather than the pseudopolitics of postmodern theory.

Both at home and abroad, the Bush years were a calamity—for the nation's economy and for its standing in the world—but a bonanza for mainstream intellectual journals like the *Nation*, the *New Republic*, *Dissent*, the *New York Review of Books*, the online bloggers, and the opinion pages of major newspapers. But the neoconservatives became the most distinctive *Jewish* current, largely because their aggressive views on foreign policy were partly motivated by their support for Israel, which sometimes came down to blanket support for the maximalist agenda of the Israeli right. The neocons were often seen as the second coming of Wilsonian idealism, trying to spread American democracy throughout the world, a theme that George W. Bush took up with gusto. But Wilson favored the dismantling of existing empires, and he was anything but a unilateralist, whereas the leading neocons, such as Paul Wolfowitz, though undoubtedly sincere in their convictions, provided rhetorical cover for policymakers whose goal was the expansion of American power in the post–cold-war world. Such an idealist cover for raw exertions of power is anything but in the Jewish tradition. Conversely, the scrupulous reflections on the moral calculus of war by writers like Walzer, Berman, and Leon Wieseltier did honor to that tradition.

4. Often to their own sorrow, Jews have been at the hinge of modern history, from the Dreyfus case, which led to the emergence of intellectuals as a class, to the Balfour declaration, the Russian revolution, the Holocaust, and the Israeli-Arab wars. This remains even more true today, with a billion Muslims angry about

Palestine and about America's role in the Middle East. For decades, the New York Intellectuals scarcely acknowledged they were Jews. Today, ethnicity is an inescapable aspect of identity, and Israel's position in the post-Holocaust world makes complex claims on every Jew. But Jewish intellectuals somehow need to honor their own traditions, American as well as Jewish, while finding ways of transcending them whenever necessary. Patriotism and tribalism have their claims, family claims, but there are also broader values at the heart of both these traditions, including a reverence for human life; a respect for the dignity of the other; a recoil from manifestations of blatant inequality and exploitation; a skepticism about false prophets and self-proclaimed Messiahs; and, especially, a disinclination to dominate others, even for their own supposed benefit. It is at once Jewish and American to intervene against genocide but not to try to spread democracy by the sword over the wishes of those whose lives are at stake. The second Bush administration witnessed an intermittent turn toward persuasion over force, not for moral reasons but because the resistance of opponents and allies alike left the nation's military overextended.

Because Jews were powerless through most of their history, as thinkers, for better or worse, they have played the role of moralists, rational analysts, and committed or disinterested critics. The career of Henry Kissinger shows how badly they can go astray on the morally barren terrain of power politics. Even the literary critics I most admire—including Jews like Trilling, Alfred Kazin, Irving Howe, Harold Bloom, and Geoffrey Hartman and honorary Jews like Wilson, F.R. Leavis, Raymond Williams, and Frank Kermode—blended their response to art with a deep moral sensitivity, an understanding that books were not simply exercises in form but morally grounded interventions in real human situations—the impressionable minds of living readers as well as the complex fate of literary characters. These critics were worldly and secular but understood how the Enlightenment had secularized our moral and religious traditions, not to explode these traditions but to salvage them in modern terms. They set out to transpose those older ideals into a new era otherwise dominated by science, technology, self-seeking commercial goals, irrational will, and a resurgent nationalism. They looked to literature as a site of endangered human values. Open to self-criticism, at their best they were moralists without being ideologues, ruefully aware of how the unpredictable ironies of history can find ways to upend our cocksure confidence. As fundamentalisms grow stronger and suicidal terrorism revives a familiar cult of action and blind belief, we need more of the bracing skepticism and the ethic of public responsibility that Jewish intellectuals like Isaiah Berlin made their own.

Peter Novick

More than one community of intellectuals has become the object of "those were the days" nostalgia: Bloomsbury in the early years of the twentieth century, Oxford philosophical circles in the thirties, the habitués of the Café Flore after the Second World War. But few groups have been as frequently celebrated as the New York Intellectuals of the 1940s and 1950s. Both individually and collectively they have been the subject of dozens of books and of almost cultish hero worship. It's a wonder that there aren't New York Intellectual trading cards. "I'll give you two Harold Rosenbergs and a Clement Greenberg for a mint condition 'Norman Podhoretz as Rookie of the Year.'" Now we have the present volume, and what is there left to say?

The first thing I can think of to say is that to speak of the New York *Jewish* Intellectuals requires some sleight of hand. Although most of the intellectuals associated with *Partisan Review* in these years were Jewish, lots of the most important ones, including Edmund Wilson, W.H. Auden, Dwight Macdonald, and C. Wright Mills, weren't. And what of the fractional cases: should we count half of Richard Hofstadter and a quarter each of Mary McCarthy and Arthur Schlesinger? If we're concerned with the *Partisan Review* community *as a community*, this sort of division makes no sense, any more than would considering the male and female members separately. I'm going to be a good soldier, and (mostly) just discuss the Jews, but—for the record—I don't think it makes much sense.

The second thing that occurs to me is that we would do well to avoid the neologism *public intellectual* when talking about these people. I don't know what they would have made of the phrase, but it certainly wasn't part of their vocabulary during the years in question. Apart from vagrant earlier uses that never took hold, the phrase entered the language when Russell Jacoby used it in his 1987 *The Last Intellectuals*—an elegy for the last *real* intellectuals, whose mark of distinction was that they weren't academics. Unlike cloistered and constrained scholars who spoke jargon to a "private" audience of fellow members of a discipline, *public* intellectuals, Jacoby wrote, were independent, free spirits who spoke in plain language to the larger public. The problems with the phrase as applied to the group we're concerned with are legion. Let me mention a few.

To begin with, many of the most important members of the *Partisan Review* group were lifelong academics. In the older generation this was true of Sidney Hook, Lionel Trilling, and Meyer Shapiro. Among those a few years younger, it was true of Hofstadter, Schlesinger, Gertrude Himmelfarb, Seymour Martin Lipset, and Mills. And, of course, as Jacoby acknowledges, by the end of the fifties practically *all* of the core members (except for the elderly) had found academic employment: Hannah Arendt, Alfred Kazin, Daniel Bell, Irving Howe, and Nathan Glazer to name just a few. There were a few elders—Edmund Wilson is the most notable—for whom staying aloof from the academy was a matter of principle. But young Jewish intellectuals like Bell, Howe, and Glazer had no animus against the academy: the only reason they didn't immediately join university faculties was a tough job market—all the tougher for them because of academic antisemitism. As the academic market improved and antisemitic barriers fell, they enthusiastically took up faculty positions.

Is it that the quality of the work of these relative late-comers to the academy declined after they found academic employment? I won't attempt to award grades to their pre- and postacademic writings, but I think the case for decline would be a hard one to make. Certainly that work didn't become noticeably narrower or more academic; most continued to write on a broad range of issues in works aimed at various audiences. (I was briefly inclined to acknowledge that previous journalistic employment—with exigent weekly deadlines—might help account for the extraordinary productivity of individuals like Bell, Howe, and Glazer. But a moment's reflection made it clear that many of those who had always been academics—Hofstadter, Schlesinger, Lipset, Mills, Himmelfarb—were just as productive.)

There is no doubt that those clustered around *Partisan Review* considered themselves *intellectuals*, but their sense of what that meant coexisted uneasily with the idea of addressing a broad public. Recall their commitment to literary and artistic modernism, which virtually insisted that work of high quality be *difficult*: that it *not* be widely accessible. To a very considerable extent those associated with *Partisan Review* were writing for each other, with outsiders being allowed, so to speak, to eavesdrop. Those members of the group with primarily literary interests often wrote for other "little magazines," but given the equally derisory circulations of those journals, this was hardly addressing "the public." Some found a slightly larger audience in magazines like the *New Leader* and *Commentary* but their appearance in such pages was as much a matter of finding paid employment as of choosing an audience. Of the four members of the group featured in the documentary *Arguing the World*, Bell had been managing editor of the *New Leader*; Glazer and Irving Kristol had been editors of *Commentary*; and both Bell and Howe wrote for it. For several years in the fifties Bell and Howe worked for Henry Luce: Bell (full-time) at *Fortune*, Howe (part-time) at *Time*. There don't seem to be any grounds for believing that they regretted leaving the world of the mass media for the academy at the end of the decade, but there is every reason to believe that they experienced the change as a liberation rather than a loss of influence.

Speaking of influence, far-reaching claims are often made for the influence of the New York Jewish Intellectuals. To cite only the most readily available example, the editor of this volume tells us in the introduction that they "achieved great influence in American society." This is not the place for a systematic examination of the claim, but it's worth asking what evidence can be cited to sustain it. Insofar as the group had a "mission" it was anticommunism: in the cultural realm, they were partisans of high modernism in opposition to the Popular Front aesthetic whose heroes were Rockwell Kent and Howard Fast; in the political realm, they stood for opposition to Stalin's blood-soaked tyranny and its American apologists. (To consider one of the least overtly political members of the group, Lionel Trilling later described his writings in the forties and fifties as driven by his opposition to "the commitment that a large segment of the intelligentsia of the West gave to the degraded version of Marxism known as Stalinism.") As a description of the political complexion of the American intelligentsia in the late thirties this was, with some allowance for hyperbole, not unreasonable. With a considerably greater allowance, the description wasn't totally off the mark in 1946 and 1947. But under the impact of world events, and not at all as a result of any intellectual influences, this was rapidly ceasing to be the case by 1948, was fading into oblivion by 1949, and was quite out of sight by 1950. (Insofar as a considerable number of Americans with illusions about the USSR came to abandon those illusions at this time, the last place they would have sought guidance would have been from those who had been regularly ridiculing them for more than a decade.) Speaking personally, as one whose political formation and continuing commitments have been firmly and strongly anticommunist, I wholeheartedly applaud (whatever my doubts about its efficacy) their self-assigned "mission," in the context in which it arose. But throughout the 1950s—and beyond—many if not most of the New York Intellectuals continued to believe that their continuing crusade against communism here and abroad constituted an "adversarial," "embattled," and "courageous" stance. As Orwell somewhere remarks, there are things so absurd that only an intellectual could believe them.

One should not, of course, reduce the question of the influence of the New York Intellectuals to their anticommunist crusade—and I'm aware that I have here only expressed skepticism and not made a detailed case for their noninfluence in that realm. But what other claims are there? What *precisely* was Lionel Trilling's influence on the study and appreciation of literature—at the time and subsequently? What is the legacy for social thought of the writings of Daniel Bell and Nathan Glazer? That phrases like "the end of ideology" were momentarily *le sound bite du jour* is surely true, but are things like that more than footnotes to the intellectual history of the twentieth century? What sort of "influence" did Howe's *World of Our Fathers* wield—apart from giving American Jews a warm "rootsy" glow at a time when such sentimental nostalgia was in fashion?

Finally, there is the often-encountered invidious contrast between the plain-spoken, accessible writing of literary critics like Howe and Trilling in the forties and fifties, and the pretentious, incomprehensible theorizing of today's academic critics. As a (not very theoretical) historian I don't have a horse in this race, but I have my doubts about the historical accuracy of the contrast. The 1952 *New York Times* review of one of Irving Howe's first works began, "If you will be charitable enough to put up with Mr. Howe's bloodcurdlingly-pedantic jargon . . . you can learn quite a lot about the novels and stories of William Faulkner." Concerning Trilling I would offer for consideration the recent observations of Louis Menand concerning the claim that Trilling's criticism was not distorted by "the theoretical." To the contrary, Menand said,

Trilling labored under a ponderous theoretical apparatus, whose elements
he took from Hegel, Nietzsche, and Freud. . . . He took works of literature to
be meditations on the issues that were important to his thinkers—negation,
the will, the "reality principle"—in much the way that a feminist or multi-
culturalist critic does today.

Narratives of declension are nowadays à la mode, whether it's a matter of
how, politically, we don't measure up to the founding fathers of the republic, or
culturally, we have failed to produce the likes of the New York Intellectuals. In
both cases this kind of invidious and ahistorical framing interferes with rather
than enhances a proper appreciation of the work of those who came before us.

Nathan Glazer

The New York Intellectuals, American Jewish Version

New York, intellectuals, Jews? How do we put them together, and why does "New
York Jewish Intellectual" have a distinctive resonance today?

New York was at the dominating center of American intellectual life for a
relatively brief period from the early twentieth century, when it displaced Boston,
to perhaps the 1960s and 1970s, when it was supplemented if not displaced by the
rapid growth and intellectual opening of American universities and by the rise of
national power in the post–World War II period, which also meant displacement
in part by Washington. (Note the move of the *New Republic* to Washington, the
later move of the *Public Interest*, the expansion of think tanks in Washington;
note how few of the reviewers of the *New York Review of Books* live in New York.)
The preeminence of New York was based in large part on the existence of a large
Bohemian quarter in Greenwich Village unrelated (in contrast to Paris's Fifth Ar-
rondissement) to New York's universities, to which nonconformists and creative
types from the rest of the country could escape and in which they could flourish.
There was a Jewish element but a relatively small one in the Greenwich Village of
the earlier period—let us say, the first twenty years of the century—and an even
smaller Jewish element in the publishing industry that had become centered in
New York. Despite Alfred A. Knopf and Simon and Schuster, who had set up
business in the 1920s, New York publishing still had very few Jews as late as the
1960s. And while I do not want to get hung up in trying to define *intellectual*, the
intellectual must be to some degree connected to publishing.

New York City by the 1920s had become almost one-third Jewish, the
effect of the mass immigration of the earlier part of the century from Eastern
Europe. The predominance demographically of a group strongly committed to
education made it inevitable that Jews would become prominent in New York

intellectual life. Jews formed overwhelming majorities of the students of the public colleges (not of the faculties) that were a unique feature of New York City. They would certainly have formed large majorities of the students of Columbia and New York University by the 1920s were it not for Jewish-restricting quotas. Although a prevailing and gentlemanly antisemitism served to limit the Jewish role in publishing, nothing prevented Jews from joining in large number the life of the Bohemian quarters. If we speak of an age of "Jewish American public intellectuals," we have in mind primarily the group around the *Partisan Review*, later the group around *Commentary*. We can add a good number of more or less closely related journals and a few publishing houses, but I speak of a defining core. This core was based on the coming together of a few historical accidents that cannot be and will not be repeated.

One was the dominance of New York City in publishing, especially of serious or semiserious journals—one must include the *New Yorker*, which paid so well and gave place to so many of the intellectuals first connected to the defining core (Harold Rosenberg, Dwight Macdonald, Hannah Arendt, and others).

A second was the dominance of Jews demographically in New York City, leading to more than dominance in the intellectual life of the city.

The third was a distinctive moment in the history of American Judaism and Jewishness, in which assimilation was dominant and almost unchallenged and in which no Jewish interests excited or involved Jewish intellectuals.

A fourth—which somewhat explains the third—was the dominance of Marxism, in political and economic thinking, and of modernism and experimentalism in literature and culture generally, in the group of free, institutionally unconnected intellectuals who gathered in New York City.

A fifth was the intellectual conservatism and ethnic exclusiveness of leading American colleges and universities, which excluded the most original minds and most Jews from faculties.

A sixth was the inflow of highly educated German and other central European Jewish scholars and intellectuals, many of whom could not establish themselves in the universities at the time. These immigrants widened the perspective of native American Jewish intellectuals coming from nonintellectual homes, who had received at best a mediocre education.

Note how time-bound almost all of these factors are: the Jewish percentage of New York City has dropped as Jews spread out to the suburbs, the West, and the South; the Holocaust and the fate of Israel have become dominant themes of culture and politics generally; Marxism has been reduced to a cult, and modernism has lost its shaping characteristics; colleges and universities are now open to all and strive to connect with the most advanced thought in all fields; and we will never again see an intellectual impact matching the tide of Central European Jewish refugees of the 1930s.

A few words about the term *intellectual* are now necessary. I believe the term comes from the conflict between Dreyfusards and anti-Dreyfusards in late nineteenth-century France. It does not mean a scholar, an academic, a novelist or poet, an artist or art critic; it means any of those engaged in such pursuits who also speak out on public affairs, who are called because of their prominence to speak out, and who respond to the call. It does not mean a political scientist, economist, or sociologist who pursues research and publication on public affairs. It may mean any such if they attempt regularly to speak to the public on issues on which they have no authority as a result of their professional calling and research. The United States has more faculty members in its colleges and universities perhaps than England, Germany, Italy, and Spain combined. That does not mean it has more public intellectuals; it very likely has fewer.

We have to think of the New York Jewish Intellectuals of the middle of the last century as a unique phenomenon caused by the conjuncture of historical events I have outlined above. But even if today books and theses are written on them and every last letter or anecdote, it seems, is noted, we should not exaggerate their influence. They were "public" in their pronouncements, but the public they addressed was miniscule. Who could have noted Dwight Macdonald and Clement Greenberg writing in *Partisan Review* at the beginning of World War II that it was an "imperialist" war and there was no reason for those fighting for a better world to choose sides? One can be sure no Washingtonian of importance noted it, and no major American columnist or commentator would have been aware of it. The "publicness" of the American Jewish intellectuals preceded their prominence. Clement Greenberg became a major figure in American art criticism, Dwight Macdonald a major figure in the criticism of popular culture, but these roles came long after their role as commentators on the large movements of the time had been abandoned.

What is interesting today is that despite the vast increase in the number of Jewish academics and cultural figures in all fields, we have no sense that they make up a distinctive political and cultural environment, a circle, a world. They are marked by the general liberalism that is characteristic of American Jews by and large. Unlike their forebears as American Jewish political intellectuals, they are scattered across all the major universities and colleges of the country. In contrast to their forebears, they accept their Jewishness—how could it be rejected after the Holocaust and the establishment of the permanently imperiled state of Israel? They do not change their names anymore (there is no longer an advantage in doing so). Their strong interest in Jewish affairs contrasts strikingly with the earlier group of Jewish public intellectuals who, along with Rosa Luxemburg, would have proudly said that Jewish problems had no greater claim on them than Chinese or Indian. The most striking thing about *Partisan Review* and the early *Commentary*, if one reads them today, is how little they were moved by Jewish tragedy, Jewish accomplishment, Jewish peril. We have to go back to the roles of Marxism and modernism to explain this oddity.

Today Jews as individuals are influential in almost every sector of American society, and proportionately more of them are influential than is the case for any other group. But that influence is not as a linked group that one can name. They are influential as individual academics, journalists, college presidents, foundation executives, etc., etc., but not as Jewish academics, Jewish college presidents, Jewish columnists, Jewish journalists.

The idea that we can find a "corporate identity" as intellectuals and as Jews linking a group of Jewish intellectuals today is found only in the case of the neoconservatives.

The term *neoconservatism* has had a strange career. It seems to have been coined by the socialist Michael Harrington to describe a group of intellectuals in the early 1970s who were moving away from not only Marxism and socialism but to some extent from liberalism itself. They were the editors and some of the writers of the *Public Interest* and *Commentary*—Irving Kristol, Norman Podhoretz, Daniel Bell, Daniel P. Moynihan, James Q. Wilson, the present writer, and others. Not all had been socialists and Marxists in their youths; not all were Jews; but the two magazines gave them a group identity as skeptics and critics over some developments in liberalism and in particular affirmative action.

The idea of neoconservatism initially described no special perspective in foreign policy. Both the neoconservatives and those who labeled them such were fierce opponents of the Soviet Union and communism, though they may have disagreed over what policies were necessary to undermine communism and limit communist expansion. The history of the word and its uses would take us far afield: today it refers to a distinctive group of hawks in foreign policy, in particular a small group, mostly Jews, who defend an activist and unilateral foreign and military policy in defense of democracy and, more than that, seek its expansion in the unlikely area of the Near East. Their critics think the stance of this group is too much affected by one dominant interest, the defense of Israel. The mere fact that they can be suspected of being motivated by such an interest shows how different they are from the original group of Jewish public intellectuals, one of whose major marks of distinctiveness was an indifference to Jewish concerns. There is no way of controlling how words are used: launched into the public domain, they come to mean what people who use them want them to mean. But some of the original neoconservatives, it should be noted, are unhappy over what the term has come to mean, and would not identify themselves with that meaning.

Beyond

What (Do?) a Transcendentalist, an Abolitionist-Women's Rights Activist, and a Race Man Have to Do with the New York Intellectuals?

Ryan Schneider

Like many of the thinkers and writers featured in the Beyond section of this volume, the three figures whose work I address here—Ralph Waldo Emerson, Frances E.W. Harper, and W.E.B. Du Bois—may not seem directly relevant to study of the New York Intellectuals. Indeed, all the essays in this section offer some response, direct or indirect, to the perception of such a disconnect. Yet these pieces constitute a collective comparison vis-à-vis the New York Intellectuals that reveals key themes and tensions, particularly in the political realm, that have shaped public intellectualism in the United States from the nineteenth century to the present.

Chief among these themes is the distinction between knowledge gained through institutional education and that acquired through individual and social experience—the latter being a crucial characteristic of what Gramsci famously called the "organic" intellectual. Defining what counts as experiential knowledge and assessing its value as a rhetorical strategy has been and remains a necessary and difficult task for U.S. intellectuals—necessary because of the anti-intellectualism that exists as a none-too-subtle subtext of American cultural expression and difficult because this subtext tends to advocate distrust or outright dismissal of knowledge not directly linked to some form of professionalism. Studying how intellectuals who lived and worked in other times and places have reckoned with this dilemma is worthwhile both for its own sake and as a means to further contextualize the various ways the New York Intellectuals perceived experiential knowledge and the extent to which they did or did not rely on it as a warrant for their cultural critiques.

Another theme underscored by the essays in this section is a tension inherent in the status of intellectuals as representative figures who speak from and for specific groups or communities (although they also may see themselves as addressing universal concerns). In basic terms: the more influential and well-known intellectuals become, the greater the risk that they will become alienated from their communities of origin. Meredith Goldsmith's essay on Anzia Yezierska's *Red Ribbon on a White Horse* illustrates how this tension manifests itself in terms of class and gender politics within the immigrant Jewish community of the 1920s, and my own analysis tracks its relation to the politics of race in the middle and latter decades of the nineteenth century.

The thinkers and writers featured in the Beyond section attempt (albeit for different purposes and to different degrees) to make political and social activism a meaningful dimension of their intellectual visions. And in doing so, they often confront not only the risk of becoming alienated from their communities of origin but also the possibility of being co-opted by the dominant or popular ideology they seek to comment upon or critique. Examining how they apprehend and deal with this potential threat to their own critical autonomy and integrity (if in fact they do see it as a threat) can again provide a rich field for comparative analysis—just as Matthew Abraham demonstrates in his reading Edward Said's concept of the "exile" subject position (with its attendant notions of critical edginess and independence) as a variation and reaffirmation of the New York Intellectuals' early rejection of dominant power structures.

My goal in this essay is to elaborate on the key themes and tensions outlined above by looking closely at the realms of art, ethics, and politics—realms that, as several other essays in this volume make clear, have always been of particular concern to Jewish public intellectuals in the U.S. I seek to add yet another dimension to the discussion of these realms by considering concepts of public intellectualism put forth by those from earlier times and different ethnic and religious backgrounds—concepts that, by and large, began germinating during the hugely popular lyceum movement of the early nineteenth century, continued to grow and develop in the hothouse of pre–Civil War reform efforts, and flowered in diverse ways during Reconstruction- and post–Reconstruction-era movements for social reorganization.

I will pause here to emphasize that I am not claiming special status for Emerson, Harper, and Du Bois—that they are somehow more worthy of consideration than other thinkers of the nineteenth and early twentieth centuries. I am attempting, rather, to create as much space as possible for provocative and useful responses to issues raised throughout this volume.

Looking back to conc pts such as Ralph Waldo Emerson's scholar-poet can, for example, enrich discussion of questions Mark Krupnick raises in his examination in this volume of the artistic dimensions and purposes of public intellectual work: "Have American Jewish intellectuals penetrated to the 'deep places of the imagination'"? "What are these 'deep places,' and why should intellectuals, Jewish or otherwise, wish to get to them?" (p. 60).

Such comparative, diachronic analysis works equally well when we shift to the realm of ethics. In the mid-nineteenth century, Frances Harper, a rising star on the antislavery lecture circuit who also spoke in support of the women's rights and temperance movements, began to create a system of ethics meant to govern public intellectual practice—a system inspired and shaped in part by the marginalization she experienced as an African American woman. As I will show, Harper's ethics—at once Christian and utilitarian—can stand in mutually revealing juxtaposition to discussions of ethical issues for Jewish intellectuals, many of whom, Daniel R. Schwarz argues in this volume, follow the Talmudic tradition of extracting moral implications from the Bible for practical application to the everyday world, resulting in a mode of thinking derived "more from practice than theology" (p. 52).

Comparative studies of the kind I am sketching out here also hold potential to supplement discussions of the political work public intellectuals perform, particularly in relation to issues of ethnic or racial identity. Most scholars of U.S. culture are familiar with W.E.B. Du Bois's concept of double-consciousness and his claim that the color-line is the "problem of the twentieth century," and most would recognize the relevance of these concepts to the study of race relations. Du Bois's work is also crucial, however, to the study of public intellectualism. He sought not only to critique the view of African American identity as problematic but also to reshape and redefine his own status as a race man—a leading black male intellectual. Du Bois's desire to find a corrective to the politics of identity that he saw as unnecessarily problematizing both his status and that of the race as a whole led him to begin serious study of communism. In this sense, his theory and practice of public intellectualism has much in common with that of many young Jewish intellectuals of the 1920s and 1930s who, Nathan Abrams argues in this volume, viewed Jewish identity as problematic and who looked outside their communities of origin—often to Marxism—for solutions (p. 19).

What follows will expand and elaborate on the issues and tensions outlined in the three analytical vignettes above. For reasons of expediency, I limit my remarks to art, ethics, and politics, treating them as independent, discrete categories despite their interdependence and capacity to account for only a portion of the broad and diverse range of work public intellectuals perform. Also, for reasons of clarity, even though each intellectual operated in all three arenas, I examine the work of only one figure as it is relevant to each category: Emerson's aesthetics and his vision of the scholar's relation to art; Harper's system of ethics and her view of the intellectual's role in shaping conduct in everyday life; Du Bois's politics of identity, specifically insofar as they influence the relation of the race man to the community of African Americans as a whole.

Intellectuals and Imagination

In his essay "Jewish Intellectuals and the 'Deep Places of the Imagination'" in this volume, Mark Krupnick poses the question of whether American Jewish intellectuals have achieved "the sublime combination of emotion and intellect characteristic of the greatest art" (p. 60)—a question initially asked by Lionel Trilling in *The Liberal Imagination* about American writers of the 1930s and 1940s whose literature was invested in issues of politics and social organization. Trilling viewed such concerns as a distraction from the kind of sustained engagement with emotion and imagination he believed was necessary for great art like that produced by the European modernists.

Krupnick takes up this standard for greatness and uses it to assess Trilling's own work along with that of Irving Howe and Alfred Kazin. In Krupnick's view, Trilling only rarely achieves the proper measure and balance of feeling and intellect, tending too much toward the latter; Howe follows suit. Kazin, conversely, doesn't achieve artistic success because his work is possessed of too much emotion and not enough intellect. Although it's possible to pick at some of Krupnick's conclusions, his critiques of the three intellectuals' failings as artists are leavened with insightful assessments of their critical acumen and ability (especially Kazin's) to help readers access literature in ways they otherwise might not have considered.

More interesting, at least for my purposes, than the debate over whether or how well these intellectuals measure up to Trilling's criteria for high art is the set of questions standing behind that debate, questions that address in more general form the relation of public intellectual work to art and emotion. Is there (should there be?) a distinction between criticism and creation? If not—and intellectuals are to be considered artists—then what place should emotions have in their work? What kinds of feelings should be expressed—and how and when should they be manifested?

Emerson, like Trilling, spent much time reflecting on the implications of intellectual forays into the deep places of the imagination. Such is clear from the artistic dimension of many of the terms he used to designate the public intellectual: poet, writer, orator, philosopher, historian, naturalist, prophet, Watcher, Thinker, Man Thinking, student of Man, and intellectual man. The terms were largely interchangeable, and Emerson deployed each of them in a variety of contexts, but he remained constant in his belief that intellectuals must see themselves as engaging in acts of creation. Moreover, they must do so with attention to the emotional component of artistic-intellectual work, particularly insofar as it links them to an audience.

In his notebooks, letters, lectures, and essays, Emerson returns again and again to the notion that scholars should employ both intellect and emotion to engage their audiences. In a journal passage that would later be reworked and integrated into his famous "American Scholar" address of 1837, he grapples with what he sees as the need to offer a "theory of the Scholar's function" and concludes that the scholar's office is to "arouse the intellect; to keep it erect & sound; to keep admiration in the hearts of the people; to keep the eye open upon its spiritual aims."[1] Combining the roles of artist and teacher, Emerson's scholar-poet relies on individual creative power to make and sustain an emotional connection to an audience without compromising the integrity of the intellectual message. Moreover, the Emersonian model conceptualizes intellectual-artistic expression as divine. Describing this phenomenon in his journals, Emerson writes, "Whoever creates is God," and goes on to suggest that the scholar-poet is capable of transcending quotidian concerns and topical issues in order to present an organic, unified vision of humankind's relation to the universe.[2]

Achieving a divine combination of intellectual and artistic expression is, of course, more difficult in practice than in theory. Emerson's scholar-poet is part and parcel of an aesthetics that is at once wildly optimistic about the redemptive possibilities of art to construct unity out of fragmentation and constantly aware that most creative expression utterly fails to achieve this ideal. Within this aesthetics, the same holds true for the status of emotion. Emerson is fascinated with its power to unify—to bring an audience together without undermining the individualism of each member. Yet he also is deeply anxious over the possibility that the linkage of intellect and emotion that underwrites expeditions into "deep places in the imagination" will result not in transformative acts of creation, divine and unifying, but rather in art that is shallow, imitative, and encouraging of conformity.

Having shown how, in his view, Jewish intellectuals have been less than successful in their art, Krupnick concludes his essay by asking why this is so: "What accounts for the relative failure of Jewish public intellectuals with regard to the imagination? How have the Jews managed in this respect in comparison with other groups such as African Americans or feminists or queer theorists or postcolonialists?" (p. 77). He suggests the answer may be found in an examination of Jewish art in light of Jewish social history and that he will leave that task to another observer.

My impulse is to respond not with social history but with a premise simultaneously less and more optimistic: no intellectual consistently plumbs the deep places in the imagination, and intra- and intergroup comparative judgments, even if they remain only propositions, rest on no viable standard of measurement. After all, to borrow Emerson's terms, "What is any man's book compared to the undiscoverable All?"[3] My sense, given his remarks about Trilling's unwillingness to define terms such as *emotion* and *imagination*, is that Krupnick would somewhat agree that we would be better off taking a broader, longer view—one that considers intellectual-artistic expression as a concept along with examining how it shapes and is shaped by social values and tensions. To do so would acknowledge that the study of intellectual work, Jewish or not, is served less by measurements of artistic failure or success and more by questions that allow for consideration of the complex and constant give-and-take between moments of imitation and conformity and moments of creative transformation.

Ethics, Ideals, and Everyday Life

The notion of a complex and constant give-and-take remains relevant when we shift our attention from the artistic to the ethical dimension of intellectual work. The oscillation here is not between the shallow and the deep or the imitative and the transformative but rather between the quotidian and the spiritual, the here and the hereafter. Also relevant is the fact that ethical dimensions of public intellectual work in the U.S. always have been shaped by a tension between concepts of divinely authored universal law (not open to individual interpretation) and pragmatic standards and guidelines for day-to-day conduct (generated through ongoing dialogue within local communities).

In his essay for this collection, Daniel R. Schwarz reminds us that these issues resonate strongly within Jewish culture because, historically, Jews have lived "on the margin—in ghettoes and shtetls, never sure of what pogroms tomorrow will bring" and, as a result, "have tended to be skeptical of sweeping universals and to dwell in particulars" (p. 51). Talmudic reading practices reinforce this worldview through emphasis on dialogic interpretation of texts and the premise that there is no pat answer to questions the texts may raise. What results, Schwarz argues, from this combination of cultural marginalization and Talmudic exegetical practice is a system of ethics that privileges concerns of day-to-day life over visions of the hereafter. This is something of a generalization, but it rings true; moreover, it invites us to continue the thread of discussion by asking how intellectuals, particularly those occupying other marginal positions in U.S. culture, might perceive the relation between universal values or laws and the necessities and limitations of everyday life and how those perceptions might, in turn, shape the work they do in the public sphere. I want to bring Frances Harper into this discussion because she is an architect of an ethical system the structure of which stands in revealing comparison to that described by Schwarz.

Born into freedom in 1825, Harper was educated at her uncle William Watkins's Academy for Negro Youth, where she received extensive instruction in biblical studies as well as the classics and elocution. The academy emphasized Christian service and political leadership, arenas in which Harper would continue to work throughout her life. She gave her first lecture, "The Elevation and Education of Our People," in 1854 and went on to achieve considerable fame as both a speaker and a writer. Arguably the most widely heard, widely read female African American intellectual of the antebellum and Reconstruction periods, she lectured constantly on an array of topics—from abolition and motherhood to temperance to women's rights. She remained active and prolific through the turn of the century and, by the time of her death in 1911, had published hundreds of pieces in nearly every genre category: poems, essays, stories, and novels.

Although Harper's subject matter shifted over the course of her career—reflecting broader changes in the U.S. cultural and political landscape—she maintained a lifelong interest in ethics; for her this meant helping members of her particular communities, African Americans and women, in their struggles to overcome everyday social, political, and economic obstacles while at the same time providing them, and humanity as a whole, with a set of spiritual ideals to help explain and justify those struggles. The foundation for those spiritual ideals is made abundantly clear in the opening sentences of an essay, first published in 1853 in *The Christian Recorder*, which brought her national attention: "Christianity is a system claiming God for its author, and the welfare of man for its object. It is a system so uniform, exalted and pure, that the loftiest intellects have acknowledged its influence, and acquiesced in the justness of its claims."[4] As the essay unfolds, Harper offers comparisons between religion and other ways of knowing—philosophy, science, poetry—all of which fall short of Christianity in their ability to meet the needs of mind, soul, and body.

Harper's promotion of Christianity as the singular remedy for humanity's ills and her belief that it provides the only answer to the search for meaning are precisely the sort of claims Jewish intellectuals generally reject. The rejection happens not so much for particular doctrinal differences between the two faiths but because the Jewish tradition privileges, to use Schwarz's terms, "the fabric of everyday life" over a specific ideology, whereas Christianity does the opposite (p. 51). Despite her own marginal status and the fact that she stayed carefully attuned for more than half a century to the everyday lives of others at the mercy of the cultural majority, Harper's ethics do not align easily or completely with those of the Jewish intellectuals Schwarz describes. She (and I do not want to be misunderstood as an apologist here) cannot privilege everyday life over ideology; ultimately, for her, ethics derived from human practice must be subsumed to a divine law.

Yet the humanist impulse so central to Jewish intellectualism is not absent from Harper's work; indeed, her writing and lectures show a preoccupation with not only identifying and examining the challenges faced by individual members of a marginal community but also formulating practical solutions. What likens Harper to intellectuals in the tradition Schwarz describes is an attention, sustained throughout her career, to ethical questions and answers relevant to the here-and-now.

Her antebellum and Reconstruction-era poems often speak of ordinary people performing extraordinary acts of heroism under slavery's regime, and among her most compelling characters are mothers struggling to do right by holding their families together under impossible conditions. Harper's favorite genre—the ballad—was the most accessible and popular of nineteenth-century forms; it helped guarantee that her readers would not only comprehend her message but also act on it. The message was often addressed to both blacks and whites, providing the former with inspiration and practical guidelines for uplifting the race while demonstrating to the latter that their obligation to improve race relations had not ended with the Emancipation Proclamation.

Harper's status as an activist for local, marginal communities and her simultaneous advocacy of a universal, controlling ideology propelled her back and forth along a continuum of ethics that was—and continues to be—one of the most prominent and problematic elements of public intellectual discourse in the U.S.

Intellectual Politics

As part of his analysis in this volume of the history of the New York Intellectuals, Nathan Abrams describes how intellectuals of the 1920s and 1930s saw Jewishness as problematic, in large part due to U.S. cultural prejudices, and how many of them turned to Marxism because it appeared to offer an alternative to such marginalization. Both Gramsci's model of the organic intellectual—one who arises from a local community, speaking both for and to it—and Foucault's concept of the universal intellectual—a more cosmopolitan figure who speaks in support of some set of universal values—are relevant here. Abrams shows how Jewish intellectuals began a shift from the former to the latter: "Rejecting their organic origins and rejected by America, young Jewish intellectuals discovered a new community in which they were accepted, it seems, without prejudice. Marxism offered a 'sense of belonging'" (p. 20).

Abrams goes on to outline several other ways these same intellectuals transformed themselves: how eventually they took on characteristics like those of both Foucault's "specific intellectual"—one who works within a specialized field, usually performing hegemonic functions—and Gramsci's "traditional intellectual"—one who self-presents as autonomous but nevertheless works to sustain the ideals of the dominant group.

Abrams's history of the changing functions and affiliations of the New York Jewish Intellectuals provides a unique perspective on an issue that is both long-standing and highly charged for intellectuals in the U.S. tradition: what complications arise when figures choose to align themselves with groups or ideologies beyond those affiliated with their own ethnic or national origins?

To add to Abrams's insights on this issue, I turn now to W.E.B. Du Bois, whose work also reveals how public intellectuals in the U.S. have defined themselves and their relations to various communities. Examining Du Bois's own concept, which prefigures in interesting ways both the organic and universal models of Gramsci and Foucault, helps illustrate the array of problems that attend the task of defining the intellectual's relations both to a community of origin and to the cultural majority.

There has been in recent years a tremendous amount of attention—one scholar calls it "incessant"—given to Du Bois's 1903 *The Souls of Black Folk* and his concept of double-consciousness, and as a result his other, later work no doubt remains understudied.[5] Nevertheless, for all the fame *Souls* and double-consciousness have received for the perspective they provide on African American identity and black-white relations, we have not fully appreciated, I think, what they have to tell us about Du Bois's vision of public intellectualism. In fact, as

I have argued elsewhere, neither the text as a whole nor the particular notion of double-consciousness can be fully understood without considering them as products of Du Bois's attempt to reshape the liminal space he occupied as a race man—a representative public intellectual for African Americans.[6] I am not claiming that Du Bois's only concern was for his own status but rather that the identity politics of race in a broader sense were, for him, inextricably bound to his position as a representative figure, always mediating between black culture and white.

From the opening lines of *The Souls of Black Folk* Du Bois establishes that African American identity always and already has been understood by whites as a problem: "Between me and the other world there is ever an unasked question: unasked by some through feelings of delicacy; by others through the difficulty of rightly framing it . . . How does it feel to be a problem?"[7] The "me" here encompasses two identities: Du Bois's membership in the race as a whole and, just as significant, his position as observer and commentator on the problems attendant to that very membership.

The defining feature of that dual status—the essence of the me Du Bois is constructing—is its distance from whites *and* blacks, distance Du Bois takes great care to elucidate. First he tells of an incident in which, as a child, his greeting card was rejected by a white girl who "refused it peremptorily, with a glance" and how this event forced him to acknowledge the "vast veil" separating his world from that of his white peers.[8] None of this is especially surprising: we would expect such separation to exist, unjust though it is, and we would expect Du Bois, as an African American intellectual, to comment on it.

The unexpected move comes immediately afterward when he draws a sharp distinction between his response to the veil and that of his black peers. He reacted, he says, by hardening his resolve and striving to achieve the great things available to whites: "they should not keep those prizes, I said; some, all, I would wrest from them. Just how I would do it I could never decide: by reading law, by healing the sick, by telling the wonderful tales that swam in my head,—some way."[9] His black peers, by contrast, chose less promising ways to respond to the fact they were viewed as problems: "With other black boys the strife was not so fiercely sunny: their youth shrunk into tasteless sycophancy, or into silent hatred of the pale world about them and mocking distrust of everything white."[10] Du Bois asks us to understand that the veil, though it affects all members of the race, fosters for him only limited solidarity and ultimately reinforces the notion that, as a public intellectual, he exists apart from both races—most assuredly closer to one than the other but completely identified with neither.

Du Bois further elaborates the existential complexity of his position in the next paragraph: "One ever feels his two-ness,—an American, a Negro; two souls, two thoughts, two unreconciled strivings; two warring ideals in one dark body, whose dogged strength alone keeps it from being torn asunder."[11] It is this statement that most people have in mind when they refer to Du Boisian double-consciousness. Almost invariably, the emphasis is on the doubleness—the duality—more than on the consciousness—the sense of always being aware of the (negative) way one is being viewed by others. Yet I argue that the "two-ness" here also signifies a third figure: that of the public intellectual faced with the task of exposing the tension without being weakened by it—of articulating the weight of white prejudice without being crushed by it. It is a dilemma Du Bois likens a few paragraphs later to that of the black artisan who must struggle "on the one hand to escape white contempt for a nation of mere hewers of wood and drawers of water, and on the other hand to plough and nail and dig for a poverty-stricken horde—[a situation that] could only result in making him a poor craftsman, for he had but half a heart in either cause."[12]

Finding some alternative to the conditions that forced the black artisan to become a poor craftsman—some solution to the dilemma that caused him to devote "half a heart" to each of his communities—is, I suspect, one of the reasons Du Bois took serious interest in communism beginning in the 1920s. It was not simply the promise of eliminating racial inequality or transcending the irresolvable two-ness of African American subjectivity. Communism also offered Du Bois, in theory at least, a public intellectual role not drained of its creative potency by multiple affiliations and capable of addressing social and racial inequalities in meaningful ways. Such potency no doubt also appealed to the young Jewish intellectuals of the 1920s and 1930s as they sought to manage their own affiliations with various communities. That Du Bois's hopes for socialism extended beyond many of theirs—into the 1950s and through his death in 1963—is not so much a measure of his optimism (or their pessimism) but rather an indication of the diverse ways African American public intellectuals have addressed the hard facts of their positions and made vital the political elements of their work.

Multidimensional Intellectual Work

The diversity these three figures demonstrate in responding to pressures of representation and affiliation bespeaks the need for continued study of the activist tradition of U.S. public intellectualism—that is, the need for further examination of how thinkers and writers envision the movement outward from personal to universal, whether in the realm of artistic creation as imagined by Emerson, in the field of Christian ethics as exemplified by Harper, or in the arena of racial politics as theorized and practiced by Du Bois. Such comparison demonstrates the importance of assessing each intellectual's (or intellectual group's) strategies in light of their vision of the link between experience and knowledge as well as the extent to which experience is viewed as a warrant for activism.

Finally, comparative study of the kind I have begun to sketch out here can help us better understand how intellectuals imagine and actualize their status as representative figures and—perhaps even more important—better apprehend the strategies by which they manage their relations to centrist ideologies and dominant orthodoxies; for example: as critics who emerge and operate from the cultural center while seeking to critique it (Emerson), as reformers who affirm and promote mainstream beliefs in hopes of correcting the inequitable treatment of those on the social margins (Harper), or as activists who find that taking on the subject position of the exile ultimately is the most effective means of honing and maintaining one's critical edge (Du Bois). Only by taking these strategies into account can we begin to trace the myriad dimensions of work performed by intellectuals—whether nineteenth-century or twentieth-, white or black, Christian or Jew—as they attempt to negotiate the unforgiving terrain of U.S. culture and politics.

Notes

1. Ralph Waldo Emerson, *The Journals and Miscellaneous Notebooks of Ralph Waldo Emerson*, ed. William H. Gilman, Ralph H. Orth, et al., vol. 5 (Cambridge: Belknap Press of Harvard University Press, 1960–1982), pp. 364–365. All subsequent references to Emerson's journals are to this edition and will be noted as JMN followed by the volume and page numbers.
2. JMN 5, p. 341.
3. JMN 5, p. 174.
4. Frances Ellen Watkins Harper, *A Brighter Coming Day: A Frances Ellen Watkins Harper Reader*, ed. Frances Smith Foster (New York: Feminist Press, 1990), pp. 96–97.
5. Kate Baldwin, *Beyond the Color Line and the Iron Curtain: Reading Encounters Between Black and Red, 1922–1963* (Durham, NC: Duke University Press, 2002), p. 150.
6. See my "Fathers, Sons, Sentimentality, and the Color Line: The Not-Quite-Separate Spheres of W.E.B. Du Bois and Ralph Waldo Emerson," in *No More Separate Spheres! A Next Wave American Studies Reader*, ed. Cathy N. Davidson and Jessamyn Hatcher, pp. 355–376 (Durham, NC: Duke University Press, 2002). See also "How to Be a (Sentimental) Race Man: Mourning and Passing in W.E.B. Du Bois's *The Souls of Black Folk*," in *Boys Don't Cry? Rethinking Narratives of Masculinity and Emotion in the U.S.*, ed. Milette Shamir and Jennifer Travis, pp. 106–123 (New York: Columbia University Press, 2002).
7. W.E.B. Du Bois, *The Souls of Black Folk*, in *W.E.B. Du Bois: Writings*, ed. Nathan Huggins (New York: Library of America, 1986), p. 363.
8. Du Bois, p. 364.
9. Du Bois, p. 364.
10. Du Bois, p. 364.
11. Du Bois, pp. 364–365.
12. Du Bois, p. 365.

The Coming of Age of a Jewish Female Intellectual

Anzia Yezierska's Red Ribbon on a White Horse

Meredith Goldsmith

At first glance, 1920s Jewish American writer Anzia Yezierska hardly seems to fit the category of the "public intellectual," a term often used today to refer to the New York Intellectual coterie of the early to mid-twentieth century. Although like the older generation of the New York Intellectuals who came of age during the 1920s and 1930s Yezierska was a Jewish American of immigrant origins, her literary and cultural interests seem strikingly distant from those of the group who in the 1920s and 1930s were, as the title of Joseph Dorman's book on the New York Intellectuals puts it, "arguing the world."[1] Whereas many members of this group studied literature, philosophy, and politics and moved into academic professions, Yezierska had a degree in domestic science from Columbia University's Teachers College and took only a smattering of courses in the liberal arts. Although the Jewish male intellectuals of the early twentieth century criticized the burgeoning and feminized culture industry of Hollywood, Yezierska published widely in popular women's magazines and acquiesced to the Hollywood PR machine that cast her as a "sweatshop Cinderella." Yezierska's popularity in the early 1920s made her particularly susceptible to the critical barbs of the young New York Intellectuals, most notably *Menorah Journal* critic Yosef Gaer, who found her most successful novel, *Bread Givers* (1925), to pander to the "palate of the typical American."[2]

However, Yezierska's social and literary agenda was not completely disparate from that of the New York Intellectual cohort. Like the young men who

mocked—and likely envied—her success, Yezierska commented on complex political and social issues, especially at the height of her name recognition in the
1920s. However, despite Yezierska's preoccupation with a variety of similar issues
to those that concerned the New York Intellectuals, class, gender, education, and
first-generation immigrant status have occluded her from this category. Unlike
the New York Intellectuals, who addressed issues of immigration, the status of
Jews in America, and the growing consumerism of American life through their
nonfiction prose, Yezierska did so through her fiction, whose highly accessible
style made her work accessible to a larger audience. Whereas for the New York
Intellectuals the academy served as a medium for middle-class assimilation,
Yezierska ultimately underscored the affiliation with her working-class origins
that made her work possible; as she distanced herself from her working-class
background through her success, she was aware that she risked losing her audience and her voice.

If Yezierska's failed class mobility and emphasis on the language of the
popular distances her from the traditional category of the public intellectual, it
simultaneously recalls another construction of the intellectual described by Italian Marxist Antonio Gramsci, who penned the essays for which he is best known
today from a prison cell in the late 1920s and 1930s. Gramsci distinguishes between "traditional intellectuals"—academics, literary artists, and educated professionals (and thus a term more applicable to the New York Intellectuals)—and
"organic intellectuals," which any class is "capable of developing within its own
ranks" through the experience of productive labor.[3] Although Gramsci never
spells out the precise source of organic intellectuals or the means by which they
will come into being,[4] the revolutionary potential of the theory is clear. Although
conventional Western Marxism had perpetuated a binary opposition between
the intellectuals and the masses, Gramsci believed that "[A]ll men are intellectuals,"[5] thus liberating the intellectual function from the elite class alone. Organic
intellectuals may be considered, as Carl Boggs explains, "representative" of their
own class and "leaders" of it—they are able to represent their own class interests
to society at large without becoming alienated from that class itself.[6]

To read Yezierska as an organic intellectual highlights the role of class conflict throughout her work and life. Yezierska struggled with precisely the predicament Gramsci explored in his theory of intellectual formation: as she became a
successful writer, an authoritative representative of first-generation immigrant
Jews, her middle-class status distanced her from the very people whose stories
helped her find her voice. In this essay, I argue that Yezierska negotiates this
dilemma by reclaiming the position of organic intellectual in her autobiographical novel, *Red Ribbon on a White Horse* (1950). Viewing Yezierska as akin to
Gramsci's notion of the organic intellectual reframes the conflict between the
popular immigrant woman writer and the young Jewish male intellectuals of the
1920s as a debate over authority. Gaer resists Yezierska's role as "*our* interpreter of
Jewish life,"[7] alluding to the fact that her representation of the immigrant ghetto

had become the authoritative one. Yezierska cultivated her authority to represent the ghetto precisely through her opposition to those Gramsci would term "traditional intellectuals": throughout her fiction, Yezierska criticized teachers, professors, and social workers for the imposition of their ideals onto her fellow first-generation Jewish immigrants. Like Gramsci, who argues that "[S]chool is the instrument through which intellectuals of various levels are elaborated,"[8] Yezierska worries in her work over the power of education to simultaneously limit and transform: throughout her work, professors and teachers serve as vehicles of Americanization, endeavoring to replace her heroines' immigrant affect with Americanized calm and reason.[9] Yezierska struggled in her personal life with traditional intellectuals like her lover and mentor John Dewey, whom she castigated for writing in a "style lack[ing] flesh and blood" that alienated "all but the intellectual few."[10] During her participation in Albert C. Barnes and Dewey's research project on the Polish-American community of wartime Philadelphia, Yezierska frustrated the sociologists on the study with her critique of the use of impersonal approaches like questionnaires to research with living people. In Gaer's review of *Bread Givers*, one glimpses the conflict between Yezierska and a community of "traditional intellectuals" who based their authority on education rather than experience; whereas the "traditional intellectuals" resented the rawness of Yezierska's depiction of the Jewish immigrant experience, Yezierska felt stifled by the rarefied air of highbrow intellectual discourse.

The title of *Red Ribbon on a White Horse* (1950) springs from a metaphor Yezierska's father uses for the value of poverty—"poverty becomes a wise man like a red ribbon on a white horse"—underscoring what Yezierska saw by the 1950s as the centrality of her working-class identity to her life and work. Yezierska's belief in the integrity of poverty underscores the direction her work took in the late 1920s and early 1930s. Whereas Yezierska's first two novels, *Salome of the Tenements* (1923) and *Bread Givers* (1925), consider the power of consumption to facilitate the transition from immigrant to American, her latter two novels, *Arrogant Beggar* (1927) and *All I Could Never Be* (1932) demonstrate her growing cynicism about achieving a position within the American middle-class.[11] Whereas in *Salome* Yezierska's heroine triumphs in her efforts to mediate between working-class immigrant women and the wealthy through her work as a designer, by *All I Could Never Be* the heroine rejects a job as a department store saleswoman, realizing that that her efforts to remake herself for such a position constitute "selling fiction instead of writing it."[12] Written almost twenty years after Yezierska published her fourth novel, *Red Ribbon on a White Horse* documents Yezierska's ultimate dissatisfaction with the ideal of bourgeois assimilation her earlier work had propagated.

Red Ribbon on a White Horse defies easy categorizations of genre. Far from a conventional autobiography, it refuses linear narrative, moving freely backward and forward in time from Yezierska's childhood in Poland, young womanhood in the tenements, and adult experiences in Hollywood, New York, and New England. Narrated from the first person, its heroine is clearly identified as Yezierska; however, it plays with the facts of the author's life, excising any reference to her marriage or child and sexualizing her relationship with the text's John Dewey figure, here the heroine's WASP employer, Henry Scott. Yezierska's text, neither a straightforward narrative of her life nor a novelized treatment of her experience, offers a thinly disguised intellectual meditation on the role of the immigrant artist—dependent on popular acceptance for her success—in the increasingly commercialized atmosphere of the twentieth-century literary marketplace.

 Red Ribbon depicts Yezierska's search for a community based on shared intellectual and artistic interests after her success selling the scenario for her first volume of short stories, *Hungry Hearts* (1921) for the movies. The first section of the novel chronicles her brief tenure with Sam Goldwyn's studio, where she joined his group of "Eminent Authors," mostly popular writers like Elinor Glyn and Will Rogers. Although Yezierska depicts her initial seduction by the ease and comfort of Hollywood living, she soon realizes its commodifying nature. After her return to New York, she soon loses her meager savings with the stock market crash of 1929 and then finds a temporary haven with the WPA Federal Writers' Project; however, this too is soon revealed to be a factory for mass-produced art. After a brief effort to reject the literary world altogether by leaving the city for New England, the narrator finds that she can only reclaim a sense of home alone in New York City.[13] Throughout the novel, Yezierska encounters different models of successful negotiation with the literary marketplace: Will Rogers in Hollywood, Richard Wright at the WPA, and Dorothy Canfield Fisher during her sojourn in New England. In her reflection on each of these characters—Rogers, part optimist, part cynic; Wright, African American artist on the brink of success; and Canfield Fisher, educated member of the literary aristocracy—Yezierska assesses the skills necessary for a literary environment dominated by what W.H. Auden calls in the preface to the novel "the competitive spirit."[14] The diversity of this trio—a popular white male performer and writer, an African American working-class writer, and a middlebrow woman novelist and Book-of-the-Month Club judge—is telling: as Yezierska juxtaposes her own story against these survivors, the text charts the evolution of the imperatives of the publishing industry with respect to Yezierska as a first-generation Jewish American woman writer. With the end of World War II, as historians have recently argued, the popular perception of American Jews had evolved from that of racialized minorities to exemplary ethnic Americans; like the New York Intellectuals, Yezierska was no longer a consummate outsider.[15] *Red Ribbon on a White Horse* registers this shift as Yezierska becomes increasingly aware of the fading market value of the first-generation immigrant narrative.[16]

 The Hollywood section of *Red Ribbon on a White Horse* allows Yezierska to reflect on the liminality of her own class position. Thanks to a $10,000 contract for the sale of *Hungry Hearts*, Yezierska is no longer a struggling Lower East Sider; however, she must now learn to behave as a woman of means. Yezierska registers her confusion through a series of cross-class encounters and reversals;

first intimidated by the maid at the Miramar Hotel who assesses her "basement bargain"[17] clothes, she is then so frightened by the elegance of her new secretary that she envisions "waging an invisible fight with a fashion plate."[18] Similarly unnerved by her first invitation to a dinner with Sam Goldwyn's Eminent Authors group, who included Will Rogers, Alice Duer Miller, Elinor Glyn, and Gertrude Atherton, she chides herself on her lack of style in contrast to the elegant gowns sported by the women writers of her new "fellowship."[19] Although Yezierska guiltily indulges in the pleasures of leisure-class living, she is soon propelled into a renewed awareness of the realities of poverty. She learns that her secretary, Miss Young, is supporting herself and her couture outfits on only twenty-five dollars a week. Miss Young sees herself as "part of the stage-set . . . If I didn't dress the part, I'd lose my job."[20] The shades of Edith Wharton's *The House of Mirth* in this passage are telling and, I would argue, not accidental: like Lily Bart, who considers clothing the frame with which beautiful young women must advertise their suitability for marriage, the secretary needs to signal her suitability for work and ultimately for marriage through beautiful, expensive clothing. Yezierska's mounting guilt over her affluence emerges in her relationship with Miss Young, whom she alternately pities and envies: whereas Yezierska deplores a system that forces a secretary to dress like a fashion plate to hold a low-paying job, she envies that secretary's ostensible lack of ambition: "She tapped her life away, day after day, with the self-confidence of automatic efficiency. She had never been tempted to go beyond herself."[21] Hoping to capture her secretary's seemingly innate sense of style, she asks Miss Young to take her shopping. In a telling example of the contingency of class positions, Yezierska tries to perform the role of a professional writer through mimicking her working-class secretary, who simultaneously maintains her position by mimicking the costumes of a movie star: as the personnel manager says when Yezierska tries to negotiate a raise for Miss Young, "If they want to dress like the stars, it's her hard luck."[22]

Yezierska acknowledges that "it seemed I had merely reversed my position, joined hands with those who grew rich at the expense of the poor."[23] As ambivalent about her wealth as she was miserable in her poverty, she refuses her customary chauffeur-driven ride to her hotel and takes the trolley through downtown Los Angeles:

> I joined the crowd waiting for the trolley: stagehands, stenographers, nameless office workers who punched the clock morning and night. . . . I felt myself relax, for the first time at ease in Hollywood. When the trolley finally arrived, every seat was jammed. I squeezed in among the straphangers, stimulated by the crowdedness, the physical discomfort. On one side of me, a big-boned Negro washerwoman; on the other, a grimy mechanic, a lifetime's hard labor in the lines of his face.
>
> Before the trip was half over, I was exhausted. If I could only slump into a seat. And then a man in front of me got up. Before I had a chance to sit

down, a Mexican day laborer pushed past me into the seat. A smell of garlic and the sickening odor of sweat turned my stomach.[24]

In this metaphor for a multiethnic working-class society, only the Mexican man and the African American woman are marked as different from the other workers, who fade into "nameless[ness],"[25] stamped only with their personal histories of labor. Yezierska too merges with the crowd, too insignificant to be given a seat. It would be tempting to argue that the narrator's sudden immersion in multiethnic, working-class Los Angeles in this scene resuscitates her sense of class consciousness. However, by the time the trip is "half over," she is "exhausted"[26] and ends up in a cab, "watch[ing] the meter tick off the dimes and dollars."[27] As in the conclusion of *Bread Givers*, in which Sara Smolinsky claims a role in an Americanized Jewish middle-class, Yezierska here seems to seek a middle position between the day laborers and the Eminent Authors, between a secretary and a studio head. Although she imagined such mediating positions for her heroines, at this moment, she is unable to envision one for herself.

Simultaneously, she is unable to envision an identity for herself as a writer without the trappings of fame or the exigencies of poverty. When Yezierska begins her tenure at the studio, she imagines a luxurious atmosphere of self-motivated production with a desk full of paper where she once has written on "backs of envelopes."[28] "Now I could be a glutton with paper," she writes. "Write and rewrite each page a thousand times without worrying over the cost."[29] Although the studio pays ample attention to the physical materials Yezierska needs for writing, she soon learns that their attitude toward the work of writing is very different. The Eminent Authors eagerly commodify themselves: "I had the goods as the market was soaring," one gloats.[30] Yezierska's discomfort in Hollywood increases as she is asked by two studio heads—both Goldwyn and William Fox—when her next novel will be complete: "In Hollywood the whirling race toward the spotlight, the frantic competition to outdistance the others, the machinery of success had to be kept going. The clock ticked off the minutes, prodding: Produce! Produce! Produce another best seller or get the hell out of here!"[31] Here, as she will continue to do throughout *Red Ribbon on a White Horse*, Yezierska critiques the Taylorization of literary production she witnessed in both New York and Hollywood. Frederick Taylor was well known in the U.S. and Europe for *Principles of Scientific Management* (1911), which attempted to instill the doctrine of efficiency in American factories and corporations. Taylor urged companies to maximize effort through decreasing wasted energy, as does Yezierska's secretary, who minimizes movement with her "swift, efficient hands."[32] Yezierska, however, abjured such a mechanized approach to writing, even though she envied those who were able to "turn out one novel after another" with "ease."[33] Unable to view her own writing as an object of mass production, she turns down Fox's contract and returns to New York to renew her allegiance with the urban poor.

The structure of *Red Ribbon on a White Horse* obscures the several years of fame and affluence Yezierska enjoyed after her Hollywood experience: the author condenses her three years of comfort in New York into a few short chapters, devoting the bulk of her attention in the New York section of the novel to the years after the stock market crash. Frequent flashbacks effectively blur the boundary between past and present, leading the reader to take Yezierska's poverty as a governing state of her experience and diminishing the several years of fame she enjoyed in the mid-1920s. Reversing the tradition of the up-from-the-ghetto narrative that had been a hallmark of Yezierska's own success, *Red Ribbon on a White Horse* reads instead like a Jewish female immigrant version of William Dean Howells's *The Rise of Silas Lapham*—a text toward which Yezierska gestures at least once in the narrative—in which the Lapham family's economic rise engenders their moral fall and vice versa. Parts 1 and 2 engage what Yezierska calls "the myth that made Hollywood"[34]—the idea that Yezierska, and indeed any white or immigrant Jewish American—could successfully remake him or herself in the image of the wealthy elite. In contrast, however, part 3 is devoted to demonstrating the limits of that myth—Yezierska learns that the successful transformation of Jews into Americans depends upon a suppression of her Jewish and working-class origins.

After the stock market crash, the myth of Yezierska's success resonates ironically against her increasing poverty. At one point, the radio airs the tale of her $10,000 Hollywood contract as she sits in her room counting her swiftly diminishing cash.[35] Journalists who had once clamored for her attention now ignore her, and a famous bestselling author known for her charity work refuses her support, claiming that "[a] writer can get along in a slum as well as in a palace."[36] Here, as elsewhere throughout her corpus, Yezierska underscores the hypocrisy of those would claim an interest in the poor yet refuse to actually see poverty as it is; as Yezierska reports the hostility of the ostensibly charitable author, she notes that "I had brought hall rooms [in contrast to the author's luxurious apartment] too close to her."[37]

Rejected by wealthy writers and social workers, Yezierska forges a new sense of community with the "millions of unemployed"[38] of whom she now realizes she is a part. In part 3 of *Red Ribbon*, Yezierska reverses her earlier disdain for poverty and for her own working-class origins. As she narrates the expansion of the indigent class, the "old poor"[39] attain a certain amount of authority: "The old poor had nothing to lose in the failing banks and the crashing market. They had always known want. Hardened to worry, immune to fear, they good-naturedly made room for the new poor, their onetime betters. There was always room at the bottom."[40] Yezierska underscores how she finds community among the poor: "The less we had, the friendlier we grew, the gayer our laughter. Misery had found company."[41] For the first time in the text, Yezierska sees herself as a part of a collective: poverty, she suggests, ironically supplies her with the human connection that she seeks. Her experience of collectivity is augmented when

Yezierska participates in a march for jobs in Union Square that supplies her with a host of story ideas.[42] It appears that Yezierska's newfound embrace of a working-class consciousness will help restore her sense of self.[43]

Yezierska soon learns of the WPA Writers' Project, and begins the process of qualifying for relief, a prerequisite for a WPA position. Although she approaches the prospect of work with optimism, her lifelong suspicion of charity pervades her depiction of the enterprise. In order to qualify for relief, the writers and artists she meets go through a process similar to the Hollywood PR machine she despised, constructing and in some cases fabricating narratives to prove their destitution. "Relief," the title of the chapter in which Yezierska herself qualifies, is a double-edged metaphor: whereas Yezierska can get the relief she seeks in the form of a job, in order to do so she must "pass" as a "pauper."[44]

Invigorated by the community of artists afforded by the WPA, Yezierska initially characterizes the project in positive terms. The writers, no longer humiliated by the process of applying for relief, are lit with the "new job look."[45] In contrast to the Eminent Authors group, in which Yezierska felt alienated and intimidated, here she reports a genuine sense of belonging to what she describes as this "new society of arts and letters."[46] She figures the WPA group as a melting pot of intellectual and personal exchange, filled with the noise and excitement of Hester Street:

> Each morning I walked to the Project as light-hearted as if I were going to a party. . . . There was a hectic camaraderie among us, although we were as ill-assorted as a crowd on a subway express—spinster poetesses, pulp specialists, youngsters with school-magazine experience, veteran newspapermen, art-for-art's-sake literati, and the clerks and typists who worked with us—people of all ages, all nationalities, all degrees of education, tossed together in a strange fellowship of necessity.[47]

As Yezierska figures it, the mutual experience of poverty softens boundaries between old and young, high and low, and links people of different "nationality" and education. Yezierska's comparison of the "camaraderie" among the writers to that of "a crowd" on the subway—recalls her earlier experience on the trolley in Los Angeles.[48] Yezierska is trapped on the trolley in the earlier scene, threatened by the possibility of dissolving into the mass of the poor where her work as a writer has no place. In contrast, here poverty invigorates a community of artists where differences in literary taste, professionalism, and experience seem more significant than those of ethnicity or race. In her depiction of the Writers' Project, Yezierska celebrates the possibility of a literary counterculture uncorrupted by economic motives, much as the New York Intellectuals sought a similar bohemianism in the 1920s with the founding of the *Menorah Journal.* Here, her reputation as a sweatshop Cinderella—a product of the Hollywood culture industry—is irrelevant; she believes herself free to commit herself to art for survival rather than churning out stories to satisfy commercial demands.

However, the Writers' Project ultimately emerges as another, even more pernicious forum for the commodification of writing than Hollywood. The genteel John Barnes, the director of the project who tells Yezierska that "[W]riting that amounts to anything takes a lot of time,"[49] is revealed to be an alcoholic and replaced by a new director, Tashman, schooled in the Tayloresque doctrine of "efficiency."[50] Tashman attempts to instill a "new standard of production"[51] that entails the transformation of New York itself into a commodity, suspending the Creative Project and focusing all the authors' energies on writing a guidebook with which to "sell New York"[52] to middle America and requiring a daily "wordage" limit for authors. In Hollywood, where Yezierska receives the message to, "Produce! Produce!," and at the WPA, where she is told, "You haven't produced anything in years,"[53] Yezierska underscores her growing cynicism about the literary marketplace as a whole.[54]

Yezierska's depiction of two of her companions on the Writers' Project, Jeremiah Kintzler and Richard Wright, offers her another medium to reflect on her growing irrelevance as a first-generation immigrant Jewish woman author. Yezierska meets both Kintzler and Wright on her first day on the project, and she juxtaposes the experiences of those two authors throughout the WPA section of *Red Ribbon*. The eccentric Kintzler yearns for a "new National Academy of Arts"[55] to fund his project on Spinoza. A formerly respected Jewish scholar he is now "a tall, gaunt man" with tattered clothes held together with safety pins. In contrast, Yezierska notes Wright's "calm smile" and "well-modeled head on straight-built shoulders" that "stood out among the white-faced men drained by defeat."[57] Like Yezierska, Wright followed his fiction, viewed by readers and critics as an authentic document of the Southern black experience, with an autobiography, *Black Boy* (1945), which established his identity as a public intellectual. Although I cannot prove that Yezierska read Wright's work, her references to him—the only African American character in any of her fiction—are self-conscious enough to suggest her comparison of her own situation with Wright's.[58] In her portrait of Wright, Yezierska acknowledges that the construction of the minority artist in the U.S. has evolved, now epitomized by African Americans rather than first-generation immigrants like Yezierska herself. Contrasts between Kintzler and Wright underscore Yezierska's perception of the differences between past experience and future possibility: "I looked from the furrowed forehead and dream-ridden eyes of the old Jew to the smooth-faced young Negro. One reminded me of so much that I knew and wanted to forget; the other opened a new, unknown world. I wondered whether it was harder to be born a Jew in a Christian world than a Negro—a black skin in a white world."[59] Although in typical Yezierskan fashion the narrator never concludes this line of inquiry, I would argue that the question lies unanswered precisely because of Yezierska's developing state of awareness. By the late 1940s, when Yezierska relocated to the largely Puerto Rican and African American neighborhood near Columbia University, she could not have been completely unaware that she was no longer treated as a member of a despised immigrant class. *Red Ribbon* references her knowledge that the first-generation Jewish immigrant plot has outlived its social context: as she tells Barnes in reference to her earlier writing, "That immigrant stuff was so long ago, in a past existence."[60] I would suggest that Yezierska and *Red Ribbon* hover on the edge of a related realization: if immigrants and Jews are no longer white America's Other, then what are they?

Yezierska juxtaposes Kintzler and Wright throughout the WPA section of the novel. Kintzler's belief in his project—as obsessive as Yezierska's commitment to her early writing—leads him to flout the WPA rules, ignoring meetings and mandatory word counts until he is fired. Like Yezierska in her own life, he is "contemptuous of order . . . too driven by the urgency of his thoughts to stop for the slowing discipline of organization."[61] But after Kintzler dies and Yezierska reads his study of Spinoza, she is struck by its abstractions and incompetence. Kintzler, as Yezierska feared of herself, is simply "written out."[62] Yezierska's attitude toward traditional academic scholarship, the kind of work embraced by the more mainstream Jewish public intellectuals, emerges in this scene. Kintzler's work will be read by no one, in contrast to that of Wright. The elderly scholar simply ignores the tedium and make-work of the Writers' Project, displaying a highbrow contempt for commercial pursuits that in some ways matches Yezierska's own.

In contrast to her connection with Kintzler, which pulls her toward the past, her growing admiration of Richard Wright impels her toward the present: contrasting Kintzler's stasis with Wright's drive, Yezierska notes that Wright is the only project member with sufficient energy to face his own writing after a day's work. Other similarities show the link between Yezierska and Wright: like Yezierska, who rose to fame with the recognition of her short stories in Edward O. Brien's *Best Short Stories of 1919*, Wright also comes to fame through the winning of a short story contest in *Story Magazine*. And in an ironic reversal, Yezierska has proclaimed early in the text, in an echo of studio public relations, that *Hungry Hearts* will be the "*Uncle Tom's Cabin* of the immigrant."[63] The book for which Wright will become known and in which his prize-winning short story "Fire and Cloud" appears is *Uncle Tom's Children* (1937), whose prefatory page proclaims, "Uncle Tom is dead!" Where Yezierska appropriates a trope of white sentimental power, Wright ironizes it.

A poignant final moment sums up Yezierska's split identification between Kintzler and Wright. Wright informs her that he has won the *Story Magazine* contest, and in his face Yezierska senses the "double-edged thrill of his triumph. It was not only recognition for his talent, but balm for all he had suffered as a Negro."[64] While Yezierska envies his discipline, she realizes that he too has stepped onto "the treadmill from which there's no respite,"[65] the mechanized world of literary production that proved so problematic for Yezierska. The section concludes on a note of haunting ambivalence: Wright walks away, confident in his youth and success, while Yezierska goes home to burn both Kintzler's and her own unfinished manuscripts. Envying Wright's confidence, Yezierska wonders, "Did he know the source and substance of his power, the people who made him? He had climbed over their backs to reach the one opening of escape."[66] Here, Yezierska projects her own experience of "escape" from Hester Street onto Wright's experience of northern migration. As she compares Wright's success to her own, Yezierska's language becomes unusually circumspect: "I thought of Hollywood when I had been as intoxicated with the triumph over my handicaps as Wright was now, wresting first prize from a white world."[67] Referring to her Jewishness, femininity, and immigrant status as "my handicaps,"[68] Yezierska resists flattening the comparison between immigrant Jewish woman and African American man. As Wright strides off, confident in his success, this scene suggests that organic intellectuals of the mid-twentieth century—the period in which *Red Ribbon on a White Horse* was written and received—would be generated by the urban African American working class rather than the Jewish immigrant class of the early twentieth century. As we have seen before, Yezierska's speculative rhetoric regarding Wright is telling: she refuses to answer the questions as negatively as she might were they posed of herself, leaving the possibility that Wright will not experience alienation from "the people who made him"[69] as Yezierska herself did.

In her identification with Wright, Yezierska positions herself against not only the scholarly tradition represented by Kintzler but the disinterested tradition represented by New York Intellectuals like Trilling, whose *Liberal Imagination: Essays on Literature and Society* was published in the same year as *Red Ribbon on a White Horse*. Wright, as depicted in *Red Ribbon*, is hardly covert about his Southern working-class origins, and does not hesitate to perform his blackness in social settings; one day, for example, he bursts into a rendition of the slave spiritual "Rise and Shine"[70] when the writers' paychecks arrive. Although Yezierska could easily be accused of primitivist stereotyping through this portrait, what strikes me about her depiction of Wright is his openness about his African American and working-class origins. In identifying with Wright, Yezierska privileges a minority identity that cannot be hidden. In contrast, whether Jews willfully did not identify as such, particularly by the 1950s, they were able to deemphasize the importance of their ethnic background. For example, although Trilling identified as part of a self-consciously Jewish group of avant-garde thinkers in the 1920s, by the 1940s, he believed that "as the Jewish community now exists, it can give no sustenance to the American artist or intellectual who is born a Jew."[71] Whereas Trilling seemed to embrace assimilation after World War II, Yezierska was increasingly suspicious of it. For her, Wright offers a model of the organic public intellectual firmly rooted in an unabashed minority consciousness.[72]

Yezierska probably did not know that she and Wright shared a literary mentor in Dorothy Canfield Fisher, best-selling novelist and judge for the Book-of-the-Month Club. Interestingly enough, Fisher took a role in disciplining and promoting both artists; urging Yezierska to edit out her more hostile attacks on rural New Englanders in *All I Could Never Be* (1932), Fisher also deleted sexually explicit and possibly politically offensive scenes from *Black Boy* (1940) and

Native Son (1945). In the final few chapters of *Red Ribbon*, Yezierska recounts her brief friendship with Marian Foster, a New Hampshire novelist and intellectual based on Fisher, perhaps the model of an early twentieth-century female traditional intellectual in the U.S. The daughter of a professor, Fisher took a Ph.D. at Columbia, traveled extensively, and studied at the Sorbonne. For Yezierska, she may have represented something of a female, less alienating counterpart to Dewey: a member of the Anglo-American intellectual elite who successfully communicated to a popular audience. In a burst of characteristic enthusiasm, the narrator feels at peace upon meeting Foster and arriving in New England, the paradigmatic site of immigration to the U.S.: "For hundreds of years the homeless of Europe had dreamed of home. Home in America. And here at last I had found it. This was it. This gift of home."[73]

However, Yezierska quickly learns that she is not to find the community she had longed for among the Fair Oaks Villagers. Her search for "fraternity"[74] in the village is unsuccessful, as the villagers talk behind her back: "She's a Jew," one of them claims. "I knew that as soon as she spoke."[75] While her relations with the villagers are tinged with perceived antisemitism and mutual distrust, her relationship with Marian Foster dissipates quickly. At a dinner to celebrate Foster's winning of the Pulitzer Prize for her novel *Common Ground*, she is struck by the "elegance"[76] of Foster and her literary friends. These authors seem to have transcended the grasping qualities of the Eminent Authors group, whom Yezierska characterized as Hester Street fishmongers in Hollywood.[77] In contrast to her sense of alienation in Hollywood, Yezierska shares a level of cultural capital with Foster and her cohort, listening as they discuss John Galsworthy's play *Loyalties* (1922), which grapples with British antisemitism. However, despite their common cultural vocabulary, Yezierska announces her difference from this elite milieu:

> What would Zalmon Shlomoh [a fishmonger friend from the Lower East Side] say if he could see me here? . . . I could almost hear his laughter as he regarded me with his sorrowful eyes: "Jew! Jew! Where are you pushing yourself?"
>
> "I'm a Jew!" I blurted.
>
> There was a sudden click of silence. A look of embarrassment closed their faces. After an interminable pause, Mr. McCormick turned to me. "I'm an Irishman, but I don't think it's important to announce it."[78]

I read this scene as a pessimistic coda to Yezierska's exploration of the politics of literary community. In contrast to the New York Intellectuals, who represented their endeavors as that of a group—despite their internal disagreements—and moreover, a group cemented by commonality of ethnicity, class, and in most cases, gender, Yezierska argues that her working-class immigrant Jewish identity condemns her to permanent isolation. Here, Yezierska underscores that acceptance in the literary elite symbolized by Foster and her friends could only be accomplished through class and ethnic passing. This episode—written in the 1940s, taking place in the 1930s—in which characters discuss the continued relevance of a play of the 1920s, suggests that although Jews may have entered a transitional state in which their whiteness is no longer radically in question, it is legitimated only as long as their ethnicity is hidden. It seems no accident that the middle-class (and undoubtedly at least second- or third-generation) Irish American McCormick, himself a model of the transition into whiteness, polices the revelation of Yezierska's ethnicity.[79] This scene underscores that the middle-class identity necessary to remain a member of the literary elite depends on at least provisional whiteness, which in turn relies on discretion, a bourgeois value antithetical to Yezierska's frankness. In this scene, it seems impossible for Yezierska to be even a marginal member of the literary scene, an immigrant Jew, and also "white."

However, Yezierska also encounters a writer in the Vermont section of the novel who counters Marion Foster's model of the traditional intellectual with a rural, regionally specific, working-class female model of creative production. When she arrives at her New England cottage, she is amazed to find it decorated with "handmade furniture,"[80] the larder full. She is told that Mrs. Cobb, "a farmer's wife who writes poetry,"[81] baked the homemade bread she enjoys. Significantly, however, Marian Foster assumes that Yezierska—a city-bred woman exposed to the latest literary trends—will neither understand nor appreciate her work and urges her to approach her gently; interestingly enough, here Foster casts the urban Yezierska in the role of traditional intellectual. Yezierska clashes with Mrs. Cobb during a Thanksgiving Day pageant in which Yezierska's alienation from the New England community—and her developing criticism of Marion Foster—emerges. However, later on, the two women bond, as Mrs. Cobb confesses that she too is a thwarted artist who had left her post as a schoolteacher in the small village to try her hand at poetry. Giving up her ambitions, she returns to the village but not without a sense of loss: "There were times when I felt half cheated because I know so little of the world outside . . . I've been sheltered from all the things you know."[82] Yezierska perceives, however, that Mrs. Cobb's strength comes from her rootedness in her rural community and her pride in her New England legacy.[83] Whereas Marion Foster dispenses Emersonian adages, enjoining Yezierska to "take [her]self for better, or for worse, as [your] portion,"[84] Mrs. Cobb lives them. Giving Yezierska the gift of food—always a sign of genuine altruism in her fiction—Mrs. Cobb offers a model of an artist who maintains a creative identity while remaining fully rooted in her community.

Yezierska's decision to close the novel with the juxtaposition of Marion Foster and Mrs. Cobb dramatizes the conflict between organic and traditional intellectuals. In contrast to Mrs. Cobb, who is known as a poet only in her rural community, traditional intellectuals like Fisher had access to literary and cultural capital, shaping popular taste and using editorial influence to her advantage. Throughout her career, Yezierska solicited the support of powerful women writers like Mary Austin, Fisher, and Zona Gale (the subject of one of the excised chapters of *Red Ribbon on a White Horse*), but each of these relationships was marked by friction. I attribute the failure of these literary friendships not simply to Yezierska's fractious personality, as does her biographer, Louise Levitas Henriksen, but to a clash of different types of intellectual and literary identities. Yezierska, a self-styled "result of the ghetto,"[85] depended on her relation to the working-class immigrant Jewish community for her voice. Lacking a conventional education, family support, or economic affluence, her connections with her class of origins were crucial to sustaining her personal and authorial identity. Thus it is no surprise that the New England experiment fails and the novel concludes with Yezierska on a train to New York, returning to the "sanctuary" of "anonymity" and poverty.[86]

Conclusion

My previous work on Yezierska studied her first two novels, *Salome of the Tenements* (1923) and *Bread Givers* (1925), which explore the dilemma of Jewish American immigrant women endeavoring to join the Americanized middle class.[87] *Red Ribbon* can be read as Yezierska's efforts to review those texts—and the heyday of her success of the 1920s—from the sober vantage point of the post–World War II era; where her novels struggle with the seductive power of elite consumables, her autobiography exhibits a profound pessimism about the transformation of writers and art into commodities. Instead, *Red Ribbon on a White Horse* shows a deep wish for a sustainable intellectual and literary community, one that Yezierska probably sensed would be difficult to create. Yezierska's many contradictions, as revealed in *Red Ribbon on a White Horse,* placed her on the margins of elite, popular, and academic literary groups. A highbrow reader who admired Galsworthy, James, Wharton, and the modernists and eschewed her fellow Hollywood writers, she was averse to social snobbery and the cultural biases it often contained. A largely self-taught thinker who valued her father's model of rabbinic education, she also worried over the inability of traditional intellectuals to communicate with readers who did not share their training. And despite her enjoyment of popular success, she yearned for an escape from the Hollywood public relations machine that romanticized her immigrant origins and obscured her efforts as a working writer. Although the Writers' Project—the only possibility Yezierska holds out as a haven for thinkers like herself—initially smoothed over these contradictions, the New Deal optimism that allowed such endeavors to be funded was short-lived.

Privileging Yezierska's class politics by considering her as an organic intellectual underscores the centrality of class analysis to her work and links her to Jewish American women writers of the thirties as disparate as Tess Slesinger, on the one hand, and Tillie Olsen on the other. However, Yezierska's forthright embrace of her working-class immigrant Jewishness alienated her from the progressive Jewish male writers of the 1920s who would ultimately define what it meant to be an intellectual in mid-twentieth-century America. In doing so, they—in contrast to Yezierska—deliberately muted their connections to their own immigrant origins: as Morris Dickstein asserts, "when I came on the scene in the early sixties, one of the main bones I had to pick with my elders was the degree of embarrassment they obviously had with where they came from and their Jewish identity."[88] In contrast to the New York Intellectuals, Yezierska claimed that her working-class immigrant origins gave her a privileged vision of the American experience and allowed her to communicate her insights to a wide audience. For Anzia Yezierska, poverty and Jewishness were indeed, as the proverb has it, ornaments to the artist-intellectual, her own "red ribbon on a white horse."

Notes

1. Joseph Dorman, *Arguing the World: The New York Intellectuals in Their Own Words* (New York: The Free Press, 2000).
2. Yosef Gaer, "Her One Virtue," *Menorah Journal* 12 (February 1926), p. 105. Edited by Elliott Cohen, the *Menorah Journal* published several of the New York Intellectuals, Lionel Trilling, Herbert Solow, and Clifton Fadiman among them. Trilling's reviews underscore the class and gender distinctions apparent in Gaer's critique of Yezierska; for example, Trilling identifies Charles Reznikoff's *By the Waters of Manhattan* (1930) as the first narrative of the Jewish American immigrant experience of any quality, thus ignoring the work of the many Jewish American women writers to publish in the 1920s, in addition to such male authors as Abraham Cahan. Lionel Trilling, "Genuine Writing," *Menorah Journal* 19 (October 1930), pp. 88–92. Trilling's praise of Reznikoff's book, like Gaer's critique of Yezierska's, focuses on the issue of style: it is his prose, Trilling writes, that "makes Mr. Reznikoff's story not merely a finer but a truer story than previous attempts in the field of American-Jewish immigrant fiction" (p. 91).
3. Antonio Gramsci, "The Intellectuals," in *Selections from the Prison Notebooks*, ed. and trans. Quintin Hoare and Geoffrey Nowell Smith, pp. 3–23 (New York: International Publishers, 1971), p. 4.
4. Carl Boggs, *The Two Revolutions: Antonio Gramsci and the Dilemmas of Western Marxism* (Boston: South End Press, 1984), p. 226.
5. Gramsci, p. 9.
6. Boggs, p. 223.
7. Gaer, p. 105.
8. Gramsci, p. 10.
9. See JoAnn Pavletich, "Immigrant Authority and the Uses of Affect," *Tulsa Studies in Women's Literature* 19, no. 1 (2000), pp. 81–105. Pavletich has argued that affect is a particularly important trope in Yezierska's fiction, demonstrating the "tensions in early-twentieth-century United States culture between a valorized emotional reserve and a denigrated emotional expressivity" (p. 81). Pavletich suggests that Yezierska's texts, recasting the relationship between the reserve that Yezierska characterizes as "Anglo-Saxon," and the affect she attributes to immigrants, "carve out an alternative space for an impassioned, emotionally expressive intellectual" (p. 81).
10. Anzia Yezierska, "Prophets of Education," quoted in Louise Levitas Henriksen, *Anzia Yezierska: A Writer's Life* (New Brunswick: Rutgers University Press, 1988), p. 155.

11. On the importance of class in Yezierska's 1920s fiction, see Cara-Lynn Ungar, "Discourses of Class and the New Jewish Working Woman in Anzia Yezierska's *Arrogant Beggar*," *Legacy* 16, no. 1 (1999), pp. 82–92; Renny Christopher, "Rags to Riches to Suicide: Unhappy Narratives of Upward Mobility: *Martin Eden, Bread Givers, Delia's Song,* and *Hunger of Memory*," *College Literature* 29, no. 4 (2002), pp. 79–108.

12. Anzia Yezierska, *All I Could Never Be* (New York: Brewer, Warren and Putnam, 1932), p. 152.

13. Anzia Yezierska, *Red Ribbon on a White Horse* (New York: Persea Press, 1984), p. 220.

14 *Red Ribbon,* p. 16. Yezierska also cast Auden in the role of a traditional intellectual, viewing his introduction as a work of "highbrow . . . pedantry" (Henriksen, p. 271).

15. Karen Brodkin, *How Jews Became White Folks and What That Says about Race in America* (New Brunswick and London: Rutgers University Press, 1998); Matthew Jacobson, *Whiteness of a Different Color: European Immigrants and the Alchemy of Race* (Cambridge: Harvard University Press, 1998).

16. However, Yezierska documents incidents of antisemitism in *Red Ribbon* to a degree unparalleled elsewhere in her fiction. I see Yezierska's narrative encounters with antisemitism in *Red Ribbon* as part of a move on her part to reconceptualize her own Jewishness in relationship to the trauma of the Holocaust, on the one hand, and in relation to a new postwar United States, on the other, in which Jews had been granted, if as yet incompletely, "the institutional privileges of socially sanctioned whiteness" (Brodkin, p. 41).

17. Ibid., p. 37.

18. Ibid., p. 43.

19. Ibid., p. 57.

20. Ibid., p. 65.

21. Ibid., p. 74.

22. Ibid., p. 65.

23. Ibid., p. 66.

24. Ibid., p. 69.

25. Ibid., p. 69.

26. Ibid., p. 69.

27. Ibid., p. 70.

28. Ibid., p. 42.

29. Ibid., p. 42.

30. Ibid., p. 62.

31. Ibid., p. 87.

32. Ibid., p. 43. On Yezierska's critique of Taylorism elsewhere in her writing, see Martha Banta, *Taylored Lives: Narrative Productions in the Age of Taylor, Veblen, and Ford* (Chicago: University of Chicago Press, 1993), pp. 172–175.

33. Ibid., p. 60.

34. Ibid., p. 68.

35. Ibid., p. 140.

36. Ibid., p. 139.

37. Ibid., p. 139.

38. Ibid., p. 145.

39. Ibid., p. 146.

40. Ibid., p. 146.

41. Ibid., p. 146.

42. Ibid., p. 151.

43. According to Henriksen, this section of the narrative is "fiction derived from the experience of Louise's friends" (p. 259).
44. *Red Ribbon*, p. 154.
45. Ibid., p. 156.
46. Ibid., p. 161.
47. Ibid., p. 165.
48. Ibid., p. 164.
49. Ibid., p. 169.
50. Ibid., p. 173.
51. Ibid., p. 174.
52. Ibid., p. 172.
53. Ibid., p. 174.
54. Yezierska's fears about finding an audience for her work after the 1920s were not unjustified. According to Henriksen, Yezierska had been working on the manuscript of *Red Ribbon* throughout the war years and sent it out repeatedly under a series of different titles. It was rejected "numerous times" (Henriksen, p. 268) before it was accepted by Charles Scribner and Sons in 1949.
55. Ibid., p. 157.
56. Ibid., p. 156.
57. Ibid., p. 157.
58. Deeper comparisons emerge between *Red Ribbon* and *American Hunger*, the deleted chapters of Wright's original manuscript, published separately in 1977. Like Yezierska, Wright uses hunger as a central metaphor for the identity of the minority American artist. Both *Red Ribbon* and *American Hunger* are narratives of disillusionment with ideals of postwar liberalism. Whereas *Red Ribbon*, especially in its excised chapters, represents Yezierska's most consistent grappling with American antisemitism, *American Hunger* documents Wright's disenchantment with Northern racism.
59. Ibid., p. 158.
60. Ibid., p. 159.
61. Ibid., p. 191.
62. Ibid., p. 138.
63. Ibid., p. 61.
64. Ibid., p. 195.
65. Ibid., p. 196.
66. Ibid., p. 196.
67. Ibid., p. 195.
68. Ibid., p. 195.
69. Ibid., p. 196.
70. Ibid., p. 163.
71. Quoted in Mark Krupnick, *Lionel Trilling and the Fate of Cultural Criticism* (Evanston, IL: Northwestern University Press, 1986), p. 31.
72. In this way, Yezierska performs an opposite move from those performed by the Jewish American performing artists Michael Rogin discusses in *Blackface, White Noise: Jewish Immigrants and the Hollywood Melting Pot* (Berkeley: University of California Press, 1996). Where, as Rogin argues, Jewish American artists like Al Jolson claimed their own whiteness by appropriating blackface, Yezierska attempts to disavow her white Americanness—extended to Jews by the postwar period—through privileging Wright's conspicuous difference.

73. *Red Ribbon*, p. 202.
74. Ibid., p. 207.
75. Ibid., p. 207.
76. Ibid., p. 211.
77. Ibid., p. 62.
78. Ibid., p. 212. This scene closely parallels a moment in *Loyalties* in which the Anglo-Jewish Ferdy De Levis accuses the wealthy ne'er-do-well Ronald Dancy of theft. When he refuses to drop the charges, De Levis is blackballed from his gentlemen's clubs by Dancy's friends: upon accusing them of antisemitism, he is told, "You appear to have your breed on the brain. Nobody else does, so far as I know" (p. 48). McCormick implies to Yezierska that only she has her "breed on the brain"; however, as this scene makes clear, it is Yezierska's responsibility to keep her Jewishness under wraps.
79. On the whitening of Irish Americans in the nineteenth century, see Noel Ignatiev, *How the Irish Became White* (NY: Routledge, 1995).
80. *Red Ribbon*, p. 203.
81. Ibid., p. 209.
82. Ibid., p. 210.
83. Ibid., p. 208.
84. Ibid., p. 212.
85. Ibid., p. 47.
86 Ibid., p. 230.
87. Meredith Goldsmith, "'The Democracy of Beauty': Fashioning Ethnicity and Gender in the Fiction of Anzia Yezierska," *Modern Jewish Studies* 11 (1999), pp. 166–187.
88. Dickstein, quoted in Dorman, p. 198.

The (Not So) New Black Public Intellectuals, from the Nineties to the Oughts

Ethan Goffman

1. Whose Tradition Is It, Anyway?

In the fin de siecle of the 1990s, which now seems a strange and naïve interlude between violent global struggles, questions of ethnic, racial, and national status dominated. In American academia, the culture wars—insignificant as they might seem against the cold war and the war on terror—continued a long drama still undecided. Two of the key groups in this drama—blacks and Jews—found themselves in new positions in their quest for ethnic and American status. By the end of the 1980s, Jewish intellectuals had fragmented into various camps, running the gamut from socialist to neoconservative, with the vast majority united on two key issues: support for Israel's security and a feeling of comfort and influence within American society. With the key issue of civil rights long settled, Jewish intellectuals felt free to disagree about the meanings of class division within American society and the question of affirmative action. A new generation of African American intellectuals, meanwhile, was far more united in its approach to these issues; their critiques linked class, racial equality, and social justice. Educated in elite academic institutions through the new opportunities of the post–civil-rights era, these young intellectuals included such figures as Cornel West, Henry Louis Gates, Jr., bell hooks, Patricia Williams, and William Julius Wilson. Their expanding body of work and increasing national stature led Michael Bérubé to argue in a January 1995 *New Yorker* piece that "black intellectuals have become singularly influential as interpreters of this moment."[1] Bérubé goes on to portray this group as one of the few voices criticizing social injustice in an otherwise largely self-satisfied time. Shortly afterward, Robert Boynton argued in the *Atlantic* that black intellectuals "have begun taking their places as the legitimate inheritors of the mantle of the New York Intellectuals."[2]

In a bizarre confluence, another notable essay appearing in the same month expressed an opposite viewpoint. The cover of the *New Republic* trumpeted "The Decline of the Black Intellectual" to advertise an attack by Leon Wieseltier upon Cornel West. Although technically the essay is only about one figure, its historical position, in combination with the brazen cover, situates it as a rebuke to those who heralded a new status for African American thinkers; indeed, the essay coincides with a larger rebuke to an academia seen as isolated and increasingly prone to slipshod radicalism, to using racial issues as part of an attack upon Western society, extending the critique of the 1960s New Left. West thus becomes an icon of larger trends, with attacks on his work part of the ongoing culture wars.

This article will treat Cornel West, as he seems to so often be treated, as a symbol of a larger intellectual struggle, a terrain to be fought over. This is, of course, quite unfair to West but useful for illuminating key issues. West does have a way of being at the center of cultural and social controversy. Besides, he is a key member of a relatively small group that speaks powerfully to and for a large number of Americans, having garnered much praise and success within academia and having made its mark in a larger public sphere through a variety of popular media. Serious dissenters, such as Thomas Sowell, while influential and worthy of study, remain outside the African American intellectual consensus. Provisionally, I shall call the group associated with West the dominant African American public intellectuals, whose politics tend to be progressive and who use race as a focal point for approaching a range of issues, including class, gender, democracy, and American identity. The dominant African American intellectuals tend also to tie American failures regarding its black population to social class and to call for a renewed healing of old divisions.

Of course these "new" intellectuals do not exist in isolation. Whatever has been happening among African American intellectuals is only part of a split between portions of academia and mainstream American society. The battle between Bérubé/Boynton and Wieseltier largely staked out how differing white and Jewish intellectual camps situated themselves. For liberal academics, the improved African American status was the next wave in a succession that signaled how broad-minded and inclusive American academia had become. First Jews had been allowed on the hallowed ground of elite universities; then they became an integral and moving force to institutions that had once denied them entry. The next step was an expanded African American presence, a move that also fit in well with the deconstructionist mode so popular at the time, which gave preeminence to voices from the margins. African American intellectuals were seen as bringing new perspectives, new ways of thought, new life to an establishment that would otherwise ossify, lose its dynamism, fail to evolve, and become irrelevant. With deconstruction exhausting itself, in danger of becoming an empty methodological tool, a rhetoric about nothing, new blood was needed. African American studies were a crucial link, to be followed shortly by an array of multicultural and postcolonial studies.

That link, in fact, was not nearly as new as it might have seemed. Rather, it comes out of a rich history of protest, often based on Christian oratory; what

Cornel West calls "the prophetic tradition." Ryan Schneider has already chron-
icled two prominent originators of that tradition earlier in this volume. The
addition of certain rhetorical tropes, used by a young generation of black intellectuals nurtured in elite universities, allowed academia to mal   e tradition
new, to use the magic power of words—the most currently fashio able words,
used by the right academics and published in the right journals—to bequeath it
into being. One important hallmark of this trend was *"Race," Writing, and Difference*, a two-part special issue of *Critical Inquiry* published in 1985 and 1986
and subsequently as a book. Edited by Henry Louis Gates, Jr., *"Race," Writi ₃,
and Difference* featured major African American scholars along with such ce -
tral figures of cultural and linguistic theory as Gayatri Chakravorty Spivak a d
Jacques Derrida. Deconstruction, with its emphasis on the power of the margi :,
now welcomed into its fold African American academics as major spokespeople.
Essentially a hybrid of African American and European traditions, this intellectual trend would be seen by its detractors as a shallow imitation of an alrea y
corrupted European/academic discourse. The new African American intellectuals, not surprisingly, saw the matter differently, always aware of deep historical
roots. As Gates writes in the introduction, "I once thought it our most important
gesture to *master* the canon of criticism, to *imitate* and *apply* it, but I now believe
that we must turn to the black tradition itself."[3]

Even as African American intellectuals adopted the latest academic fashions, they critiqued that which they adopted. There is more than a bit of irony, for
instance, in West's complaint that, "the academic system of rewards and status,
prestige and influence, puts a premium on those few black scholars who imitate
the dominant paradigms elevated by fashionable Northeastern seaboard institutions of higher learning."[4] To acclimate within academia while maintaining a
very different tradition has been tricky. Yet in the 1990s, academia was more
than ready to welcome the new wave of African American intellectuals, and acceptance was fulsome. Once publication in the most prestigious journals legiti-
mized the new intellectuals, it was only a short step to such magazines as the *New
Yorker*. Within academia, certainly, Jewish Americans had broken barriers and
paved the way for a broader acceptance of African American scholarship. Beyond that, numerous Jewish American scholars, from Franz Boas to Irving Howe
to Sander Gilman, had worked actively to promote black literature, as well as to
initiate African Americans into the previously whites-only halls of academia and
toward broader cultural acceptance.

Yet no matter how well intentioned, such efforts are forced, by the irony
of historical situation, to maintain an edge of patronage if one believes the thesis
advanced by Ralph Ellison and Toni Morrison, among others, regarding black
centrality in American cultural and social history. As Ellison puts it, "Materially,
psychologically, and culturally, part of the nation's heritage is Negro American,
and whatever it becomes will be shaped in part by the Negro's presence."[5] There
is a certain absurdity, then, that European Jews, those late arrivals to American

shores, are posited as precursors to the African American public intellectual voice. The facts of American history have made it a necessity for Jewish intellectuals and professionals to work for the inclusion of blacks; certainly from a legal standpoint civil rights for blacks have also improved rights for Jews. Along with this has come a virtual moral necessity to promote the cultural inclusion of blacks.

By the 1990s, the initiation of African American intellectuals into academic and cultural institutions seemed in its final stages. Employing a touch of deconstructionist rhetoric, Boynton's "The New Intellectuals" portrays black intellectuals as the logical heirs to the largely Jewish New York Intellectuals, "oppositional figures who prized their place on the margins, dissenting from conventional wisdom."[6] Jewish Americans, although incorporated in society and particularly academia, romanticized their earlier outsider status, which they saw reenacted in the African American intellectuals who delivered an alternative and oppositional view and expanded the boundaries of what it means to be American. And if the New York Intellectuals had "synthesized socialist politics and literary modernism,"[7] the African American intellectuals similarly spoke up for a version of social justice and a trend-setting literary movement, in this case multiculturalism. The core functions of the public intellectual tradition are transferred to a new setting. If the old intellectuals spoke to "a small literate public," the new intellectuals employ a variety of media to speak to "a larger educated public whose post–cold-war concerns about race, gender, and economic security have little to do with the ones that shaped the world half a century ago."[8]

With the cold war over, the battles between communism and democratic capitalism were at an end. In a global world, (at least) two key questions remained: how to reconcile an array of national and ethnic differences and whether the new global order would deliver material security to all. In a world driven by neoliberal policies of globalization, the African American intellectuals had little to offer on the economic front, although they voiced strong support for older notions of economic justice. However, despite some contrary claims and despite deep divisions on campuses, these intellectuals were crucial in developing a rhetoric that both acknowledged and transcended the unique history of multiple racial and ethnic groups. Boynton may be a bit idealistic in arguing the African American scholars of the 1990s have been instrumental in developing a "new paradigm" with an "explicit rejection of identity politics and the victimology that so often lies at the heart of efforts to mobilize the allegiances of racial or ethnic groups."[9] Although some of these scholars relied implicitly or explicitly on racial politics, overall they were crucial in developing a broader version of American identity that evolved in concert with a larger movement among academics and thinkers.

Boynton further explores how African American intellectuals extend issues of concern to Jewish Americans in the interplay between ethnic identity and a politics of inclusion. In a move particularly important for the post–civil-rights era, many broke away from the divisiveness of black nationalism. "By pointing out the pitfalls of rigid identity politics," these new intellectuals "have sought to distance themselves from the notion of victimization that has so dominated race-and ethnicity-specific rhetoric."[10] If the New York Intellectuals early effaced their ethnic history under the rubric of a universal culture and often of socialism and only dealt with Jewish identity late in their development, African American intellectuals followed an opposite trajectory. Circumstances necessitated that they speak first for their race while they were given little credence regarding other issues. Building upon Ellison's thinking, Boynton writes, "Although the New Yorkers are perhaps best known for their Jewishness . . . it wasn't until relatively late in their careers that they made their ethnic heritage a conscious component of their intellectual lives. In contrast, most black intellectuals have had the concept of blackness at the very center of their thinking from the start."[11]

This quote implies more agency than was, in fact, present. The actuality of academia, and of most academic organs, necessitated that Jewish thinkers begin from a position of (theoretical) universality to achieve recognition as serious intellectuals. By contrast, in both academia and more popular formats, African Americans have been encouraged first and foremost to write as exemplars of their race. This is a double-edged sword. As Bérubé puts it, "if black intellectuals are legitimated by their sense of a constituency, they're hamstrung by it, too: they can be charged with betraying that constituency as easily as they can be credited with representing it."[12] Furthermore, if on the one hand African American intellectuals are granted a stance and an audience, on the other they are often constrained to it, given less credit when they speak outside the confines of "black" topics. With some exceptions, only recently has space opened up for blacks in a wider conception of the public intellectual. Whether these efforts by such thinkers as Stephen Carter in religion, John McWhorter in linguistics, Hilton Als on theater, and Henry Louis Gates, Jr., on a variety of issues, maintain a core of "African American thought" is debatable. Certainly socialism had earlier provided a powerful framework for Jewish American intellectuals, a coherent ideology allowing them to speak as universal intellectuals. For African Americans, issues of diversity, identity, and social justice may offer a unifying rubric but an amorphous one. Still, many African American intellectuals—including West—continue to believe in some form of socialism.

To other thinkers, socialism is the problem. Wieseltier's attack on West comes out of the group that broke most fiercely from the Jewish intellectual attachment to socialism: the neoconservatives, who rebelled from academic orthodoxy, from which they remain estranged. By contrast also with the mainstream liberal Jewish tradition, for the neoconservatives American identity and Jewish identity trump universalism. Because America has been good to the Jews, the neoconservatives feel themselves quintessentially American. Blending Jewish and American identity politics, they view Israel as, like themselves, an embattled embodiment of American democracy. Although during the Reagan administration and again today the neoconservatives have seen as much influence as any group of public intellectuals, within intellectual society they have always felt themselves a small, embattled minority. If, to Wieseltier, Cornel West functions as a stand-in for black intellectuals, black intellectuals themselves act as a stand-in for the academia into which they were being initiated. To the neoconservatives, African American intellectuals are merely the latest incarnation of a phony intelligentsia drenched in cheap rhetoric and knee-jerk radicalism.

In excruciating contrast to Boynton, Wieseltier considers oppositional status optional for the public intellectual. His attack on West as a superficial practitioner of "the prophetic tradition," whose works are "almost completely worthless," comes from a perspective in which Jewish Americans, now quite comfortable within American society, speak as guardians of academic standards under assault. West provides an opportunity for Wieseltier to simultaneously attack two bastions of academia—postmodernism and Marxism: "West's books are monuments to the devastation of a mind by the squalls of theory"[13] and "This is not Stalinism. This is silliness."[14]

Most important, though, is Wieseltier's attack on West's use of the Christian prophetic tradition. Suspicious of mixing religion—and particularly Christianity—with government, Wieseltier simply speaks from a different historical experience than does West. "The alliance of religion with power," claims Wieseltier, "is a long and miserable story."[15] From the Jewish perspective of Spanish Inquisition and pogroms, this is as self-evident as the statement that "gravity pulls you down." In the African American experience, however, Christian oratory has been a powerful tool of resistance, one that has often appealed to state intervention, notably in the gains of the civil rights movement and in affirmative action.

For West, unlike Wieseltier, biblical tradition may be the theological core around which a rationalist argument is built. According to Wieseltier, West "is a historicist, and the prophets were the early enemies of historicism, who chastised the temporal in the name of the eternal."[16] West, by contrast, explains that "my conception of Christian faith is deeply, though not absolutely, historical."[17] The African American prophetic tradition conceives of the temporal as an iterative route to the eternal, the history of the Jewish Exodus, of wandering in the desert followed by redemption, repeated in the suffering of Jesus Christ and again in the black exodus from slavery with its wandering toward an as-yet-unrealized promised land. Wieseltier continues with his Old Testament perspective: "the Bible did not prescribe that we look at the world through the eyes of its victims. It prescribed that we seek justice. That is not the same thing."[18] In the New Testament tradition, however, it is very much the same thing. Redemption comes through suffering. Justice without empathy is a kind of shell of justice, a blind following of commandments without understanding.

If Wieseltier misunderstood the historical context behind West's thought, the entire debate about African Americans as heirs to the Jewish American public intellectual tradition—itself largely predicated on the European rationalist tradition—risks overlooking the deeper history behind the dominant black intellectuals. They are heirs to an activist, oratorical African American tradition dating back several hundred years, with a strong religious basis. As African Americans gained access to higher education, they incorporated the language and methodology of academia into already existing traditions of prophetic resistance. Although African American intellectuals have a hybrid ancestry with some debt to Jewish Americans, they are best understood within the framework of the oratorical and activist tradition epitomized by Frederick Douglass, Frances E.W. Harper, W.E.B. Du Bois, James Baldwin, Angela Davis, and many others. For many African American intellectuals, "the university" is merely a vehicle for expressing an earlier struggle played out in a variety of landscapes.

Certainly, the university has hybridized with the African American protest tradition in creating the current group of black intellectuals. To an extent, Jewish Americans have served as middlemen in this process, one observed cynically in Harold Cruse's *The Crisis of the Black Intellectual*. In an expanded version of this view, the process of interrogation faced by Phillis Wheatley, the need to prove her humanity and intellect through mastering European forms—what Nellie McKay calls the "Wheatley Court"—is simply recycled time and again. Henry Louis Gates, Jr., describes this as "the primal scene of African American letters"[19]; as William Banks puts it, "the mere existence of a black poet symbolized a challenge to whites."[20] Immanuel Kant succinctly stated the then prominent European view of blacks: "not a single one was ever found who presented anything great in art or science or any other praiseworthy quality."[21] Hauled before a committee of leading citizens, Wheatley proved a thorough grounding in the European classics, enough so that she was judged capable of writing her poems.

Wheatley's success and others that follow, however, have built-in limitations, depending upon copying white styles and forms. Wheatley never convinced Thomas Jefferson, who believed that her poems "are derivative, imitative, devoid of [the] marriage of reason and transport."[22] This has been the double bind of the African American intellectual: ability to imitate white forms is demanded to prove intellectual worth, but such works are then derided as merely imitative. Some 200 years later, the charge that black intellectuals are derivative continued, by this point in the writing of black nationalists, mirroring racialist assumptions that blacks are fit only to write about blacks. Harold Cruse, for instance, judged black intellectuals in the Communist Party as falling victim to "cheap militancy, imitative posturing, and a blind evasion of Negro realities."[23] Cruse has a similar problem with James Baldwin, whom he believes to have been preempted by Jewish intellectuals. The cycle in which criticism of an inability to master European thought alternates with criticism of not being "black enough" continues to this day. Echoing Cruse, Adolph Reed declares the black intellectuals praised by Boynton and Bérubé—a group from which he is notably absent—to be in the tradition of Booker T. Washington as "the singular, trusted informant to communicate to whites what the Negro thought, felt, wanted, needed."[24] "When we consider that these performances are directed to white audiences," Reed continues, "their minstrel quality stands out."[25] Black artists and intellectuals find themselves in a double bind; they may be judged harshly whatever route they take, even by other black intellectuals.

McKay believes that black scholars have "continued to find themselves defendants in the same court of opinion that had judged Phillis Wheatley two centuries earlier,"[26] to be judged through a perspective that considers itself universal, does not realize its own grounding in a specific historical framework. Cruse, for instance, points out the Eurocentricism in critics who argue that "Negro shows were not art"; rather, he argues, they have "severely distorted native American standards by over-glorifying obsolete European standards."[27] Where blacks continue the European tradition, as in West's philosophical work, they are derided as merely derivative. Conversely, where blacks forge ahead in African American or Pan African traditions they may be judged as outside the grand—implicitly European—traditions of academia. So jazz has been judged as inferior to classical music because it lacks the latter's grand harmonies. The reasoning here is circular: classical music has already been judged as the best that has ever been thought, written, or played, and therefore all music must be judged by the standards of classical music, on its terms.[28] Updating Jefferson's judgment of Wheatley, Wieseltier finds West lacking because he has only absorbed the European philosophical tradition in a superficial way, almost like a parrot.

Paradoxically, then, Cruse and Reed prefigure Wieseltier in their critique of certain African American intellectuals. A more comprehensive analysis fuses the development within African American oratorical traditions and the displacement of this tradition to a larger American public using a number of tools, including the European-originated academic tradition. So Michael Eric Dyson describes how intellectuals take the work of "everyday people who interpret, analyze, and reflect on black culture" and cause "the process of critical scrutiny to become explicit, and at times, systematic."[29] And West explains that "Martin Luther King, Jr., was the most significant and successful organic *intellectual* in American history. Never before in our past has a figure . . . linked the life of the mind to social change with such moral persuasiveness and political effectiveness."[30]

Between the crucial baby steps initiated by Wheatley and the sweeping oratory of King lies a history of prophetic preaching and public intellectual work far too complex to be examined here in all but the sparsest detail. The history has been one of repeated iterations of having to prove and reprove the basic humanity, intellect, and cultural worth of blacks. So Frederick Douglass recalled, "how he would be marched out before audiences to detail his suffering and degradation, the floggings, the random cruelties. All analysis and interpretation, he noted, were reserved for the white antislavery speakers who followed."[31] In 1897, as W.D. Wright explains, a group of black intellectuals including Alexander Crummell established the American Negro Academy. Believing that "the [race] battle in America [was] to be carried on in the world of minds,"[32] Crummell understood the necessity of developing a strong African American intellectual presence. Subsequent African American intellectuals, realizing that their work risked

languishing in a vacuum, continued the work of institution building. Pseu_)-
scientific research declaring "negroes" to be intellectually inferior mandated a
strong African American response, albeit one often ignored by mainstream a(.-
demia. Such journals as the *Crisis* and the *Messenger* provided outlets for disc.s-
sion and debate, whereas churches and black colleges constituted institutional
support for the organic and academic poles of the endeavor.

African American writing, too, though often overlooked by academia,
played a role in creating theoretical structures of American intellectual thought.
Most notable is W.E.B. Du Bois's *The Souls of Black Folk*, published in 1903; the
book's theory of double consciousness has been used extensively, particularly
in the 1980s and 1990s, as a tool for understanding African Americans, ethnic
Americans, and an expanding array of hyphenated peoples. As with much of African American thought, this conceptual breakthrough was ignored by academia
for years. From within, African American intellectuals were compelled to deal
first and foremost with the race issue, whereas from without the rich and contra-
dictory aspects of African American discussion were reduced to the thoughts of
a few key spokespeople.

Although throughout the twentieth century an increasingly rich black intellectual community wrote for and reached broader segments of the public, African
American intellectuals nevertheless continued to be seen first as spokespeople
of their race in both white and black communities. So, argues Scott MacPhail,
"The black artist and intellectual must serve the audience appointed to them by
birthright and shared suffering."[33] Little wonder, then, that in a perverse mirror of
white social construction, a forceful group of black artists and intellectuals, notable among them Amiri Baraka and Larry Neal, were at the forefront of a black
nationalist tide just as the civil rights movement crested. This trend obscured the
multicultural vision of American identity sketched in nascent form by Ralph Ellison and James Baldwin until the 1980s and the start of the new culture wars.
Fought over questions of insider and outsider status and high and low culture,
the culture wars solidified the African American position in academia yet also
helped to marginalize academia within the larger society, with such discourses as
deconstructionism and multiculturalism providing juicy targets for a network of
conservative institutions and commentators.

Aside from the conservatives, at least one current thinker, Eugene F.
Rivers, finds today's black intellectuals lacking, co-opted by the twin villains of
mainstream academia and a media relying on a star system. Citing "the first At-
lanta Conference, held in 1896," Rivers explains that "nearly 100 years ago, a
Black intelligentsia—endowed with few resources, facing every imaginable form
of racial disenfranchisement, living in a world of routine lynching—conducted
an intellectually serious program of cooperative and engaged research, focused
on the basic life conditions of Black Americans."[34] By contrast, Rivers asks how
today's far more privileged black intelligentsia have failed "to produce a coherent
and coordinated research agenda addressing the contemporary devastation of

the Black community?"[35] To Rivers, today's lauded black intellectuals look small compared to the longer history of African Americans writing, organizing, and arguing themselves into being in the face of hostility and silence. It is probably unfair to ask scholars in such fields as literature and philosophy to engage in a sociological project. Yet the vexing question of the role of cultural studies, and of the public intellectual, remains. Most of the current crop seems to feel it is their obligation to speak in public media forums and, in academia, to create a discourse of resistance and empowerment, but institution building is a more scattershot affair. In the world of scholarly and public discourse, the example of conservative institutions such as the American Enterprise Institute and the Cato Institute has not been matched by African Americans or by a broader progressive intellectual movement.

During the 1990s, however, at least one potent institution was built in that wellspring of academic respectability, Harvard University. There the African American portion of the culture wars seemed triumphant in the creation of an academic "dream team" led by Henry Louis Gates, Jr. The illusory nature of this triumph, its isolation within an academic bubble, its vulnerability to external criticism was to be revealed in a strange drama between Harvard's newly appointed president, Lawrence Summers, and Cornel West, who once again played the role of stand-in for larger cultural issues. In January 2002, Summers summoned West for a private meeting. All the details of what happened will never be known. By West's own account, he was accused of lacking academic credentials, engaging in trivial and embarrassing activities, and shirking his duties as a teacher.[36] From one perspective, West was replaying the court of Phillis Wheatley, being called before a private authority, forced to defend himself, and judged. Implicitly believing the charges against him to have been based on race, West charged on a radio interview, "The level of disrespect, the level of being dishonored—his attack on me was the wrong person, the wrong professor, and the wrong Negro."[37] As Sam Tanenhaus explains it, this statement is uncharacteristic of West, who has been notable throughout his career for refusing to play the race card, at least regarding his own status.[38]

Another perspective, however, sees West as exemplifying the criticism that much of academia, and particularly African American public intellectuals, played up a few stars and encouraged groupthink. According to West's critics, his academic work had become overly broad and slipshod while his activities putting out a rap album and campaigning for activist presidential candidate Al Sharpton lacked intellectual seriousness. Certainly, the conservative critics were having a field day at West's expense. Claimed one *National Review* essay, Summers "was well known for offending people based on (a perhaps hasty assessment of) the content of their character rather than the color of their skin. So there was no warrant to call him a racist just because he was being unpleasant, confrontational, and even inquisitorial in a single meeting. Unless, that is, you take an a priori approach to racism."[39] The trope has become a common one, the claim that today's black intellectuals—at least those in academia—do not measure up to the illustrious words of Martin Luther King, Jr., that people be judged by the content of their character and, implicitly, by their achievements. The charge of racism is seen as too easily used to mask incompetence.

West's conservative critics bash him in other quarters. "West is a good mimic," claims Roger Kimball in the *National Review*. "He sounds very much like an angry postmodern intellectual."[40] On the one hand, West is here a vehicle for an attack on an academia seen as striking pretentious poses. On the other, he is derided as unworthy even of these lowered standards. The rhetoric directed against Wheatley reemerges: blacks can only imitate European standards. Yet West is also attacked for the ways in which he engages in African American society, for rap music and political activism. Evidently, African American academics are to remain well isolated from the public sphere despite a black tradition of social activism. In describing his own position as being "much more of a public teacher than a public intellectual,"[41] West implicitly acknowledges a contrary tradition of public service.

Kimball echoes Wieseltier in attacking not just specific positions of West but in reducing him to a rhetorical construct—"the postmodern intellectual." The reader is assumed to be able to pick up that this is by its very nature bad—shallow, derivative, flimsy. This is poisoning the well, associating the object attacked with a metaphysical something understood to be odious, thereby undercutting the need for deeper analysis. Like so much political argument these days, this attack relies—with a knowing wink and a nudge—on reducing its object to a kind of stereotyped miniature rather than on seriously engaging the issues.

Reversing the direction of this attack, it might be more accurate to say that today's political discourse is shallow, lacking knowledge of and appeal to historical experience and sociological analysis. Today's African American intellectuals, by contrast, parallel and extend the Jewish American tradition of merging the literary, the social, and the political. As Irving Howe explains it, an essay written during the prime period of the New York Intellectuals "was likely to be wide-ranging in reference, melding notions about literature and politics, sometimes announcing itself as a study of a writer or literary group but usually taut with a pressure to 'go beyond' its subject, toward some encompassing moral or social observation."[42] Yet it is the larger African American tradition of biblical oratory, social activism, and the drive for literary mastery, that leads to this parallel. The mistake made by some analysts of today's African American intellectuals is not to compare them to their Jewish predecessors but to situate the New York Intellectuals as the primary predecessor group. Today's black intellectuals, rather, represent a hybrid, drawing upon African American tradition (as well as contemporary culture) but working from a keen awareness of European academic and of Jewish intellectual traditions. These have been crucial but incomplete tools in the process of creating a black American intelligentsia who are themselves a crucial but incomplete part of today's public intellectual dialogue. To attempt to place one group, either Jewish Americans or African Americans, as the singular vanguard of the public intelligentsia is to misunderstand the complex, multivocal nature of American society.

2. Where Are They Now?

Since the culture wars of the 1990s, what has happened to the vaunted African American public intellectuals? Have they been relegated once again to the margins? Superficially, they seem to have disappeared, silenced by the ferocious clamor of an ever more partisan politics and the violence of terrorism and war. In 20/20 (or twenty-first century) hindsight, this is hardly a surprise. When it came to actual influence on policy, these intellectuals hardly had a chance. As Bérubé puts it, "the new black intellectuals will have a significant influence on the American political agenda when, and only when, a national party runs on the slogan 'It's the social justice, stupid.'"[43]

This is not quite true, at least when it comes to rhetoric. Following the attacks of 9/11, multicultural discourse—grounded in the work of African American intellectuals and even more so in the civil rights movement—provided the rhetorical material for President Bush to speak healing words to the Muslim community at the Islamic Center of Washington, D.C.: "These acts of violence against innocents violate the fundamental tenets of the Islamic faith. . . . America counts millions of Muslims amongst our citizens, and Muslims make an incredibly valuable contribution to our country. Muslims are doctors, lawyers, law professors, members of the military, entrepreneurs, shopkeepers, moms and dads. And they need to be treated with respect."[44] Without Martin Luther King, Jr., one wonders if such words could have been spoken.

Of course words and actions are two different things. That, in subsequent months, Muslims—many of whom voluntarily registered with the U.S. Justice Department—were detained without cause and held without due process shows an enormous gap between rhetoric and reality. If we grant, then, that today's African American intellectuals have little effect on current policy, given the dramatic shift in emphasis of the new century do they have something unique to contribute to our current perplexities? In a brief and sketchy tour of a few intellectuals, this section will begin to explore this question.

In the wake of 9/11 and the electoral triumph of a strange political alliance of free market and Christian fundamentalists, West has written *Democracy Matters*. Grounded in American history and political philosophy and in the African American tradition, the book begins to piece together a critique of our country's internal state, touching also on the related external problems with which we are currently struggling. Like such thinkers as James Baldwin, West is troubled by a false American innocence, a naiveté almost willfully ignorant of those violent aspects underlying our history that continue to shape us. He traces a skeptical appraisal of the underside of American history to Herman Melville, who "expressed a radical suspicion of the capacity of the American empire to cast aside its childish innocence and confront its nihilistic violence."[45] West believes that the situation is worsening today, decrying a "troubling deterioration of democratic powers in America,"[46] depicting a country beset with plutocratic elites, a distorted fundamentalism, and imperial overreach. He extends his earlier discussion of African American nihilism to include all Americans, arguing that market materialism has corrupted our values, resulting in "psychic depression, personal worthlessness, and social despair."[47] Yet West also perceives hope in a "deep democratic" tradition, a vision delineated by such thinkers as Emerson. American self-criticism is crucial here; West continues the public intellectual tradition of dissent, of decrying the enormous breaches in the American promise of freedom while voicing hope for the continuing ability of our tradition to renew and widen itself for yet another rebirth.

West also calls for an end to tribalist and fundamentalist division, for spreading deep democratic traditions to new parts of the world. He renews his tough criticism of Israel while also strongly supporting that state's right to exist free of terrorism. He supports a movement among Muslim intellectuals to reconcile their religion with democracy. In grappling with these issues, he renews a tradition of intellectual dissent followed only sporadically by today's Jewish intellectuals. His basic assumptions about both the possibility of social transformation and the nature of American society are more pessimistic. For African Americans far more than for Jews, the balance of hope and desperation that America represents leans on the side of desperation, of promises broken. Having experienced the brutal misunderstandings of race in this country, West calls for dialogue, honest dissent, and hard work. His vision of the United States' role in the world is grounded in an America that understands democracy and freedom as "not something that can be so easily imposed from the outside, not the least by an arrogant superpower."[48]

To West's critics, *Democracy Matters* is undoubtedly a trivial and ideological work. And West's heavy-handed prose does, at times, impede his argument. By the conclusion, for instance, the word *prophetic* has become a kind of general-use prefix attached to any individual or cause that West finds agreeable. It is this kind of rhetorical sloppiness that had earlier opened West to Wieseltier's ridicule. Yet, as this article has shown, *prophetic* does have a potent meaning emanating from the African American tradition. And throughout the book, West is making a crucial argument—albeit one not unique to him—about the woeful state of American democracy, an argument that people of all political beliefs should consider. Although ridicule and personal attacks have always played their part in American dialogue, we are at an unfortunate time in which they seem to have eclipsed real argument and hard consideration of multiple perspectives. As West warns in one of his more eloquent passages, "if we lose our precious democratic experiment, let it be said that we went down swinging like Ella Fitzgerald and Muhammad Ali, alive with style, grace, and a smile that signifies that the seeds of democracy matters will flower and flourish somewhere and somehow."[49]

West's narrative of democratic hope and loss echoes, and is echoed by, numerous others. Discussing alternative classroom pedagogy, for instance, bell hooks digresses: "If mass media had chosen to focus on the incredible national and religious diversity of the victims of 9/11 (including the many Muslims who were killed), it would have been impossible to create the sentimental narrative of us against them, of Americans against the world."[50] Implicitly, hooks calls for a return to the ideas of Bush's speech at the Islamic Center, so quickly dropped. Like West, hooks employs an African American perspective, enhanced by the ideals of cultural diversity, to show how American cultural shortcomings lead to simplistic analysis and hence short-sighted foreign policy. Also paralleling West, hooks believes that powerful but misleading images in the mass media generate social nihilism: "No wonder, then, that so many people feel terribly confused, uncertain, and without hope. . . . Despair is the greatest threat."[51] Such descriptions of alienation extend a healthy skepticism of mainstream culture dating back at least to Max Horkheimer and Theodor Adorno, skepticism once prevalent in our intellectual discourse, now too often forgotten.

An intellectual perspective on the obliterating power of media images and the harm it does to displaced peoples is voiced also by Patricia Williams: "We are submerged in an image-driven culture with no long-term memory, as well as in a diasporic world full of wandering refugees, displaced by violence, searching for simulacra of home."[52] Alienation amidst materialism conjoins with the anxiety of misplacement faced by so many in a shifting world, the angst-ridden side of multiculturalism and of globalism. Is it too much to say that Williams describes the society against which Osama Bin Ladin rebels in his fundamentalist search for a nationalist identity? Can an African American critique help us as a country to understand our worst enemy? And does this fundamentalist enemy of a cosmopolitan globalism live in our country, albeit in disguise? Williams goes on to argue that Christian identity and Jim Crow have often been connected: "God's supremacy and white supremacy are still very much confused in many people's minds."[53] Would Wieseltier, with his distrust of an alliance between religion and government, agree here? Surely Williams's critique is unfair to many, many Christians, yet also accurate in describing a streak in American life. Our world seems divided between a mythic fundamentalism and a rootless modernism, a division that is interrogated by the African American presence and that black intellectuals may, therefore, have a special place in addressing.

Like so many intellectuals today, African Americans have of late been largely confined to academia, often writing in an abstract prose that many find alienating, a prose alternately isolated from, and attacked by, mainstream and conservative media. Paradoxically, when our society was more self-critical, when talk of alienation and commercialism was more widespread, this may have indicated a certain health, a society actively inoculating itself against the diseases of passivity and self-satisfaction. That we have become so self-satisfied is one sign of our current malaise, our inability to correct our course, our dependence on blaming an outside force, whether a strangely altered vision of "liberalism" or terrorists who hate freedom. Granted, we certainly have brutal enemies, but we no longer seem able to understand how or why our actions affect the outside world. And African American intellectuals are one of a limited number of voices that may have something to offer to help change that.

Like the Jewish New York Intellectuals, no single black public intellectual stands out as representative. Their voice is stronger, and their impact greater, as a group than as a collection of individuals. It is doubtful whether there are today any African American figures as important as James Baldwin or Martin Luther King, Jr.—or George Orwell, to cite an Anglo example. Yet from Henry Louis Gates, Jr., to bell hooks, to Patricia Williams, to Michael Eric Dyson, to a host of others, there is no doubt that they are read and listened to, that they are meaningful in people's lives, that they create a collective awareness (albeit one currently ignored by the political powers that be and marginalized by much of the mass media). No singular figure, then, dominates today's African American intellectuals; they act as a kind of democracy of voices, working together and in counterpoint to make meaning and to act as one strain of the American conscience. In this, they follow the musical tradition of Duke Ellington and Miles Davis, whose music—and meaning-making—depended upon an assemblage of voices.

Insofar as the turn toward African American studies in particular, and ethnic studies in general, has been one of tribalist division, it has nothing whatsoever to offer American society. Insofar as the arc of these studies is toward mutual understanding, and a reinvocation of universalist principles grounded partly in the rationalist tradition—but only when it avoids a European ethnocentrism—and in the actual histories of numerous peoples, it may offer the only hope. The last thing the United States and, indeed, our planet needs is a global conflict between an Islamic fundamentalism and a Christian and U.S. nationalist fundamentalism, yet this seems to be what we are getting. As African American poet and public intellectual June Jordan says, reflecting upon the meaning of 9/11 just after that horrible event, "I do believe that fundamentalist conflict burns at the core of our international fratricide. I do believe we cannot even aspire towards safety without respectful reckoning with completely different, religious, world views, embraced by most of humanity."[54] She goes on to plead for a recognition that "it is the law which reigns as the supreme organizing governance of our experiment, our United States. That is the humane secular basis for a democratic state."[55] Jordan synthesizes the best impulses of the United States as reflected in its constitution and traditions with the promise of the civil rights movement. She expresses not the victimology and division claimed by critics of multiculturalism but unification.

Such a vision, however, is no longer sufficient if enacted only on a national stage. Culturally uniting two continents, African American intellectuals, to be effective, must use their hyphenated position as a springboard to a global vision, one moving beyond a few elites to include the disenfranchised. Exemplifying this we come to a different kind of African American, one more literally African, in

Kwame Anthony Appiah, who was raised in Ghana—as well as in England. An immigrant to America, Appiah's *Cosmopolitanism* thus reflects a multiple identity, nomadic and multicultural in a literal way. If more conventional "African Americans" live, at least metaphorically, a bifurcated existence, they may also retreat to an insular perspective in a way unavailable to Appiah.

Appiah defines a global identity through the term *cosmopolitanism*, which "dates at least to the Cynics of the fourth century BC, who first coined the expression cosmopolitan, 'citizen of the cosmos.'"[56] Such citizenship is not a free-floating universalism; it proceeds from a particular place, a *polis*, but moves beyond it. A cosmopolitan is faced with multiple paradoxes in balancing local and universal values. Humans, after all, are genetically the same: "there really are some basic mental traits that are universal—in the sense that they're normal everywhere."[57] We can, it seems, use these commonalities to grope for some set of universal principles: sharing food with the hungry, not killing the innocent, seeking a just society. Still, given vast cultural differences, for instance on the question of female circumcision (discussed elsewhere in this volume and by Appiah), such knowledge and values are slippery, in need of constant reevaluation. Appiah thus interrogates the assumptions of both cultural relativists and moral conservatives: "It is not skepticism about the very idea of truth that guides us; it is realism about how hard the truth is to find. One truth we hold to, however, is that every human being has obligations to every other."[58]

Cosmopolitanism faces perhaps its greatest challenge in fundamentalist terrorism. Appiah describes an international organization with a powerful Internet presence, one that scorns boundaries yet lacks the value of toleration: "The community these comrades are building. . . . is open to all who share their faith. They are young, global Muslim fundamentalists; they are the recruiting grounds for Al Qaeda."[59] The ability to bridge borders clearly isn't enough; one must also bridge perspectives, bridge cultures. Appiah points out that, "universalism without toleration, it's clear, turns easily to murder."[60] Perhaps central to the maze of paradoxes in defining cosmopolitanism is the question of toleration, of how those who believe in understanding and coexisting with other societies deal with societies that lack the value of toleration.

The answer is not an easy turning inward. Appiah's analysis suggests a response to 9/11 and the subsequent crisis of terrorism shared by other African American intellectuals: if the United States fails to explore, to strive to understand other cultures, to engage in dialogue, we will fail. As he explains, "thoroughgoing ignorance about the ways of others is largely a privilege of the powerful."[61] This is our greatest danger, that we seek to impose our way of life through blunt dominance rather than understanding, dialogue, and evolution. A United States that insists on others' learning English while we fail to reciprocate continues a dangerous pattern of cultural isolationism. If we give insufficient attention to teaching Arabic, to learning about the Koran, to the history and cultures of the Middle East, in the end we will pay the price. And African Americans are in a powerful experiential and moral position to advocate for an intercultural United States. How deeply this will go, and whether they will be listened to, is another question.

It is too early to say. West, Williams, hooks, Jordan, and Appiah represent a nascent reaction to our new world living under terrorist threat, fighting a brutal insurgency in Iraq, with an America harshly divided both within itself and from the world and with a decreasing respect for civil liberties. But if today's African American intellectuals can become spokespeople for a unitary vision, perhaps their legacy will be something more than that of the scattered, overhyped pseudomovement their critics might conceive them as. Such an approach must stem from an acute awareness of the limitations of an America that refuses to acknowledge how the unsavory parts of its past reflect upon its present. African American intellectuals have a special experience regarding the role of minorities, of nationalism, of frustrated peoples who feel overlooked, who have grown bitter enough to turn to violence. To remain relevant, African American intellectuals must fight the nihilism that historical experience can bring, must fulfill the tricky balancing act of relentless criticism and an expansive vision of democracy through dialogue, of a society in which all participate. Without dissent—without constant criticism of its shortcomings—our country will inevitably succumb—is in the midst of succumbing—to a shallow nationalism based upon misunderstanding. If somehow today's black public intellectuals can regain public notice, perhaps they will fulfill the legacy left them by the Jewish intellectuals and by earlier African American activists and intellectuals.

Notes

1. Michael Bérubé, "Public Academy: A New Generation of Black Thinkers Is Becoming the Most Dynamic Force in the American Intellectual Arena since the Fifties," *New Yorker*, January 9, 1995, pp. 73–80, p. 76.
2. Robert, Boynton, "The New Intellectuals," *Atlantic Monthly*, March 1995, p. 56.
3. Henry Louis Gates, Jr., introduction to *"Race," Writing, and Difference*, ed. Henry Louis Gates, Jr., and Kwame Anthony Appiah (Chicago: University of Chicago Press, 1992), p. 13.
4. Cornel West, *Race Matters* (1993; repr. New York: Vintage Books, 2001), p. 62.
5. Ralph Ellison, "What America Would Be Like without Blacks," in *Going to the Territory* (New York: Random House, 1986), p. 111.
6. Boynton, p. 54.
7. Ibid.
8. Ibid., p. 56.
9. Ibid., p. 66.
10. Ibid., p. 57.
11. Ibid., p. 60.
12. Bérubé, pp. 77–78.
13. Leon Wieseltier, "The Unreal World of Cornel West: All and Not' at All," *New Republic*, March 6, 1995, p. 32.

14. Ibid., p. 33.

15. Ibid., p. 34.

16. Ibid., p. 33.

17. Cornel West, "The Making of an American Radical Democrat of African Descent," in *The Cornel West Reader*, pp. 3–18 (New York: Basic Civitas Books, 1999), p. 13.

18. Wieseltier, p. 33.

19. Henry Louis Gates, Jr., *The Trials of Phillis Wheatley* (New York: Basic, 2003), p. 5.

20. William Banks, *Black Intellectuals: Race and Responsibility in American Life* (New York: W.W. Norton, 1996), p. 25.

21. Quoted in Gates, *The Trials of Phillis Wheatley*, p. 25.

22. Ibid., p. 49.

23. Harold Cruse, *The Crisis of the Negro Intellectual: A Historical Analysis of the Failure of Black Leadership* (1967; repr. New York: Quill, 1984), p. 147.

24. Reed Adolph, "The Current Crisis of the Black Intellectual," *Village Voice*, April 11, 1995, p. 32.

25. Ibid., p. 35.

26. Nellie McKay, "Naming the Problem that Led to the Question 'Who Shall Teach African American Literature?' or, Are We Ready to Disband the Wheatley Court?" *PMLA* 113, no. 3 (1998), p. 362.

27. Cruse, p. 98.

28. Although much of the American intelligentsia has come to accept jazz, blues remains suspect, whereas rap faces a repeat of the court of Wheatley. Granted, much rap plays up its gangster elements and thus reinforces negative stereotypes, yet the music's more complex musical juxtapositions and sardonic social commentary are often ignored.

29. Michael Eric Dyson, "More than Academic: Seamless Theory, Racial Disruptions, and Public Intellectuals in the Ivory Tower," in *Open Mike,* pp. 61–78 (New York: Basic, 2003), p. 74.

30. Cornel West, "Prophetic Christian as Organic Intellectual," in *The Cornel West Reader*, pp. 425–439 (New York: Basic Civitas Books, 1999), p. 426.

31. William Banks, *Black Intellectuals: Race and Responsibility in American Life* (New York: W.W. Norton, 1996), p. 24.

32. W.D. Wright, *Black Intellectuals, Black Cognition, and a Black Aesthetic* (Westport: Praeger, 1997), p. 14.

33. Scott MacPhail, "June Jordan and the New Black Intellectuals," *African American Review* 33 (1999), p. 60.

34. Eugene F. Rivers III, "Beyond the Nationalism of Fools: Toward an Agenda for Black Intellectuals," *Boston Review*, October/November 1995, p. 2, http://www.boston review.net/BR20.3/rivers.html (accessed March 2008).

35. Ibid., p. 3.

36. Cornel West, *Democracy Matters: Winning the Fight against Imperialism* (New York: Penguin Press, 2004), pp. 192–194.

37. "Cornel West Outlines 'Pull toward Princeton' and 'Push from Harvard' in Exclusive Interview with NPR's Tavis Smiley," April 15, 2002, National Public Radio, http:// www.npr.org/about/press/020415.cwest.html (accessed March 2008).

38. Sam Tanenhaus, "The Ivy League's Angry Star," *Vanity Fair*, June 2002, pp. 201–223.

39. Matt Feeney, "West of Everything: A Professor's Approach to Disagreement," *National Review Online*, August 13, 2002, http://www.nationalreview.com/comment/ comment-feeney081302.asp (accessed March 2008).

40. Roger Kimball, "Dr. West and Mr. Summers: A Harvard Tale—Cornel West vs. Larry Summers," *National Review*, January 28, 2002, p. 25.
41. Tanenhaus, p. 222.
42. Irving Howe, "The New York Intellectuals," in *Selected Writings, 1950–1990*, pp. 240–280 (San Diego: Harcourt, Brace, Jovanovich, 1969), p. 261.
43. Bérubé, p. 80.
44. George W. Bush, Speech to the Islamic Center of Washington, DC, November 17, 2001, the White House, http://www.whitehouse.gov/news/releases/2001/09/20010917-11 .html (accessed March, 2005).
45. West, *Democracy Matters*, p. 88.
46. Ibid., p. 2.
47. Ibid., p. 26.
48. Ibid., p. 104.
49. Ibid., p. 218.
50. bell hooks, *Teaching Community: A Pedagogy of Hope* (New York: Routledge, 2003), p. 12.
51. Ibid.
52. Patricia J. Williams, *Open House: Of Family, Friends, Food, Piano Lessons, and the Search for a Room of My Own* (New York: Farrar, Straus, Giroux, 2004), p. 8.
53. Ibid., p. 99.
54. June Jordan, "Some of Us Did Not Die," in *Some of Us Did not Die: New and Selected Essay of June Jordan*, pp. 3–16 (New York: Basic Books, 2002), p. 4.
55. Ibid., p. 14.
56. Kwame Anthony Appiah, *Cosmopolitanism: Ethics in a World of Strangers* (New York: W.W. Norton, 2006), p. xiv.
57. Ibid., p. 96.
58. Ibid., p. 144.
59. Ibid., p. 138.
60. Ibid., p. 140.
61. Ibid., p. xvii.

Simply Said

Edward Said and the New York Intellectual Tradition

Matthew Abraham

> If it wasn't for this offense done to the Palestinians in 1947 and 1948, Edward would have become what he basically already is: a New York Jewish intellectual.
> —Christopher Hitchens

Introduction

In an interview in the summer of 2000, where they were discussing the 1947–1948 Palestinian dispossession at the hands of the yet-to-be-formed Israeli Defense Forces of the Haganah and the IZL (Irgun), *Ha'aretz*'s Ari Shavit and the famed cultural critic Edward Said reflected on the possibilities of an Israeli-Palestinian binational state, something Said had advocated on behalf of for quite some time—much before the failure of the Oslo Accords and Camp David II. This interview took place just a few months before the outbreak of violence that began the Second Intifada in the occupied territories, a possible reaction to the failure of the Camp II talks where, brought together by then-President Bill Clinton, Ehud Barak, had supposedly offered (in exchange for the Palestinian recognition of "Israel's right to exist as a Jewish state") Arafat nearly 80 percent of the West Bank for a viable Palestinian state, "a deal of a lifetime," although many considered the offer a call for Palestinian submission to a Bantustan arrangement reminiscent of the South African national territories.[1]

As he came to fully understand Said's nuanced position, which clearly placed reconciliation between the Israelis and the Palestinians ahead of revenge or retribution for either group's historical grievances, and the identification of a mutual interest in peace and coexistence in a future binational state before the assignment of blame, Shavit proclaimed, "You sound very Jewish." Said replied, "Of course. I'm the last Jewish intellectual. You don't know anyone else. All your other Jewish intellectuals are now suburban squires. From Amos Oz to all these people here in America. So I'm the last one. The only true follower of Adorno. Let me put it this way: I'm a Jewish-Palestinian."[2]

The concept of a "Jewish-Palestinian," clearly provocative and intriguing in its attempt to employ notions of exile, loss, and refugeehood to understand the historical suffering of two peoples that are engaged in a seeming death struggle in the Middle East, articulates a condition of loss, longing, and hopelessness for the modern age. A Jewish-Palestinian does not attempt to privilege the historical wrongs committed against one of the peoples within this binary over another, employing a superior sense of victimhood to deny the suffering of the other side, but instead recognizes the singularity of each people's oppression and dispossession. Shavit's observation suggests that to be Jewish ("to be a Jew") is to occupy a specific political-historical space, a space within which someone appreciates the condition of exile and the insights it brings to the human experience. Historically speaking, to be a Jew is to be an exile. To be a Palestinian at this historical moment does not hold the same meaning, even though the stateless Palestinian living under occupation may know something more about what it means to be an exile than an Israeli or American Jew. I do not intend to employ the term *Jew* as a caricature but instead to articulate how a concept of "Jewishness" can be used to understand all human suffering, even Palestinian suffering.

As a condition, Jewishness has signified the capacity to empathize with suffering, homelessness, wandering, and powerlessness. Can one honestly describe Jews—at this present historical moment—as suffering, homeless, wandering, and powerless? Ironically, these adjectives aptly describe the Palestinian condition under Israeli occupation; however, when one understands that antisemitism and Orientalism are different sides of the same coin of age-old hatreds directed against distinct populations, whether these are Jewish or Muslim, an interesting complementarity emerges. Antisemitism, as a European-generated hatred directed against Jews, has been effectively transferred to the Palestinian Arab in his or her resistance against Israeli occupation. Palestinian Arab resistance to Israeli occupation is configured as antisemitism because the occupiers of what was previously Palestinian land are Jewish. Orientalism, as a discourse that essentially constructs the "existence" of Eastern peoples such as Arabs, is also a European creation that allowed for colonial domination through the wedding of power and knowledge. The domestication of the East and its peoples through Western social sciences such as anthropology and linguistics created discursive targets through which to understand and control non-Europeans. Said described this process in great detail in his *Orientalism*:

[B]y an almost inescapable logic, I have found myself writing the history of
a strange, secret sharer of Western anti-Semitism. That anti-Semitism and,
as I have discussed it in its Islamic branch, Orientalism, resemble each other
very closely is a historical, cultural, and political truth that needs only to be
mentioned to an Arab Palestinian for its irony to be perfectly understood.[3]

The Jewish embrace of the state of Israel signals an end to the Jewish Question and the beginning of the Palestinian Question; however, can one say that the
Jewish Question ever really ended? Zionism, as a form of Jewish nationalism, has
ironically ensured the perpetuation of the Jewish Question and concomitantly the
Palestinian Question. Both questions, as Joseph Massad has suggested in his *The
Persistence of the Palestinian Question*, are intimately connected; one question can
not be solved without turning to the other. Analyzing the Palestinian condition,
then, requires a precise accounting of the place of non-Jews within the economy of
Zionism, a task that Said made both personal and professional.

Although some have argued that Said compromised his status as a public intellectual because of his embrace of Palestinian nationalism, the evidence
suggests a far more complicated picture.[4] Said's commitment to bearing witness
to grave injustice (not just the injustices committed against Palestinians) as well
as documenting the intellectual evasions surrounding difficult human questions
about neglect and dispossession (and not just the Palestinian Question) stands
as a testament to his special type of intellectual style that was reminiscent of the
early New York Intellectuals such as Hannah Arendt. Arendt, because of her critical statements about Zionism as outlined in *Eichmann in Jerusalem: A Report of
the Banality of Evil* and an essay titled "Zionism Reconsidered," was plagued by
controversy in the later part of her life for questioning the foundations of Jewish
nationalism and the necessity of a Jewish state. Her most controversial work interrogated the role of the *Judenräte* (Jewish Councils) in cooperating with the Third
Reich, as these Councils delivered Jews over to the Nazis for eventual extermination in the concentration camps.[5] That Arendt tackled such taboo and explosive
subjects as part of her intellectual work suggests that she was committed to exposing the contradictions and inconsistencies within lachrymose and easily formulated narratives about the Holocaust and Jewish suffering; her doing so provides
greater insight into the human condition. Said approached the problems of Zionism from a far different subjectivity but with the same acumen. His "American Zionism: The Last Taboo" raises disturbing questions about how Israeli nationalism
has always been perverted by rampant militarism, which has had the potential
to compromise the moral integrity of American Jews who support Israel as an
exclusively Jewish state.[6] In writing what they have about Zionism from their very
different positions, Arendt and Said assumed an almost pariah-like status among
segments of the public intensely focused on promoting Israelism, if not Zionism.
Such a status is a prerequisite for moral rebellion and intellectual responsibility.
Arendt explained her own perspective in a letter to Gershom Scholem:

What confuses you is that my arguments and my approach are different
from what you are used to; in other words, the trouble is that I am independent. By this I mean, on the one hand, that I do not belong to any organization and always speak only for myself, and on the other hand, that I have
great confidence in Lessing's *selbstdenken* [self-thinking] for which, I think,
no ideology, no public opinion, and no "convictions" can ever be a substitute. Whatever objections you may have to the results, you won't understand
them unless you realize that they are really my own and nobody else's.[7]

This sort of intellectual independence and refusal of intellectual orthodoxy
characterized Arendt's positions on Zionism and Israel throughout her career.
Ironically, she and Noam Chomsky—who has been considered (for over fifty
years) a virulent critic of Israeli policies toward the Palestinians—were proud
Zionists in the 1940s before the actual founding of Israel in 1948, at which point
it became known that there could be no rapprochement with the Arabs because
of the UN partition and growing Jewish immigration into what was once considered Palestine.

In his *The Politics of Dispossession*, Said writes "I go so far as to be convinced
by Rosa Luxemburg's statement that one cannot impose one's own political solution on another people against their will. As a Palestinian who has suffered loss
and deprivations, I cannot morally accept regaining my rights at the expense of
another people's deprivation."[8] As perhaps the last true follower of Adorno, Said
brought an enlightened skepticism toward all nationalisms, including Palestinian
nationalism, realizing the necessity of creating conditions for noncoercive community through the bringing together of discrepant experiences, an indication of
his commitment to exposing how nationalism and its attendant cultural discourses
often separate people from one another based upon little more than territorial divides. Explaining the almost religious fervor with which such divides are policed
and protected became Said's enduring passion, an effort that permeated both his
literary criticism and his political work on behalf of the Palestinian people.

Said, Arendt, and the New York Intellectuals

If we view the New York Intellectuals as representing a group of committed individuals devoted to working against the grain of mainstream culture and society
while exploring how dominant values and modes of conceptualization come into
being through art and literature, as well as politics, we should evaluate how the
conditions of exile and marginality—and sometimes pariah status—inform their
social analyses. There are inherent contradictions in describing Edward Said as an
outsider because his academic position allowed him to command cultural capital
and to take advantage of an academic location that has largely dissolved in the
contemporary academy; he operated within a circuit of immense prestige and
influence where one can move into expert (nonacademic) social spaces, while he
was also taken seriously as a critic and commentator. For Said, this positionality

allowed him to speak on the subjects of Islam, the Question of Palestine, and the relationship of each to the terrorism industry, all of which were far outside his formal academic training but firmly within the grasp of his social predicament as an Arab Palestinian. He was alert to the ways in which knowledge reifies human experience, reducing it to something that can be quantified, analyzed, and removed from crucial contexts that give it meaning and shape. Zionism has successfully done such a thing to Judaism. The Palestinian intellectual, schooled as a New York Intellectual, becomes something other than Jewish; he becomes capable of using Jewish experience to explore other human experiences, extending senses of Jewish suffering to the suffering of others. One recognizes the ambivalence in Said as he speaks of confronting Zionist aggression, being careful to underscore that Zionism is not Judaism and that Palestinian resistance is directed at Zionists and not Jews qua Jews. Although this is most definitely a complicated and hazardous task, it was necessary for Said to make distinctions where others had left the political field unanalyzed, allowing violence to reign where understanding and reconciliation should have entered.

In this section, I would like to draw some parallels between Said and Hannah Arendt, someone occasionally mentioned as being part of the New York Intellectual scene. Arendt, like Mary McCarthy, was one of the few women considered as part of this male-dominated group. Arendt achieved notoriety with her coverage of the Eichmann trial in 1961 in a series of articles for the *New Yorker* that took form as a controversial book titled *Eichmann in Jerusalem*, which reached the startling conclusion that Adolph Eichmann was far from the epitome of evil many had reckoned him to be; instead, he was, in Arendt's estimation, the banality of evil—someone quite average caught between his career ambitions as a Nazi bureaucrat who was attempting to please his superiors and a lack of scruples that prevented him from confronting the horrors of the bureaucratic machinery of which he was a part. Arendt, who during her early life was a Zionist, became very skeptical of Zionism because of what she witnessed at the Eichmann trial, where she saw the aims of Israeli nationalism rather than those of universal justice being served.

The book created a firestorm of controversy that occupied Arendt for many years because she was forced to defend herself against accusations of antisemitism and self-hatred while witnessing most of what she wrote in the book being distorted and misread. The most damning accusation lodged against Arendt was that she had betrayed the Jewish people with the book, providing non-Jews with an excuse to not pay attention to the moral gravity of the Holocaust due to her depiction of Eichmann as an ordinary man, a man who could have been any of us. Perhaps Arendt's most controversial claim in the book involved the Judenräte councils that were complicit in aiding the Nazis to bring Jews to their eventual deaths in the concentration camps. That Arendt confirmed that there was widespread cooperation between Jews and Nazis to kill fellow Jews highlighted a tragic and unspoken about aspect of the Holocaust. This aspect of Arendt's commentary in *Eichmann in Jerusalem* continues to be a point of fierce contention and debate. In some sense, this book made her a pariah within the

Jewish community. The word *pariah* means something more than outcast; it is meant to emphasize that someone is the lowest of the low, beneath contempt and unworthy of notice. This designation is usually reserved for the unforgivable sinner, the violator of some taboo, or the transgressor of some sacred principle. However, those who tell deeply unpopular truths—prophets—face similar ostracism because they erode a community's confidence in a vital myth, creating crisis and uncertainty about the past and one's identity as a result of that past. Arendt became a pariah in the Jewish community because of her unwillingness to uphold Zionist myths for the sake of the nation. She sought complexity where others demanded simplicity and orthodoxy in the name of nationalism.

Ostracized by those who demanded that he toe a line with respect to Palestinian nationalism, Said often had to go it alone in his struggle to humanize the Palestinian people for a Western audience in the United States. After serving on the Palestinian National Council for fourteen years, Said resigned in protest in 1991, mainly due to his dissatisfaction with Yasser Arafat and the PLO, both of which in his estimation had begun to betray the Palestinian people for personal privilege and comfort. In short, the PLO had become an extension of Israeli domination, acting as the comprador arm of the Israeli government, which seeks to destroy all vestiges of Palestinian culture through a form of politicide, to borrow a term of the Israeli sociologist Baruch Kimmerling.[9]

Like Arendt, Said was suspicious of nationalism, nationalistic impulses, and the consequences of both for colonized peoples. Arendt viewed Zionism as placing the future of the Jewish people in jeopardy because it would place Jews living in Palestine in a compromised position of having to rely upon the generosity of a superpower to maintain itself militarily, politically, and diplomatically. In this sense, Arendt was predicting Zionism's future predicaments as it sought to secure and guard land on behalf of a colonial power. Most find comfort and solace in nationalism; it is an indication of home, comfort, and friends. To be an exile is to be without a nation, a nationality, a home, and security. Nationalism, in Said's estimation, is a God that always fails because it reduces human experience and lines of solidarity between people to territories and borders that in reality carve up the world in unproductive and destructive ways. To be an exile is to relate to all people regardless of their country of citizenship or point of origin, nationality, or birth. This catholicity of thought, this openness to different forms of social experimentation, allows for the type of worldliness, spontaneity, plurality, and natality characteristic of both Said and Arendt. The rejection of crippling orthodoxies that reduce human action to *Realpolitik* allows for human action to change the world, deep commitments that Said and Arendt worked toward throughout their careers and lives.

Restlessness, Alienation, and the Intellectual Spirit

As part of his efforts to create such conditions through his literary and political work, Said's notions of "worldliness," "exile," "secular criticism," "contrapuntal reading," and "structures of attitude and reference" find a specific place in the New York Intellectual tradition because these concepts contribute to a harnessing of critical energy to progressive social movements, whether Marxist, postcolonial, Trotskyite, or anticommunist. While the "postcolonial"—as a rubric representing a commitment to the liberation of Third World peoples—never held a place in the New York Intellectual's imagination, especially by the time the Vietnam war rolled around, Said, of course, is recognized as the founder of postcolonial studies, even though he never claimed this for himself.

Said's Adornian discomfort with mass culture suggests that an oppositional stance to the dominant forces within a society is necessary for an engagement and serious critique. The critic requires a constant sense of alertness, of not quite being at home, an uneasiness with facility and clichés. Said's restlessness, his guardedness against sleep, his easy movements between—and his attempts to fuse together—the genres of personal and academic writing, suggest a cosmopolitan fluidity that sought to upset established conventions and easygoing platitudes. The New York Intellectuals, a group that was initially comprised of unassimilated Jews, felt a similar sense of alienation as they wrote about and critiqued American culture, which is perhaps why they share the term *diaspora*, increasingly adopted by dispossessed groups. To this end, Said felt most at home on a plane, never being part of anything for very long, while stating that he could never have lived anywhere but New York, a city of many cultures that never sleeps, embracing all those who come within its borders. As the city that set the pace in publishing and media throughout the twentieth century, New York has long been a natural draw for writers and intellectuals. Especially for those who have no place or are searching for a place, New York presents opportunities to recreate one's sense of self and relation to the dominant mode—its polyphonic character and fast pace allow for a reinvention of the self and one's relation to the past; this was certainly true in Said's case.

There is a desire to recoup family stories and histories as one comes to construct one's personal history; this is particularly true as one enters one's later life, or in Said's case, when you're handed a death sentence like leukemia. Edward Said's relationship to the city of New York figures prominently in his attachment to the phenomena of "exile," "homelessness," and "in-betweeness": all are states of restlessness, anxiety, and uncertainty that marked much of Said's life, even his childhood years, as he writes in the opening paragraph of *Out of Place*:

> All families invent their parents and their children, give each of them a story, a character, fate, and even a language. There was always something wrong with how I was invented and meant to fit in with the world of my parents and four sisters. Whether this was because I constantly misread my part or because of some deep flaw in my being I could not tell for most of my early life. Sometimes I was intransigent, and proud of it. At other times I seemed to myself to be nearly devoid of any character at all, timid,

uncertain, without will. Yet the overriding sensation I had was of always being out of place.[10]

Said's sense of being "out of place," his discomfort with his personal, social, and political surroundings, created—to a degree—the very conditions of his possibility as an exiled critic. The pain accompanying a loss of home and identity, along with the alienation that comes with embodying the Palestinian Other within the West, which has yet to come to grips with what a Palestinian identity might mean and be, buoys the critic against the trappings and seductions of the larger culture. As an outsider-cum-by-virtue-and-education-learned-insider to Western culture, Said assumed a certain Du Boisian double-consciousness, turning a mirror on the epistemological categories and assumptions of the West as he stood outside and criticized them—seeing both himself and those who objectified him. In the introduction to his now-famous *Orientalism*, Said speaks of the cruel and punishing destiny of a Palestinian in the West in these terms:

> The life of an Arab Palestinian in the West, particularly in America, is disheartening. There exists here an almost unanimous consensus that politically he does not exist, and when it is allowed that he does, it is either as a nuisance or as an Oriental. The web of racism, cultural stereotypes, political imperialism, dehumanizing ideology holding in the Arab or the Muslim is very strong indeed, and it is this web which every Palestinian has come to feel as his uniquely punishing destiny.[11]

With the creation of the state of Israel in 1948 seeming to resolve the Jewish Question and the persistence of the Palestinian Question—along with the demonization of much of the indigenous population of the Middle East—throughout the latter half of the twentieth century into the present, a current of postcolonial thought now argues that Arabs have become the new "Jews."[12] Orientalism, as antisemitism's "secret sharer," deploys many of the same vile stereotypes against Arabs as antisemitic discourse deployed against European Jews. As a new Jew, Said could have easily laid claim to the New York Intellectual heritage; in fact, the comparison has been made by some. In his *Edward Said and the Politics of the Limit*, Moustapha Marrouchi writes, "Edward Said may be the last of a special breed of wide-ranging literary-political-aesthetic New York intellectuals, who are grouped around *Raritan*, one of America's most prestigious and influential voices of high culture."[13] Although his detractors branded him an ardent Palestinian nationalist, he was an inheritor of Enlightenment's most cherished values: reason, tolerance, noncoercive community, and mutual coexistence; like the New York Intellectuals he blended study of high culture, largely European, with a genuine concern for injustice and dispossession. As Irving Howe claimed, "The New York Intellectual [had] a fondness for ideological speculation; [he] strive[s] self-consciously to be 'brilliant.'"[14]

Said lived up to Howe's expectations of the New York Intellectual: they were radicals; had a fondness for ideological speculation; wrote literary criticism with a strong social emphasis; reveled in polemic; strove self-consciously to be brilliant; and by birth or osmosis, they were Jews.[15] In a way, these expectations—with the exception of the last one—could be seen in the "two conflicting impulses of [Said's] own literary career" as he excelled as a literary critic and a spokesperson for the Palestinian cause.[16] To a degree, the public intellectual grew out of the New York Intellectual tradition of the early and mid twentieth century. Said, as a Palestinian, has never really been considered part of this overwhelmingly Jewish intellectual movement. Despite this, Said did have close personal ties to some of the most prominent New York Intellectuals, such as F.W. Dupee, to whom he dedicates his massive *Reflections on Exile*, and Lionel Trilling, for whom Said held immense respect and admiration.

In Between Worlds, *Out of Place*, and Outside the Intellectual Fold

Said's education in the United States and his relatively comfortable life as an academic at Columbia occupied his early adulthood and midlife. Despite these comforts, he came to identify with lost causes that one supports—or believes in—because one cannot experience hope and achievement without them.

> The time for conviction and belief has passed, the cause seems to no longer contain any validity or promise, although it may once have possessed both. But are timeliness and conviction only matters of interpretation and feeling or do they derive from an objective situation? But there is no getting around the fact that for a cause to seem or feel lost is the result of judgment, and this judgment entails either a loss of conviction or, if the sense of loss stimulates a new sense of hope and promise, a feeling that the time for it is not right, has passed, is over.[17]

This theme of lost causes was most attributable, of course, to the Palestinian struggle to which Said became most attuned while a professor at Columbia in the city of New York. Edward Said's relationship to the city of New York merits an examination particularly as it explains his attachment to the phenomena of exile, homelessness, and in-betweeness: all are states of restlessness, anxiety, and uncertainty that marked much of Said's life, even his childhood years. In the introduction to *Reflections on Exile and Other Essays*, Said remarked that

> [w]hen [he] arrived in New York [in the fall of 1963] there was still some vitality left in its most celebrated group of intellectuals, those clustered around *Partisan Review*, City College and Columbia University, where Lionel Trilling and F.W. Dupee were good friends and solicitous colleagues of [his] in the Columbia College English Department. . . . Very early on, however, [he]

discovered that the battles the New York intellectuals were still engaged in over Stalinism and Soviet Communism simply did not have much interest for [him] or for most of [his] generation, for whom the civil rights movement and the resistance against the U.S. war in Vietnam were much more important and formative.[18]

Those who took part in the civil rights movement and the resistance against the U.S. war in Vietnam were not central players in the New York Intellectual movement. The implications of the civil rights movement and the cultural resistance to the Vietnam War for U.S. culture were, of course, instrumental in shaping the trajectory of Said's thought and work and connected quite naturally to Said's abiding concern, Palestinian self-determination. Each issue became a consciousness-raising exercise requiring a consideration of the rights of minority peoples and the legitimacy of their response and resistance to white supremacy, imperial hegemony, or settler-colonialist expansion. The political turn in Said's work came in 1967 as the Arab-Israeli War and Israel's occupation of the West Bank and Gaza forced him to confront his Palestinian identity in a new way.

The experience of 1967, the re-emergence of the Palestinian people as a political force, and my own engagement with that movement was what in a sense made it possible for me to live in New York, despite the frequent death threats, acts of vandalism, and abusive behavior directed at me and my family. In that rather more agitated and urgent environment than the one fussed over tiresomely by the New York intellectuals . . . a wholly different set of concerns from those of the *Partisan Review*—for who I wrote one of the early essays in this book—gradually surfaced in my work coming to an explicit statement first in my book *Beginnings: Intention and Method*, then in *Orientalism*, then still more insistently in my various writings on Palestine. These concerns, I believe, were magnified and made clear by the other New York, that of the diasporic communities from the Third World, expatriate politics, and the cultural debates, the so-called canon wars, that were to dominate academic life in the 1980s and after.[19]

Nineteen sixty-seven, then, represented a crucial year in Said's thinking and development, particularly as he conceptualized the New York Intellectuals and the failures of the movement. It was a time of great social ferment, and yet the New York Intellectuals instead of remaining true to their renegade beginnings had settled down into close readings of modernist poetry and novels, an indication of an accommodationist turn in their political aspirations. No longer standing in distinct opposition to the status quo, the New York Intellectuals had become apologists for the American power establishment. Interestingly enough, just as Said was beginning to grapple with the implications of being a Palestinian because of the Arab-Israeli Six-Day War in 1967, U.S. intellectuals began their intellectual love affair with Israel. A distinct interest in Israel, Israelism, and Jewish nationalism began at this historical moment in the wake of Israel's impressive military victory against multiple Arab enemies, proving the possible effectiveness of Israel as a U.S. strategic asset in containing Arab nationalism. This "turn," if you will, resonated in the lives of Jewish and Palestinian Americans.

Compare Said's statement about his coming to recognize his out-of-placeness as a Palestinian to Irving Howe's assessment of the New York Intellectuals as "Jewish writers com[ing] out of the immigrant milieu":

> The New York intellectuals comprised the first group of Jewish writers to come out of the immigrant milieu who did not crucially define themselves through a relationship to memories of Jewishness. They were the first generation of Jewish writers for whom the recall of an immigrant childhood seems not to have been unshakeable. They sought to declare themselves through a stringency of will, breaking clean from the immediate past and becoming autonomous men of the mind. If this severance from immigrant experience and Jewish roots would later come to seem a little suspect, the point needs nevertheless to be emphasized when the New York intellectuals began to cohere as a political-literary tendency around *Partisan Review* in the thirties, Jewishness as an idea or sentiment played only a minor, barely acknowledged role in their thought.[20]

To what degree Said self-identified with the populations being devastated in Vietnam or discriminated against in the United States is perhaps impossible to know. Recognizing the connections between the Palestinian struggle and the liberatory struggles of other oppressed peoples (the Vietnamese and African Americans) Said began to lay the theoretical ground for an expansive study of how Western culture represents and subjugates difference through the prism of culture. Ironically Jews also often claim a similar position, although detractors now argue that this is paternalistic, that the Jewish experience is no longer comparable to that of oppressed minorities.

As the purported founder of the field of postcolonial studies, Said sought to create noncoercive communities through the fusing of the discrepant experiences of ethnic minorities whether African-American, Vietnamese, or Palestinian. Although the New York Intellectuals did not focus primarily on these issues, one can argue that Said extended the soul-searching ethos of this overwhelmingly Jewish movement; as Jews struggled to cope with the challenges of assimilation in the early twentieth century, Said recuperated the experiences of other types of minorities, particularly people of color. Therein, I believe, rests Edward Said's legacy as a New York Intellectual. Abdul Jan Mohammed labeled Said a "specular border intellectual" in that he turned a mirror on the West, revealing its structural underpinnings, erasures, and commitments that have excluded ethnic minority voices. Said's recuperation of such colonial subjects as Fanon, James, Antonius, Kanafani, and his contrapuntal placement of those voices against and within the West stands as an unparalleled critical achievement.

Said's literary and very public intellectual career also fit quite squarely, albeit somewhat uneasily, within an intellectual tradition shared by such figures as Lionel Trilling, Sidney Hook, Philip Rahv, Irving Howe, and Norman Podhoretz. Although certainly sharing many of the same intellectual commitments that define the New York Intellectual—fierce intellectual independence, an enforced self-isolation from political power and the corruptions of the mainstream, and a rejection of a gregarious tolerance for present circumstance—Said can be viewed as defining the very characteristics of the engaged public intellectual while actively pursuing a political agenda that often put him at direct odds with the New York Intellectual tradition's most important figures, such as Michael Walzer.

Exodus, Statehood, and Empowerment

Although it is important not to view Walzer as in any way a representative of all New York Intellectuals, who shared a diversity of opinions and political views, one can catch a glimpse in Walzer's later political writings of how Jewish nationalism or Zionism came to occupy a central place among many Jewish writers who styled themselves as New York Intellectuals. In Walzer's writing, Said claims, one can find the following strategy:

> One: he finds a contemporary situation in the world that could, if it isn't immediately addressed, affect Israel's standing adversely; Two: he does that [deals with the discredited appearance of Jewish fundamentalism and continued colonial rule over many Arabs and Arab land] initially by appearing to condemn something close at hand, which progressives can also condemn without much effort and for which an already substantial consensus exists; Three: he shows how certain rather provocative aspects of Jewish and/or Israeli history and/or related episodes in, say, American or French history, do not at all fit the condemned instances, although some obviously do. Four (the really important intellectual move): Walzer formulates a theory and/or finds a person or text—provided that none is totally general, too uncompromising, too theoretically absolute—that provides the basis for a new category of politico-moral behavior. Five: he concludes by bringing together as many incompatible things as possible in as moral-sounding as well as politically palatable a rhetoric as possible."[21]

By documenting Walzer's strategy of apologetics for Israel as a liberal democracy in *Exodus and Revolution* and other works such as *Just and Unjust Wars*, Said traces the connection between Zionism and U.S. nationalism, which permeates the outlooks of those who would come to represent the Neoconservative movement (Podhoretz, Peretz, Kristol, Krauthammer, etc.). Said states, "If Jews were still stateless, and being held in ghettoes I do not believe Walzer would take the positions he has been taking."[22] In contrast to earlier figures labeled New York Intellectuals, such as Hannah Arendt, who expressed strong skepticism toward Zionism, a later group of intellectuals who experienced a political turn that aligned them with anticommunist movements opposing social change emerged. This group found itself toeing the line of the CIA, the Committee for Cultural Freedom, and other reactionary cultural forces attempting to stifle internal dissent against the U.S. intervention in Vietnam. Although the New York Intellectuals may have had their roots in Jewish radicalism, by 1950 they had become ensconced well within the American establishment. By that point, figures such as Norman Podhoretz, Irving Kristol, Sidney Hook, and Dwight Macdonald were praising the worldwide benefits of American militarism. How did the New York Intellectuals, a group that had its beginnings in intellectual independence, become so seemingly dependent upon the judgments of the corridors of power in such a relatively short time?

Said's debate with Walzer, which will be discussed in the latter half of this essay, highlights his sharp differences with the New York Intellectuals as he defends the Canaanites, not just Palestinians, but the indigenous populations of other times and contexts: Algerians, Vietnamese, and others. These native blacks and browns, he argues, have been pushed out, repressed, and forgotten. In perhaps Said's most visible exchange with a New York Intellectual, he refuses to allow Walzer to conduct this tidy inventorying of Exodus's history without forcing a recognition of the pain and the costs endured by indigenous populations through settler-colonialism, even when that settler-colonialism is tied to the national aspirations of a persecuted people such as the Jews in the wake of the Holocaust, i.e., the founding of Israel. Although *Exodus and Revolution* claims to be a liberatory narrative for all people, Said finds this assertion to be nonsensical and purblind to the realities of what the Canaanites have suffered. He reminds Walzer that native resistance is the natural reaction to settler-colonial domination, while condemning intellectuals who rationalize the latter with concepts such as the "connected critic," a reference to Camus's capitulation to the seduction of French nationalism. "No one would deny that critics belong to a community, work in a sphere, are connected to people. What Walzer cannot see is that there is considerable moral difference between the connectedness of a critic with an oppressing society, and a critic whose connection is to an oppressed one."[23] Said's exchange with Walzer highlights the difficulties of maintaining a critical consciousness when the life and livelihood of one's own people face destruction.

Lost Causes

The New York Intellectuals sought to create a union between critical consciousness and political conscience. Irving Howe writes, "Throughout the thirties the New York Intellectuals believed, somewhat naively, that this union was not only a desirable possibility but also a tie both natural and appropriate."[24] Throughout his career, Said's commitment to and enactment of worldliness surpassed the New York Intellectuals' attempts to link literary criticism and political activism.

Said's public interventions, his search for solutions to seemingly intractable international problems and conflicts, refused the oft-portrayed and often easily formulated and bandied about image of the impotent literary critic. The skills of the engaged critic, if deployed in the spirit of withering critique and in the context of "lost causes" can contribute to the overturning, or at least an unsettling of destructive orthodoxies that often pass as almost "natural," for example, the current state of affairs. Through an exertion of will and a great refusal of what mere mortals accept as necessary evils or an unfortunate state of affairs, the engaged critic resists, unsettles, and defiantly seeks alternative explanations, histories, narratives, and solutions to create a culture and climate of coexistence. The erasure and deliberate forgetting of nondominant voices and perspectives creates the continual production of an overwhelming common sense that, when challenged, makes the critic appear silly or Martian-like, as the critique cannot be understood within the dominant idiom. Said championed "lost causes":

> But does the consciousness and even the actuality of a lost cause entail that
> sense of defeat and resignation that we associate with the abjection of capit-
> ulation and the dishonor of grinning or bowing survivors who opportunis-
> tically fawn on their conquerors and seek to ingratiate themselves with the
> new dispensation? Must it always result in the broken will and demoralized
> pessimist of the defeated? I think not, although the alternative is a difficult
> and extremely precarious one, at least on the level of the individual.[25]

Never satisfied by the approval of a boss's nod, the promise of a guild prize, or even an ambassadorship to some exotic place, the committed critic seeks to tell the truth regardless of whom he may embarrass or expose; he sits back and accepts the repercussions—whether they be personal or professional—as they come, often seeking to "shock" well-entrenched stakeholders, for whom *Realpolitik* is a religion rather than an easily identifiable codeword for "the American establishment," into a recognition of the too often damaging effects of the corrupt application of power in the world. As Said writes in his *The Politics of Dispossession*,

> [And] orthodoxy quickly arms itself with such self-confirmations as "re-
> sponsible," "realistic," and "pragmatic," which lay upon the intellectual the
> burden to "stop questioning our values and threatening our privilege." "Our"
> in this sentence is the possessive of the apologist, who will pay any moral or
> intellectual price in order not to trouble himself with the radical issues.[26]

Using Raymond Williams' "structure of feeling" as the basis for a critical heuristic that he came to call "structures of attitude and reference," Said exposed the subtle ways through which the sheer power of empire exercised a definitive control over not only geographic space but also the literary and literal imagination—the structuring of social space through narrative enclosures and the very forms through which narratives can be told. Empire, the overwhelming suzerainty of imperialism, controls the structure of stories and the outlook of the characters contained therein, as Said demonstrates with respect to Austen's *Mansfield Park*. The exclusion of resistant voices and dissenting views is enabled by the structure of the narrative itself, facilitating a sutureless presentation of imperial dominance that extends political-military might into literary spaces. Within such a tightly controlled public space that so completely controls who may speak as an "expert" on terrorism or American foreign policy, those who reject the facile formulations—so often found in the "clash of civilizations" thesis and "you are either with us or against us" formulations, Said enacts a brand of public intellectualism that recaptures the spirit of speaking the untrammeled truth to power, the consequences be damned.

Said's notion of exile, an out-of-place-ness that endows one with a critical edge and fierce independence so very necessary to casting criticism and judgment from afar, matches the New York Intellectual's 1930s-style commitment to staying out of power's entrapment: its material rewards and attractive sinecures that are surely meant to co-opt any and all into the ideology of the status quo.[27]

> The greatest single fact of the past three decades has been, I believe, the vast human migration attendant upon war, colonialism, and decolonization, economic and political revolution, and such devastating occurrences as famine, ethnic cleansing, and great power machinations. In a place like New York, but surely also in other Western metropoles like London, Paris, Stockholm, and Berlin, all these things are reflected immediately in the changes that transform neighborhoods, professions, cultural production, and topography on an almost hour-to-hour basis. Exiles, émigrés, refugees, and expatriates uprooted from their lands must make do in new surroundings, and the creativity as well as the sadness that can be seen in what they do is one of the experiences that has still to find its chroniclers, even though a splendid cohort of writers that includes such different figures as Salman Rushdie and V.S. Naipaul has already opened further the door first tried by Conrad.[28]

The exile can see what others, intoxicated by the rewards of orthodoxy, no longer can: the general corruption of the guild structure and its embarrassing willingness to suppress rather than to reveal unpleasant truths about the nation-state.

> What remains is an immigrants' and exiles' city that exists in tension with the symbolic (and at times actual) center of the world's globalized late capitalist economy whose raw power, projected economically, militarily, and politically everywhere, demonstrates how America is the only superpower today.[29]

A contrast can be seen between what Said does in *Out of Place* and what someone like Norman Podhoretz does in *Making It* and *Breaking Ranks*. A parallel can be drawn between Said's post-1967 experience living as a Palestinian in the United States while coping with the indignities of anti-Arab sentiment, which has historical roots in the Orientalism Said analyzed with such precision, and the prevalent antisemitism of the America of the thirties and forties. This replays the experience Irving Howe demonstrates in *World of Our Fathers*—understanding what it means to be an ethnic minority within a larger American culture where one has to assimilate into or isolate oneself from the larger homogeneous mass.

This aspect of Said's criticism, its relationship to Said's "Oriental" identity and the inevitable ways in which it trafficked in but never directly engaged antisemitic caricatures and stereotypes, deserves more critical attention. If it is in fact the case that Palestinian-Arabs are the new Jews, Said, in writing the history of Orientalism, has—by the same logic—written the history of the new antisemitism, not the new antise. /tism trumpeted so loudly by the ADL and World Jewish Congress but instead the racial hatred directed against Arabs within a cultural climate where it is sanctioned and quietly condoned. While striving to write the history of Orientalism, Said quite naturally wrote the conditions of his own possibility. Driven by an enduring commitment to placing "c ⸱icism before solidarity," Said continually rejected the easy-going style of the p ⸱ dit and the "Orwellian terminology" of the up-and-coming-establishment figⱥ re, qualities that no doubt establish him as a New York Intellectual while also assuring him an anomalous place within the same tradition.

Resisting the Trappings of Power

In his lifelong search to bring together the insights of literary criticism and t⸱ e far-reaching implications of a directly engaged and necessary political activis⸱n, Edward Said traversed many disciplines and modes of thought, often upsetting well-entrenched interests and the ideological ruses that hide and make the⸱ 1 more palatable and less unsettling. What made Edward Said's life and career s⸱ extraordinary was the way in which he challenged the dry-as-dust criticism ⸱f his day to be something more than textual exegesis bent upon preserving idealized abstractions devoted to the preservation of aesthetic imperatives. Like the earlier New York Intellectuals, Said moved literary criticism into the world, where the life-preserving function of secular criticism—unhampered by the divine edicts and metaphysical absolutes that drive various types of religious enthusiasm—might grapple with the concerns of the day. The retreat of various literary specialists, seemingly bent on avoiding sensitive political issues and the commitments that come along with resolving them, into schools of criticism that promote the production of precious terminologies, finely crafted to highlight textual operations, suggests the abandonment of the one-time oppositional function that many engaged critical intellectuals such as Sartre and Chomsky have found so dear: the continual monitoring and withering criticism of centers of concentrated power. The old "New Critics" shared this trait, in contrast to the New York Intellectuals, who were largely a renegade group in the 1950s.

Said asks, "What does it mean to have a critical consciousness if . . . the intellectual's situation is a worldly one and yet, by virtue of that worldliness itself, the intellectual's social identity should involve something more than strengthening those aspects of the culture that require mere affirmation and orthodox compliancy from its members?"[30] He contends that exposing those aspects of a culture that promote stifling orthodoxies, that soften and tame the critical sense, will contribute to human freedom and fulfillment. He implores his fellow critics to understand that "[c]riticism must think of itself as life-enhancing and constitutively opposed to every form of tyranny, domination, abuse; its social goals and non-coercive knowledge produced in the interests of human freedom."[31]

The individuals who conduct these critiques upset the comfort level of those regulating the types of criticism that become tamed by institutions and orthodoxies. Those who resist the idée rescues and strike out on their own to find out the truth about the structures of domination that soften the critical sense in lesser men are labeled as "agitators," "a set of interfering, meddling people, who come down to some perfectly contented class of community and sow the seeds of discontent among them," Said contends. "That is the reason why agitators are so completely necessary."[32] Being comfortable or feeling at home reduces the very conditions of possibility for the exile's existence: uneasiness, restlessness, uncertainty, out-of-placeness, and a constant state of alertness. This vigilance arises out of the awareness that at any moment conditions may change such that the exiled critic will be forced to flee from state authorities because of a specific statement he has made or a specific commitment he has honored. Abuse, slander, and even death threats only embolden the dedicated critic as he seeks, at any cost, to avoid Benda's *trahison des clercs*. Although the New York Intellectuals aspired to Said's level of commitment with respect to engaged social critique, they clearly did not, and perhaps could not, meet his standard. As the quintessential specular border intellectual, Said traversed the often self-imposed fiefdoms that hamper the professional literary critic's career, daring to take up the cause of populations long forgotten by academics and politicians, fad and fashion.

Predicting the vagaries of intellectual culture represents a daunting, if not impossible, task: the politics of one era are swept away and replaced by another, clearing the intellectual horizon and posting new challenges and obstacles. The volatility of the New York Intellectual scene from the 1930s to the 1950s certainly merits close examination, with particular emphasis placed upon the shift from clearly demarcated Marxist positions to rabid anti-Stalinism and liberal anti-communism. Many of the New York Intellectuals in the course of their careers drifted from the Communist Party to Trotskyism, to anti-Stalinism, to liberal anti-communism, and finally to conservatism, Sidney Hook being perhaps the most prominent example of this intellectual trajectory. Adept popular intellectuals are able to measure the winds of fashion and change while gauging the survivability of any one political position. Convictions are easily replaced by pragmatic considerations such as economic livelihood and professional popularity. Although it might be easy to conclude that many of the later New York Intellectuals were not intellectuals at all but merely sham intellectuals, such a judgment does not adequately take into account the political pressures attending the material conditions governing intellectual work during the 1950s and 1960s. Although Said came upon the scene somewhat later, he managed to enter the "political fray" after 1967, when his own identity as a Palestinian could be neither ignored nor hidden: in some sense, he saw little choice in his "decision" to become an engaged intellectual.

An urgency and restless energy pulse through Said's political essays, tampering with the normalcy of the everyday, undermining its unity and simpleness: a contrapuntal reading reveals the ruthlessness with which empire structures time, space, and sense. Said's alertness, his ability to strip away all of the layers of camouflage that conceal the brutalities that often attend abuses of power in the world and its excessive cruelties and insidious reach; his own sense of displacement, loss, and migration permeated this work—the essay form itself worked through the sense of torment and anguish, relieving Said of his obligation to bear witness to his people's suffering. Despite his training as a high humanist, Said struggled with the narratives and histories of those who fell out of humanism's reach—those who due to an epistemological willfulness had no identity: "They cannot represent themselves. They must be represented" (Marx). This epigraph from *Orientalism* captures quite perfectly the modern Palestinian predicament. Although it is true that Said was a Palestinian representing Palestinians, as well as an Arab representing Arabs, he found his destiny wrapped up in making these intellectual representations to a Western audience woefully ill-informed about either. Said's recuperation of the Arab as an idea involves, what Abdirahman Hussein calls an "activated agonistic dialectic," pours a corrosive acid on Western traditions, customs, and discourses that have for centuries "spoken to and for" Arabs through Orientalist discourses.[33]

Resisting Accommodation

Like many of the early New York Intellectuals such as Herbert Solokow and Max Eastman, Said quite naturally adopted an oppositional stance toward the dominant American culture, seeking a leveraging position through which to not only conduct critique but also to create a cognitive dissonance among those in power—a recognition that willful domination brings with it a price for whole populations and pieces of geography. Unlike the New York Intellectuals, however, Said refused the temptations of power and never committed the apostasy so central to the New York Intellectuals' evolution. The excision of the New York Intellectuals' revolutionary beginnings, and the deradicalization of the movement, demonstrates the immense strides the movement took to avoid being associated with the anti-Stalinist left—although many of them had belonged to it. The amnesia of the New York Intellectuals on this point suggests the enormity of the political stakes involved: to admit the shift in position would have meant to admit being pulled in by power's centripetal force.

Encounter, the Committee on Cultural Freedom, and other CIA-backed venues gave the New York Intellectuals a way to ideologically manage the rapid changes in American culture. Racial issues, the rise of feminism, protests against U.S. involvement in Vietnam, and the growing resistance culture forced the New York Intellectuals to shift rightward, suggesting that their real interests resided not with the people of color and other marginalized groups—with whom they previously allied, at least theoretically—but instead with the white, power establishment. As Jewish writers prior to assimilation, they stood in opposition to this establishment and critiqued its chauvinism and the alienation it produced. The seemingly paradoxical history of the New York Intellectuals, with the deradicalization of the movement's leading figures throughout the cold war, is just now being rewritten. As one-time radicals such as Sidney Hook and Phillip Rahv traded in their revolutionary garb for the trappings of power that came along with CIA-front money, they consciously rewrote the fabric of their political convictions while maintaining that their belief systems had remained consistent across the years of change that swept the country in the fifties. Although it is true that Stalin's purges did play a part in their shift away from communism, some intellectuals used this shift to reinvent themselves in extremely self-serving ways, and it is difficult to disentangle motives on this front. Nonetheless, the vehemence with which New York Intellectuals such as Diana Trilling resisted opinions that hinted at anything to the contrary suggests that the politics of apostasy brings with it many a bitter pill. As Frances Stone Saunders writes in *Who Paid the Piper? The CIA and the Cultural Cold War*:

> That former left-wingers should have come to be roped together in the same enterprise with the CIA is less implausible than it seems. There was a genuine community of interest and conviction between the agency and those intellectuals who were hired, even if they did not know it to fight the Cultural Cold War. The CIA's influence was not always, or often, reactionary and sinister, wrote America's pre-eminent liberal historian, Arthur Schlesinger, "In my experience its leadership was politically enlightened and sophisticated."[34]

In light of the neoconservative self-portrait being created by many of the New York Intellectuals, one is tempted to conclude that they have had a stake in perpetuating an amnesia that avoids a forthright disclosure of their previous political history as revolutionary but anti-Stalinist Marxists.[35] Wald writes:

> In fact, only by understanding the peculiar nature of their transformation can one come to grips with the most contradictory and confusing aspects of the New York intellectuals: that a group of individuals who mainly began their careers as revolutionary communists in the 1930s could become an institutionalized and even hegemonic component of American culture during the conservative 1950s while maintaining a high degree of collective continuity. This pendular evolution by so many New York intellectuals suggests, from a radical point of view, that their politics were deceptive from the beginning.[36]

Although it is true that many of the New York Intellectuals fell victim to the "God that failed" syndrome, the dimensions of their intellectual treason should be measured in increments:

> It was by successive stages that the New York intellectuals moved from a distinct variety of communism in the 1930s to a distinct variety of liberalism in the 1950s; from advocating socialist revolution to endorsing capitalism. Anti-Stalinism became a catchall phrase in the U.S., representing a resistance to social change. In the 1950s the formerly radical New York intellectuals defended themselves against an onslaught by attacking those further to their left, sometimes using the theory of "totalitarianism" to claim that the concepts "left" and "right" had lost their traditional meanings. Essentially they purged from the pale of respectability those adhering to ideas fundamentally at odds with Cold War liberal ideology, starting with all variants of Leninism.[37]

As Wald argues, "the logic of pure and simple anti-Stalinism is to move its adherents toward an anticommunism that views the imperialist practices of the United States as a lesser evil in a world conflict of two 'camps.'"[38] By the time Edward Said came onto the political scene in the late sixties, these camps were on a collision course.

Saidian Resistance

Edward Said dedicated his scholarly career to exposing how systems of thought create exclusions dividing human beings, who might otherwise find lines of connection and mutuality between one another, along filiative lines such as blood, ethnos, and nation, and affiliative ones such as professions, alliances, and organizations. Said's critical concern for the ways in which cultures erase the voices of ethnic minority figures, evident throughout his scholarly corpus, restored the faces to the victims, particularly victims of imperial violence and erasure. Occupying an in-between space that was the condition of the New York Intellectuals in an even more special way, Said echoed Adorno that the exile sees what others cannot see. If nothing else, the history of the New York Intellectuals ultimately represents a cautionary tale about how allegiance to power can corrupt the intellectual mission in a very serious way. When adherence to a party line and doctrinal truths becomes the calling card of a group of intellectuals rather than the unfettered pursuit of truth, Benda's cry of "*trahison des clercs*" is in order. Said's career avoided the pitfalls to which many New York Intellectuals eventually succumbed.

Said's sense of self, his ability to use his own human agency in the world, signaled a larger than life person. He wished to write his life and identity into existence. One gets the sense in *Out of Place* that Said is coming to know himself for the first time. This follows the path of many New York Intellectuals, who understand what it meant to be a minority within a larger American culture where one has to assimilate or isolate oneself. The ability of the individual to *begin*, to break free of tradition and to start anew—either as a writer or as a burgeoning sign of critical consciousness—represents a radical act of freedom, a necessary act of resistance that occurs between culture and system. Affiliative loyalties replace filiative relationships; in this sense, one can refashion an identity through relations unconnected to birth, relations that can be invented according to time and circumstance.

It is this individual effort, in Said's estimation, that allows a breaking free from the constraints of a textual tradition or a disciplinary apparatus, or a departing from the cliché-ridden dictates of a cynical *real politick* manufactured for the benefit of a crippling conformism. This effort can have a numbing effect upon the critical mind as it navigates between the Charybis of independence and the Scylla of communal acceptance. The condition of exile, as Said so powerfully demonstrated, provides a site—a stance or state of mind—through which to remain alert to the seductions and trappings of power, attractions that often reduce the most perceptive critic to a mere state functionary. In his *Representations of the Intellectual*, Said writes:

> Nothing in my view is more reprehensible than those habits of mind in the intellectual that induce avoidance, that characteristic turning away from a difficult and principled position which you know to be the right one, but which you decide not to take. You do not want to appear too political; you are afraid of seeming controversial; you need the approval of a boss or authority figure; you want to keep a reputation of being balanced, objective, moderate; your hope is to be asked back, to consult, to be on a board or prestigious committee, and so to remain within the responsible mainstream; someday you hope to get a honorary degree, a big prize, perhaps even an ambassadorship.[39]

The constant intellectual vigilance necessary for resisting the desperate longing for mainstream acceptance and the creature comforts that so often can tame the critic brings with it a loneliness and isolation that become difficult to sustain. The pressures of career, family, and the day-to-day drudgery associated with contemporary life often relegate the embrace of the critical attitude to an unreachable and impractical ideal: only a handful of intellectuals can live up to Julian Benda's critical model that calls for resisting *trahison des clercs*. Standing against daunting odds, going against the cultural flow, and not engaging in the massive, selective amnesia that is so much a part of the American cultural landscape requires constant effort, an energy and sense of purpose that never longs for a pep rally, a sign of acceptance and reassurance. When one receives such a sign, it's high time to change course, to reevaluate one's position in relation to the larger culture, and to chart a new direction that avoids the idée rescues that reduce the complexity of the human community to a facile formulation of "us" and "them." Said speaks out against a tolerance for the status quo and flight from controversy:

For the intellectual these habits of mind are corrupting *par excellence*. If
anything can denature, naturalize, neutralize, and finally kill a passionate
intellectual life it is the internalization of such habits. Personally, I have encountered them in one of the toughest of all contemporary issues, Palestine,
where fear of speaking out about one of the greatest injustices in modern
history has hobbled, blinkered, and muzzled many who know the truth and
are in a position to serve it.[40]

The ability of the individual to make an impression, a mark, on the collection of civilization's accumulated texts and traditions signals the importance
of human agency in forging intellectual resistance against discourses such as Orientalism, imperialism, and the luxuries of a culture's selective amnesias. Through
the trope of Blackmur's "technique of trouble," Said created trouble along disciplinary lines, subjecting the cult of expertise—whether that of the Orientalist or
the literary critic—to radical unsettling. Said's career-long belief that the individual could still emerge through these mazes of discourses—while attempting
to awaken an intellectual community from its self-induced philosophical slum-
ber—finds repeated expression from *Conrad and the Fiction of Autobiography*
through to *Freud and the Non-European*. The importance of the individual's relying upon, while also resisting tradition, found such repeated articulation in Said's
work because it was directly tied to Said's self-construction as a critical intellectual: as Said wrestled to understand how the West constructs its Other, in this
case the Oriental, he mastered the major figures of the Western canon, coming
to a deep understanding of how the most prominent figures in the history of European thought managed, and to a degree contained, the conditions of possibility
of difference's expression. Unlocking the master code of Orientalism, locating
the unarticulated Manichaeism that propels the separation of cultures while in
fact such cultures are interdependent, stood as Said's most valuable achievement
as he strove to write between culture and system.

Systems of thought, such as Orientalism, rely upon the creation of my-
thologies, which must be held in place through intellectual omissions, excisions,
and amnesias. The perversity of knowledge systems contributes to the creation
of discursive divisions that undermine human unities. Said claims that Orientalism, for example, was an intellectual and human failure because it demonstrated
how knowledge can be deployed to undermine human divisions instead of high-
lighting human commonalities. Obviously, the *Orientalism* project was deeply
personal for Said:

> Much of the personal investment in [*Orientalism*] derives from my aware-
> ness of being an "Oriental" as a child growing up in two British colonies. All
> of my education, in those colonies (Palestine and Egypt) and in the United
> States has been Western, and yet that deep early awareness has persisted.
> In many ways my study of Orientalism has been an attempt to inventory
> the traces upon me, the Oriental subject, of the culture whose domination

has been so powerful a factor in the life of all Orientals. . . . Along the way, as severely and as rationally as I have been able, I have tried to maintain a critical consciousness, as well as employing those instruments of historical, humanistic, and cultural research of which my education has made me the fortunate beneficiary. In none of that however, have I ever lost hold of the cultural reality of, the personal involvement in having been constituted as, "an Oriental."[41]

For Said, the task of the responsible intellectual should be to upend knowledge's reificatory and place-holding power, while articulating the commonalities in humans' discrepant experiences; doing so is the key to forging the conditions for "non-coercive" human communities. Nationalism, one of the most destructive forces of the twentieth century, remade the outlines of the world and relied upon the creation of narrative stories to support its development. The Exodus story, the biblical story of Moses leading the Israelites out of Egypt to the Promised Land, represents just such a narrative in that intellectuals have seized upon it in the course of explaining national liberations.

The Said-Walzer Exchange

The publication of Michael Walzer's *Exodus and Revolution* in 1986 sparked a vitriolic and protracted exchange between Walzer and Edward Said in the journal *Grand Street*, pitting two well-established academics, one Jewish and one Palestinian, in a conflict of interpretations over the biblical text Exodus. Walzer can be seen as a prototypical New York Intellectual. A long-time contributor to *Dissent* magazine and the *New Republic*, Walzer has earned a reputation as liberalism's respectable voice, a man of the left who knows well the pitfalls of radicalism and has frequently written about them. Walzer dedicates *Exodus and Revolution* to the *New Republic*'s longtime editor, Martin Peretz.

Why did Walzer turn his critical arsenal upon this particular biblical story? He presents Exodus's supposed linear structure with oppression, promised land, redemption, the crushing of antirevolutionary violence in the Golden Calf episode, and so forth, as a divine warrant for Israel's creation and the resulting destruction of the Canaanite Palestinians. In *Exodus and Revolution*, Walzer argues that the Exodus story represented a narrative-basis for contemporary liberation politics that provided hope for oppressed peoples. He claims, using the argument within Exodus, that "Wherever you are it's probably Egypt; the departure from Egypt requires a march through the wilderness; we can march to the Promised Land by joining arms and marching together; this story forms the basis of all modern liberatory movements, including the African-American civil rights movement." Said viewed Walzer's argument as a bad-faith, Zionist attempt to justify the expulsion of over 750,000 Palestinians in 1947 and the creation of Israel in 1948. He argued that Walzer must take Israel-Palestine out

of the colonialism-anticolonialism discussion so as to avoid indicting Israel in
the same way the U.S. was indicted in Vietnam. The Israeli occupation in 1967
made this increasingly difficult, leading to a whole industry of Israeli apologetics
and historical revision.

Walzer's compact and tidy history of Exodus politics in *Exodus and Revolution* suggests a complete "blindness" to the oppression of those who have suffered under the Israeli military occupation: the Palestinians of the West Bank,
the Gaza Strip, and the Golan Heights. Said's indignation is apparent in the following quotation:

> [But] the one thing I want Walzer to remember is that the more he shores
> up the sphere of Exodus politics the more likely it is that the Canaanites
> on the outside will *resist* and try to penetrate the walls banning them from
> the goods of what is, after all, partly their world too. The strength of the
> Canaanite, that is the exile position, is that being defeated and "outside,"
> you can perhaps more easily feel compassion, more easily call injustice "in-
> justice," more easily speak directly and plainly of all oppression, and with
> less difficulty try to understand (rather than mystify or occlude) history and
> equality.[42]

In its general outlines, the Said-Walzer debate over Exodus was reminiscent of the Sartre-Camus debate over the *pied noirs* in Algeria, Frenchmen who
lorded it over a native majority, and the legitimacy of colonial regimes and the
resistance that native populations often direct against them. In 1952, Camus
and Sartre, who had worked together as part of the French resistance against
the Nazis, broke their friendship due to a series of events centering around the
Communist Party's stance on anticolonial violence. Camus took a decidedly
anti-Marxist stance, becoming a darling among cold-war liberals, while Sartre
joined the Communist Party. Camus rejected the politics of the engaged critic
for the distance of what he called the connected critic, an intellectual who admits
his ties to an ethnic community while realizing that these ties may condition
and compromise his ability to criticize or condemn that community's actions,
particularly when they exert colonial dominance. Whereas Sartre condemned
the French *pied noir* community of Algeria, even going so far as to label the
native resistance against it "legitimate," Camus chose "his mother over justice,"
deciding not to condone anticolonial violence, in direct contrast to Third World
revolutionaries such as Franz Fanon and C.L.R. James.

Said harshly judges Walzer's tidy reading of Exodus, which excises in-
convenient aspects of the Israelites' escape from Egypt and bondage, a blatant
apology—similar to Camus' evasions on Algeria—for the expulsion of the Palestinians prior to Israel's creation, excusing the creation of a neocolonial depen-
dency that seeks to blot out the memory of the Canaanites. In his response to
Said's "Michael Walzer's Exodus and Revolution: A Canaanite Reading," Walzer
amazingly compares the Palestinians to the *pied noirs*, whom Camus eventually

encouraged to leave Algeria because of the native uprising. Said writes: "Walzer can't distinguish between the victims and the conqueror-colonizers. Is this the sort of analysis we should expect from a professor at Princeton's Advanced Institute?" This debate with Walzer is Said's most heated with a New York Intellectual and reveals a great deal about how the New York Intellectuals drifted toward Jewish nationalism and the pitfalls they encountered in the course of embracing a strong identity politics. Walzer, amongst all the New York Intellectuals, worked quite hard to distinguish Israel's wars against the Arab states, and in particular against the Palestinians, from America's adventure in Vietnam.

- According to Walzer, Jewish liberation provides a model for all liberatory movements.
- Israel's creation, and the destruction of the Canaanite Palestinians, was legitimate and biblically ordained.
- Without explicitly stating so, Walzer strategically connects secular and religious worlds. How?
- Walzer wishes to present Exodus as secular and progressive, about liberation and against oppression and as a paradigm for radical politics. Said asks, "Why is Walzer so undialectical, so simplifying, so ahistorical and reductive?" According to Said, the first answer is that he really is not and that Walzer's argument in *Exodus and Revolution* has an altogether different, and quite complex, trajectory from the one presented on a surface reading.

The material in Walzer's work that touches upon Israel's predicament since 1967 (*Just and Unjust Wars, Thick and Thin: Moral Argument at Home and Abroad, Spheres of Justice*, and *Exodus and Revolution*) is made to shore up the more unpleasant aspects of Israel's founding through philosophical arguments while serving a resolutely political (and not philosophical) agenda. Its path is marked by repeated words and phrases: *progressive, moral, radical politics, national liberation, oppression, liberalism, liberal subject, community, democracy*. It is necessary, in order to understand Said's multilayered reading of the text, to quote at some length from his "Michael Walzer's Exodus and Revolution: A Canaanite Reading." He begins by discussing Walzer's redeployment of Jewish myth and history:

> Considered as a group, the provenance of these [progressive, moral, radical politics, national liberation, oppression] is not Exodus. The terms enter American and European political vocabulary after the Second World War, usually in the context of colonial wars fought against movements of national liberation. The power of "liberation" and "oppression" in the works of those Third World militants like Cabral and Fanon, who were organically linked to anticolonial insurrectionary movements, is that the concepts were later able to acquire a certain embattled legitimacy in the discourse of First World

writers sympathetic to anticolonialism. The point about writers like Sartre, Debray, and Chomsky, however, is that they were not mere echoes of the African, Asian, and Latin American anti-imperialists, but intellectuals writing from within—and against—the colonialist camp.[43]

Like Sartre, Debray, and Chomsky, Said wrote from within—and against— the colonialist camp, presenting a perhaps even more compelling portrait as an embattled Palestinian spokesperson. After the 1967 Arab-Israeli Six-Day War, the New York Intellectual was forced to question his relationship with his Jewishness and Israel, just as Said was forced to confront his identity as a Palestinian within a context of loss and dispossession. The Jewish intellectual, like the Palestinian intellectual, sought to understand his relationship within a national or aspiring national community, measuring the pitfalls of blind loyalty to an unreflective nationalism. Such blind loyalty leads to a *trahison des clercs*, a treason Said finds Walzer guilty of committing throughout *Exodus and Revolution*:

> Although most commentators recognize that that period is now practically over (largely because the anticolonial movements were victorious), only a little attention has been devoted to the ideological aftermath in Europe and America. A "return" to Judeo-Christian values was trumpeted; the defense of Western civilization was made coterminous with general attacks on terrorism, Islamic fundamentalism, structuralism and communism. . . . Much retrospective analysis of the colonial past focused on the evils of the newly independent states—the corruption and tyranny of their rule, the betrayed promise of their revolutions, the mistaken faith placed in them by their European supporters. The most striking revisionist has been Connor Cruise O'Brien, whose total about-face found him an entirely new audience . . . extremely eager to hear about the evils of black or brown dictators and the relative virtues of white imperialism.[44]

As American liberals worked hard in the midst of the cold war to condemn the excesses of dictatorial rule in Soviet-backed regimes, their stances with respect to countries where the United States backed harsh and repressive regimes—while often directly interfering with the formation of democratic rule and worker participation—were quite different. A noticeable silence attended U.S. intellectual discourse with respect to bloody U.S. interventions in Nicaragua and South Africa during the 1980s. Similarly, a silence has attended U.S. intellectual discourse with respect to U.S. support for Israel's thirty-nine-year military occupation of the West Bank and Gaza.

> The revival of anti-imperialist and liberationist language in discussions of Nicaragua and South Africa is one major exception to this pattern. The other major exception has been the rhetoric of liberal supporters of Israel. I speak here of a rather small but quite influential and prestigious group that since 1967 has conducted itself with—from the perspective of students of

rhetoric—considerable tactical flexibility. All along, in the face of considerable evidence to the contrary, members of this group have tried to maintain
Israel's image as a progressive and wholly admirable state.[45]

The upshot of Said's exchanges with the New York Intellectuals revolves
around the responsibility of the intellectual and the difficult issues that attend a
committed criticism, which often forces one to leave ethnic loyalties behind while
affirming an oft-cited but frequently avoided dictum: "criticism before solidarity."
This debate highlights the war, or "conflict of interpretations"; in this case, the
text in contest is Exodus. Said's and Walzer's stances, vis á vis Sartre's and Camus'
stances toward Algeria, act as a proxy for their stances toward Israel-Palestine.
For Said, there can be no Jewish march through the wilderness out of the oppression of Egypt, culminating in the creation of Israel, without the destruction of the
Canaanite-Palestinians. Although Walzer has long argued that there are instances
when ethnic minorities, caught between the borders of a nation where they are
not wanted, "must be helped to leave," he makes the seemingly inexplicable error
of comparing the Palestinians to *pied noirs*, who in Said's words "battened themselves by force on an overseas possession whose natives were abused, exploited,
repressed until those natives rose up and sacrificed one million dead in the process of liberating themselves from French settlers."[46] In this exchange, one can
easily see how historical representations of Jewish suffering and the struggle for
Palestinian self-determination in the American public sphere can create violent
intellectual confrontation.[47]

I see this exchange between Said and Walzer, as a New York Intellectuals, to
be among Said's most interesting and provocative contemporary debates. We see
Said's and Walzer's stances on colonial violence and native resistance, exchanges
between dominating and subjugated populations, and—of course—Said's and
Walzer's varying stances on Israel's creation and its relationship with the Palestinians. "[Walzer] has the gall to say that I am represented by 'Arafat, Habash,
and Abu Musa,' mixing together the one acknowledged symbol of Palestinian
nationalism with two of his bitterest, most implacable enemies. Well, who represents Walzer, the Israeli pilot who drops cluster bombs on children in Beirut, or
Generals Sharon and Eytan?"[48] In this question, Said implies that American Jews,
in their "embrace of the state" and state power, are no longer powerless and can
indeed make victims of others in the name of Jewish nationalism. The deaths of
nearly 20,000 Palestinians between June and September 1982, with nearly 3,000
Lebanese-Palestinians killed by Israel's Phalangist allies at the refugee camps of
Sabra and Shatila, with IDF troops purportedly overseeing the massacre, led to a
great deal of soul-searching in Israel about the specific aims of the invasion into
South Lebanon. The apologetics for the invasion among left-liberals in the United
States has been well-documented.[49] Said asks, "Whom does one respect more, in
the accredited Western and Judaic traditions, the courageously outspoken intel-
lectual or loyal member of the complicit majority?"[50]

With the New York Intellectuals' drift away from the Com͵ ͺunist Party through to Trotskyism and eventually to liberal anticommunism leading to conservatism, we see a shift in their view of colonialism and antiliberation movements, for example, Vietnam and Israel. In fact, Walzer has been viewed as one of the leading liberal voices within the United States for nearly thirty years. ͺ ͺs *Spheres of Justice*, *Just and Unjust Wars*, and *Thick and Thin: Moral Arguments* ͺt *Home and Abroad* have contributed greatly to left-liberal thought in the U.S. A ͺ-ticommunism, a U.S. nationalist version of liberalism, has, with respect to Ame ͺ-can foreign policy, camouflaged military adventurism and colonial exploitation by describing them in more palatable ways, "defensive wars," "occupation," anͺ the like. Neoconservatism, then, really became a "middle way" between libeͺ l anticommunism and right-wing conservatism. Although the pitfalls of Vietnaͺ were recognized, great efforts were made to show that "Israel was not Vietnam," reinforcing the purity and necessity of Israel's birth in the wake of the Holocaust.

Through his writings, Said projects an anguish and despair at the state of contemporary intellectual culture; at the same time, however, there is in Paul Bové's words an attempt to attain "hope and reconciliation."[51] Without hope it's impossible to fight for a lost cause, a cause that represents a discrepant experience and disentangling them from the grips of highly mediated discourses.

Said's persistent efforts in criticizing the ayatollahs and imams of the Middle East while also leveling withering critiques of U.S. presidents, PLO leader Yasser Arafat, and Israeli prime ministers suggest that he was capable of living out the highest ideals of the committed intellectual: possessing the capacity to extend the application of a principle to friend and foe equally, regardless of the consequences. In rejecting the cult of expertise and the policy intellectuals who proffer the peace of the powerful, Said challenged the easy-going collegiality of the academic guild and the sycophantism of those abiding by a constant *Realpolitik*. While the public rhetoric of "us versus them" and "the clash of civilizations" is consumed by the jingoists and the newsmakers, Said cautioned us against enjoying the collective comforts of nationalism and its attendant patriotic fervor.

As went the American power establishment, so went the New York Intellectuals, bringing accommodation politics to a new level. As Alan Wald points out, the erasure of this accommodationist style from the New York Intellectuals' history has allowed the movement's leading figures to maintain that they've held a consistent politics when in fact they drifted quite far across the thirties to the fifties from communism to Trotskyism, liberal anticommunism, finally to conservatism. The "politics of memory" game has made the telling of the New York Intellectuals' history a complex task, indeed. Edward Said's engagement with and within that history forms a unique chapter in American intellectual life.

Notes

An abbreviated version of this essay appeared under the title of "History, Memory, and Exile: Edward Said, the New York Intellectuals, and the Rhetoric of Accommodation and

Resistance" in "History, Memory, and Exile," ed. Michael Bernard-Donals, special issue, *MMLA* (Spring 2007).

1. See Clayton Swisher's *The Truth about Camp David: The Untold Story about the Collapse of the Middle East Peace Process* (New York: Nation Books, 2004).

2. Gauri Viswanathan, ed., *Power, Politics, and Culture: Interviews with Edward W. Said* (New York: Pantheon Books, 2001), p. 458.

3. Edward Said, *Orientalism* (New York: Vintage, 1979), p. 28.

4. See Mark Krupnick in "Edward Said and the Discourse of Palestinian Rage," *Tikkun* (November–December 1989) 4, no. 6 (1987), pp. 21–24, and Michael Walzer "An Exchange: Michael Walzer and Edward Said," *Grand Street* 5, no. 4 (1986), pp. 246–252 (1986, reprinted in William Hart, *Edward Said and the Religious Effect of Culture* [Cambridge: Cambridge University Press, 2000]).

5. There is an interesting parallel with Said's views on Palestinian collaborators. The punishment of death for Palestinians who collaborate with the Israeli government is protected under international law, obviously creating serious repercussions for betrayal of one's "own people." See Said's exchange with Robert Griffin and the Boyarin Brothers in "An Exchange on Edward Said and Difference," *Critical Inquiry* 15, no. 3 (Spring 1989), p. 641.

6. See "American Zionism," http://fromoccupiedpalestine.org/node.php?id=530 (accessed March 3, 2007).

7. Hannah Arendt, *The Jew as Pariah: Jewish Identity and Politics in the Modern Age*, ed. Ron Feldman (New York: Grove Press, 1978), p. 20.

8. Edward Said, *The Politics of Dispossession: The Struggle for Palestinian Self-Determination, 1969–1994* (New York: Vintage Books, 1995), p. 175.

9. See Baruch Kimmerling's *Politicide: Ariel Sharon's War against the Palestinians* (London and New York: Verso, 2003).

10. Edward Said, *Out of Place: Out of Memoir* (New York: Vintage, 1999), p. 3.

11. Said, *Orientalism*, p. 27.

12. See Joseph Massad, "The Persistence of the Palestinian Question," *Cultural Critique*, Winter 2005, pp. 1–23.

13. Moustapha Marrouchi, *Edward Said and the Politics of the Limit* (New York: SUNY, 2003), p. 43.

14. Irving Howe, *Decline of the New* (New York: Harcourt, Brace, and World, 1963), p. 212.

15. Howe, p. 212.

16. Marrouchi, p. 43.

17. Edward Said, *Reflections on Exile* (Cambridge: Harvard University Press, 2001), pp. 527–528.

18. Said, *Reflections on Exile*, pp. xii–xiii.

19. Said, *Reflections on Exile*, pp. xii–xiii.

20. Irving Howe, *World of Our Fathers: The Journey of the East European Jews to America* (New York: Harcourt, 1989), p. 599.

21. Edward Said, *Blaming the Victims: Spurious Scholarship and the Palestinian Question* (London and New York: Verso, 2001), pp. 172–173.

22. Said and Hitchens, *Blaming the Victims*, p. 176.

23. Hart, p. 194.

24. Howe, *Decline of the New*, p. 217.

25. Said, *Reflections on Exile*, p. 527.

26. Said, *The Politics of Dispossession*, p. 324.

27. Although it's true that many New York Intellectuals remained aloof from power in the 1930s, by the 1950s many surely took sides as they aligned themselves with U.S. military adventurism, joined the Committee on Cultural Freedom, worked for CIA-front magazines like *Encounter*, etc. By the time Said enters the scene, he's kind of a throwback to what the New York Intellectuals once *were*.

28. Said, *Reflections on Exile*, pp. xii–xiv.

29. Said, *Reflections on Exile*, pp. xi–xii.

30. Edward Said, *The World, the Text, and the Critic* (Cambridge: Harvard University Press, 1983), p. 24.

31. Said, *The World, the Text, and the Critic*, p. 29.

32. Said, *The World, the Text, and the Critic*, p. 78.

33. Abdirahman Hussein, *Edward Said: Criticism and Society* (London and New York: Verso, 2002).

34 Frances Stone Saunders, *Who Paid the Piper? The CIA and the Cultural Cold War* (New York: Granta, 2002), p. 3.

35. Alan Wald, *The New York Intellectuals* (Chapel Hill and London: University of North Carolina Press, 1987), p. 9.

36. Wald, p. 70.

37. Wald, p. 348.

38. Wald, p. 367.

39. Edward Said, *Representations of the Intellectual* (New York: Vintage, 1994), p. 11.

40. Said, *Representations of the Intellectual*, pp. 100–101.

41. Said, *Orientalism*, p. 26.

42. Said and Hitchens, *Blaming the Victims*, p. 178.

43. Said and Hitchens, *Blaming the Victims*, p. 170.

44. Said and Hitchens, *Blaming the Victims*, pp. 170–171.

45. Said and Hitchens, *Blaming the Victims*, p. 171.

46. Edward Said, quoted in Hart, pp. 197–198.

47. In "Caliban's Triple Play," Houston Baker writes that "[it] is difficult to hear a Palestinian voice separate from the world of Jewish discourse." In Henry Louis Gates, ed., *Race, Writing, and Difference* (Chicago: University of Chicago Press, 1984), p. 388.

48. Said, quoted in Hart, p. 197.

49. Noam Chomsky, "The Peace for Galilee," in *The Fateful Triangle: The United States, Israel, and the Palestinians,* chapter 5 (Boston: South End Press, 1983).

50. Said and Hitchens, *Blaming the Victims*, p. 175.

51. Paul Bové, "Hope and Reconciliation: A Review of Edward W. Said," *boundary 2* 20, no. 2 (Summer 1993), p. 266.

Feminist (and "Womanist") as Public Intellectuals?

Elfriede Jelinek and Alice Walker

Tobe Levin

Le silence est la forme civilisée du génocide.
—Régis Debray

Creative writers have functioned as public intellectuals at least since the Bible or, less controversially, since Euripedes' *Lysistrata* featured women's first sex strike for peace. Fiction is among the most effective whistle-blowers, drawing society's attention to its evils in the hope of effecting *tikkun olam,* or "healing the world." Indeed, Toni Morrison, discussing the aptitude of the imagination to elucidate slavery, contends that "some things only artists can do—and it's their *job.*"[1] Like an earlier generation of New York Intellectuals, Morrison links aesthetics, politics, and ethics with profound effect in her most popular novel, *Beloved.* The interview cited above reveals how, initially inspired by the historical Margaret Garner, Morrison sought to fill a gap in understanding of "the peculiar institution." Certainly, she agreed, there is a lot of history but nothing in the heavy tomes to "get close to." She speculated that instead of a broad, sweeping approach she would try something personal, "narrow and deep." Rewarded by a Nobel Prize, Morrison apparently succeeded.

The feminist project is similar, of course, defined as intricate engagement to generate change, and its clarion call in the seventies—the personal is political—resulted in the elevation of emotion and anecdote to complement analysis. Just as the New York Intellectuals wedded belles lettres to a more traditional essay

243

form, so too have many feminists placed autobiography, or "the authority of experience," at the heart of their public presence.

European and, in particular, German feminism provided one alternative definition of the public intellectual, reserving a spectacular place for the narrative artist. Whereas in the United States nonfiction such as Betty Friedan's *The Feminine Mystique* (1963) prompted a movement, it was storytelling that inspired women's organizing in Germany and Austria. By word of mouth alone, Verena Stefan's slim underground volume—*Häutungen*[2]—reached best-seller status while Elfriede Jelinek's early novels laid solid groundwork for the Nobel Prize winner's reputation as an outspoken critic of complicity between the economic and ideological systems. Inspired by the Frankfurt School, Jelinek's first three works of fiction demonstrate how rhetoric disempowers the working classes by placing them in a double-bind. Her heroines live in the superficially unscathed world delineated by imported sitcoms. In thought, Jelinek's protagonists cannot escape from the template provided for viewers' understanding of themselves. In the best of all possible media worlds, with affluence attainable and resolution steady, class conflict becomes literally unthinkable and change impossible unless, deploying irony and other sophisticated exegetic skills required to enjoy her prose, a reader dives beneath the surface.

In this sense, fiction, because it can provoke analytic and emotional thinking that leads to action, appears as a genre of choice for German-language feminist authors. Literary strategies significant for Jelinek, for instance, include the Brechtian alienation effect; Althusser's interpellations that call into being forces for progress; or Hans Magnus Enzensberger's consciousness industry illuminating how advertising saturates the public mind, dangling promises before those who, however, are systematically excluded from enjoying the fruits of their labor. Needless to say, the sources reveal a solid footing on the left, although women's concerns are not considered a "secondary contradiction." If Marxism offers a universalist theory of human rights, Jelinek implicitly critiques its hijacking by male spokespersons dismissive of the more personal perspective.

For women clearly face a specific gendered burden, one in which the body becomes a vehicle for marking oppression. Public intellectuals, therefore, extend their classic role of speaking truth to power, and speaking for the oppressed, by intervening on the terrain of the body. Critics of pornography, such as the late Andrea Dworkin, probe the fraught relationship between representations of women as prostitutes—the etymology of pornography—and its effects on actual females. Or in Elfriede Jelinek's analysis, "Pornography is the exercise of violence against woman aimed at humiliating . . . her. If, for example, in a hardcore novel or film, a man is whipped, he remains an individual freely choosing to degrade himself. But when a woman is dishonored . . . she is not violated as herself, as an individual. Rather, all women are debased along with her. A member of the oppressed caste is a stand-in, so to speak, for all the rest. That's the decisive thing."[3]

In other words, sexual violence, disseminated by a billion-dollar porno industry, remains pervasive in our times.

Postcolonial and antiracist writers, among them Alice Walker, confront a similar violence, often disguised, that denies individuality to various subordinated groups. In both Walker and Jelinek the female body is aggressed against, the agent either outside or within as part of an internal struggle with the norms of dominant society. Although in marked contrast to Jelinek in style and tone, Walker, in fiction and essays, remains concerned with women's equality and dignity, combining empathy for women with reclaiming majesty for African Americans and Africans—men included—subjected to a "Western" gaze. Just as women have found it challenging to secure an audience among men who refuse to take their intellectual contributions seriously, so, too, have disempowered groups such as the descendants of slaves been excluded. In other words, as Orlando Paterson describes it, not only women but also men in discriminated populations suffer "social death."[4]

Because the philosophical and aesthetic choices of the American and Austrian diverge so significantly, their juxtaposition may at first seem strained. Although both aim to ensure justice for women, Jelinek appears less hopeful than Walker that this can, indeed, be done. To Jelinek, uncovering the mechanisms that mute women's voices is a first step, the second being to disarm those structures. But can they be defeated? Will the public accept the Other? Defined by its maleness, which excludes femininity, civil society requires a private realm to which women are confined, and Jelinek doubts whether the resulting entrapment by language—the master's tools—can ever be breached. Walker, unlike Jelinek, displays exuberant defiance of such seeming truth.

For the roots of this distinction emerge from geography and history. Jelinek, an equality feminist, aspires to full participation in the polity as it developed out of the Enlightenment with a new, euphoric emphasis on individual rights. The fact that these rights were not extended to women then, and have only been begrudgingly granted since, suggests that the system itself is flawed and the challenge to repair it great, if not impossible. For Walker, nothing is impossible. Hers is a utopian vision.

We therefore enjoy a study in contrasts: Jelinek's pessimism versus Walker's optimism; Jelinek's nihilism versus Walker's constructivism; Jelinek's atheism versus Walker's pan-spirituality and god-driven language; Jelinek's objective, impersonal irony versus Walker's subjective, personal, even down-home discourse. The result is also a contrast in audience, Jelinek readers tending to be well-schooled rebels from the *Bildungsbürgertum*, or educated middle class, Walker's from a broader, possibly less comprehensively schooled social segment.

Yet instructive analogies exist. Both belong to minorities with traumatic histories, slavery for Walker, the Holocaust for Jelinek. Both experienced personal trauma, Walker in the form of a gunshot wound that blinded one eye,

Jelinek in her upbringing, which she has called "psychological torture."[5] Both have been acclaimed, Walker awarded a Pulitzer, Jelinek the Nobel Prize. Both Marxist/socialist in orientation, they are feminists bold enough to write about female genital mutilation (FGM), and both have been victims of debilitating, hostile criticism for having done so. "I am Vienna's persona non grata," Jelinek once lamented to me,[6] while Walker was immeasurably hurt by the negative response given by African women resident in the U.S. to her work against FGM, so much so that, regrettably, she muted her engagement, though not without a fight. I paraphrase: in the time it takes you to stone the messenger, she has told her critics, thousands of girls will be cut.[7]

Quite literally, women have been and continue to be cut off, cut down, cut out. They have been systematically ignored, their voices refused. For this reason, when we think of public intellectuals, relatively few women come to mind, and those that do tend to steer clear of violence against women as both a sign and agent of women's public silence. The option of following a pattern characteristic of the (male) New York Intellectuals who shed an ethnic specificity—their Jewishness—to assume a mantle of universality is not open to women, even though both Jelinek and Walker wrestle with and find original solutions to this dilemma. Jelinek's answer is the more realistic. As we will see in tracing its evolution through *The Piano Teacher*,[8] her novel featuring genital mutilation, she universalizes sex.[9] That is, the privileged signifier—the lord is one—is male. Walker, in contrast, explodes this essentially mono-gendered viewpoint: not one, but a multiplicity of sexes confounds the would-be universalist, Walker's inclusiveness based on claims to human rights. Like the New York Intellectuals in their emphasis on social class, Walker and Jelinek speak for the marginalized. But unlike male privilege to subsume the human, oppositional racial and gender identities remain out on the edge.

Elfriede Jelinek: Subversion and Somatophobia

"Do you love Scholten, Jelinek, Häupl, Peymann, Pasterk . . . or art and culture?" This question, posed on an Austrian billboard by Jörg Haider's right-wing party, "honors" the progressive mayor of Vienna, the Austrian minister of culture, a well-known theatre director, another respected media figure, and Elfriede Jelinek as proponents of "degenerate art." Perhaps "only" 20 percent of Austrian voters take Haider's side, but he represents a broad resistance to immigration and feminism.

"A dauntless polemicist with a website . . . poised to comment on burning issues,"[10] Jelinek has always been an incisive critic of the status quo. Her earliest pieces unmask the culture industry, its saturation and imprisonment of thought, denying the possibility of individuality: "women [and other characters are unable] to fully come to life in a world where they are painted over with stereotypical images."[11] Or as the *Münchner Literaturarbeitskreis* notes, Jelinek's figures are not "psychological, but typological, representative of their class or upbringing."[12] Thus, language itself—as she's called it, "the never-ending wound"—is the first of three major, interlocked themes, the others being fascist Austria and misogyny. To illustrate: the very word *whore* and the concept behind it invalidate all efforts to rehabilitate females, trapped in the inflexible meshes of violent social hierarchies.

The violence needed to literally keep women in their place experiences periodic overflow onto groups that only seem to include men. Sander Gilman shows how antisemitism first effects the feminization of, for instance, the Jewish male and ripens the seedlings of enmity against him that grow with murderous results. Logically, Jelinek's second angry thrust targets Austria as an antisemitic and xenophobic country, these two hatreds rooted in a consuming masculine militaristic bias. As the Nobel Prize committee notes, "With special fervour, Jelinek has castigated Austria, depicting it as a realm of death [particularly] in her phantasmagorical novel, *Die Kinder der Toten* [Children of the Dead] (1995)."[13] Even earlier, in the drama *Wolken. Heim* (1989), Jelinek dared unveil the Nazi past of a theater icon, Paula Wessily, who, in the notorious propaganda film made under Hitler in 1941, *Heimkehr,* pronounces the words, "We don't buy from Jews."[14]

But Jelinek's broad jump from a favorite of literati to best-seller and pariah status came with *Lust* (1989), a novel in which, according to the Swedish Academy, she "lets her social analysis swell to fundamental criticism of civilization by describing sexual violence against women as the actual template for our culture."[15]

Enormous brouhaha surrounded *Lust* due to what many perceived as deceptive marketing, the book cast as "female porn" that soon revealed itself as the opposite, composed of weary and repetitive stage directions for copulative acts, scripted to the point of mechanical reproduction and sucked dry of any visible titillating aura.

The plot is deceptively simple. Because AIDS has penetrated even the most remote Alpine village, our protagonist, a factory boss, realizing that he will have to give up promiscuity and prostitutes, turns to his wife Gerti to satisfy his needs. She tries to escape the sexual attacks, the deadly repetition of the constantly-the-same, only to fall in with another man, this time a young law student. But her urges remain unreciprocated because female lust deflates male desire. Her caresses elicit brutality. Nor can she as a mother live out her sexuality, motherhood and sex canceling each other out. Ultimately, both maternity and heterosexual coupling fail the female; limited by an imposed biological destiny, Gerti is without alternatives other than self-annihilating ones. In a final symbolic gesture, she suffocates her child with a plastic shopping bag.

In an attempt to claim an individualism and sexual agency equivalent to the masculine, Jelinek had taken Georges Bataille, De Sade, Sacher-Masoch, and Pauline Réage as her models to experiment with a woman's porn. "I wanted to find a female equivalent of obscene language," Jelinek told critic Sigrid Loeffler (1989), "but the very writing of such a text destroyed me—as a subject and in my intention to write pornography. I came to recognize that a woman can't do this, at least not given the present situation."[16] Although one may suppose that she ends up replicating what she rebels against because she meets it on its own terms, her aesthetic choices neutralize this danger: she has applied overkill. After all, we learn again and again (and again) which anatomical appendages are inserted into which receptacles. Now, the voyeur goes to the screen specifically for repetition, but on paper only tedium results. Jelinek's "porn," if it doesn't disgust you, puts you to sleep.

In an interview with Alice Schwarzer, the Nobel laureate explains why she failed to create a text able to stimulate desire in a woman. First, to escape the "exclusively male envisioning of women's bodies" that dismembers them, she would substitute a female gaze, but this didn't work because erotica was forced to cede to violence. "For women, sexuality IS violence," Jelinek insists. "But only women know this; men, not yet."[17] Thus, in Jelinek's oeuvre, women under patriarchy cannot be the subjects of their own desire because once a woman tries to place herself in the subject position vis-à-vis a man her insubordination turns him off. His loss of lust then triggers an escalation of brutality—as in the novel *Lust* but also in the earlier *Piano Teacher*. For instance, the following portrays one of Jelinek's better heterosexual encounters, Erika and her student Klemmer still desirous to meet. Yet,

> The very instant that both have become physical for each other, they have broken off any reciprocal human relations. . . . And the deeper one goes, the more intensely the flesh rots, becoming light as a feather and flying away from these two mutually alien and hostile continents, which crash into each other and then collapse together, turning into a rattling thing with a few canvas tatters that dissolve at the slightest touch, disintegrating into dust.[18]

Dust to dust: almost Biblical in her evocation, if not downright Tertullian, Jelinek's conclusion drawn from male sexual hegemony is the same as O's: women are scripted for annihilation, a closure that logically conforms to the female's assignment, to hate herself. The theory's narrative embodiment emerges from a typical passage in *The Piano Teacher* presenting the failed artist Erika:

> No sooner does the sound of the closing door die down than she takes out her little talisman, the paternal all-purpose razor. SHE peels the blade out of its Sunday coat of five layers of virginal plastic. She is very skilled in the use of blades . . . [and] This blade is destined for HER flesh. This thin, elegant foil of bluish steel, pliable, elastic. SHE sits down in front of the magnifying side of the shaving mirror; spreading her legs, she makes a cut, magnifying the aperture that is the doorway . . . Her hobby is cutting her . . . body.[19]

Thus the protagonist, a cutter, fits the clinical description of the psychological disorder whose victims relieve unbearable tension, anger, or anxiety.[20] But she is also symbolic of a larger ill, literally carried out on approximately 150 million females alive in the world today who are victims of genital cutting.[21] This move from individual pathology to cultural *Überbau* is the work of the work of art.

In an interview, Jelinek links the fictional razor wielded here on a European woman to reality:

> Müller: The most horrible scene you invented to illustrate the theme of self
>   hatred in the novel is the cutting.
> Jelinek: I didn't invent it.
> Müller: I mean where the woman in the book cuts her vagina with a razor.
> Jelinek: I've done it.[22]

Why?

One puzzle piece emerges from a 1997 ARTE film produced by Jochen Wolf, *Die gehaßte Frau Jelinek/Une femme à abattre*," which I translate as "Jelinek despised." It presents the author as a controversial intellectual and examines the effect of stressful young years on her art. A highly ambitious but frustrated mother projected her needs onto the child, required to train for a musical career studying violin, viola, flute, piano, composition, and organ at the Vienna Conservatory when only fourteen. Her mother's motive?

> She buried me in so many . . . things which she would have liked to do
> herself. My mother had a wonderful, powerful voice. She would certainly
> have become a great singer . . . She had done a business *abitur* and studied
> economics. And this sort of business high school was attended almost ex-
> clusively by Jewish girls from entrepreneurial families. . . . And after school,
> these Jewish girls were the only ones who sang, made music, put on plays.
> But [my mother's] mother never let her join in. So she wanted me, as her
> substitute, to have these opportunities. But she put terrible pressure on
> me. . . . She stole my childhood and my youth.[23]

In Jelinek's words, "I experienced my childhood and teen-age years as . . . a night-mare. You could truly say I was a tortured child."[24]

Vacation, though hours of practice were still enforced, offered the young Jelinek at least a change of scenery. She visited her grandparents in an isolated region that would become a favored venue in her art:

> And what was most decisive for my writing, during those summers, I came
> into contact with the rural proletariat, this male proletariat. This world of
> lumberjacks, handymen, unemployed, alcoholics, whom I studied minutely,
> and this saved me, my contact with the real world of productivity, not only
> the middle class world of my *gymnasium*. Then I realized this desire to write
> it down precisely; here I learned objective language.[25]

Regarding Jelinek's Jewish father, Friederich, credited with having honed her talent for analyzing language and cracking open the world with linguistic hu-mor, she wrote, "Papa could have been a king, yet he died so miserably."[26] He had

survived the Nazi terror as a chemist for the war industry, but afterward, a challenging marriage became more and more difficult. Jelinek would write, "[Mental]
illness transformed him from an unbelievably intelligent person to a complete
idiot."[27] He died in a psychiatric hospital in 1969, another significant blow to the
daughter who in *The Piano Teacher* would dramatize the slippage between child
and male parent. The girl's identification with the father authorizes her public persona; despite the desperate circumstances, he seems to have given her agency.

Containing perhaps Jelinek's entire corpus, *The Piano Teacher* can be
seen as a gesture of solidarity with the father and "an act of revenge against the
mother. Had the mother forced her to write poetry, she would most certainly
have become an accomplished organist."[28] Like the real daughter, the "literature
works only in opposition." Jelinek affirms: "I rub myself raw on the status quo in
a kind of raging bitter comic mode."[29]

Jelinek as Whistle-Blower, or Women against Themselves

Where does one find the language to transmit both comedy and rage? To borrow
from Booker T. Washington, the precocious teen "dropped her bucket where she
was," opening her career with the first full-length pop novel in the German language, *wir sind lockvögel baby!* (*we're decoys, baby!*), that parodies the media in a
pastiche of episodes taken from comics (Batman and Robin), teenage magazines
featuring stars and other plastic idols (the Beatles), romance and film (James
Bond, horror and sci-fi), homogenized in such a way that individuality dissolves,
genre is exploded, and the programming of consciousness is revealed. *We're Decoys, Baby!* asks to be read with one eye on the text and the other on its models.
As critic Reinhard Urbach notes, "In form, the book is a collage of clichés from
pulp fiction, soap opera and comics, but the content illustrates the flip side of
innocence. Where one expects romance, rape occurs. And cynicism takes the
place of pathos. The form is in constant conflict with the content."[30] The same
can be said of *The Piano Teacher*. It implodes the bildungsroman, soap opera,
Harlequin, in sum, any conventional boy-meets-girl plot.

Let's return then to the mutilating incident above: the passage preceding it
generated the negative feelings to be purged by cutting, the viewpoint on women
expressed by a young male music student the pianist finds attractive. Without
"the strength to track down her femininity which lies buried in the debris[,] he is
of the opinion that a woman is a woman. Then he makes a little joke about the female sex, which is known for its fickleness: oh, women! Whenever he cues HER
to play, he looks at her without really perceiving her. He does not decide against
HER, he simply decides without HER."[31] Now, as we have seen, Jelinek's mother
decided for her and without her input. Can it be that, in the author's symbolic
imagination, the earlier experience of maternal objectification provides the template for masculine abuse? It appears that Jelinek's personal suffering, similar to
Walker's injury, oils the wheels of her social critique.

Throughout Jelinek's oeuvre, then, we encounter this indifference, erasure, annihilation, or "dissing" of women by men for whom women appear not to count, an attitude that then—faute de mieux—becomes the palimpsest for women's deletion of themselves. Called cunts, women in Jelinek disappear into their own organ, which must be violated in order to receive them. Attempts at agency backfire, the only possible outcome self-harm. As we learn about Erika, razor at the ready, "She is entirely at her own mercy, which is still better than being at someone else's mercy. It's still in her hands."[32]

Thus, the convex meets the concave, or an activity, connoted masculine, drives the excavation of a passage into the feminine. The protagonist goes at her unfeeling carcass in the spirit of exploration and creation:

> The opening is caught in the retaining screw of the mirror, an opportunity for cutting is seized. Quick, before someone comes. With little information about anatomy and with even less luck, she applies the cold steel to and into her body, where she believes there ought to be a hole.[33]

First looked at from the agent's point of view, perspective is displaced and projected onto the disassociated organ in a parody of Luce Irigaray's famous feminist tract, "Quand nos lèvres se parlent." A trio of voices, the self and dual genital, results:

> The aperture gapes, terrified by the change, and blood pours out. This blood is not an unusual sight, but presence doesn't make the heart grow fonder. As usual, there is no pain. SHE, however, cuts the wrong place, separating what the Good Lord and Mother Nature have brought together in unusual unity. Man must not sunder, and revenge is quick. She feels nothing. For an instant, the two halves, sliced apart, stare at each other, taken aback at this sudden gap, which wasn't there before. They've shared joy and sorrow for many years, and now they're being separated! In the mirror the two halves also look at themselves, laterally inverted, so that neither knows which half it is. Then the blood shoots out resolutely. The drops ooze, run, blend with their comrades, turning into a red trickle, then a soothingly steady red stream when the individual trickles unite. The blood prevents HER from seeing what she has sliced open.[34]

Whereas Irigaray offers a positivist revaluation of leg lips tonguing in erotic affirmation, Jelinek suggests the violence of separation, the absence of feeling, and the eventual obstruction of vision—meaning understanding and orientation but also castration—by the carnal flood of traditionally mystified fluid. Evoking both menses and childbirth as organ-obliterating events, the cutter intensifies the loss of self that patriarchy displaces onto the organ: "It was her own body, but it is dreadfully alien to her."[35]

Or rather, it has become alienated by a thick mesh of social and economic meanings, all pointing toward the deadly metaphor, woman equals cunt. Funneled into a capitalist system of exchange, the truncated woman becomes a commodity, in bourgeois society as decorative; in the underbelly of pornography as consumable.

Furthermore, in the aftermath of self-invasion, it is logical that a sanitary product should secure erasure:

> In order to stem the flow of blood, SHE pulls out the popular cellulose package whose merits are known to and appreciated by every woman. . . . The queen's crown suddenly slips into her panties, and the woman knows her place in life. The thing that once shone forth on the head in childlike pride has now landed where the female wood has to wait for an ax. The princess is grown up now, and this is a matter of opinion on which opinions diverge. One man wants a nicely veneered, not-too-showy piece of furniture; the second wants a complete set in genuine Caucasian walnut. But the third man, alas, only wants to pile up huge heaps of firewood.[36]

It's not difficult to see why, even before *Lust, The Piano Teacher* had garnished such dubious encomiums as "Sure Shot with Poison," "On the Heels of Lust," "Trained for Self-Destruction," "Your Evil Eye, Elfriede"—all (translated) titles of reviews. Among feminists Jelinek is lauded, of course, for handling such controversial themes as female masochism, rape fantasies, and the maternal misuse of power. As critic Sigrid Loeffler points out, *The Piano Teacher* "can be read as the story of an unsuccessful artist, as the vivisection of the mother-daughter bond in a claustrophobic petit bourgeois milieu, as the etiology of sex-pathological behavior, or as a feminist treatment of the theme, 'destruction of female sexuality.'"[37]

As we have seen, this latter topos, literal in Jelinek, is also, ethnographically speaking, a widespread custom in Sub-Saharan and the Horn of Africa as well as in Egypt. Now, admittedly, an adult's voluntary slicing differs from the excision of children, often brutally forced. Still, a remarkable number of features are shared by European and tropical practitioners. These include the surgery's compulsive and ritualistic nature, the razor's association with the Father, the mothers' complicity in suppressing their daughters' sexuality, and the daughters' acceptance of their mothers' teaching. Not unlike African girls who look forward to the rite, Erika has embedded her mother within herself—"Mother and child have exchanged roles"[38]—most strikingly dramatized in what Jelinek calls the "lesbian rape scene of the mother,"[39] a "parasexual, cryptosexual"[40] attack.

Following the father's exit to an asylum for the mentally ill, Erika had begun to share the marital bed with her mother. In a penultimate scene, the piano teacher has been beaten up—instead of made love to—by the student Klemmer, who had been pursuing her and whose interest had been briefly returned. But his lust becomes violent once Erika attempts to take control via a letter giving step-by-step instructions for the masochistic treatment she desires. Wounded, she lies in bed next to her mother, where she "mounts a half-hearted love attack"[41] but is "carried away" by the onset of kissing.

Erika keeps pressing her wet mouth into Mother's face, holding her in steely arms so Mother can't resist. Erika lies halfway, then three-quarters upon Mother, because Mother is starting to flail her arms seriously, trying to thrash Erika. With hectic thrusts of her head, Mother's mouth tries to avoid Erika's puckered mouth. Mother wildly tosses her head around, trying to escape the kisses. It's like a lovers' struggle, and the goal isn't orgasm, but Mother per se, the person known as Mother.[42]

Immediately preceding the daughter's initiative, her mother is said to have been thinking of "a separate bed for Erika."[43]

Apart from the almost slapstick quality in the scene above, psychoanalytic and Lacanian critics read the passage as translating into story form an incomplete parting of mother and child. This pervasive textual syndrome is theorized by "the psychologist of narcissism and ego development," Erika's namesake Heinz Kohut, who "comment[s] on the destructive effects of a symbiotic mother/daughter relationship, in which the merger with an idealized object prevents successful separation from the primary other, the mother."[44] Now, within the phallogocentric order suppressing feminine alterity, such complicity can only prove dysfunctional.[45]

Jelinek, therefore, unveils the quisling mother, the one who colludes in her daughter's mutilation in millions of literal cases each year. But, as Nawal el Saadawi knows, excision is a shared oppression, for in Jelinek's texts, a clitoris or a vagina, when literally and metonymically erased, snuffs out and thereby paradoxically creates a female caste based on somatophobia and misogyny. Those identified as women, wherever they inhabit patriarchal space, have been divided even unto our most intimate bonds.

Jelinek thus uses the discourse on women to evoke women's absence from discourse showing that, where two sexes may be expected we have only one, the male (an echo certainly of the Church fathers for whom women were merely defective men). In Katrin Sieg's terms: "Woman . . . an image with no 'substance' . . . is revealed as a male phantasm. [Jelinek implies] that women . . . cannot speak because they are always already spoken for and about. [She refuses] to represent female identity."[46]

If, however, the female cannot be known, the question becomes, what effect does this have on real lives? "Language [is] the site at which sexual difference is inscribed and performed,"[47] Sieg goes on. In other words, at a certain profound level, idiom molds bodies. As Judith Butler contends, "'naturalness' [is] constituted through discursively constrained performative acts that produce the body through and with the categories of sex."[48] Jelinek, reliably denaturing Nature, embodies this challenging assertion in her text, in particular in acts of mutilation that ironically construct and deconstruct.

These scenarios include (1) genital mutilation proper; (2) metaphors and metonymies of mutilation; and (3) gynocidal erasures that conflate women with their genitals, negating both.

For instance, consistently transgressive in the role of masculine consumer yet returned incessantly to alienation and passivity, Erika visits peep shows where, "here, in this booth, she becomes nothing. Nothing fits into Erika, but she, she fits exactly into this cell. Erika is a compact tool in human form. Nature seems to have left no apertures in her. Erika feels solid wood in the place where the carpenter made a hole in any genuine female."[49] The "genuine" females are, of course, those playing hide-and-seek with their twats on the turn-table revealed when slots are fed the appropriate coins. Only by refusing the inversion can she differentiate herself from them, an option made attractive by their reduction to their genitalia.

Language effects this de-feminization by cunning application of metonymy, making intelligible the link between the first sentence (in which Erika is nothing) and the first clause in the second (in which nothing fits into Erika): necessarily reduced to a penile sheath, that is, vagina, Erika proves to be impaired as an encasing, which in turn only confirms her phallic status. In a play on Lacanian thought whereby the man HAS but the woman IS the phallus, Erika becomes the instrument, insinuating her whole self into the cell—any small, enclosed space that bids entry. But the metamorphoses aren't over yet: now resembling a cyborg—in a clear allusion to E.T.A. Hoffmann and other romantic forerunners of the life-sized mechanical partner—Erika's lack of slits is logical. She has been neutered, that is, castrated, neither giving (shelter) nor receiving (through her entrance hall). In this respect, she differs from "real women."

Clear enough, it seems to me. But the passage continues dismantling the category "woman" via a healthy flirt with Sartre:

> Erika's wood is spongy, decaying, lonesome wood in the timber forest, and the rot is spreading. Still, Erika struts around like a queen. . . . The man at the entrance bravely addresses her as "Ma'am." Please come in, he says, welcoming her into his parlor, where three small lamps glow tranquilly over boobs and cunts, chiseling out bushy triangles, for that's the first thing a man looks at, it's the law. A man looks at nothing, he looks at pure lack. After looking at this nothing, he looks at everything else.[50]

Although the translation is good, this last line maintains another important dimension in the origin. Zuerst schaut er auf dieses Nichts, dann kommt die restliche Mutti auch noch dran.[51] After the void, he takes the rest of the little mother in . . .

Erika the totem, opening this passage, had just emerged from the preceding paragraph as sealed shut. But wait! What do we understand as spongy, decaying, spreading rot if not the process of creating holes? Thus, the phallic woman ends up perforated, so that privileges of class and race are merely camouflage. Inviolability and control remain illusory, policed by authority's delegate, the mother: "Erika feels nothing, and has no chance to caress herself. Her mother sleeps next to her and guards Erika's hands. These hands are supposed to practice, not scoot under the blanket like ants and scurry over to the jam jar."[52]

A perishable product, the unstable category woman dissolves. For instance, in this same scene, "the cleaning women *are* women, but they don't look like women."[53] Or, later, when Erika interrupts a young male student's enjoyment of movie posters advertising a soft porn flick, "one would never believe that she and the women in the photos belong to one and the same sex, namely the beautiful. . . . Indeed, a less sophisticated person might even conclude, just from her outer appearance, that the piano teacher belongs to an entirely different subcategory of the human species."[54] Well, no. Really only the more sophisticated, postmodern thinker might think so.

However, we can agree that the colloquial "nothing" opening the peep show passage echoes in the Master Narrative's "nichts" or nothingness at its close, the Nothing men—or at least men buying into a cartoon version of the masculine narrative—see as a woman. Nothing then—not-woman—is the counterpart to man, with Jelinek's text supporting those who argue for one discursive sex, the male. In Jelinek, you see, "there are no 'women.'"[55]

These themes—women's complicity in their erasure and acceptance of the horror their genitals inspire—reoccur in a strongly worded passage offering Erika's thoughts while Klemmer stalks her. Fearing that the "porous, rancid fruit marking the bottom of her body" will soon putrefy "the whole genital area," killing her,

> Erika imagines that one day she will dissolve under the earth, transforming into a 75 centimeter long hole in a coffin, the organ she had . . . detested and neglected taking possession of her. She has become Nothing. And nothing awaits her.[56]

The final nothingness, conflating high philosophy with the *larmoyance* of daytime soaps, tempers with the wit of code switching the gloom of an otherwise suicidal passage playing with the trope of woman as illness. For although the hyperbole can be read as satire, the nothingness to which woman is consigned both reflects and enacts a gynocidal threat turned in against the female self.

Concerning the origin of this projection, Jelinek tells an illustrative tale (borrowed, I think, from Freud): "A small boy is bathing with his mother. On seeing the water run down the drain, he begins screaming uncontrollably, because he sees in the black hole sucking the water away the black hole that belongs to his mother which he fears could suck him in again, just like that. A strong image, it offered me insight."[57]

In *The Piano Teacher*, because the whole body inevitably falls prey to a female's cavity, the victim finds complicity attractive as the only possible form of agency: "Erica is in love with the young man and expects Salvation [*Erlösung*] through him . . . She wants him to suck her in until nothing is left,"[58] clearly a reversal of the little boy's drainage angst. If then the male can kill—and "Erika . . . wants him as the instrument of her eradication,"[59] the man has become—the mother.

For this nihilism echoes in the relationship with the maternal. As noted, we often encounter the daughter's wish for internal immigration, that is, to resettle herself in the mother's flesh. At one point she is "a fish in the tropical maternal waters"[60] or, again, "Erika would rather simply crawl back in."[61] More often, however, the matriarch herself originates the threat of reingestion: "this maternal hovering could swallow her whole."[62] The cannibal progenitor is a "leech . . . sucking her marrow from the bone,"[63] an act of infanticide to reinforce the claim that the mother, too, is male: "The mother is a phallic figure, father and mother in one."[64] With the daughter also phallic and the male, maternal, then clearly the feminine is gone.

Jelinek has said about her mother as Frau Kohut's model, "I think that she had the feeling, in *The Piano Teacher* I had killed her. We never discussed it but I heard about remarks she made to other people, so I know she saw it as murder. Still, I could only survive by means of this assassination. If I hadn't done it . . . and I'm always hearing from women who thank me for killing my mother as an ersatz for them, so they didn't have to kill theirs . . . Still, this phallic 'occupation of the mother' had for me a 'bitter dialectic' because for my mother, I was the phallic one."[65]

Alice Walker: More Subversion, Less Somatophobia

When in 1982, Alice Walker won the Pulitzer Prize, becoming the first black American to do so, not many were surprised, though some would be angry. The Georgian had just published *The Color Purple*, which later, in Stephen Spielberg's hands, became a blockbuster of sorts. The epistolary novel innovated in transcribing black Southern dialect and—the more controversial part—in revealing dysfunctional postslavery families characterized by male violence against women and including (presumed) incest, bigamy, lesbianism, and more than a hint of Walker's iconoclastic attitude toward gender. In contrast to Jelinek, for whom gender is unitary and male, Walker sees gender as mercurial and multiple, its changing shapes limited only by imagination. In *The Color Purple*, for instance, Mr. _____, male treachery incarnate, is tamed—but not before the furor, black voices raised in protest against Walker's "washing dirty laundry in public"—parallel to the taunt "Nestbeschmützer" aimed at Jelinek accused of betraying Austria. Walker, however, was charged with painting all African American males with a violent brush—an untrue allegation but one that tarnished of itself her ability to represent the black minority in the sense that public intellectuals would try to do. For if Walker really was anti-male, how could she speak for the group?

Walker weathered the storm of criticism fairly well. Worse by far was the reception eleven years later of a film, *Warrior Marks* (1993), produced with Pratibha Parmar that followed up on a somewhat less criticized novel, *Possessing the Secret of Joy* (1992). Here the subject was female genital mutilation. Although in *The Color Purple*, the (invented) Olinka perform "a bit of bloody cutting around puberty,"[66] the actual excision remains muted. In *Possessing the Secret of Joy*, Walker revisits a figure from the earlier work, Tashi, who, spared by her Christian parents, decides to undergo infibulation because her "leader" (modeled on Jomo Kenyatta) sees it as the marker of ethnicity and its acceptance as rejection of the colonizer's values. Incapacitated by the operation, Tashi soon understands how she, as a woman, has been a political and cultural scapegoat. After marrying her missionary boyfriend Adam, moving to the U.S., and Americanizing her name, Tashi/Evelyn breaks down. Her mental instability brings her for psychotherapy to Switzerland with a physician resembling Karl Jung. Under his care, Tashi/Evelyn approaches health but only after confronting the unarticulated trauma occasioned when she witnessed her deceased sister Dura's excision. Once the supposedly accidental death is recognized as murder, an agent emerges: the Tsunga, Walker's term for the excisor. Tashi's activism consists in returning to Africa and taking the operator's life. As a result, she is hanged.[67]

Typical of the mild early criticism of *Possessing*—in comparison to that panning *Warrior Marks*—is the viewpoint expressed by Gay Wilentz in the *Women's Review of Books*. Wilentz deplores Walker's poetic license fantasizing Africa, for the Olinka are an invented tribe uniting characteristics of many ethnic groups. In anticipation of the popular but ethically suspect satire "How to Write about Africa,"[68] Wilentz accuses Walker of "misunderstanding . . . African culture" in her "polemic":

> [D]riven by a belief that not only African . . . but all societies actively thwart women's sexuality and control over their bodies [*Possessing*] tends to efface difference and will be problematic for readers acquainted with African history [because] Western stereotypes of "Africa" [may be] reinforce[d].[69]

Not without some justification, Wilentz questions Walker's imprecision: no single tribe, let alone the composite Olinka, can legitimately represent a diverse continent. Nonetheless, Wilentz argues less convincingly when she asserts that use of the "most extreme form of female circumcision" lends "an aspect of voyeurism [to] Walker's approach; [and that] her taking such liberties unfortunately puts her in the company of other Western writers before her for whom 'Africa' merely represented the exotic or grotesque" because "infibulation is practiced extensively *only* [emphasis mine] in Mali, Somalia and Sudan, and rarely in Kenya and most other black African countries."[70]

Now, even if we oppose "only" the 15 percent of all mutilations that involve infibulation, the large numbers warrant protest—which is what Walker does. In the MLA's *Profession 2004*, Cathy N. Davidson and David Theo Goldberg insist that "the humanities" make a "unique and irreplaceable contribution to bettering the human condition."[71] What better bettering can there be than engaging literature to put an end to torture?

Some well-meaning people ask, however, whether the West should deploy a lexicon of horror to convey what takes place. Critics, among them many anthropologists, don't like to call it "mutilation," contending the term is judgmental and insulting—as it undoubtedly seems to many who have faced the knife.

Typical is the reaction of Fadumo Korn in *Born in the Big Rains, a Memoir of Somalia and Survival.*[72] As vice president of the nongovernmental organization (NGO) FORWARD—Germany, she accepts the acronym FGM but takes care to differentiate between the procedure and its victims who choose not to be treated with the condescension often reserved for "cripples." An immigrant from Tanzania backs her up: "If you ask me if I'm circumcised, I'll say yes. If you ask me if I'm mutilated, I'll say no."[73] Removal of a healthy sexual organ is, nonetheless, by medical definition, mutilation. FGM, therefore, is a brutal act, not a state of being. African activists, politicians in Europe and Africa, international agencies, and development NGOs agree.[74]

Although in the international arena Walker's example proved inspiring, as recently as fall 2005 a volume of essays opened another page in the troubled reception of Walker's accomplishment. The collective authors in Obioma Nnaemeka's *Female Circumcision and the Politics of Knowledge* return time and again to both *Possessing the Secret of Joy* and *Warrior Marks* in order to deplore Walker's complicity with Western-inspired opposition, calling "interventionist" even those texts written by African activists. A second volume, *Female Circumcision: Multicultural Perspectives*, edited by Rogaia Mustafa Abusharaf, confirms in its very title this broad antagonism—significant only in the United States—to the officially accepted terminology that *Warrior Marks* underwrites.[75]

Clearly a public intellectual in taking courageous and groundbreaking stands, speaking truth to (here patriarchal) power, Walker's decades-long impact, like Jelinek's, is evident in this continuing discussion, much of it contentious, and much also based on emotion, not reason. Here's one example that could stand in for many.

An academic, not an activist, Vicki Kirby critiques Sudanese physician Asma el Dareer and Somali midwife Raquiya Abdalla, pioneers whose books, both published in 1983 by Zed Press, mine their respective professional fields.[76] Similar in tone to nearly all the essayists in Nnaemeka's anthology, Kirby reproaches el Dareer and Abdalla for their "medical discourse," calling it inappropriately universalizing. Yes, medicine provides the "red thread through [a] cluster of texts"[77] including Walker's. And FGM is undeniably a medical issue. The problem then? Echoing Wilentz, Kirby contends that "A biological reductionism, Reason's disinterested arbiter of 'what a body is,' translates cultured specificity through a universalizing template of sexuality. Although clitoridectomy and infibulation are practiced in thirty countries in Africa alone, the diversity of its cultural, political and historical experience is summarily negated [by] medical discourse."[78]

In the above, the spirit of Walker's critics becomes clear: not FGM—not, let me specify, the razoring of girls' genitalia *à vif* and the resultant morbidity and mortality—but "diversity of . . . cultural, political and historical experience" should remain in the forefront of discussion. Reminiscent of the question often implicitly raised by the New York Intellectuals concerning the validity or desirability of dismissing ethnic distinctiveness in favor of universal principles,

Walker has been consistently berated for taking a human rights—in this case the right to health—stance.

Given the heralded study, "Female Genital Mutilation and Obstetric Outcome: WHO Collaborative Prospective Study in Six African Countries" published in the prestigious British medical journal *Lancet* on June 2, 2006, such criticisms really should be laid to rest, because to continue "stoning . . . the messenger"[79] is to follow a dubious ethics. What did the World Health Organization find? Basing its results on a statistically reliable sample of just under 30,000 respondents in five West African countries, it uncovered an increase in mortality among parturient women and babies if the mothers had been excised. In other words, "circumcision" can be lethal, in the short and long term.

In *Warrior Marks*, Nigerian midwife Comfort Ottah refuses to bury this truth under euphemism. For Ottah, any analogy to the male procedure, implied by the very use of the term *circumcision*, is misleading. Seen protesting the motion by a Brent Counselor to legalize "female circumcision" in Great Britain, Ottah contends that "this is not cultural. It's torture. And these girls suffer for life."[80]

The viewpoint is shared by a number of memoirists, fiction writers, and filmmakers: three Senegalese Khady [Koita] in *Mutilée*; Pierrette Herzberger-Fofana, Erlangen City Councilwoman and FORWARD–Germany board Member; Awa Thiam, author, politician, and speaker in Walker and Parmar's *Warrior Marks*; Ghanaian Annor Nimako in *Mutilated*—among the most aggressive and adamant abolitionists; Nigerian Dr. Irene Thomas, vintage activist and powerhouse behind *Beliefs and Misbeliefs*, a no-holds-barred film made and disseminated by the Inter-African Committee; Egyptian Nawal el Saadawi, novelist and physician; Somalis Nura Abdi, Waris Dirie, Ayaan Hirsi Ali; and other African women and men—most recently, of course, Senegalese Ousmane Sembène, whose *Moolaadé*, the first feature-length film against FGM, has already become a classic of the genre.

I invoke these mentors—many of whom have been associates for decades—because it remains essential if you're not from Africa to credential your "right" to speak out. Neither Pratibha Parmar, of Indian parentage, nor Alice Walker, an African American, is free of "Western" taint when it comes to this issue. In fact, Walker's minority status, invoked in the United States as a source of empathy and authority, appears particularly galling to critics from Africa now employed at U.S. universities whose class origins tend to be far higher and who were assuredly not descendents of slaves. "There was a sense of competition, of jealousy, an image issue on the part of the African elite," a West African colleague told me. "For in my view, anyone genuinely interested in changing the situation [opposing FGM] should have welcomed [Walker's] efforts. It was the U.S. experience [of misrecognition] and [the nation's] general lack of knowledge of development issues" that led to the condemnation of Alice Walker by African women in the U.S.

This split between Africans and African Americans in the United States has not been duplicated in Western European countries whose scapegoated minority was Jewish, and this accounts in some measure, I think, for the very different approaches to understanding FGM on either side of the Atlantic, with serious consequences for conduct of the international movement against it.

Increasing though Still Deficient Knowledge

Despite the fact that many West Africans and other global residents now have some idea of what these operations entail, people remain underinformed about infibulation, the type of intervention nearly universal in the Horn of Africa, represented in *Possessing the Secret of Joy* and alluded to by Efua Dorkenoo in *Warrior Marks*.

What, then, are we really talking about? Because Walker omits the stage directions offered by a number of African activists, among them Nura Abdi, I give you passages from *Tränen im Sand* (*Desert Tears*, 2003, not available in English; translations of selected passages are mine), the memoir by a Somali immigrant to Germany dedicated "To all the world's women, victims and non-victims of FGM (Female Genital Mutilation)"—the term left in English in the German. Here Nura describes what happened to her.

One increasingly hot morning, a drama unfolds in the author's Mogadishu courtyard, where first Nura's elder sister Yurop, then neighbors and cousins Ifra, Fatma, Muna, Suleiha, and Nasra make desperate efforts to escape, are caught and, "with fanatical violence," are hurled onto the crate that had once held oranges. "When my turn came," Nura writes, "I burst into tears. . . . 'I don't want to!' [I shrieked, but] that didn't help at all. They grabbed me, dragged me to the box . . . held me down"—and cut. "The sound, like sharp scratching or knifing of burlap . . . filled my head, louder than all the [women's] screams" intended to disguise the victim's.

"But the worst was yet to come," Nura goes on. "The worst is when they sew you up."

> Sweat poured out of me. . . . I was nauseous and felt like throwing up while between my legs someone was busy with a needle in an open wound. It was as if with all my senses, wholly conscious, I was being slaughtered.

The child faints. But before being bound, she comes to, only to experience "a new pain this time, the *halaleiso* rubbing herbs on the fresh wound. . . . It felt like . . . being held over an open fire." Again, she loses consciousness but recovers it and notes

> I remember: when they carried me away . . . blood on the floor and those parts . . . hacked off . . . What had been sawed off all of us . . . The *halaleiso* had tossed them in a pile in the bowl. Later I learned that someone had dug a hole and buried them somewhere in the courtyard. Exactly where we were

never to learn. "What do you need to know for?" was all they would say. "It's long gone to where it belongs. Under the earth."[81]

A burial aptly concludes this scene, interment of female sexuality.

As Abdi's witnessing implies, she appeals to a universal standard of justice in her advocacy of abolition, as does Alice Walker, and in a monument to Walker's influence as a public intellectual speaking for an increasingly recognized concept of international law and human rights, no less significant a venue than the German Bundestag cites her in consideration of specific legislation. As that Berlin body states in the government's answer to a major interpellation (Drucksache 14/5285) posed in the thirteenth legislative period by MdB Rudolf Bindig, Lilo Friedrich, Angelika Graf, Dr. Angelika Köster-Lossack, Irmingard Schewe-Gerigk, Claudia Roth, and the Green Party Caucus:

> In vielen Aspekten kommt Genitalverstümmelung der Folter gleich und verletzt das Menschenrecht auf Körperliche Unversehrtheit. [In many respects, genital mutilation resembles torture and violates the human right to bodily integrity.]

The paragraph continues:

> Menschenrechtsorganisationen wie Terre des Femmes und Menschenrechtlerinnen wie Alice Walker [footnotes Walker, Alice/Parmar, Pratibha, *Narben oder die Beschneidung der weiblichen Sexualität*, Hamburg 1996] tragen das Thema seit Jahren in die Öffentlichkeit. [Human rights organizations like Terre des Femmes and human rights activists like Alice Walker (with *Warrior Marks* explicitly footnoted) have been pushing the theme into public awareness for years.]

Although Nawal el Saadawi, well known in feminist circles, had in the early seventies already condemned her own clitoridectomy, her authority was limited. It wouldn't be until the 1990s that as both activist and artist Alice Walker would become the first personality of world renown to publicly oppose female genital mutilation. Her novel and documentary (with Pratibha Parmar) did more than decades of international and grassroots agitation by "ordinary" citizens to bring the dimensions of the problem to the attention of law- and policymakers in and outside of Africa, suggesting the power of a popular international author.

Before the 1990s, FGM could still be considered a taboo subject, the number of academic and general articles remaining shamefully small. True, in 1982 Elizabeth Passmore Sanderson published an eighty-two-page bibliography, but ethnographic work, which constituted the bulk of listings, addressed university faculty, not policy- and lawmakers, citizens, or activists. And anthropologists, to put the best possible construction on it, tend to be blinded by goodwill—toward those in power, which means patriarchal privilege over women. But in my view, partisanship on this issue is unavoidable, and to abstain from ethical judgment on grounds of cultural relativity or anticolonialism *is* ipso facto *to take sides against activists*. As Efua Dorkenoo has told me, if "outside intervention" may be suspect, passivity can as easily be understood as racist, for apologetics in the name of neutrality amounts to a morally dubious double standard. What would not be tolerated if systematically practiced on white girls, "they" can simply go on doing to their own.[82]

Anthr/apologists notwithstanding, Walker's intervention brought results. Efua Dorkenoo explained in *Cutting the Rose*: "Alice Walker's work has sparked much interest and debate on the subject,"[83] influencing, among others, A.M. Rosenthal who, in 1992, launched "a regular column on FGM in *The New York Times*."[84] It is also more than coincidence that the two major international conferences, Vienna on human rights (1993) and Cairo on population (1994), came so closely on the heels of Walker's efforts. Both accepted FGM as a major humanitarian challenge.

Yet in the United States, where girls of African origin remain at risk, problems in reception of Walker's book and film immediately surfaced. Now, Walker knew to be fearful. In *Anything We Love Can Be Saved: A Writer's Activism*, she records her apprehension. Visiting Jung's home in Bollingen, the final quaff of inspiration taken, she notes, "This was the last journey I had to make before beginning . . . *Possessing the Secret of Joy*, a story whose subject frankly frightened me. An unpopular story. Even a taboo one."[85]

Whereas the U.S. gave the novel mixed reviews at best, the film incurred outright hostility. *Newsweek*, for instance, quoted Sudan's premier female surgeon, Nahid Toubia, alleging that only because Walker's popularity had suffered did she take on FGM; a "falling star," she was trying to get "the limelight" back.[86] More to the point, Walker, it was said, failed at empathy, her accusatory finger not illuminating but condemning and, therefore, alienating the African immigrant audience she claimed to address.

How affected Walker was by her critics can be teased out of the speech, referred to above, that opened *Warrior Marks*' tenth screening on February 24, 1994, in Oakland. Charged with having portrayed only victims, she exhorts, with a veneer of irony, "If in fact you survive your mutilation, and the degradation it imprints on soul and body, live it with fierceness, live it with all the joy and laughter you deserve."[87] In other words, she's talking to survivors, inviting allies, and interpolating enemies: "What can *you* do?" she asks: ". . . refrain from spending more than ten minutes . . . malign[ing] the messenger. Within those minutes thousands of children will be mutilated. Your idle words will have the rumble of muffled screams beneath them."[88] Yes, of course, she concedes, "We know that women and children who suffer genital mutilation will have to stand up for themselves, and, together put an end to it. But that they need our help is indisputable."[89] Walker's compassion, however, mined from African-*American* suffering, what she calls "our centuries-long insecurity,"[90] is troubling. Presuming an identity more likely to be rejected than embraced, she dares her audience to know "who we are, . . . what we've done to ourselves in the name of religion, male domination, female shame or terrible ignorance."[91] But who are "we"?

One thing unbearable to Walker's African critics but incontrovertibly central to events is named by German writer Verena Stefan in a chapter devoted to Tashi in *Rauh, wild & frei: Mädchengestalten in der Literatur*[92] (Rough, wild and free: Images of Girls in Literature). Stefan reads the murder of the Tsunga as a dagger to the shibboleth, reverence for the matriarch, a form of emotionally anchored respect with which many African daughters are raised that differs from adult-child egalitarianism in less traditional, less hierarchical societies, that is, the West.[93] Walker uncovers "betrayal of girls by their mothers" and targets "control the older wield over the younger."[94] Furthermore, in a revealing contrast, Stefan takes the rapport between Celie and Shug in *The Color Purple* as the other side of clitoridectomy's perfidy: "Während einer Beschneidungszeremonie herrscht auch geteilte Intimität zwischen Frauen und Mädchen, die Intimität des Horrors: Frauen betrachten und berühren das Geschlecht eines Mädchens, um es zu verstümmeln."[95] ("In the circumcision ceremony, we also have shared intimacy between woman and girl, the intimacy of horror. Women observe and touch a young girl's genital—to mutilate it.")

In *The Dynamics of African Feminism: Defining and Classifying African Feminist Literatures*, Susan Arndt raises the issue of homophobia, fear of which propels Stefan's observations and may also account in part for Walker's negative U.S. reception. In particular, two theorists of African womanism—Mary E. Modupe Kolawole and Chikwenye Okonjo Ogunyemi—frankly come out as homophobes by dismissing out of hand any possible relevance of a gay (and by implication bi- or transgender) movement to African realities. Arndt writes, with inappropriate neutrality, "I do not know of any feminist theoretician in the West who dissociates him- or herself explicitly from lesbianism. . . . [So] it is a novelty within . . . feminist discourse that theoreticians of gender issues like Ogunyemi and Kolawole reject lesbian love explicitly, generally and firmly."[96] What is really troubling, however, is that they have not been called on the carpet for it.

Now, homophobia kills—and understanding the role it plays in sustaining FGM is crucial. Lesbianism in particular poses a serious threat to female subordination in a patriarchal system that thrives by policing a binary system of sex and gender. Where Jelinek focuses on the overwhelming power of the male signifier to absorb all differences into itself, Walker explodes it, making room for a plethora of options. Pierre, for instance, in *Possessing*, is a pan-sexual figure and arguably the author's *porte-parole*. Hetero-normativity is rejected.

Was it homophobia, at least in part, that made offensive to many critics *Possessing the Secret of Joy*? Were they troubled by the lesbian subtext doubtless present in *Warrior Marks* as well? Pratibha Parmar, after all, lives an openly lesbian lifestyle and, although "a film maker first and last"—not a "lesbian filmmaker," in her interviewer's words—she has, for instance, in her short documentary "'Jodie: An

Icon'... looked at ways in which ... Foster has been constructed ... for lesbians in her various screen personas."[97] To borrow a conclusion from my earlier study, "Alice Walker: Matron of FORWARD," Buchi Emecheta charges Western feminists, including, ironically, Walker, with concern only for "issues ... relevant to themselves ... transplant[ed] onto Africa. Their own preoccupations—female sexuality, lesbianism and female circumcision—are not [African women's] priorities."[98]

Say what? Emecheta may be telling it like it is for the majority, but, for instance, Fanny Ann Eddy, a thirty-year-old human rights activist, had founded a lesbian and gay association in 2002 in Sierra Leone. On September 29, 2004, she was murdered, having earlier told the Human Rights Commission of the United Nations in Geneva how dangerous it was for lesbians, gays, bi- and transsexuals to remain invisible in African society. Clearly, it is equally dangerous for them to make themselves visible.[99]

Invisible, too, had been FGM. But breaking taboo has its price, and Walker suffered for her courage. After all, she intervenes for other, important, abuses and "insists upon the necessary and strong relationship between spirituality, activism and art."[100] Was she still ill at ease with FGM so many years down the road? Would her retirement be permanent? To find out, I phoned Walker's friend, Efua Dorkenoo, OBE, interviewed in *Warrior Marks* and credited as an advisor to the film. "What, if any, were Walker's reasons for abandoning campaigns?" I asked. Mainly, Efua told me, Walker had been hurt by African women critics having "charged her with not knowing Africa, with having self-serving interests. ... After all, she had spent more than seventeen years thinking about the issue before writing about it, using her talent as an artist to bring the subject to the world."

It is a pity that Walker has attenuated activism because the task remains, as Senegalese author Awa Thiam points out. Having also been attacked for talking publicly about excision, she answered Pratibha's question—"How do you feel about us coming here and making this film?" with the following: "You know, I work ... in the belief [in] universal sisterhood, that we are all in this together. ... For us, ... female genital mutilation [takes] priority. You can help ... it on[to] the world's agenda."[101]

The taboo-breaking this entails remains a challenge. I'm thinking of Yari Yari Pamberi, that remarkable gathering in New York City in October 2004, including Walker's presentation on a star-studded panel. Not a word about FGM. To his credit, NYU's Manthia Diawara, editor of *Renaissance noire* and conference convener, gave a few militant words to the issue. But apparently the elite among African and African-American intelligentsia continues wrapping the issue in silence.[102]

How different has been reception in Europe, birthplace of the Universal Declaration of Human Rights out of the ashes of the Holocaust. Particularly in Germany, where 20,000 African girls are at risk, Walker's input has not only been welcomed and praised but also transformed into concrete action. As we have seen, in addition to the *Antwort der Bundesregierung*, the executive's answer to parliament following a major interpolation in 1998, Walker is named as an inspiration in asylum debates.[103] The decision to offer sanctuary to African women fleeing the threat of excision is, in part, based on Walker's work. Or even earlier, in 1997, at a preparatory multipartisan hearing organized by the Green Party in Bonn, Dr. Angelika Köster-Lossack, MdB (Member of Parliament), included the German title of Walker's film—*Narben*—in the title of her talk. Alice Schwarzer, Germany's "first" feminist, TV personality, and author, has featured Walker and *Narben* in her magazine, *Emma*'s, pages. Indeed, a phalanx of intellectuals and celebrities has lauded the film. As a result, *Warrior Marks* has been distributed throughout the nation; nearly every major university and *gymnasium* has it in its archives or has shown it at film festivals and other events. This diffusion has met with the approval of many resident Africans, for they are engaged in the NGOs feeding into governmental agencies concerned with refugees, foreign aid, and women. Even the president of Germany, Dr. Horst Köhler, is involved. On April 18, 2005, the GTZ (Gesellschaft für Technische Zusammenarbeit—German Technical Cooperation, similar to U.S. AID), coordinator of INTEGRA, a network of NGOs against FGM in Germany, announced that Köhler had agreed to become the patron of the movement.

No parallel to this concerted effort exists in the United States despite an estimated number of girls at risk higher than 100,000 and excised or infibulated women with special health needs running into the tens of thousands.[104]

In sum, what has made such a difference? Why has Alice Walker been shunned in the U.S. for dealing with this issue but celebrated in Europe, especially in Germany? The complex reasons have to do with the development of the women's movement on both continents; on what has been learned, in Germany, from the Holocaust; on what is permitted in terms of who may speak "for" whom; and on the preference for human rights discourse in Europe as opposed to poststructuralist shattering of needed coalitions in the U.S. with its stubborn, divisive, essentialist stance on "race." The question has been posed, is multiculturalism good for women? Cultural relativism? In the case of Walker as an activist against FGM, clearly not.

Jelinek and Walker

"After I read *Possessing the Secret of Joy*," Efua Dorkenoo told me, "I wrote to Alice. You see, FORWARD counsels women like Tashi, whose mental anguish has become unbearable. Tashi is so real that I wanted to let Alice know and invite her to be patron of FORWARD. Of course, she agreed if we called her matron."[105] On June 3, 1995, FORWARD-U.K.'s board thanked Walker for the welcome of Dorkenoo's testimony before the U.S. Congress in 1993; for information that reached Edward Kennedy, propelling him "in[to] the forefront of international advocacy on FGM with UN Specialized Agencies and the US Missions in Africa"[106]; and for inspiring congresswomen Patricia Schroeder and Barbara Rose Collins's bill (H.R. 3247) against FGM in the United States.[107]

Yet in a 1993 *New York Times* editorial, African residents in the United States take issue with Walker. The video, they charge, is "emblematic of the Western feminist tendency to see female genital mutilation as the gender oppression to end all oppressions . . . a gauge by which to measure distance between the West and the rest of humanity."[108] These criticisms occur despite Walker's having made "a deliberate effort to stand with the mutilated women, not beyond them."[109] In a BBC interview she tells Juliane Greenwood that she wrote the novel out of concern for "the women who have had this done to them," yet she anticipates, correctly, "a lot of sadness, a lot of pain, disguised as embarrassment and . . . anger."[110]

Jelinek has also angered her audience, though for somewhat different reasons. In the study *Elfriede Jelinek in the Gender Wars: Newspaper Reception of "The Piano Teacher" and "Lust,"* Anja Meyer teases out one source of hostility expressed by both male and female readers. The inability of most reviewers to engage her on the intellectual level at which she operates—that is, they tend to be journalists untrained in influential postmodern theories, analysis, or hermeneutics—leads to an over reliance on narrative plotting, the least important of Jelinek's literary strategies. Reduced to what happens without attention to how it sounds (that is, to the ironies and implosive metaphors of representation), Jelinek's writing feeds aggressive pens of apologetic sexists—including women. For instance, at the 1976 "Schreib das auf, Frau" conference in Berlin, one of the first to draw together fiction writers of the new women's movement, Jelinek was accused of lacking empathy for her working-class female figures. Misunderstood as realistic characters, they were not seen as deliberate stereotypes and ironized media images. Readers mistook Jelinek's genre.

Walker's African critics in the U.S. also misread her genre, for *Warrior Marks* is not a straightforward documentary. Yes, it's about female genital mutilation, but equally important, it shows the coming-to-awareness of an activist, writer, and public intellectual willing to take on and encourage others to oppose a dangerous but entrenched custom. *Warrior Marks,* then, is a kind of bildungsroman. Not unlike the New York Intellectuals who pioneered a hybrid genre, personalizing the essay with literary touches that jeopardized them in the scientific world, so too does Walker feature not only FGM but the artist's emotions when confronting it. Yet the New York Intellectuals were mainly men, and this returns us to an earlier thorny issue. Can women function as public intellectuals as effectively as men? Already considered overemotional and therefore exercising dubious command outside the domestic sphere, can they indulge in drama and yet retain authority? Are they listened to? Jelinek thinks not. Regarding the hostility of Austrian critics she notes, "They kicked and spit on Thomas Bernhard, too, but they put on his plays. The work of a man simply has a different valence from that of a woman. She's much easier to dismiss."[111]

In her *LA Times* review of *Possessing the Secret of Joy*, Tina McElroy Ansa shares an anecdote to back this up:

> Months ago, [she] heard an African-American male scholar/writer say in the manner of a comic throwing away a line, "Hey, did you hear that Alice Walker dedicated her latest novel to ['] the innocent vulva[']?" He sort of pursed his lips and looked slowly around the room. Then, . . . rais[ing] one eyebrow, [he] . . . chuckled and went on to another subject. As if to say, "'Nough said." His gesture was part amusement, part embarrassment, part incredulity, part derision.[112]

Amusement, embarrassment, incredulity, derision—these are emotions that have governed readings of both Jelinek and Walker who, despite the intention of such barbs to silence them, have remained prolific and provocative if not unanimously loved. Both place the female body at or near the center of their works, which automatically drives a wedge between them and their male—and female—audiences. Both subscribe to an activist understanding of art. Both want to influence policy.

Yet the differences between them are instructive. Jelinek, for instance, a "double-agent of feminist aesthetics," highlights women's self-destructive hatred and impaired agency,[113] Walker their potential for self-love and strength. Indeed, Walker names her feminism "womanism," implying faith in black women's positive power.

Jelinek, however, is not so sanguine, the tribulations of her preference for the negative illuminated by critic Sigrid Loeffler. Regarding *The Piano Teacher's* fraught reception, Loeffler writes:

> It's got to be shockingly misunderstood. From *Penthouse* to *Playboy*, the sex-media industry will sniff out pornography and welcome it; the literary critics will smell an autobiographical rat. Male readers will suspect misandrony, female readers misogyny; mothers will discover the hatred of mothers and feminists, a renegade sister. For how is the "awful truth"—that many women do indeed entertain [self-destructive] fantasies—to be brought into harmony with campaigns to abolish sexual violence? When the public must be convinced that women do NOT desire to be raped and beaten, how can a feminist novel inscribing these wishes in reality be useful? Such a book will certainly be misunderstood.[114]

Jelinek requires her readers to decode the bitter irony she deploys to defend female rights to their own physical and intellectual personhood, but in the last analysis she remains wrapped in dissonance, disappearing into the "void" projected by male experience onto the female body. If Jörg Haider assimilates her to chaos—on the billboard he opposes Jelinek to culture—she appears to agree. The public intellectual can only disrupt, not build. As John Champagne writes about the filmed version of Erika, "[she] is in effect saying to the patriarchy, 'You want me to be castrated; well, I am."[115] Although disrupting authority and undermining ideology are certainly traits of the public intellectual, when deployed in women's interest those interests become men's. For Jelinek, "repressive sexuality incites to gynocide."[116]

In contrast, Walker's optimistic vision is nowhere more striking than in Nyanda, a little statue ironically found in the excisor M'Lissa's hut. In a photograph brought to Tashi in prison, the figure is captured "smiling broadly, eyes closed, and touching her genitals. If the word 'MINE' were engraved on her finger, her meaning could not be more clear."[117]

Walker, therefore, rehabilitates desire. Yes, Tashi kills the excisor but by doing so unleashes a movement whose slogan is the last thing the condemned prisoner sees: "RESISTANCE is the secret of joy."

Public intellectuals agree.

Notes

I would like to acknowledge the generous support of Professors Shulamit Reinharz and Sylvia Barack Fishman, and to thank them for the time they gave me as a scholar-in-residence at the Hadassah-Brandeis Institute, Brandeis University, spring 2006, to work on this chapter.

1. Toni Morrison, *Toni Morrison*, BBC video, 1988.
2. Verena Stefan, *Häutungen* (Munich: Frauenoffensive, 1975).
3. Elfriede Jelinek, unpublished interview by Tobe Levin, November 19, 1991. My translation.
4. See Orlando Patterson, *Slavery and Social Death* (Cambridge, MA: Harvard University Press, 1982).
5. Jochen Wolf, *Die gehaßte Frau Jelinek / Une femme à abattre*, television documentary, ARTE, 1997. Also, William Vlach offers a comment helpful to understanding the Erika figure. "The symptoms of Post Traumatic Stress Disorder (PTSD) include the traumatic event being persistently re-experienced, e.g. 'flashbacks,' persistent avoidance of the event, e.g., 'psychic numbing,' and increased arousal, e.g., 'hypervigilance.' One who has been vicariously traumatized may become anxious, depressed, cynical, and increasingly sensitive to violence. This process occurs via empathy for the victim." William Vlach, "When Saviour Becomes Serpent: The Psychology of Police Violence," in *Violence: "Mercurial Gestalt*," ed. Tobe Levin (Amsterdam: Rodopi, 2008), p. 227.
6. Jelinek interview, 1991.
7. Alice Walker, "Heaven Belongs to You," in *Revisioning Feminism around the World*, pp. 62–63 (New York: The Feminist Press at CUNY, 1995), p. 63.
8. *Die Klavierspielerin*, translated into English as *The Piano Teacher*, has been made into a film, *La Pianiste* (2002) directed by Michael Haneke and starring Isabelle Huppert and Annie Girardot. It won Best Film, Best Actor, and Best Actress at the Cannes Film Festival. See John Champagne, "Undoing Oedipus: Feminism and Michael Haneke's *The Piano Teacher*," *Bright Lights Film Journal*, April 2002, issue 36 http://www.brightlightsfilm.com/36/pianoteacher1.html (accessed February 13, 2006).
9. Ironically, as we will see, Walker is explicitly accused of doing this.

10. Svenska Akademien, http://nobelprize.org/literature/laureates/2004/jelinek-bibl.html (accessed February 13, 2006).

11. Ibid.

12. Münchner Literaturarbeitskreis, "Gespräch mit Elfriede Jelinek," in *mamas pfirsiche—frauen und literatur* 9/10, pp. 170–181 (Münster: Verlag Frauenpolitik, 1978), p. 176.

13. A highly controversial figure in her homeland, she participates in a long tradition of "sophisticated social criticism" including "Karl Kraus, Ödön von Horváth, Elias Canetti, Thomas Bernhard and the Wiener Group." Svenska Akademien. http://nobel prize.org/literature/laureates/2004/jelinek-bibl.html (accessed February 13, 2006).

14. Quoted in Jochen Wolf, "Die gehaßte Frau Jelinek/ Une femme à abattre," TV documentary, 1997, ARTE.

15. Svenska Akademien, http://nobelprize.org/literature/laureates/2004/jelinek-bibl .html (accessed February 13, 2006).

16. Sigrid Loeffler, "Die Hose Runter im Feuilleton," *EMMA*, May 1989, p. 4.

17. Alice Schwarzer, "Ich bitte um Gnade," *EMMA*, July 1989, p. 51.

18. Elfriede Jelinek, *The Piano Teacher*, trans. Joachim Neugroschel (New York: Grove, 1988), p. 116.

19. Jelinek, *Piano Teacher*, p. 86.

20. As psychologist Armando R. Favazza notes, more women cut than men, reflecting "ambiguity, paradox, and discontinuity in females' experiences of their bodies." *Bodies under Siege: Self-Mutilation and Body Modification in Culture and Psychiatry* (Baltimore: Johns Hopkins University Press, 1996), p. 51. Self-slicing may then be an attempt "to own the body, to perceive it as self (not other), known (not uncharted and unpredictable), and impenetrable (not invaded or controlled from outside)" (p. 51). Or in Jelinek's terms "Sie ist für sich selbst tabu" [She's taboo to herself]. Elfriede Jelinek, *Die Klavierspielerin* (Reinbek bei Hamburg: Rowohlt, 1983), p. 70.

21. "Despite many decades of campaigns and legislation, female genital mutilation (FGM) is still highly prevalent in the areas where it has traditionally been practiced and is still practiced [on] girls from these areas now living in Europe [and elsewhere in diaspora]. FGM comprises any procedure where parts of the female genitals are removed without medical indication," usually without anesthesia. Susan Elmusharaf, Nagla Elhadi, and Lars Almroth, "Reliability of Self Reported Form of Female Genital Mutilation and WHO Classification: Cross Sectional Study," *BMJ* [British Medical Journal] Online, DOI:10.1136/bmj.38873.649074.55 (published June 27, 2006), http://bmj.bmjjournals.com/cgi/content/full/333/7559/124 (accessed July 17, 2006). Although hospitals and clinics are known to perform clitoridectomies, excisions, and infibulations under more sanitary conditions to spare girls pain in the short term, long-term side effects remain. These include but are not limited to painful intercourse, scar formation, loss of vaginal elasticity, and unwonted tearing during childbirth that increases danger to both mother and child. Elevation in maternal morbidity where FGM is practiced has been corroborated by the largest UNICEF/ WHO study undertaken to date, published in *Lancet*, June 2, 2006.

22. André Müller, "Ich lebe nicht: André Müller spricht mit der Schriftstellerin Elfriede Jelinek," *Die Zeit*, June 22, 1990, p. 55.

23. Wolf. My translation.

24. Ibid.

25. Ibid.

26. Ibid.
27. Ibid.
28. Ibid.
29. Ibid.
30. Reinhard Urbach, review of *Michael. Ein Jugendbuch für die Infantilgesellschaft* by Elfriede Jelinek, Hessischer Rundfunk, July 6, 1972, n.p. Often Jelinek's fiction capitalizes on this discrepancy between expectations and poetic forms, playing on a technique of mind control that Elizabeth Janeway identifies as randomness. In her analysis of television Janeway asks, "What does the Media Establishment assume that we assume about the way this world functions?" In her viewing she found "a consistent, insistent demonstration of randomness, a statement that life is unpredictable and out of control." Applied as we know in the Gulag and in concentration camps, disruption of prisoners' normal expectations, severing action from consequence, led victims to conclude that safety, if it is anywhere, lies in "passivity and hiding." The effect on the status quo is clear, for "if the powerful can divide the majority of ordinary folk into disconnected, self-protecting [persons], they need not fear organized resistance." This is precisely Jelinek's concern in *Decoys* and her two subsequent novels, *Michael: A Children's Book for the Infantile Society* (1972) and *Women as Lovers* (1975). Elizabeth Janeway, "Soaps, Cynicism and Mind Control," *MS.*, 1983, 14/1), p. 118, quoted in Tobe Levin, "Introducing Elfriede Jelinek: Double Agent of Feminist Aesthetics," *Women's Studies International Forum* 9, no. 4 (1986), p. 437.
31. Jelinek, *Piano Teacher*, p. 85.
32. Ibid., p. 86.
33. Ibid.
34. Ibid.
35. Ibid.
36. Ibid., p. 88.
37. Sigrid Loeffler, "*Die Klavierspielerin*," ORF Ex-Libris, 2. Courtesy of Rowohlt Verlag, March 26 and April 2, 1989.
38. Elfriede Jelinek, *Die Klavierspielerin* (Reinbek bei Hamburg: Rowohlt, 1983), p. 293.
39. Schwarzer, p. 51.
40. Elfriede Jelinek, *Die Klavierspielerin* (Reinbek bei Hamburg: Rowohlt, 1983), p. 293.
41. Ibid, p. 232.
42. Ibid.
43. Ibid.
44. Sigrid Berka, "D(e)addyfication: Elfriede Jelinek," in *Elfriede Jelinek: Framed by Language*, ed. Jorun B. Johns and Katherine Arens, pp. 229–254 (Riverside: Ariadne, 1994), p. 231.
45. From this point, two pages, or eight paragraphs, are adapted from "*Die Klavierspielerin*: On Mutilation and Somatophobia," in "*Other*" *Austrians: Post-1945 Austrian Women's Writing*, ed. Allyson Fiddler, Proceedings of the Conference, Post-1945 Austrian Women's Writing, University of Nottingham, April 18–20, 1996, pp. 225–234 (Berne: Peter Lang, 1998). Because this publication was bilingual, it required knowledge of German. Here all quotes appear in translation, making the discussion available for the first time to those who cannot read German.
46. Katrin Sieg, *Exiles, Eccentrics, Activists: Women in Contemporary German Theater* (Ann Arbor: University of Michigan Press, 1994), pp. 151–152. See also Tobe Levin, "Jelinek's Radical Radio: Deconstructing the Woman in Context," *Women's Studies International Forum* 9, no. 4 (1991), pp. 435–442.

47. Sieg, p. 170.
48. Judith Butler, *Gender Trouble: Feminism and the Subversion of Identity* (London: Routledge, 1990), p. x.
49. Jelinek, *Piano Teacher*, p. 51.
50. Jelinek, *Piano Teacher*, pp. 51–52.
51. Jelinek, *Klavierspielerin*, p. 67.
52. Jelinek, *Piano Teacher*, p. 52.
53. Ibid.
54. Ibid., p. 99.
55. Tobe Levin, "Jelinek's Radical Radio: Deconstructing the Woman in Context." *Women's Studies International Forum* 14, nos. 1 & 2, (1991), p. 91.
56 *Klavierspielerin*, p. 247. My translation.
57. Elfriede Jelinek, with Jutta Heinrich and Adolf-Ernst Meyer, *Sturm und Zwang. Schreiben als Geschlechterkampf* (Hamburg: Ingrid Klein, 1995), p. 37.
58. *Klavierspielerin*, p. 257. My translation.
59. Ibid., p. 270.
60. Ibid., p. 73.
61. Ibid., p. 95.
62. Ibid., p. 147.
63. Ibid., p. 125.
64. Schwarzer, p. 54; see also Berka 1994, p. 143.
65. Wolf.
66. Alice Walker, *The Color Purple* (New York: Simon & Schuster, 1982), p. 237.
67. Ngugi wa Thiong'o's 1955 novel *The River Between* probably inspired at least two major elements here, a young woman's choice of FGM for tribal reasons and a sister's death from the procedure. Ngugi's is the first novel of which I am aware that makes "female circumcision" a central theme. The author opposes it by allowing his protagonist, known as "The Teacher," to take an Irigu, or uncircumcised bride. See my article "Women as Scapegoats of Culture and Cult: An Activist's View of Female Circumcision in Thiong'o's *The River Between*," in *Ngambika. Studies of Women in African Literature*, ed. Carole Boyce Davies and Anne Adams Graves, pp. 205–221 (Trenton, NJ: Africa World Press, 1985).
68. Binyavanga Wainana, "How to Write about Africa," *Granta 92. The View from Africa*, http://www.granta.com/extracts/2615 (accessed March 18, 2006).
69. Gay Wilentz, "Healing the Wounds of Time," review of *Possessing the Secret of Joy* by Alice Walker and *Bailey's Café* by Gloria Naylor, *The Women's Review of Books* 10 (February 1993), p. 16.
70. Ibid.
71. Cathy N. Davidson and David Theo Goldberg, "Engaging the Humanities," in *Profession 2004*, pp. 42–62 (New York: MLA, 2004).
72. Fadumo Korn, with Sabine Eichhorst, *Born in the Big Rains: A Memoir of Somalia and Survival*, trans. Tobe Levin (New York: The Feminist Press, 2006).
73. Gritt Richter, "'Ich bin nicht verstümmelt!' Betroffene Frauen auf der Suche nach Sensibilität und Respekt—eine Erfahrungsbericht," in *Schnitte in Körper und Seele. Eine Umfrage zur Situation beschnittener Mädchen und Frauen in Deutschland*, ed. Berufsverband der Frauenärzte, Terre des Femmes, UNICEF, pp. 13–14 (Köln: UNICEF, 2005), p. 13.
74. Fran Hosken (1920–2006) coined the term FGM (female genital mutilation) in the 1970s.

75. Rogaia Mustafa Abusharaf, ed. *Female Circumcision: Multicultural Perspectives* (Philadelphia: University of Pennsylvania Press, 2006). A regional conference of the Inter-African Committee (AIC) in Addis Ababa proposed altering the terminology. In 1991, the UN Seminar on Traditional Practices Affecting the Health of Women and Children, held in Burkina Faso, recommended the term "female genital mutilation," or FGM, which is now codified in World Health Assembly Resolution WHA46.18 and other international instruments, including documents approved during the Fourth World Conference on Women in ⸗eijing, China, September 1995 (WHO J2). The European Network for the Prevention and Eradication of Female Genital Mutilation (EuroNet FGM), at its January 2004 meeting in Paris, drafted a press release affirming that the operations constitute a mutilation and should be so named. In Bamako, at the triennial gathering of the Inter-African Committee in April 2005, the IAC also urged continued use of FGM, which had been the official language of the UNFPA and UNICEF until influenced by the United States suggesting that "mutilation" be repl   by "cutting." See also the "DECLARATION: on the Terminology FGM; 6th IAC Ge   al Assembly, April 4–7, 2005, Bamako/Mali," aka "The Bamako Declaration," http://www.iac-ciaf .org/index.php?option=com_content&task=view&id=28&Itemid=44&PHPSESSID= ccab7400b78c4c9a3d1c37b99817fa52 (accessed November 15, 2006).

76. Both activists, El Dareer cooperated with German women's groups in the late seventies and early eighties and spent several weeks in 1991 as my houseguest. Abdalla   n be seen in a photograph shot by FORWARD–Germany's managing director, Dr. A li Barre-Dirie, in Somalia in January 2006. Abdalla continues as a militant.

77. Vicki Kirby, "Out of Africa: 'Our Bodies Ourselves?'" in *Female Circumcision a d the Politics of Knowledge: African Women in Imperialist Discourses*, ed. O. Nnaeme a, pp. 81–96 (Westport and London: Praeger, 2005), p. 83.

78. Ibid.

79. Alice Walker, "Heaven Belongs to You," in *Re-Visiting Feminism around the Wo l,* pp. 62–63 (New York: The Feminist Press, 1995), p. 63.

80. Pratibha Parmar, director. *Warrior Marks.* Producer Alice Walker. Distributor Women Make Movies, 1993.

81. Excerpts in *Feminist Europa: Review of Books* 3, no. 1, (2003) and 4, no. 1 (2004). See http://www.mtholyoke.edu/~tflevin (accessed March 18, 2006).

82. Efua Dorkenoo, interview by Tobe Levin, June 1994.

83. Efua Dorkenoo, *Cutting the Rose: Female Genital Mutilation: the Practice and Its Prevention* (London: Minority Rights Group, 1994), p. 81. This point is also repeatedly made by attorney Linda Weil-Curiel.

84. Ibid., p. 82.

85. Alice Walker, *Anything We Love Can Be Saved: A Writer's Activism* (New York: Random House, 1997), p. 126.

86. David A. Kaplan, Shawn D. Lewis, and Joshua Hammer, "Is It Torture or Tradition?" *Newsweek*, December 20, 1993, p. 124.

87. Walker, *Heaven*, p. 63.

88. Ibid.

89. Ibid.

90. Walker, *Activism*, p. 150.

91. Ibid.

92. Verena Stefan, *Rauh, wild & frei: Mädchengestalten in der Literatur* (Frankfurt: Fischer, 1997).

93. See Dympna Ugwu-Oju, *What Will My Mother Say? A Tribal African Girl Comes of Age in America* (Chicago: Bonus Books, 1995).

94. Stefan, p. 108.

95. Ibid.

96. Susan Arndt, *The Dynamics of African Feminism: Defining and Classifying African Feminist Literatures* (Trenton: Africa World Press, 2002).

97. "Identities, Passions, and Commitments: An Interview with the British Filmmaker Pratibha Parmar," *Lola Press, International Feminist Magazine*, November 1999–April 2000, p. 38.

98. Thelma Ravell-Pinto, "Buchi Emecheta at Spelman College," *SAGE: A Scholarly Journal on Black Women* 2, no. 1 (Spring 1985), p. 50.

99. Anke Guido, "Menschenrechtsverletzungen an lesbischen Frauen," *TdF Menschenrechte für die Frau*, 2 (2005), p. 13.

100. Farah Jasmine Griffin, "The Courage of Her Convictions," review of *Anything We Love Can Be Saved: A Writer's Activism*, by Alice Walker, *The Women's Review of Books* 15, no. 4 (January 1998), p. 23.

101. "Identities, Passions, and Commitments," p. 36. And Pratibha comments, "It was refreshing for me to hear her, [Thiam] having come from the late 80s and early 90s talk of post-feminism, with so much cynicism around the bankruptcy of feminism. It was good to meet a woman who still has that wonderfully optimistic belief in the idea of universal sisterhood, which many of us held in the 70s, but which got lost along the way as we got more fragmented and disparate." "Identities, Passions, and Commitments," pp. 36–37.

102. Another distressing example: Ada Uzuamaka Azodo, in "Issues in African Feminism: A Syllabus," includes nothing on FGM—in 1997! The course was offered at Indiana University Northwest.

103. http://www.ak-kipro.de/fgm_bundestag200107.html (accessed July 17, 2004).

104. Another example of the difference between the U.S. and Europe: Dr. Pierre Foldès pioneered clitoral reconstruction, has been offering the procedure to hundreds of women in Paris, and has begun training other surgeons to perform it. Hubert Prolongeau, *Victoire sur l'Excision. Pierre Foldès, le chirurgien qui redone l'espoir aux femmes mutilées* (Paris: Albin Michel, 2006). And whereas there are already dozens of well-woman clinics serving victims of FGM in Britain, only the overworked Dr. Nawal Nour at Brigham and Women's Hospital in Boston can be found to systematically offer a similar service in the United States.

105. Dorkenoo interview, 1994.

106. Dorkenoo, *Rose*, p. 82.

107. Tobe Levin, "Alice Walker: Matron of FORWARD," in *Black Imagination and the Middle Passage*, ed. Maria Diedrich, Henry Louis Gates, Jr., and Carl Pedersen, pp. 240–254 (New York: Oxford University Press, 1999), p. 241.

108. Seble Dawit and Salem Merkuria, letter to the editor, *New York Times*, December 7, 1993.

109. Walker, *Warrior Marks*, p. 13.

110. Juliane Greenwood, moderator, *The South Bank Show*, BBC 2 (11 October 1992).

111. Anja Meyer, *Jelinek in der Geschlechterpresse. Die Klavierspielerin und Lust im printmedialen Diskurs* (Hildesheim: Olms-Weidmann, 1994), p. 158.

112. Tina McElroy Ansa, review of *Possessing the Secret of Joy*, by Alice Walker, *Los Angeles Times*, July 5, 1992. Reprinted in *Alice Walker: Critical Perspectives Past and*

Present, ed. Henry Louis Gates, Jr., and K.A. Appiah, pp. 32–34 (New York: Amistad, 1993), p. 33.

113. The 2001 Sundance Festival Grand Jury Prize went to a modern version of the Weiniger biography, Henry Bean, director, *The Believer,* produced by Fireworks Pictures and Peter Hoffman. It portrays a Jewish Nazi.

114. Sigrid Loeffler, "Ohnmacht—Ein Aphrodisiakum?" *Profit* 8 (February 28, 1983), p. 73. My translation.

115. John Champagne, "Undoing Oedipus: Feminism and Michael Haneke's *The Piano Teacher,*" *Bright Lights Film Journal,* April 2002, http://www.brightlightsfilm.com/36/pianoteacher1.html (accessed April 13, 2008).

116. Levin, "Introducing," p. 436.

117. Walker, *Possessing,* pp. 196–197.

Town Whores into Warmongers

The Ascent of the Neoconservatives and the Revival of Anti-Jewish Rhetoric in American Public Discourse, 1986–2006

Susanne Klingenstein

> Very plausible schemes with very pleasing commencements have often
> shameful and lamentable consequences.
> —Edmund Burke

The Rocky Ascent of the Neoconservatives

In October 1988, a short month before the election that would transfer power from an ever-optimistic Ronald Reagan to a thin-lipped, parsimonious George Herbert Walker Bush and bring about the neoconservatives' first fall from grace, Russell Kirk, author of *The Conservative Mind* (1953),[1] a founding text of postwar American conservatism, gave a lecture at the Heritage Foundation, a conservative think tank specializing in legislative policy analysis that feeds information into Washington's "decision-making loop."[2] Kirk offered two soothing predictions about the neoconservative "interlopers,"[3] who had garnered third- and second-tier appointments in the Reagan administration: "[I]t appears to me that . . . President Bush will not be eager to obtain the services of this little Sacred Band—which made itself exclusive, and now finds itself excluded. . . . I predict that within a very few years we will hear no more of the Neoconservatives: some will have fallen away, and others will have been merged with the main current of America's conservative movement, and yet others' pert loquacity will have been silenced by the tomb."[4]

During the Reagan era, American conservatism was on the cusp of becoming profoundly transformed by the neoconservatives. The seeming congruence of their views on domestic and foreign policy with those of Reagan and their success at garnering appointments, albeit not in the administration's inner sanctum, created deep resentment among paleoconservatives[5] because they believed themselves to be "the real architects of the Reagan victory."[6] Kirk was a dyed-in-the-wool paleoconservative who felt unjustly marginalized. In his talk he identified the source of the threat to his status and expressed his hope that the newcomers would now be shown the door by a man of the right experience and social class.

Kirk's metaphor of the "little Sacred Band" was a veiled allusion to the Jews. At the heart of Kirk's rhetorical attack, concealed by the quaintness of his lexicon, lay the old reproach against the Jews: self-confident aloofness and exclusive in-group bonding based on the conviction of being the Chosen People. This reproach, often articulated in conjunction with suspicions of secrecy, conspiracy, and an undermining of the established order, is a classic trope in antisemitic literature.

In this essay I examine the perplexing phenomenon that the rise of the neoconservatives to political influence was accompanied by a rise in anti-Jewish rhetoric. Usually at a very low hum in American politics, anti-Jewish rhetoric was quite audible between the 1880s and the late 1930s but went underground in the aftermath of World War II. In the late 1980s, however, it was reemerging. In the spring of 2006 it moved from the political fringe into the academic mainstream in a "working paper" two academics published on an official Harvard University Web site. The two professors, one of whom was well known as a conservative "realist," used themes and rhetorical strategies long familiar from the rhetoric of leftwing anti-Zionism, which, in turn, had emerged in the wake of Israel's victories in the wars of 1967 and 1973, that is, in the wake of another perceived empowerment of the Jews.

The dynamic here is a familiar one. Since the eighteenth century and the tentative Enlightenment promise of integrating the Jews into European society with full civil rights (not realized until the late nineteenth century), a perceived (that is, real or imagined) empowerment of the Jews frequently elicited a rise in antisemitic rhetoric. When in 1799 a spokesman for Berlin's wealthy Jews offered the conversion of several well-off and enlightened Jewish families to Christianity (because political emancipation was not in the offing), the response by Prussia's Protestant elite was not joy at the Jewish souls' imminent salvation. Rather, the offer spurred a series of anti-Jewish polemics culminating in 1803 in a learned exposé of the Jews' perpetual scheming to attain world domination and of their current desire to subjugate Prussia economically and intellectually. Karl Wilhelm Friedrich Grattenauer's tract "Wider die Juden" (against the Jews) is one of many indirect precursors of the professorial essay on the "Israel Lobby" posted on Harvard's Kennedy School of Government Web site in March 2006.[7]

In this essay I will examine the rhetorical responses to the most recent perceived political "empowerment" of Jews. The facts of the neoconservatives' ascent to political influence have by now been fairly well established.[8] Many books either maximize or pointedly neutralize the involvement of Jews in the evolution of neoconservatism but don't manage to leave it alone altogether.[9] Fair enough because neoconservatism turned out to be the trajectory that, for the first time in American history, brought a sizable group of smart and articulate Jews with bold ideas into positions of real political power.[10] What has not been examined is the escalating reaction to the *perception* of American Jews in power. America is no stranger to antisemitism,[11] but the rebirth of its old tropes among educated men since the 1980s is particularly fascinating to observe. In this essay I describe the political ascent of the neoconservatives from the perspective of those who most distrust them and examine the rhetoric that articulates the distrust.

In his 1988 presentation at the Heritage Foundation, Russell Kirk was quite right about the ouster of the neoconservatives by the incoming Bush administration from their perches in the Reagan government, where, it was said incorrectly and with barely concealed hostility, they had dominated the "foreign, defense, and educational policy areas."[12] George H.W. Bush, flustered by the "vision thing" and, unlike Reagan, without a clear ideological agenda of his own, gave a wide berth to eggheads who believed that democracies did not arise but were created and that America should make the "promotion of democracy its main objective."[13] The elder Bush shut out the neocons and alienated them by promoting and pursuing a foreign policy that left much of the "responsibility for maintaining regional stability to multilateral institutions," such as the European Union and the United Nations, whom the neocons deeply distrusted.[14] Measured by the fiery and expansive ideas of the neocons, the administration of Bush 41 appeared cheerless and dispirited. Nevertheless, it was a largely meritorious presidency of "dutiful public service,"[15] which in its "view of what was doable was determined pre-Reagan."[16] It became irreversibly loathsome to the traditionalist Right only when the elder Bush broke his promise and raised taxes.

Although a handful of neoconservatives had snared juicy appointments because the administration wanted their "intellectual ballast"[17]—most notably that of William Kristol, who served Vice President Dan Quayle as domestic adviser[18]—the neocons were largely out of the loop. Russell Kirk assumed that a combination of weakening commitment, assimilation, and death would now eliminate the obnoxious neocons from the conservative scene. He could not have been more wrong.

The neocons disappeared into think tanks and universities, where they redefined their political vision (challenged severely by the seeming collapse of the Soviet Union beginning in 1989). For them the twelve years of enforced exile from power during the elder Bush and Clinton administrations were a blessing in disguise. It allowed them to adjust to the new political realities with full concentration and to transform themselves from single-minded anti-Soviet ideologues into "force-based 'hard' Wilsonians focused on foreign policy" in a broader, more general way.[19] In those twelve years the neoconservatives created an extensive intellectual network—consisting of think tanks, journals, and publishing houses—and financial support system.[20] In addition, they secured the succession of a younger generation of neoconservatives that was more ready to engage in Republican politics (the first generation of neoconservatives tended to stay with the Democratic Party). The younger cohort was not averse to abandoning the complex moral-philosophical discussion and social policy thinking of their elders for a somewhat simplified foreign policy agenda of actively spreading American-style democracy abroad backed by high-tech weapons systems.[21] When Bush 43 assumed power in January 2001, a younger generation of neocons, equipped with a view of foreign policy shaped by their minute study of the failure of multilateral warfare and diplomacy in Bosnia, Somalia, and Kosovo and annoyed by the equivocal result of the first Gulf War, stood ready to make its move and to give a perplexed and fairly inexperienced president all the right answers.

Most important, however, the neoconservatives had used the elder Bush and Clinton years to build a strong alliance with the Evangelical Christians (one of the most fruitful and lasting connections was that between Gary Bauer and William Kristol). The neocons recognized the evangelicals' potential power as a grass-roots movement and despite massive ideological differences[22] fervently wooed them. The gentlemen of the Old Right, in contrast, spurned the evangelicals on account of their perceived intellectual crudity and "lowbrow imitation of what the Old Right represents." The paleoconservatives were class- and culture-conscious aesthetes rather than strategists.[23] The neocons, however, were self-made urban pragmatists. The paleoconservatives, mentally stuck in the 1950s, were neither able to muster the requisite tolerance nor to hold their noses at opportune moments and thus failed to hitch the political evangelicals' potential to their wagon.[24] As the elder Bush began his administration, the paleoconservatives felt painfully that they had become a marginal, powerless group in post-Reagan conservatism.[25] They vented their frustration by lashing out at their rivals.

The Rhetoric of Defeat

Small-scale attacks by Old Right conservatives on the neoconservatives, say, by Joseph Sobran, senior editor of *National Review*, had been a regular feature of paleoconservative journalism since the beginning of the Reagan administration. The first all-out attack on the neocons took place in the *Intercollegiate Review*, the magazine of the Intercollegiate Studies Institute, the oldest national conservative organization, in its "State of Conservatism" symposium in the spring of 1986. In his introduction Gregory Wolf announced that "distinguished conservative scholars," by which he meant men who valued "order and organic community, class and natural aristocracy," and men who regarded "Christian belief as the foundation of morality and law,"[26] were dismayed at seeing conservatism in America, "the only force competent to articulate the first principles which are the prerequisite for any genuine social and political reform," suffer from "attenuation," "apostasy," and a "sense of malaise."[27] He cited four reasons for the paleoconservatives' despair: the emergence of the neocons as a result of the radicalization of the 1960s; the rise of the populist and evangelical New Right as a result of society's accelerating moral decay; the attraction of "pragmatists and camp followers to the seats of power and privilege" in the wake of conservative successes at the polls; and the "liberal-dominated" media's pigheaded insistence that the neoconservatives, who like old liberals continued to be plagued by utopian schemes, were now the conservative enemy. The paleoconservatives thought the media ignored them and pushed them "out of existence" (*IR*, p. 4). In politics, as elsewhere, it is better to be reviled than to be ignored. Yet as newly converted neocons, ragamuffin New Righters, and opportunistic hangers-on were storming through the gates of Washington, the Old Right felt it had much to complain about.

The encroachment metaphor was taken further by Clyde Wilson, a history professor at the University of South Carolina and editor of *The Papers of John C. Calhoun*: "[W]e have simply been crowded out by overwhelming numbers. The offensives of radicalism have driven vast herds of liberals across the border into our territories. These refugees now speak in our name, but the language they speak is the same language they have always spoken. We have grown familiar with it, have learned to tolerate it, but it is tolerable only by contrast to the harsh syllables of the barbarians over the border. It contains no words for things that we value. Our estate has been taken over by an impostor, just as we were about to inherit" (*IR*, p. 6).

The target here is not the Christians of the New Right but the neoconservatives, many of whom were descended from Eastern European Jews who had arrived as immigrants around the turn of the twentieth century. Although Wilson's metaphor alludes to their abandonment of left-liberal positions in the early 1960s, his metaphor also encodes their immigrant history as observed by an old-stock American who in the 1910s would have perceived the arriving Jews as "herds" of Yiddish-speaking "refugees" fleeing from the "offensives" of mob violence in tsarist Russia. Their efforts at assimilation, such as learning the language of their new country, are of course deceptive and doomed to fail because a leopard cannot change its spots. Just as their forebears may speak a Yiddish-accented English but retain a Jewish mindset, so the neoconservatives may now speak a conservative lingo but without subscribing to any of the conservative values and continuing instead to cherish their old liberal ideas.

At the beginning of the century Eastern European Jews were considered unassimilable. Similarly Wilson considers the neoconservatives essentially unchanged liberals and thus calls them "impostors" attempting to usurp the paleoconservatives' inheritance (or access to power). In a subsequent paragraph Wilson takes the idea of the "impostor" a step further. Referring to the Civil War, when a captured Confederate soldier who preferred service in the Union army to languishing in jail was called a "galvanized Yankee," Wilson calls the neocons "galvanized conservatives." To a Southerner, a galvanized Yankee is a traitor. One of the stereotypes that attached to Jews and looms behind the term *galvanized* is that of men whose loyalty is dictated by opportunity and who will betray their fatherland at the drop of a dime. Echoes of that stereotype can be heard clearly when Wilson writes, "[T]he Old Guard cannot help but catch on the wind from the Potomac a faint but unmistakable odor of opportunistic betrayal" (*IR*, p. 7).

The themes of opportunism, usurpation, power hunger, deceit, and perversion of conservative thought are sounded by several contributors to the symposium, most notably by M.E. Bradford, who had a specific axe to grind and wielded it with gusto against the neoconservatives. In 1981, Bradford, a professor of English at the University of Dallas, had campaigned to become chairman of the National Endowment for the Humanities. But the neocons, especially Irving Kristol in his magazine *Public Interest*, backed William Bennett and mercilessly attacked Bradford for his scorn of Abraham Lincoln, for his opposition to the 1964 Civil Rights Act, and for his support of the Alabama segregationist George Wallace as presidential candidate in 1968 and 1972. Bennett acceded to the NEH chairmanship, but in 1985, Bradford became president of the Philadelphia Society, an organization of conservatives founded after Barry Goldwater's 1964 defeat. Bradford organized the first meeting with himself at the society's helm around the subject of neoconservatism and invited comrades-in-arms as speakers.[28]

Toward the end of the *Intercollegiate Review* symposium, George A. Panichas, a professor of English at the University of Maryland, produced the old chestnuts of the materialism, hedonism, modernism, and spiritual aridity of the Jews, a staple of the Catholic antisemitism of George Santayana and T.S. Eliot and of the genteel craziness of Brooks and Henry Adams.[29] America's spiritual culture, Panichas argued, had been assaulted by modernism and was in retreat. The vacuum had been filled by a "sham conservatism [that] merely temporalizes and trivializes and dissimulates spiritual laws and truths" (*IR*, p. 23). The "*chic* politicized conservatism" developed by the pragmatic newcomers, a "tinsel, opportunistic, and hedonistic conservatism," may be temporarily successful in a "technological-Benthamite world" but will fail to redeem it because it "fails to acknowledge spiritual needs that coalesce in God and the soul" (*IR*, p. 23). Echoing Santayana and T.S. Eliot on the modern Jew, Panichas characterizes the neoconservatives hiding behind their "sham" confection as spiritually barren wreckers of traditional culture.[30]

A similar note was sounded by University of Michigan professor Stephen Tonsor at a meeting of the Philadelphia Society in May 1986. Tonsor defined modernism as a "revolutionary movement in culture which derived from a belief in man's radical alienation, in God's unknowability or non-existence, and in man's capacity to transform the conditions of his existence."[31] He then claimed that the "social and political consequence of modernity is totalitarianism" and that the "denial of the existence of order as the ground of being, and the rejection of the transcendent are a one-way street to Dachau. . . . Hitler did not need to give a specific command for the 'final solution.' Himmler and the members of the SS Einsatzgruppen knew the 'final solution' was implicit in their conception of reality" (*NR*, p. 55). At first glance this seems not to make much sense. While it is true that Nazi ideology had no use for the traditional Christian God, it had a very precise sense of order and how it wanted to arrange the world. What Tonsor means by the modernists' "denial of the existence of order" becomes clearer when he talks about the composer protagonist in Thomas Mann's novel *Doktor Faustus*:

> Because [Adrian] Leverkühn [a composite of Nietzsche and Arnold Schönberg] could not accept an order which, modernist that he was, he felt to be meaningless, he imposed a new order, rational and cleanly articulated as the music of Bach but lacking Bach's attachment to the divine and reconciliation to the human. Leverkühn's achievement was a great technical triumph but only a triumph of technique. It is fitting funeral music for a culture that died of pride. (*NR*, p. 56).

Having established his interpretation of modernism—"rational technique in the pursuit of irrational ends [such as the Nazis' industrialized killing of the Jews]; that suggests the modern condition"—Tonsor applied his reading of modernity to contemporary politics. Because the "neoconservatives are or have been cultural modernists [they] are so inventive and often correct in dealing with the realm of technique. . . . What the neoconservatives have done is to divorce technique from ends in an effort to maintain their cultural modernism while rejecting its social and political implications" (*NR*, p. 56). What all this technical wizardry amounts to is that it allows the neoconservatives to avoid having to locate "themselves in a body of principle that makes life worth living, or that one would die defending" (*NR*, p. 56).

In Tonsor's view, then, the neoconservatives are godless rationalists who arrogantly indulge in the mastery of technique regardless of the human cost. They are unfettered by the higher ideals for which more humble people would lay down their lives. Pride, of course, is the infernal sin of the Jews. Thus we are prepared when Tonsor finally tells us who the neoconservatives are—New York Jews (and some auxiliaries):

> Neoconservatism is above all a transmogrification of "the New York intellectuals," . . . who . . . reflected the instantiation of modernity among secularized Jewish intellectuals. Neoconservatism is culturally unthinkable aside from the history of the Jewish intellectual in the twentieth century. (*NR*, p. 56).

In his essay Tonsor constructs a cultural lineage that connects the Nazis, Mann's Adrian Leverkühn (i.e., a fusion of Nietzsche and Schönberg), and the godless Jews of New York. In order to detract from the patent absurdity of his mental construction, Tonsor posited at the outset of his essay that as a result of modernity, there was no longer any difference other than "style and slogans" between the far right and the far left: "The Right that is born of modernity is a radical revolutionary Right, which cannot in any important degree be distinguished from the revolutionary Left" (*NR*, p. 55). Hence the conversion from the left to the right that the neoconservatives claimed they had undergone and that now entitled them, they said, to play a leading role in the GOP and the Reagan administration was immaterial. It was the arrogance of the newly converted sinner that irked Tonsor most of all, and he articulated his upset in a metaphor that managed to be simultaneously homey, funny, and insulting:

> It has always struck me as odd, even perverse, that former Marxists have been permitted, yes invited, to play such a leading role in the Conservative movement of the twentieth century. It is splendid when the town whore gets religion and joins the church. Now and then she makes a good choir director, but when she begins to tell the minister what he ought to say in his Sunday sermons, matters have been carried too far. (*NR*, p. 55)

Those familiar with the history of American conservatism will enjoy the irony here. Many of the saintly Old Right founders of postwar Conservatism had deep roots in Marxism. Not only had Whittaker Chambers been a communist before his conversion, but so was Frank Meyer, an important writer for *National Review* in the early 1960s; Russell Kirk himself had supported the socialist Norman Thomas; and Willmoore Kendall, Buckley's mentor at Yale, had also begun his intellectual career on the left.[32] Tonsor's outburst is an instance of the pot calling the kettle black.

Two and a half years after Tonsor's presentation at the Philadelphia Society, Russell Kirk, the doyen of American Conservatism, gave his talk at the Heritage Foundation in which he summed up the position of the Old Right on the neoconservatives. Kirk was an elitist who put little stock in ordinary people. He saw in class hierarchy a bulwark against the decline of moral values. Echoing the Southern Agrarians and T.S. Eliot's lecture series *After Strange Gods* (1933), Kirk indulged in neofeudal dreams. He "wished for an aristocracy of rule over a traditional culture. His elite—gentlemen and scholars—would defend values, not interests. Their status would derive from class and personal cultivation; they would conserve civilization against the onslaught of the masses demanding cheap and shoddy goods."[33] In such a concept of society, there is little room for those associated with modernity, technology, and immigration. In Kirk's 1988 speech, the anti-Jewish thrust appeared somewhat muted because it was tempered by a grudging appreciation of what the neocons had achieved. But ultimately, Kirk, though more civil than Tonsor, was just as hostile. For Kirk, too, the neocons were a "horde of dissenters . . . of Jewish stock," who, though talented, suffered from earnestness and intellectual hubris.[34] Earnestness used to be a strike against the hard-working immigrant kids at gentlemen's colleges, and intellectual hubris is a long-standing Christian complaint against the Jews. Kirk noted further that the neocons "skillfully insinuated themselves into the councils of the Nixon and Reagan Administrations!" Focused on "seeking chiefly place and preferment," that is, being opportunists who lack principles to die for, they have not "made many friends." They have "no true political constituency" and "have shown no great literary skill: I fear that not one book by a neoconservative will still be read in the year 2000" (*RK*).

Worse yet, clever as the neoconservatives may be, having no principles and ideals, they also "lack those long views and that apprehension of the human condition which form the basis for successful statecraft" (*RK*, p. 4). They may thus be able technocrats and be "possessed of considerable knowledge of the world about us. But in the understanding of the human condition and in the apprehension of the accumulated wisdom of our civilization, they are painfully deficient" (*RK*, p. 4). George Santayana once described his Jewish fellow students at Harvard College, Charles Loeser and Bernard Berenson, in very similar terms. They were friendless outsiders to the fellowship of the college. They had acquired so much technical expertise (through industrious study) that they were not only conversant in the culture but could even make their living by brokering and selling the trappings of the culture to its rightful heirs (Loeser and Berenson became art dealers who settled near Florence); yet they remained outside the culture because they lacked a true human (i.e., Christian) understanding of Western (i.e., Christian) civilization.[35]

What the Jews lacked in humanity, they made up for in "infatuation with ideology," which Michael Novak, a Catholic neocon, defined as a "guiding vision of Future social action" (*RK*, p. 6). What was wrong with the neocons' guiding vision was that it promulgated "an ideological manifesto that offers nothing better than a utopia of 'democratic' creature comforts" (*RK*, p. 7). Here Kirk is referring to the neocons' idea (based on the thinking of Adam Smith) that the marginally comfortable will be too keen on preserving and multiplying their hard-won possessions to go out and make trouble. To paleoconservatives the notion that material comforts can override commitment to moral ideas is a threat to religion because it suggests that "man could create himself . . . , that he is not . . . dependent on God, but the master of his own soul and destiny" (*RK*, p. 6).

Kirk expected that the neoconservatives as former leftists would "address themselves to the great social difficulties of the U.S. today, especially the swelling growth of a dismal urban proletariat, and the decay of the moral order." But true to (Jewish) type, instead of thinking ethics, they were thinking money: "[T]heir concern has been mainly with the gross national product and with 'global wealth'" (*RK*, p. 8). Nor are they "champions of diversity," but as modern technocrats "they aspire to bring about a world of uniformity and dull standardization, Americanized, industrialized, democratized, logicalized, boring. They are cultural and economic imperialists, many of them" (*RK*, pp. 8–9). In this assessment the Old Right shakes hands with the New Left. In short, clever and glib, the neocons are "committed to an ideology and devious at attaining their objects" (*RK*, p. 9).

It struck Kirk as a "reasonable presumption that Mr. Kristol and certain of his colleagues would prefer to install in the White House some person, not at all a fine gentleman, who might be deviously manipulated by Neoconserva⁺⸱ e ideologues." But the opportunity for the "hijacking of the American presidenc ," and pulling the wool over an "inexperienced" president's eyes did not arrive ur il 2001.[36] Good Americans were saved from the wiles of the neocons by the electi⸱⸱a in 1988 of the elder Bush who, according to Kirk, had "far too much practical experience of federal office to be so managed by the 'first-class academic "brai 1 trust'" that Mr. Kristol desires to establish in the White House" (RK, pp. 9–1⸱⸱(. And thus, Kirk's conclusion, the "little sect" was fated finally to disappear.

Though Kirk was right about the elder Bush, he was wrong on other counts. It was the Democrats who installed in the White House a "person, not at all a fine gentleman," whose behavior galvanized conservative voters. The neocons did not melt away but regrouped, built alliances, studied foreign policy, developed new views, wrote position papers and founded journals, most notably the Weekly Standard (in 1995). The neocons persisted, and so did the suspicions and conspiracy theories about them. What is most interesting about Kirk's remarks is that they articulate a perception of the neocons as a small, elitist, deceitful, manipulative, opportunistic cabal bent on accruing power to further its sinister (Jewish) goals. This perception resurfaced with a vengeance both in America and Europe in the wake of 9/11, when President George W. Bush adopted neoconservative foreign policy ideas and launched the war in Iraq.

Minor Skirmishes Before and After 9/11

A week after the 1986 meeting at the Philadelphia Society the editorial board of National Review discussed the case of Joseph Sobran, one of its senior editors. National Review, the first modern conservative magazine, was founded in 1955 by William F. Buckley, who is credited with having single-handedly revived conservatism as a modern intellectual alternative to leftwing thought by purging paleoconservatism not only of "its most extreme and bigoted elements,"[37] meaning its racism, but also of its mind-numbing dullness.[38]

Sobran's comments on Israeli politics in NR had been consistently and openly hostile. His column about Ronald Reagan's controversial 1985 visit to the military cemetery in Bitburg, which contains also the remains of several SS men, had included snide remarks about the "Jewish lobby." Sobran's subsequent columns on Israel were even more daringly tinged with antisemitism. In addition, he had accused the Jews of persecuting Christians and had praised an overtly racist-nativist magazine as "often brilliant" and as the only magazine in America that "faces the harder facts about race."[39] Buckley and the other members of the editorial board resolved to dissociate themselves "from what we view as the obstinate tendentiousness of Joe Sobran's recent columns. We are confident that in the [future he will] argue his position in such a fashion as to avoid offending our natural allies."[40] Sobran fell silent for a while but then resumed his attacks on Jews and Israel. In the fall of 1990, Buckley was ready to fire him and wrote the necessary letter; preempting its delivery and receipt, Sobran stepped down on his own accord.[41] For the patrician Buckley, whose original editorial board for *National Review* included five Jews,[42] it was essential that American conservatism stay modern, which meant untinged by any form of racism.

Patrick J. Buchanan, a Catholic pundit and presidential candidate with a deep appreciation for the isolationist and populist conservatism of Father Coughlin in the 1930s, picked up where Sobran had left off. Although as a television commentator Buchanan heckled the neoconservatives relentlessly, the neoconservatives chose to ignore him as an incurable crank. But in 1990, when the Gulf War was brewing and public opinion on Israel and the Jews became crucial, Buchanan's rhetoric had to be curbed. The occasion arrived when Buchanan said on the television pundit show *The McLaughlin Group* that "[t]here are only two groups that are beating the drums for war in the Middle East—the Israeli Defense Ministry and its amen corner in the United States."[43]

Buchanan's fellow pundits on the show did not pick up on this remark. But three weeks later on September 14, 1990, A.M. Rosenthal made it the subject of his *New York Times* column and it became a cause célèbre. Buchanan had identified the warmongers who were arguing for the ouster of Saddam Hussein as A.M. Rosenthal, Richard Perle, Charles Krauthammer, and Henry Kissinger. "They have in common many things," wrote Buckley, "but in the context of the polemical offensive by Buchanan, the most conspicuous of these is that they are all Jewish."[44] There were plenty of gentiles who argued then for the ouster of Saddam Hussein, among them Frank Gaffney, John Bolton, Alexander Haig, and George Will, but Buchanan's point was that the Jews were pushing America toward war for the sake of Jewish interests. The issue was taken up by a handful of journalists,[45] but produced no reprisal against Buchanan. He continued as commentator on several pundit shows. This was in part due to the contemporaneous outbreak of raw antisemitism in the black community, which in August 1990 led to the murder of an orthodox Jew in Brooklyn. The antisemitic rhetoric and outbursts of physical violence among African Americans made Buchanan's malicious rhetoric appear genteel and manageable by comparison.[46]

Although Buchanan's unguarded moment came to be regarded as a mere gaffe and he escaped unscathed, observers of conservatism registered Buchanan's public return to the rhetoric and concepts of the paleoconservatism that Buckley had worked hard to overcome. Buchanan's dare-devil rhetoric triggered two long-term consequences. The first evolved because the increasing incidences of anti-Jewish utterances had began to bother Buckley, not only because they revealed the troubled relationship of the Old Right to Jews but also because they threatened to undo his work in modernizing conservatism. Buckley decided to take this bull by the horns. In December 1991, he published an unusual forty-two-page essay in *National Review* scrutinizing not only Sobran's columns and Buchanan's remarks, but also anti-Jewish incidents at the *Dartmouth Review* (where young right-wingers honed their skills) as well as Gore Vidal's antisemitic diatribe from the left.[47] He concluded that none of this should be tolerated. He called Israel "a point of light"[48] and closed ranks with Irving Kristol on the need for more religion in America. Buckley and *National Review*, which had served for so long as a clearinghouse for conservative ideas, were moving toward the neocons, just as the neocons were preparing to endorse some of the pet causes, among them religion and abortion, of the traditional conservatives. It was Buckley's endorsement that signaled to the Old Right that the neocons were here to stay.[49]

The second consequence of Buchanan's unguarded public moment was that, like Buckley, the evangelical leadership realized that Buchanan's nativist sympathies were not in synch with the general mood and thus relegated his supporters to an "angry chorus on the sidelines." The evangelicals were just learning to be pragmatic. As Buchanan conservatives were becoming compromised, they became unattractive as political allies despite Buchanan's media savvy, and the road opened to an alliance, or marriage of convenience, between evangelicals and neoconservatives.[50] Buckley's endorsement was encouraging, and the neocons' pragmatic endorsement of religion certainly helped in fomenting and cementing the alliance, but more important, probably, were the evangelicals' missionary roots. The evangelicals' missionary impulse seemed to click easily with the neoconservatives' "ideas of forceful external interventionism." During the Clinton administration evangelicals and neoconservatives joined forces to argue for an American engagement in the Balkans. Supported by the evangelical grass roots, endorsed by Buckley, largely unopposed by the marginalized isolationists, the "neo-conservatives were able to nibble away at the Republican realist school to the extent that, in the wake of September 11, they found themselves in the ascendant."[51]

However, building alliances with other conservatives was a necessary but not sufficient condition to assure neoconservative success. More important was the presence of neoconservative policy papers and policy makers in the bowels of the administration. What the alliances ensured was only the lack of public opposition among conservatives when the neoconservative reorientation of American foreign policy actually occurred in the wake of 9/11. The work of preparing and engineering the reorientation was done, some observers argued, by neoconservative apparatchiks who had worked in government since the Reagan administration.

The "Hijackers" of American Foreign Policy

The key issue for future historians of American politics is to puzzle out the reasons, motivations, and mechanisms behind the sudden change in American foreign policy in the wake of the attacks on New York and Washington on September 11, 2001. In the anti-Jewish rhetoric that emerged in America as the situation in Iraq started to deteriorate in the summer of 2003 and began to adversely affect American prestige and perceptions of its power, the blame was squarely placed on a group of neoconservative Jewish operatives, often said to be disciples of the hard-to-understand German Jewish refugee philosopher Leo Strauss. It was argued that the neocons had "hijacked" American foreign policy.[52]

Whether President George W. Bush changed psychologically on, or shortly after, September 11, 2001, is a matter of much conjecture.[53] That his approach to foreign policy changed in a way that "certain long-held neoconservative desires articulated before [9/11] lined up with U.S. strategy after that date"[54] seemed obvious to some analysts. One observer speculated that Bush suddenly clicked with the neocons, that he suddenly had the right mental receptors for them.[55] After 9/11 he shared with them clarity of purpose and the confident expression of moral certainty.[56] Others, in contrast, noted precisely here a continuity of Bush's Texan and Christian cultural disposition and thus argued for a happy confluence of neoconservative and presidential missionary zeal. It was incontrovertible, however, that Bush's prepresidential record had registered no strong interest in foreign policy.

On the campaign trail, candidate Bush outlined a foreign policy characterized both by humility and self-interest. By this he meant that unlike President Clinton, who had been carried away by global do-gooding, he was determined not to use American soldiers for social work around the world. Bush emphasized repeatedly that he did not see "military intervention as the answer to every problem"[57] and argued that American "troops ought not to be used for what's called nation-building."[58] Most observers were convinced that Bush entered neither the presidential race nor the White House with a fully scripted foreign policy and certainly not one inclined toward a neoconservative agenda. Bush was ridiculed for knowing too little about the world outside the United States. Those who perceived Bush as a tabula rasa in foreign affairs were later most inclined to assume that his post 9/11 policies were due to the neoconservatives' usurpation, or "hijacking," of an empty slate.[59] More careful observers noted Bush's intense foreign policy tutelage by pragmatic veterans of past Republican administrations, foremost among them Condoleezza Rice, a protégé of Brent Scowcroft, a member of the elder Bush's cabinet.[60]

After the election, the neoconservatives had to struggle to get significant appointments. Neocon stalwart John Bolton's difficult confirmation as undersecretary of state for arms control and international security made clear that "nominating neo-conservatives to the Bush administration was not a walk in the park."[61] One key figure, however, though not a neoconservative himself, guaranteed that neoconservatives would not be overlooked by the Pentagon and the State Department. That figure was Vice President Dick Cheney, whose active role in the Bush White House many observers have tried to pinpoint, ultimately assigning him the role of the great villain in the Bush presidency.[62]

When the dust of the appointment period settled, it turned out that a fair number of neoconservatives with extensive administrative and foreign policy experience had received excellent appointments. Apart from Bolton, the key players included Paul D. Wolfowitz, Douglas J. Feith, Dov Zakheim, Peter Rodman,

Elliott Abrams, Abram Shulsky, David Wurmser, and several others. I. Lewis "Scooter" Libby, the "neocons' neocon," a former student of Wolfowitz's and co-author with him of a 1992 guidance memorandum on post–cold-war defense policy,[63] became the vice president's chief of staff. Cheney then assembled his own small team of foreign policy experts.[64] Richard Perle had taken himself out of the running and instead of an administrative appointment accepted the chairmanship of the Defense Policy Board.[65]

In the arguments that set out to prove the "hijacking" of American foreign policy after 9/11 or, more precisely, to prove that neoconservatives *"drove* the U.S. shift in foreign policy"[66] from the pursuit of Al Qaeda to the invasion of Iraq, the element that became important was that these men were interconnected, that they formed a "cabal" of some sort. It was easily apparent, of course, that they had already worked with each other since the 1970s. The central figures were perceived to be Libby, Wolfowitz, and Perle and the non-neocon Cheney. By the 1990s they held highly specific views on foreign and defense policy, including the assessment that Iraq was a menace to its neighbors (based on Wolfowitz's work in the 1970s), and the suggestion that toppling Saddam Hussein was a key move in the pacification of the Middle East.[67]

As the American occupation in Iraq was failing and Americans were beginning to ask why they were in Iraq, observers and analysts undertook to connect the dots (who had worked with whom, who had authored which paper when, who was Jewish and who was not, who had studied with Strauss and who had studied with Albert Wohlstetter,[68] and so on). Then they constructed interpretations that seemed to fit the bill. In the most vociferous of the public blame games surrounding the Iraq "adventure," the machination of the Jews to assure the security of Israel came to dwarf the securing of oil as the ultimate explanation for the invasion of Iraq.[69]

Small Skirmishes

Patrick J. Buchanan remained among the most vocal critics both of Bush's unilateral, preemptive, interventionist foreign policy and of the neoconservatives, whom he held responsible not only for the American engagement in Iraq but also for America's continued support of Israel, demonstrated once again during the Israel-Hezbollah War in August 2006.[70]

Buchanan is not easily discouraged by defeat. In 2000 he presented himself for the second time as a presidential candidate and was rewarded with 438,487 votes, roughly half of one percent of all votes cast. This signaled to him that he still had a following. In the spring of 2002, disturbed by what appeared to be a strong endorsement of neoconservative ideas on foreign policy by the Bush administration, Buchanan founded a new magazine, the *American Conservative,* "to publicize his view that the neoconservatives had hijacked both the conservative movement and American foreign policy."[71] Buchanan, so often associated with the rear-guard, was suddenly in the forefront of a national trend among Bush critics on the left and right.

In the spring of 2003, American forces invaded Iraq, defeated its army, and ousted its president. In May 2003, major military operations were declared over, and the reconstruction and political transformation of the country was supposed to begin. Chaos ensued as ethnic and radical religious forces, set free by the American army and reinforced by fighters infiltrating Iraq from other Muslim countries, turned against American troops and their allies as well as against newly trained Iraqi police and civilians of different persuasions wreaking daily havoc through suicide bombings, kidnappings, and executions. The Americans persisted in their efforts to build democratic institutions in Iraq and to restore its infrastructure. Voting took place on January 31, 2005, and with difficulty Iraqis established a functional government implementing the results of the election. Violence continued and increased; the number of Americans killed in Iraq rose steadily; security in Baghdad deteriorated; American expenses rose. Countries such as Iran and Korea took advantage of the American engagement in Iraq to pursue their nuclear weapons programs. America allowed Europe to lead negotiations with Iran (which failed) and was seen to prefer diplomacy over military action[72]; simultaneously American prestige in the world declined rapidly; criticism at home mounted.

The old fault lines among American conservatives, plastered over in the immediate aftermath of 9/11 and during the buildup phase of the wars in Afghanistan and Iraq, had been reopening since the beginning of the insurgency in Iraq in the summer of 2003. Once again, Nixon-Ford-Reagan-Bush-41 realists and neoconservative interventionists were sharply divided.[73] Traditional conservatives complained loudly that arrogant neoconservatives were perverting Reagan's foreign policy and doing a great disservice to the "cause of true conservatism."[74] The neoconservative camp itself was severely shaken by desertions, most notably that of Francis Fukuyama, a protégé of Paul Wolfowitz and a leading neoconservative thinker. Fukuyama's doubts were focused by a speech Charles Krauthammer delivered at the American Enterprise Institute in February 2004 that praised the doctrine of preemption and argued that the removal of Saddam Hussein had made America safer. Fukuyama, puzzled by the sustained applause for Krauthammer, announced his dissent in a searing critique of the neocons' argument for war in the summer 2004 issue of Irving Kristol's *National Interest*. Two years later he demolished *Present Dangers*, one of the seminal neoconservative foreign policy books, edited by William Kristol and Robert Kagan, in his analysis *America at the Crossroads*.[75]

While sophisticated policy battles and internecine warfare raged among professional conservatives in the administration and the media, the men and women in the American heartland were beginning to wonder what America was doing in Iraq and what their sons and daughters were dying for. Populists sensed their chance. On May 6, 2004, the Democratic senator from South Carolina,

Ernest "Fritz" Hollings, published an op-ed piece in the *Charleston Post and Courier* in which he presented "The answer: President Bush's policy to secure Israel."[76] Thus Hollings identified Israel as the central reason for America's going to war. In a CBS interview with Steve Kroft, retired marine General Anthony Zinni argued similarly that a "group of policymakers within the administration known as the neoconservatives . . . saw the invasion of Iraq as a way to stabilize American interests in the region and strengthen the position of Israel."[77] The idea that the neoconservatives were largely Jewish and therefore particularly interested in the security of Israel was establishing itself in public discourse.

There was a more refined way of blaming the neoconservatives, above all, the singularly confident (Jews) Richard Perle, William Kristol, and Paul D. Wolfowitz. Tucker Carlson, once a frequent contributor to the *Weekly Standard*, suddenly remembered his classical conservative roots. "I supported the [Iraq] war and now I am feeling foolish," he said; "I'm just struck by how many people like me who were instinctively distrustful of government forgot to be humble in our expectations. The [neoconservative] idea that the federal government can quickly transform the Middle East seems odd to me for a conservative."[78] Humility in foreign policy was, of course, what Bush had campaigned on in 2000, and hubris, humility's opposite, had always been the most irksome of the sins of the Jews on the Christian books. Hubris became a favored title for books about the activist foreign policy of the Bush administration.[79]

Bush's loyal speechwriter Michael Gerson, an evangelical Christian,[80] certainly got the message. In Bush's address to the nation on May 24, 2004, the president came across as steadfast but somewhat reduced in stature. "Gone is the hubris," commented Fouad Ajami, who admitted to his own misjudgment in the build-up to the Iraq war in the same column. "The unspoken message of the speech was that no great American project is being hatched in Iraq. If some of the war's planners had thought that Iraq would be an ideal base for American primacy in the Persian Gulf, a beacon from which to spread democracy and reason throughout the Arab world, that notion has clearly been set aside."[81] Bush's speech subsequently fostered speculation about the ouster of the neoconservatives should he manage to be reelected for a second term in November 2004.

In August 2004, three months before the election, Fukuyama seceded from the neocons. Unlike other critics, he did not ask what motivated the neocons, and he continued to express his loyalty to certain neoconservative principles. He was most upset by the neoconservatives' unwillingness to find anything wrong with the war in Iraq. Among Fukuyama's parting shots was his pointing out that Krauthammer's views "on how the United States should deal with the Arabs" were colored by his long years of thinking about the Israeli-Palestinian conflict and "his views on how the Israelis need to deal with the Palestinians."[82]

As the security of American troops in Iraq deteriorated in the months before the presidential election, questions about the neocons' motivation for completing the American mission in Iraq became more frequent and more pressing. Less than two months before the election, the *New York Review of Books*, a mainstay of the critical left, published a weighty issue that was a clever omnium gatherum of critical voices. In a review of three books Arthur Schlesinger, Jr., addressed the issue of motivation because two of the books suggested particular answers that sounded true to liberal ears. The editors chose to adorn Schlesinger's review with a nasty 2003 David Levine caricature of Paul Wolfowitz in which a large-nosed Wolfowitz was seen baring big teeth and laughing unpleasantly into two hairy, wolfish paws.

Schlesinger noted that James Mann and James Bamford, the authors of two of the books under review, agreed in their "skepticism about the neocon fantasy that the establishment of democracy in Iraq will have a domino effect and democratize the whole Islamic world."[83] In probing the roots of and motivations for this "fantasy," Schlesinger uncritically endorsed the two commonplaces that by then had become firmly associated with the neoconservatives: the influence of Leo Strauss and their special concern for Israel because of their Jewish descent. "Mann," Schlesinger wrote, "attributes the visionary delusions of the neocons to the influence of Leo Strauss (1899–1973), the German refugee philosopher . . . at the University of Chicago. . . . He approved of Plato's 'noble lies,' disliked much of modern life, and believed that a Straussian elite in government would in time overcome feelings of persecution."[84] Having exposed "Strauss's German windbaggery," Schlesinger moved on to ask how nice traditional conservatives could suddenly have turned into neoconservative philosopher kings. He found the answer in Anne Norton's polemical book on the Straussians: "Perhaps it was the hubris bred by too much power obtained too quickly."[85] Wolfowitz's hideous grin (courtesy of David Levine) loomed large above the quote.

Turning to James Bamford's book *Pretext for War*, Schlesinger pointed out that "Bamford places considerably more emphasis than Mann does on the role of Israel in getting us into this mess."[86] In order to preempt criticism Schlesinger declared that "Bamford and Norton confront the Israel question frankly and without a trace of anti-Semitism." To throw light on the "Israel question," Schlesinger turned to Norton's assessment of Paul Wolfowitz's post-September 11 strategic plan: "This strategy," Norton claimed, "could be understood as advancing American interests and security only if one saw those as identical to [sic] the interests and security of the state of Israel."[87] Schlesinger then latched on to the thinnest of evidence in Bamford's book to concoct his conclusion that "the deceit apparently practiced on the US government by the Likud regime in Israel is pertinent to the imperial dreams, and delusions, of the Straussians. The neocon vision is that the United States as the supreme military superpower is bound to work its will on the rest of the world."[88]

At the very moment Schlesinger penned his review, news of an Israeli mole in the Pentagon broke. CBS picked the weekend before the Republican National Convention in New York City to run a story about an FBI investigation of Lawrence Franklin, an analyst working in the office of the neoconservative Undersecretary of Defense for Policy Douglas Feith, the Pentagon's number-three man after Rumsfeld and Wolfowitz. Franklin was suspected to have given classified information on Iran policy to the American Israel Public Affairs Committee, which passed it on to Israeli officials. A short media feeding frenzy ensued but subsided when leaks about the investigation dried up.[89] Feith's office, long suspected by critics to have had a guiding hand in the alleged manipulation of pre-war intelligence to create a compelling case for war, was again in the spotlight and with it all the questions of the neoconservatives "special relationship" to Israel that had been asked for years in blogs and mainstream publications.

It was in this context that Patrick J. Buchanan's full-scale attack on the neoconservatives *Where the Right Went Wrong: How the Neoconservatives Subverted the Reagan Revolution and Hijacked the Bush Presidency,* published on September 1, 2004, became briefly a bestseller. Buchanan, whose mind was among the sharpest in the pundit business, had learned from his experiences in the 1990s, when his hostile remarks about Jews had backfired (although without injuring him too badly). In his new book he avoided pointing out that the neocons and warmongers were Jews who had Israel's interests at heart. He didn't have to do that anymore because that association was now firmly established in the culture. Buchanan could be content to name names: Krauthammer, Perle, Wolfowitz, Irving Kristol, and William Kristol. Readers would draw their own inferences. One Amazon.com reviewer rushed to Buchanan's defense before any fingers had been pointed: "We can expect the usual boring, predictable litany of verbal assaults borrowed straight from Lenin's handbook: Anti-Semite, isolationist, protectionist, etc."[90] Liberal reviewers noted Buchanan's "perpetual irritation with American Jews" and remarked that his "roster of warmongers is made up exclusively of Jews," sparing Rumsfeld, Cheney, Rice, and the president himself, "who sent all those armed Americans into Iraq."[91]

Buchanan's indictment, because it came from a known polemicist against the Jews, made some waves on the Web but was largely ignored by the educated mainstream and the political elite. Buchanan's polemic turned out to be chump change compared to the attack that was to appear on a Harvard University Web site in the spring of 2006.

Meanwhile the "outing" of the connection between Jewishness, neoconservatism, and neoconservative foreign-policy ideas regarding the Middle East was becoming cultural entertainment. During the Republican National Convention in New York City, Leo Katz's satire "Dubya and the Gang of Seven" was performed several times. It featured Paul Wolfowitz wearing a star-spangled yarmulke and dancing to klezmer-infused music.[92] Shortly afterward, a Hanukkah greeting card made the rounds that showed a smiling Bush 43 with a blue yarmulke on his head (blue for the State of Israel) underneath the Yiddish lettering (slightly misspelled) "a freylekhn khaneke," saying, "Of course I am Jewish." Inside the card explained: "Didn't you ever hear of the Hanukkah BUSH?" A Hanukkah-bush is a self-mocking way of referring to a Christmas tree in an assimilated Jewish home.

Neoconservatives were usually careful not to portray themselves as Jews. In the Thanksgiving 2004 issue of the *Weekly Standard* one found the neocons caricatured as brutal Vikings (rather than brainy Jews) storming the State Department.[93] Finally, the editors of the *Weekly Standard* decided to have a little fun with the neocon-Jewish-megalomania-world-domination association that was becoming a mainstream staple. The *New Republic*, following the *Nation*'s lead, had announced its own first cruise, but then pulled out of the project in June 2003 ("We decided not to do it," said editor Martin Peretz, "because it's really tacky"[94]). The *Weekly Standard* responded in July 2003 by running a parody of an advertisement for its own cruise. It showed the neoconservatives in top form. Under the banner "Join Us as We Conquer the World" appeared the picture of a battleship (*USS Benevolent Hegemon*) and the headshots of the entertainers during the "eight imperial days & seven unilateral nights": Cheney, Perle, Ariel Sharon, Abrams, Rumsfeld, Wolfowitz. The "daily ports of call" played on the supposed Straussian underpinnings of neoconservatism and the Jewish roots and dreams of its major *makhers*: "Friday: The University of Chicago (Orientation); Saturday: Fly to Athens; Sunday: Athens to Jerusalem; Monday: Greater Israel (Hebron, Amman, Damascus); Tuesday: Liberated Iraq; Wednesday: Iran; Thursday: Not-yet-Liberated North Korea (tentative stop); Friday: Claremont College (debriefing)." In a smaller box below, readers were informed of the "Titular Ship's Captain: George W. Bush/Actual, Behind-the-Scenes Captain: Abram Shulsky, Dept. of Defense." In a crowning mockery of the popular perception of the neocons the parody ad announced that there were "Two Dining Plans Available: Kosher and Glatt Kosher."[95] Of course, no one requiring glatt kosher food would actually fly to Athens on a Saturday, which just goes to show that the neocon creators of the parody were not punctiliously observant Jews themselves.

It's pretty clear, at least to this reader, that with its July 2003 parody the *Weekly Standard* editors were enjoying themselves. The parody picked up on the rapidly hardening association of neoconservatives and Jews, added the established association of Jews with Israel, and spiced the whole thing up by throwing in the old canard of the Jews' craving for world dominance (wherein Jewish and neoconservative goals supposedly met). To the editors in Washington, the result of the concoction was utterly absurd. Outside the beltway, however, a trajectory of thought was hardening from conjecture into certainty that the Jews were behind it all to protect their own kind.

Occasionally, small warning signs of this development surfaced in the mainstream press. In October 2003, James Woolsey, director of the CIA in the Clinton administration and a Presbyterian, wrote in the *Jerusalem Post*, "I sometimes get asked these days if I'm Jewish—it's my neoconish views on defense and foreign affairs, I suppose."[96] A year and a half later, Dutch politician Frits Bolkestein was getting "Wolfowitzed," by which the writer meant Bolkestein was accused of being a plotter in a cabal.[97] One was certainly used to conspiracy theories circulating on right- and left-wing blogs and Web sites.[98] This was, after all, the time when Dan

Brown's book *The Da Vinci Code*, which plays with the Jesuits' exclusive organization Opus Dei, became an international bestseller. When in March 2006 such views surfaced in the Ivy League, however, it came as a tremendous surprise.

What had gone before to make such views credible was the persistent association of neoconservatives with Jews; the decades-old linking in the public mind of Jews with Israel; the absence of the weapons of mass destruction in Iraq that had been the American government's stated reason for the invasion; the growing doubts about the U.S. government's motivation for going to war; the subsequent review of the government's rhetorical shift from the pursuit of Al Qaeda (as perpetrators of 9/11) to invading Iraq; the "discovery" that neocons had been pushing American administrations to take on Iraq at least since the early 1990s; the neocons' identity as Jews; the Jews' identity with Israel; Israel's identity with Likud (under Ariel Sharon) and its desires for a Greater Israel; and finally the "discovery" of Likud's "amen corner" and financiers in America. This chain of evidence seemed to make so much sense that it displaced other staples of suspicions, such as corporate interests in securing oil supplies. Finally the Likudnik-American conspiracy theory received its Ivy League imprimatur.

The Big Battle

In March 2006, the left-leaning *London Review of Books* dropped a bombshell. Its March 23 issue featured an essay titled "The Israel Lobby" by two political science professors, John J. Mearsheimer and Stephen M. Walt. The essay was a condensed version of an eighty-two-page working paper (forty-two pages of text, forty pages of footnotes) that had been posted on the Web site of Walt's home base, the Kennedy School of Government at Harvard University under the equally inflammatory title "The Israel Lobby and U.S. Foreign Policy." The paper made two distinct main claims, one, that America's all-out support of Israel was not in America's own best interest but was in fact a "strategic liability" or "burden"[99]; and, two, that for years America's foreign policy choices had been manipulated, unduly influenced, and ultimately distorted by the "Israel Lobby," whose core "is comprised of American Jews who make a significant effort in their daily lives to bend U.S. foreign policy so that it advances Israel's interests."[100]

Three elements made the paper by Mearsheimer and Walt a loose cannon that exploded all over the Internet and set off a firestorm of positive responses on the right and the left. The first element was the suggestive combination of the two claims. Tony Judt argued that each claim can be debated on its merits.[101] A powerful pro-Israel lobby does exist in Washington. Its core is the American Israel Public Affairs Committee (AIPAC).[102] It is also true that from a theoretical Nixon-Ford-Reagan-Bush-41 realist point of view, one can debate the value of Israel as a strategic ally in the Middle East and the demerits of supporting it financially to assure its stability. But the Mearsheimer and Walt combination of the two claims argued that American Jews (under the influence of a foreign country, Israel) ruthlessly manipulated the American executive in its foreign-policy thinking to the effect that America would take military actions in the Middle East that were to Israel's advantage and America's obvious disadvantage. Hidden in that claim was the old canard of the double loyalty of the Jews.

The second element was the paper's mode of arguing its points: seemingly clear, easily accessible, and well documented, it weaved a conclusive historical narrative about a large-scale conspiracy involving manipulative Jews, ruthless neoconservatives, and biased media (including the *New York Times*[103]). The tone appeared cool, detached, and scientific. One had to know the political and historical material the authors covered fairly well to detect to what degree quotes had been taken out of context and facts distorted.[104] What was unmistakable, however, was the paper's overall aggressive pitch against the Jews.

The third element assuring the paper's success was the time and place of publication. In March 2006 Americans were getting very troubled by the continued violence in Iraq, which devoured American lives and treasure at a rate that caused many Americans to demand a cost-benefit analysis. At that time the rhetorical image of Jewish neoconservatives as warmongers was already well established, but its provenance on the right and left fringe had suffused it with the sour odor of the perpetual malcontents. The beauty of the timing was that the Marsheimer-Walt narrative dovetailed not only with the anti-Jewish and antimainstream media rhetoric on the political fringes but also with mainstream stories about the manipulative lying of the Bush 43 White House, the lying of the biased media, the stupidity of "Dubya," the evil intent of his vice (!) president, and the general disorientation about who knew or had known what and what had been done for exactly what reason.[105] Why, really, was America in Iraq? Mearsheimer and Walt seemed to offer a coherent answer that made a lot of sense even to someone as scholarly as Tony Judt, who was moved to write in a *New York Times* op-ed piece that "it will not be self-evident to future generations of Americans why the imperial might and international reputation of the United States are so closely aligned with one small controversial Mediterranean client state."[106]

The beauty of the place of publication, both in the respected *London Review of Books* and, even better, on a Harvard Web site, was immediately apparent to all concerned. The Kennedy School logo on the paper, as well as the Harvard and University of Chicago affiliations of the authors, seemed to validate their claims. White supremacist David Duke was the first to point out that the elite establishment was finally catching up with what he had been saying for years.[107] The Harvard paper was also praised and distributed by Hamas and the Muslim Brotherhood, as well as various Arab, Iranian, and American left-wing Web sites. As a consequence, Harvard first removed its logo from the Mearsheimer-Walt paper and then opened the Kennedy School Web site to rebuttals written by full-time Harvard faculty.[108]

David Duke was right when he pointed out that the "Harvard report contain[ed] little new information."[109] The central assertions about the "Israel

Lobby" had already been rehearsed in Stephen Walt's 2005 book *Taming American Power: The Global Response to U.S. Primacy*. The book, according to analyst Gary Rosen, was a "blistering critique in the form of an academic treatise" and Walt himself no liberal academic blushing at the thought of American power but a hard-core realist without "moral compunctions about the pursuit of American interests."[110] Yet like a classic isolationist, he recommended in his book that America "reduce the overall 'footprint' of its military power, especially in Europe and the Middle East . . . leaving the maintenance of stability in key regions to 'local actors.'"[111]

Walt was a charter member of the Coalition for a Realistic Foreign Policy, a conservative anti-Bush advocacy group that aimed to get the realists' point of view across to the administration, especially their determined opposition to the war in Iraq. There were many legitimate reasons to oppose the American military presence in Iraq; however, American politics is not governed by reason alone but also by the election cycle (thus the Republican senator from Nebraska, Chuck Hagel, then suspected to be a contender for the 2008 GOP presidential nomination, joined the realist opposition to Bush), as well as by deep-seated emotions, of which disappointed expectations of loyalty are one.

Gary Rosen was certainly correct to point out that the group most profoundly shocked by Bush's 9/11 conversion from a "candidate who had mocked 'nation building' and recommended an international posture of 'humble' strength" to a president who articulated "unapologetically neoconservative convictions" were the realists, who in the fall of 2001 and the planning of the American response to the Al Qaeda attacks found themselves suddenly relegated to the sidelines, disempowered, marginalized, neglected. With America at war, the bitterness of that experience had to be kept under a tight lid, but in Walt's book of 2005 and in the coauthored 2006 Harvard working paper it finally erupted in a lashing out against a classic scapegoat—the Jews.

During the first critical firestorm that publication of their "working paper" had evoked, John Mearsheimer had been remarkably quiet, perhaps because his own views were less hardened than Walt's.[112] But on August 28, 2006, he participated with Stephen Walt in a panel discussion hosted by the Council on American-Islamic Relations (CAIR) on "The Israel Lobby and the U.S. Response to the War in Lebanon" at the National Press Club in Washington, D.C. During the discussion, which was carried live on C-SPAN, Walt and Mearsheimer claimed that "Israel had planned the war many months in advance, had obtained the administration's approval and waited for an excuse to launch it."[113]

The CAIR event garnered very little attention, yet observers were concerned that the rhetorical strategies that Mearsheimer and Walt moved from the fringe into the mainstream were accruing legitimacy because the two professors were serious and highly respected scholars.[114] On the cover of its July–August 2006 issue, *Foreign Policy* asked whether the Israel Lobby, now used without quotation marks, had too much power. The magazine allowed Mearsheimer and Walt to restate their claims and invited four men to discuss (support or rebut) them. Thus the central argument that "neoconservatives inside and outside the Bush administration, as well as leaders of a number of prominent pro-Israel organizations, played key roles in making the case for war"[115] was now established as acceptable (that is, debatable with pro and con possibilities) in American mainstream discourse.[116] The unstated subtext was that a closely cooperating band of Jews had taken over American foreign policy.

In the Tanks: The Descent of the Neoconservatives

While Jewish leaders worried about the long-term effects of the Mearsheimer-Walt paper and in May 2006 asked the White House to speak less loudly about protecting Israel,[117] neoconservatives largely ignored the professorial assault. By 2006 they had bigger headaches. The security situation in Iraq was desperate, and the country was sliding toward a full-blown civil war. The neoconservatives' ideas appeared to have foundered on the ethnic, religious, and historically grown realities of Iraq, and their nation-building plans seemed in tatters.

In November 2004, President Bush had been elected by a comfortable enough margin to warrant arguing that he had won a mandate to stay the course in the Middle East and to pursue the neoconservative vision of establishing a functioning democracy in Iraq that would give neighboring Arab populations an inkling of what was possible with American help.[118] Bush's second inaugural speech, written by Michael Gerson and immediately christened "Freedom Speech," was a strong affirmation of the neoconservative ideals: "The survival of liberty in our land increasingly depends on the success of liberty in other lands. The best hope for peace in our world is the expansion of freedom in all the world. America's vital interests and our deepest beliefs are now one. . . . So it is the policy of the United States to seek and support the growth of democratic movements and institutions in every nation and culture, with the ultimate goal of ending tyranny in our world."[119] Tom Wolfe, significantly, called these lines the "fourth corollary to the Monroe Doctrine."[120]

Although neoconservatives rejoiced[121] and prepared to return into public view, from which they had been largely banished during the election campaign, this wasn't going to be easy. The conservative press moved immediately into damage-control mode. Its analysts made clear that no second neoconservative hijacking of the president was taking place; rather, the ideals articulated in the second inaugural address were closely linked to those in the first inaugural address, and those in turn were linked to Bush's famous Citadel speech delivered on September 23, 1999.[122] Liberals comforted themselves that it was all "hopelessly vague and without a time frame," whereas neocons mounted a valiant defense of their principles.[123]

But it was clear that as long as the president was besotted by the idea that the goal of American foreign policy was to spread democracy for its own sake (thus unmooring his pursuits in the Middle East from the war on terrorism), he would continue to alienate traditional conservatives as well as his Republican base. The neocons would have to be ousted publicly to create the appearance that the most radical elements were being removed from the Bush administration.

The first to announce his departure, a few days before the January 31 election in Iraq, was Douglas J. Feith, undersecretary of defense for policy and lightning rod for many intelligence issues relating to Iraq.[124] Bush's State of the Union address on February 2, 2005, again called for an expansion of freedom around the world but focused on the overhaul of Social Security,[125] and the general sense was that an overhaul of his administration was in the offing.

The neocons' demise had been predicted as early as the summer of 2004, when policy analysts began to declare that the "preemption doctrine is dead" (Philip Stephens), that the Bush doctrine was "a spent force" (James Mann), that the neoconservative approach to foreign policy "lies buried in the sand of Iraq" (*Foreign Policy* editor Moisés Naím).[126] But when Bush reshuffled his cabinet, appointing National Security Adviser Condoleezza Rice to replace realist Colin Powell as secretary of state, neoconservatives were pleased because Rice had supported Bush's move from realism to neoconservatism, thus betraying her realist mentor Brent Scowcroft. But Rice disappointed neocon expectations by rebuffing John Bolton as second in command and picking instead trade negotiator Robert B. Zoellick, who had served under the elder Bush's secretary of state, James Baker III, and built a reputation as a pragmatic and skillful diplomat.[127] Bolton subsequently went as U.S. ambassador to the United Nations (after a lengthy and contentious nomination hearing and an initial recess appointment that ran out in December 2006). Paul Wolfowitz, on whom, in the assessment of analysts and historians of the Iraq war, the onus of having intellectually paved the way for Bush's invasion of Iraq had come to rest, was moved from his number-two post at the Pentagon to the World Bank, replacing president James Wolfensohn, who was to oversee Israel's withdrawal from Gaza.[128] A year later, the *Wall Street Journal* announced the ouster of the neoconservatives and the softening of Bush's foreign policy on its front page.[129]

The removal of Wolfowitz, "Mr. Architect of the Iraq War,"[130] certainly had had an overall soothing effect on Republicans and the press, though liberals now worried about his potential villainy at the World Bank[131] (within a year Wolfowitz drew complaints about being too tough on bribery in the developing world[132]). James P. Rubin, however, Clinton's assistant secretary of state, defended Wolfowitz's appointment to the World Bank, arguing that "the neoconservative movement is distinctive in part for its willingness to expend American resources—military and economic—to promote democratic change." Although Wolfowitz "has shown poor judgment in significant military matters," at least his ideology prepared him "not to undermine the World Bank's central mission of alleviating poverty."[133] Here, at long last, the liberal roots of neoconservatism seemed to be shining through. Unfortunately, Wolfowitz also showed poor judgment at the World Bank when he signed off on a salary raise for his companion, Shaha Ali Riza. This induced the witty *New York Times* columnist Maureen Dowd to proclaim Wolfowitz more con than neo.[134] Although the bank's twenty-four-member board publicly cleared Wolfowitz of wrongdoing and ethical improprieties, he was still forced to resign his presidency in May 2007, largely because the Europeans continued to resent Wolfowitz's role in the planning of the Iraq war and chafed under his American hardball and play-it-close-to-the-vest management style.[135] Wolfowitz's successor was former trade envoy Robert B. Zoellick, who had meanwhile become an executive at Goldman-Sachs.[136]

On the domestic front things weren't going too well either for the neo-conservatives. The poor outcome in Iraq would seem to have deprived them of the moral standing and intellectual authority to make any recommendations on how to counter the threat of Iran's nuclear armament. More important, with American personnel and treasure tied up in Iraq and the American people worried about the economic consequences of a prolonged engagement in the Middle East, the Bush administration's freedom to act on any foreign policy recommendations the neoconservatives were likely to make regarding Iran, for example, was extremely curtailed.[137] The neoconservatives seemed finished, but rumors that they were pushing for aggressive action vis-à-vis Iran persisted and drew sustenance from articles and editorials in the *Weekly Standard*.[138]

The nadir of the neoconservative movement was the moment both for the potential resurgence of the traditional realist principles of the GOP as cultivated by Senator Chuck Hagel and a "clutch of realists based at the Nixon Center"[139] and for the renascence of William F. Buckley's modernized classical conservatism. In December 2005, President Bush had been written off as a fuzzy-hearted Wilsonian who "rushes optimistically ahead." In the spring of 2006, the paleoconservative Intercollegiate Studies Institute published its fat *American Conservatism: An Encyclopedia,* into which both Leo Strauss and neoconservatism had been unremarkably subsumed as minor irritants. In July 2006, conservatism's living éminence grise, William F. Buckley, pronounced the Iraq War a failure and Bush's problem as "the absence of [an] effective conservative ideology—with the result that he ended up being very extravagant in domestic spending, extremely tolerant of the excesses by Congress and in respect to foreign policy, incapable of bringing together such forces as apparently were necessary to conclude the Iraq challenge."

Asked about President Bush's foreign policy legacy, Buckley buried him: "There will be no legacy for Mr. Bush. I don't believe his successor would re-enunciate the words he used in his second inaugural address because they were too ambitious. So therefore I think his legacy is indecipherable."[140] These were Buckley's final words on the younger Bush's claim to history. Buckley died suddenly on February 27, 2008.

In the intellectual vacuum in the days after 9/11, the neoconservatives had hitched their wagon to the presidency of George W. Bush, and they will share his fate in the history books, which depends on the eventual outcome of the Iraq

War. But after twenty years in the trenches of American politics, the neoconservatives had not only professionalized their movement by establishing strong
institutional bases; they had also become "battle-hardened fighters"[141] who did
not give up easily. After the Iraq Study Group under the leadership of former
Secretary of State James A. Baker III and Lee H. Hamilton presented its December 2006 report recommending the withdrawal of American combat forces from
Iraq and direct U.S. dialogue with Syria and Iran about Iraq and the Middle East,
the neoconservatives played another ace in January 2007. They came up with the
idea of the "surge." In a fifty-two-page paper titled "Choosing Victory: A Plan for
Success in Iraq," Frederick W. Kagan, resident scholar at the American Enterprise
Institute, argued that victory was still possible "at an acceptable level of effort" if
America adopted a "new approach to the war and implement[ed] it quickly and
decisively."[142] The plan recommended beefing up American forces in Iraq and
balancing the training of Iraqi forces with securing the Iraqi population, clearing
violent Sunni neighborhoods, and restoring infrastructures to ensure a return to
normal life. Although the Iraq Study Group implicitly conceded the American
defeat in Iraq, the Kagan report conceded at most weakness of will. The neoconservatives were, once again, plucking the right cords because the president, who
had so much wanted to be Ronald Reagan's rather than his father's presidential successor, opted for optimism rather than defeat and authorized the surge.
Whether it turns out to be a failure or a success is, at this moment, still uncertain. What is certain, however, is that despite massive attacks on all fronts, including the sophisticated use of anti-Jewish rhetoric, the neoconservatives have
demonstrated a surprising staying power in American politics that was beyond
the imaginative scope of Russell Kirk, who in October 1988 had delivered the
exaggerated report of their demise.

Notes

1.   Russell Kirk, *The Conservative Mind: From Burke to Eliot*, 7th ed. (New York: Regn-
     ery, 2001).
2.   Burton Pines, then vice-president for research at the Heritage Foundation, quoted
     in Sidney Blumenthal, *The Rise of the Counter-Establishment: From Conservative Ide-
     ology to Political Power* (New York: Times Books, 1986), p. 49. Other writers have
     called the Heritage Foundation "an advocacy organization, plain and simple, a well-
     informed pressure group committed to changing policy." John Micklethwait and
     Adrian Wooldridge, *The Right Nation: Conservative Power in America* (New York:
     The Penguin Press, 2004), p. 77.
3.   This was Melvin E. Bradford's term for the neoconservatives. See M.E. Bradford,
     "On Being Conservative in a Post-Liberal Era," *The Intercollegiate Review* 21 (Spring
     1986), p. 15. Bradford (1934–1993) was a southern traditionalist.
4.   Russell Kirk, "The Neoconservatives: An Endangered Species," Heritage Lecture 178
     (Washington: Heritage Foundation, 1988), pp. 3, 4.
5.   Micklethwait and Wooldridge reserve the term paleoconservatism for positions held
     by the right edge of the GOP and articulated most vociferously by Patrick Buchanan.

The Right Nation, p. 102. I'm using the term *paleoconservatism* somewhat more loosely for all conservative positions before Reagan so as to distinguish it from modern conservatism "meaning the conservatism that took hold of the Republican Party with Ronald Reagan." Cf., James W. Ceasar, "Providence and the President," *Weekly Standard*, March 10, 2003, p. 31. On other definitions see Franklin Foer, "What It Takes," *New Republic*, October 13 & 20, 2003, pp. 23–31.

6. Stefan Halper and Jonathan Clarke, *America Alone: The Neo-Conservatives and the Global Order* (Cambridge: Cambridge University Press, 2004), p. 70.

7. Michael Brenner, Stefi Jersch-Wenzel, and Michael A. Meyer, eds., *Deutsch-jüdische Geschichte in der Neuzeit*, vol. 2, *Emanzipation und Akkulturation 1780–1871* (München: C.H. Beck, 1996), p. 29ff.

8. Several of the notable histories of neoconservatism are cited throughout this essay. Other valuable sources are Irving Kristol, *Reflections of a Neoconservative Mind: Looking Back, Looking Ahead* (New York: Basic Books, 1983), and Irwin Stelzer, ed., *Neoconservatism* (London: Atlantic Books, 2004); this book is marketed in the United States as Irwin Stelzer, ed., *The Neocon Reader* (New York: Grove Press, 2004). Jacob Heilbrunn's excellent, detailed account *They Knew They Were Right: The Rise of the Neocons* (New York: Doubleday, 2008) appeared in mid-January 2008, just as this essay was going to press. Hence Heilbrunn's perspective, supporting evidence, and interesting conclusion could not be fully integrated into this essay. To date, Heilbrunn's critically distanced yet magnificently researched work is the most informative book on the neocons' rise and demise, which Heilbrunn prefers to call a "return to exile" (p. 274).

9. Murray Friedman, *The Neoconservative Revolution: Jewish Intellectuals and the Shaping of Public Policy* (Cambridge: Cambridge University Press, 2005), maximizes Jewish involvement, especially in the early phase of neoconservatism. Halper and Clarke, in contrast, point out that "neoconservatism attracts adherents from a wide variety of religious backgrounds" (*America Alone*, p. 58).

10. For a historical perspective on the integration of Jews into American politics, see L. Sandy Maisel and Ira N. Forman, eds., *Jews in American Politics* (Lanham, MD: Rowman and Littlefield, 2001).

11. Robert Michael, *A Concise History of American Antisemitism* (Lanham, MD: Rowman and Littlefield, 2005).

12. Gary Dorrien, *The Neoconservative Mind: Politics, Culture, and the War of Ideology* (Philadelphia: Temple University Press, 1993), p. 11. For a dissenting view, see Halper and Clarke, *America Alone*, pp. 68–73.

13. Joshua Muravchik, quoted in Halper and Clarke, *America Alone*, p. 80.

14. Halper and Clarke, *America Alone*, p. 81.

15. Micklethwait and Wooldridge, *The Right Nation*, pp. 96, 33, 102. David Halberstam, *War in a Time of Peace: Bush, Clinton, and the Generals* (New York: Touchstone, 2002), p. 147.

16. Grover Norquist, quoted in Bill Keller, "Reagan's Son," *New York Times Magazine*, January 26, 2003, p. 30.

17. Dorrien, *The Neoconservative Mind*, p. 13.

18. James Atlas, "The Counter-Counterculture," *New York Times Magazine*, February 12, 1995, p. 38.

19. Halper and Clarke, *America Alone*, p. 74.

20. See esp. Halper and Clarke, *America Alone*, pp. 103–111. An inimical view of the media's shift to the right during the same time is presented in David Brock, *The*

Republican Noise Machine: Right-Wing Media and How It Corrupts Democracy (New York: Crown, 2004).

21. Cf., Halper and Clarke, *America Alone*, chap. 3, "The Nineties: From Death to Resurrection" (pp. 74–111). This chapter analyzes the gradual redefinition of the neoconservatives' political agenda. Written from a conservative libertarian point of view, it is among the best analyses of the neoconservatives in the 1990s. See also James Pierson, "Investing in Conservative Ideas," *Commentary*, May 2005, pp. 46–53. Pierson outlines how, in comparison to classical conservatism, neoconservatism "never developed a full-blown theory of government, economics, or society" (p. 51).

22. The difficulty of imagining just how such an alignment between deeply religious and deeply secularist forces would work is reflected in David Frum's puzzled look at the Religious Right in his book about the transformation of the Republican Party. Because he can't bring the two together in his mind, Frum underestimates the political potential of the Evangelicals, whose turnout was crucial in electing Bush 43 to a second term in November 2004. David Frum, *Dead Right* (New York: Basic Books, 1994), pp. 159–173. On the galvanizing of Christian evangelicals by Michael Horowitz, a Jewish neoconservative, see Peter Waldman, "Evangelicals Give U.S. Foreign Policy an Activist Tinge," *Wall Street Journal*, May 26, 2004: A1, A8.

23. A good perspective on classical or paleoconservatism is offered by Bruce Frohnen, Jeremy Beer, and Jeffery O. Nelson, eds., *American Conservatism: An Encyclopedia* (Wilmington, DE: Intercollegiate Studies Institute, 2006), and George H. Nash, *The Conservative Intellectual Movement in America Since 1945* (Wilmington: Intercollegiate Studies Institute, 2006).

24. Micklethwait and Wooldridge, *The Right Nation*, pp. 185–189.

25. This profound change in American conservatism was felt all the way down to non-party individuals. In a letter to the editor of the *New Yorker*, Kenneth E. Moore, a retired professor of anthropology at the University of Notre Dame, responded to an October 24, 2005, article by Tom Reiss about the intellectual state of modern conservatism. Moore wrote, "My understanding of Edmund Burke began with the works of Russell Kirk, [Peter] Viereck's contemporary. Regarded as the 'father of American conservatism,' he opposed the senior Bush's Gulf War, ridiculed the National Rifle Association, and was a passionate environmentalist. It is unfortunate that the current Republican Party has cast aside the formidable understanding of conservatism formulated by these two men." *New Yorker*, December 12, 2005, p. 8.

26. John B. Judis, "The Conservative Wars," *New Republic*, August 11 & 18, 1986, p. 16.

27. Gregory Wolf, "Introduction to the State of Conservatism," *Intercollegiate Review* 21 (Spring 1986), p. 3. Subsequent references to this issue will be cited in the text and indicated by the letters *IR*.

28. Judis, "The Conservative Wars," p. 16.

29. See Allen Guttmann, *The Conservative Tradition in America*, chaps. 5 and 6 (New York: Oxford University Press, 1967). Susanne Klingenstein, *Enlarging America: The Cultural Work of Jewish Literary Scholars, 1930–1990* (Syracuse, NY: Syracuse University Press, 1998), chap. 1.

30. It is important to note that several paleoconservatives, including Gerhart Niemeyer, George Carey, and Paul Gottfried, managed to write critically about the neoconservatives without resorting to anti-Jewish stereotypes (*IR*, pp. 9–14, 18–21).

31. Stephen Tonsor, "Why I Too Am Not a Neoconservative," *National Review*, June 20, 1986, p. 54. This is a condensed, cleaned-up version of Tonsor's presentation at the meeting. Further references to this essay are cited in the text indicated by the letters

NR. None of the other talks appeared in print. Summaries of the talks are presented in Jeffrey Hart, "Gang Warfare in Chicago," *National Review,* June 6, 1986, pp. 32–33.

32. Cf. Franklin Foer, "Once Again America First," *New York Times Book Review,* October 10, 2004, p. 22.

33. Blumenthal, *The Rise of the Counter-Establishment,* p. 22.

34. Kirk, "The Neoconservatives," p. 2. Further references to this essay will be cited in the text indicated by the letters *RK.*

35. Klingenstein, *Enlarging America,* pp. 5–19.

36. Micklethwait and Wooldridge, *The Right Nation,* p. 203; Halper and Clarke make the case for the neoconservative domination of Vice President Dick Cheney (*America Alone,* pp. 120); see also the argument laid out in James Mann, *Rise of the Vulcans: The History of Bush's War Cabinet,* esp. chap. 7 (New York: Viking, 2004); James Mann, "The Armageddon Plan," *Atlantic Monthly,* March 2004, pp. 71–74; Spencer Ackerman and Franklin Foer, "The Radical," *New Republic,* December 1 & 8, 2003, pp. 17–23. The "neo-conservative hijacking of U.S. foreign policy" at the beginning reign of an inexperienced president is the central contention in Halper and Clark, *America Alone,* see pp. 138–156; esp. 156.

37. Friedman, *The Neoconservative Revolution,* pp. 87, 132.

38. Micklethwait and Wooldridge, *The Right Nation,* pp. 50–51; Jeffrey Hart, *The Making of the American Conservative Mind: National Review and Its Times* (Wilmington, DE: Intercollegiate Studies Institute, 2005). See also William F. Buckley, Jr., *Did You Ever See a Dream Walking? American Conservative Thought in the Twentieth Century* (Indianapolis: Bobbs-Merrill Company, 1970).

39. Quoted in William F. Buckley, "In Search of Anti-Semitism," *National Review,* December 30, 1991, p. 27. Buckley presents a detailed analysis of the Sobran case.

40. Buckley, "In Search of Anti-Semitism," p. 24.

41. Buckley, "In Search of Anti-Semitism," p. 31.

42. Friedman, *The Neoconservative Revolution,* p. 85.

43. Quoted in Buckley, "In Search of Anti-Semitism," p. 31.

44. Buckley, "In Search of Anti-Semitism," p. 32.

45. See Joshua Muravchik, "Patrick J. Buchanan and the Jews," *Commentary,* January 1991, pp. 29–37; "Letters from Readers: Buchanan Pro & Con," *Commentary,* May 1991, pp. 4–7, 10–14; David Frum, "The Conservative Bully Boy," *American Spectator,* July 1991, p. 12; "Special Correspondence: Robert Novak on Pat Buchanan," *American Spectator,* August 1991, p. 7.

46. Jonathan Rieder, "Crown of Thorns," *New Republic,* October 14, 1991, pp. 26–31; Alessandra Stanley, "City College Professor Assailed for Remarks on Jews," *New York Times,* August 7, 1991, p. B1; Daniel Wattenberg, "A Venomous Tree Grows in Brooklyn," *Insight,* October 7, 1991, pp. 18–20; Helle Bering-Jensen, "Bonfire of the Bigotries," *Insight,* September 2, 1991, pp. 38–39; Henry Louis Gates, "Black Demagogues and Pseudo-Scholars," *New York Times,* July 20, 1992, p. A15.

47. Gore Vidal, "The Empire Lovers Strike Back," *Nation,* March 22, 1986, pp. 350–353.

48. Buckley, "In Search of Anti-Semitism," p. 55.

49. Such a turn was nothing new for Buckley, who had been an isolationist as a very young man. He switched to interventionism with the heating up of the Cold War and with the help of Senator Joseph McCarthy's persecution of suspected Communists, the modernist cosmopolitans whom the old isolationists had battled. Cf. Foer, "Once Again America First," p. 23. See also George H. Nash, *The Conservative Intellectual Movement in America since 1945* (New York: Basic Books, 1976), and Frederick F.

Siegel, *Troubled Journey: From Pearl Harbor to Ronald Reagan* (New York: Hill and Wang, 1984).

50. The offspring of this uneasy union, largely radical Christians trying to catch up with modern American conservatism, were called "theocons." Cf. Damon Linker, *The Theocons: Secular America under Siege* (New York: Doubleday, 2006); Sidney Blumenthal, "Theocons vs. Neocons," *Salon*, March 4, 2004. http://dir.salon.com/story/opinion/blumenthal/2004/03/04/culture_war/ (accessed September 1, 2005). In addition to citing the date Web-based material was accessed, I will also cite the date articles and documents were posted so as not to obfuscate the chronology of the discussion.

51. Halper and Clarke, *America Alone*, p. 70.

52. In the eyes of Patrick J. Buchanan, the neocons had "hijacked" more than foreign policy as indicated in the subtitle of his book *Where the Right Went Wrong: How Neoconservatives Subverted the Reagan Revolution and Hijacked the Bush Presidency* (New York: St. Martin's Press, 2004).

53. Observers on the left tend to argue that 9/11 did not change but reinforced characteristics and tendencies that Bush had displayed before, among them a Texan can-do attitude and determination, and divinely inspired missionary zeal derived from his born-again religious experience that helped him get a grip on drinking. Cf. Eric Alterman and Mark Green, *The Book on Bush: How George W. (Mis)leads America* (New York: Viking, 2004), pp. 188–192; Ronald Kessler, *A Matter of Character: Inside the White House of George W. Bush* (New York: Sentinel, 2004). For a description of Bush's immediate reaction to 9/11 see Bob Woodward, *Bush at War*, chaps. 1 and 2 (New York: Simon and Schuster). Other observers tend to concede Bush an intellectual growth spurt. Cf. Frank Bruin, *Ambling into History: The Unlikely Odyssey of George W. Bush* (New York: HarperCollins, 2002). Daniel Cass, "Is Bush a Conservative?" *Commentary*, February 2004, pp. 19–26, examines the complaints classical conservatives have against Bush.

54. Halper and Clarke, *America Alone*, p. 149.

55. This theory ignores the influence of Vice President Cheney and his group of advisers on the president's policy decisions.

56. Keller, "Reagan's Son," p. 30. See also, Ron Suskind "Without a Doubt," *New York Times Magazine*, October 17, 2004, pp. 44–51, 64, 102, 106.

57. Halper and Clarke, *America Alone*, p. 133.

58. Quoted in Halper and Clarke, *America Alone*, p. 135.

59. Alterman and Green, *The Book on Bush*, pp. 193–197. See also Jacob Heilbrunn, "The Neoconservative Journey," in Peter Berkowitz, ed., *Varieties of Conservatism in America*, pp. 105–128 (Stanford, CA: Hoover Institution Press, 2004), p. 106.

60. Ivo H. Daalder and James M. Lindsay, *America Unbound: The Bush Revolution in Foreign Policy* (Washington, DC: Brookings Institution, 2003), pp. 17–34. Daalder and Lindsay vehemently oppose the idea of the neoconservative hijacking and suggest instead that Bush came into the presidency with a strong and coherent worldview that was evident during his presidential campaign. See also Kiron K. Skinner, "Study the Words," *Wall Street Journal*, February 2, 2005, p. A14. Skinner argues that Bush had a detailed policy plan before he became president.

61. Halper and Clarke, *America Alone*, p. 115. Halper and Clarke's clear analysis of the nomination process highlights the difficulties.

62. Cf. John W. Dean, *Worse than Watergate: The Secret Presidency of George W. Bush* (New York: Little Brown, 2004); see esp. chap. 4, which comments on the "Cheney/Wolfowitz World Dominance Philosophy" (p. 97). See also Lou Dubose and Jack

Bernstein, *Vice: Dick Cheney and the Hijacking of the American Presidency* (New York: Random House, 2006).

63. Richard H. Curtiss, "I. Lewis ('Scooter') Libby: The Nexus of Washington's Neocon Network," *Washington Report on Middle East Affairs*, September 2004, pp. 18–20, http://www.washington-report.org/archives/Sept_2004/0409018 (accessed September 7, 2006). John Dickerson, "Who Is Scooter Libby," *Slate*, October 21, 2005, http://slate.com/id/2128530 (accessed September 7, 2006).

64. Robert Dreyfuss, "Vice Squad," *American Prospect*, May 3, 2006, http://www.prospect.org/web/page.ww?section=oot&name=viewPrint&articleID=11401 (accessed September 7, 2006).

65. For a speculation about the reasons, see Seymour Hersh, "Lunch with the Chairman," *New Yorker*, March 17, 2003, pp. 76–81. Thomas Powers, "Tomorrow the World," *New York Review of Books*, March 11, 2004, pp. 4–6.

66. Halper and Clarke, *America Alone*, p. 149.

67. On the political backgrounds and earlier administrative work of neoconservatives active in the Bush administration, see Halper and Clarke, *America Alone*, pp. 116–156; Mann, *The Rise of the Vulcans*; George Packer, *The Assassins' Gate: America in Iraq*, chap. 1 (New York: Farrar Straus and Giroux, 2005); and more far-reaching, Seymour Hersh, *Chain of Command: The Road from 9/11 to Abu Ghraib* (New York: HarperCollins, 2004).

68. Two books in particular stoked the fires of a conspiracy of neoconservative fellow Straussians: Shadia B. Drury, *Leo Strauss and the American Right* (New York: St. Martin's Press, 1999), and Anne Norton, *Leo Strauss and the Politics of American Empire* (New Haven: Yale University Press, 2004). The Straussian witch hunt finally induced confessed neocon Robert Kagan to write a very funny column, "I Am Not a Straussian," *Weekly Standard*, February 6, 2006, pp. 16–17, arguing the nonsensical nature of the Straussian conspiracy theory. Two rigorous critical studies of Strauss further undermine theories of a Strauss-inspired neoconservative cabal. They are Heinrich Meier, *Leo Strauss and the Theologico-Political Problem* (Cambridge: Cambridge University Press, 2006), and Steven B. Smith, *Reading Leo Strauss: Politics, Philosophy, Judaism* (Chicago: University of Chicago Press, 2006).

69. Stefan Halper and Jonathan Clarke are two analysts who squarely lay the blame on the neoconservatives' long-standing goal to bring about regime change in the Middle East, but they steer clear of accusing them of pursuing special interests as Jews. But because they do not push their argument beyond suggesting that the neoconservatives "had adopted the notion of remaking the Middle East" (pp. 155, 297), they give the impression that they stop asking too soon. They suggest that the natural next question to ask would be: why did the neoconservatives want to change the Middle East? But they don't go that way.

70. Patrick J. Buchanan, "No, This Is Not 'Our War,'" July 21, 2006, http://www.Antiwar.com (accessed September 7, 2006).

71. Micklethwait and Wooldridge, *The Right Nation*, p. 204. See also the mission statement of the *American Conservative* at http://www.amconmag.com/aboutus.html (accessed September 9, 2006).

72. Helene Cooper and David E. Sanger, "With a Talk Over Lunch, a Shift in Bush's Iran Policy Took Root," *New York Times*, June 4, 2006, pp. A1, A12.

73. As early as February 2004, when Bush presented his budget proposal to Congress, the so-far-loyal pundits George F. Will and Peggy Noonan, a former speechwriter for Ronald Reagan, demurred. They vocally criticized the budget deficit Bush endorsed

to pay for the Iraq War. As classical conservatives they drew the line at national debt. Other classical conservatives took longer to voice their dissent. The leading voice in the classical conservative/realists' dissent was Brent Scowcroft, who had been opposed to the Iraq War from the start. Cf. Jeffrey Goldberg, "Breaking Ranks: What Turned Brent Scowcroft against the Bush Administration?" *New Yorker*, October 31, 2005; Richard W. Stevenson and Douglas Jehl, "Leak Case Renews Questions on War's Rationale," *New York Times*, October 31, 2005, pp. A1, A22; Gary Rosen, "Bush and the Realists," *Commentary*, September 2005, pp. 31–37. Richard N. Haass, "Is there a Doctrine in the House?" *New York Times*, November 8, 2005, p. A31. See also Gary Rosen, ed., *The Right War? The Conservative Debate on Iraq* (Cambridge: Cambridge University Press, 2005).

74. Stefan Halper and Jonathan Clark, "Would Reagan Have Attacked Iraq," *American Spectator*, posted on the magazine's Web site June 15, 2004; the article first appeared in print in the April edition of *American Spectator* under the title "Neoconservatism Is Not Reaganism." John Tierney, "The Hawks Loudly Express Their Second Thoughts," *New York Times*, May 16, 2004: section 4, p. 5. On the front page of the Week in Review section, Tierney's article was billed as "Out with the Neo." See also Bruce Bartlett, *Impostor: How George W. Bush Bankrupted America and Betrayed the Reagan Legacy* (New York: Doubleday, 2006).

75. Francis Fukuyama, "The Neoconservative Moment," June 30, 2004, www.national interest.org/2004 (accessed September 9, 2006); Robert Kagan and William Kristol, eds., *Present Dangers: Crisis and Opportunity in American Foreign and Defense Policy* (San Francisco: Encounter Books, 2000); Francis Fukuyama, *America at the Crossroads: Democracy, Power, and the Neoconservative Legacy* (New Haven: Yale University Press, 2006). See also Robert S. Boynton, "The Neocon Who Isn't," *The American Prospect Online Edition,* October 10, 2005. Francis Fukuyama, "After Neoconservatism," *New York Times Magazine*, February 19, 2006, pp. 62–67. Francis Fukuyama and Adam Garfinkle, "A Better Idea," *Wall Street Journal*, March 27, 2006, p. A16; David D. Kirkpatrick, "Battle Splits Conservative Magazine," *New York Times*, March 13, 2005, section 4, p. 12. Charles Krauthammer, "The Neoconservative Convergence," *Commentary*, July–August 2005, pp. 21–26.

76. The full quote reads, "The answer: President Bush's policy to secure Israel. Led by Richard Perle, Paul Wolfowitz, and Charles Krauthammer, for years, there has been a domino school of thought that the way to guarantee Israel's security is to spread democracy in the area." Ernest F. Hollings, "Why We Are in Iraq," May 7, 2004, *State.com,* www .thestate.com/mld/state/news/opinion/8609339.htm (accessed September 9, 2006).

77. Quoted in Liel Leibovitz, "Tales of the Neocons," *Jerusalem Report*, June 28, 2004, p. 28. Similar views were presented in Michael Scheuer's anonymously published book *Imperial Hubris: Why the West is Losing the War on Terror* (New York: Brassey's Inc., 2004).

78. Quoted in Tierney, "The Hawks," p. 5.

79. Michael Scheuer, *Imperial Hubris: Why the West Is Losing the War on Terror* (Washington: Potomac Books, 2004); Michael Isikoff and David Corn, *Hubris: The Inside Story of Spin, Scandal, and the Selling of the Iraq War* (New York: Crown, 2006).

80. Jeffrey Goldberg, "The Believer," *New Yorker*, February 13 & 20, 2006, pp. 56–69. Gerson resigned his tenure as George W. Bush's speech writer on June 25, 2006.

81. Fouad Ajami, "Iraq May Survive, but the Dream Is Dead," *New York Times*, May 26, 2004, p. A25.

82. Fukuyama wrote, "Krauthammer has not supported strongly engaging the Arab world through political strategies. In the past, he has put forward a particular view of Arab psychology, namely, that they respect power above all as a source of legitimacy. As he once said in a radio interview, if you want to win their hearts and minds, you have to grab a lower part of their anatomy and squeeze hard." Fukuyama, "The Neoconservative Moment," pp. 5–6.

83. Arthur Schlesinger, Jr., "The Making of a Mess," *New York Review of Books*, September 23, 2004, p. 40. Schlesinger does not comment further on James Mann's *Rise of the Vulcans* in this review.

84. For a refutation of Strauss as purveyor of foreign policy ideas to the neocons see Thomas G. West, "Leo Strauss and American Foreign Policy," *Clarendon Review of Books*, Summer 2004, pp. 13–16. For connections between Strauss and Pentagon neocons see Seymour Hersh, "Selective Intelligence," *New Yorker*, May 12, 2003, pp. 44–51. For a left-liberal view of the influence of Strauss on the neoconservatives see Shadia Drury, *Leo Strauss and the American Right* (New York: St. Martin's Press, 1999), and Anne Norton, *Leo Strauss and the Politics of American Empire* (New Haven: Yale University Press, 2004). In a proposal for a special issue of *Boundary2* about Straussianism, Joseph A. Buttigieg and Paul A. Bové wrote, "[O]nce the vectors of Straussian ideas appear, the horrendous consequences of current arrangements, properly now understood as Straussian stand out with terrifying clarity, demanding analysis and opposition." Email to the author, November 14, 2003.

85. Quoted in Schlesinger, "The Making of a Mess," p. 40. When Schlesinger's review appeared, Norton's book had actually not yet been published, and it was not one of the three books he had been asked to review.

86. Schlesinger, "The Making of a Mess," p. 40. James Bamford, *A Pretext for War: 9/11, Iraq, and the Abuse of America's Intelligence Agencies* (New York: Doubleday, 2004).

87. Quoted in Schlesinger, "The Making of a Mess," p. 40.

88. Schlesinger, "The Making of a Mess," p. 41.

89. Marc Perelman, "Neocons Blast Bush's Inaction on 'Spy' Affair," *Forward*, September 10, 2004, pp. 1, 10; Ori Nir, "As Leaks Dry Up in FBI Investigation, Activists Still Fear Jury Probe," *Forward*, September 17, 2004, pp. 1, 5. Edwin Black, "Feeding Frenzy," *Jerusalem Report*, October 4, 2004, pp. 28–30; Edwin Black, "Spat Erupts between Neocons, Intelligence Community," *Forward*, December 31, 2004, p. 4; Ori Nir, "U.S. Aide Arrested amid Signs that Lobby Probe Widens," *Forward*, May 6, 2005.

90. Andrew Westphal, "Brave and Honest Exposé," posted as a review of Buchanan's book on amazon.com on September 1, 2004.

91. Michael Kazin, "The Good Old Days," review of *Where the Right Went Wrong* by Patrick J. Buchanan, *New York Times Book Review*, September 12, 2004, p. 21.

92. Jason Zinoman, "With Jaundiced Eyes and Barbed Tongues," *New York Times*, September 4, 2004, p. 25.

93. David Horsey, "The Last Bastion of Resistance Falls," *Weekly Standard*, November 29, p. 7.

94. Quoted in Gabriel Sanders, "From Port to Starboard, Magazines Take to High Seas Towing the Party Line," *Forward*, November 26, 2004.

95. "Parody," *Weekly Standard*, July 7/July 14, 2003, p. 48.

96. James Woolsey, "We Are All Jews," *Jerusalem Post*, October 3, 2003, online edition (accessed September 10, 2006).

97. Philologos [Hillel Halkin], "Getting Wolfowitzed," *Forward*, April 15, 2005, p. 14.

98. On a progressive Web site Kurt Nimmo wrote, "Obviously, it will be easier for the U.S. (at the behest of the Likudites in Israel) to lord over small mini-states than deal with larger entities . . . or for that matter an Arab world united behind a common cause, namely (as Osama bin Laden supposedly wants) reducing the influence of the West in the Middle East and uniting to fight against its perennial enemy, Israel.

"This is precisely what the Straussian neocon war against Islam is all about, regardless of all the highfalutin talk about democracy and modernizing Arab and Iranian societies. As Norman Podhoretz understands, in order to accomplish this objective the United States will need to follow Israel's lead—that is to say launch brutal invasions and terrorize entire populations, as the Israelis are currently doing in the Gaza Strip. The Iraqi 'quagmire' will need to be replicated in Iran and Syria—and sooner before later, as Podhoretz urges.

". . . So, the question is: Are you ready to donate your kids or yourself to fight Israel's war against the Muslim world, currently pegged at over a billion people? Are you ready for generations of ceaseless war—as Bush promised—and the possibility of thousands, maybe hundreds of thousands of U.S. kids slaughtered in the name of Greater Israel?" Kurt Nimmo, "Rumours of Neo-Con Decline Greatly Exaggerated," October 9, 2004, Progressivetrail.org/articles/041009Nimmo.shtml (accessed September 11, 2006). Nimmo is referring to Norman Podhoretz, "World War IV: How It Started, What It Means, and Why We Have to Win," *Commentary*, September 2004, pp. 17–54.

99. John J. Mearsheimer and Stephen M. Walt, "The Israel Lobby and U.S. Foreign Policy," John F. Kennedy School of Government Faculty Research Working Paper Series, March 2006, http://ksgnotes1.harvard.edu/Research/wpaper.nsf/rwp/ RWP06-011/$File/rwp_06_011walt.pdf, pp. 3–7 (accessed April 19, 2006). All references to the Mearsheimer and Walt paper will be to this posting rather than to the shortened version in the *London Review of Books*, March 23, 2006.

100. Mearsheimer and Walt, "The Israel Lobby," p. 14.

101. Tony Judt, "A Lobby, Not a Conspiracy," *New York Times*, April 19, 2006, p. A23.

102. Nonorganized, ordinary Jews have, of course, a well-established liberal track record and have been vocal in articulating their disapproval of Bush. In 2000, Bush got 19 percent of the Jewish vote; in 2004, it was a scant 24 percent. But such facts cut little ice with conspiracy theorists. Ami Eden, "Bush Vote: Boom or Bust," *Forward*, January 14, 2005.

103. Mearsheimer and Walt, "The Israel Lobby," p. 20–21.

104. Alan Dershowitz, "Debunking the Newest—and Oldest—Jewish Conspiracy: A Reply to the Mearsheimer-Walt 'Working Paper,'" April 6, 2006, http://www.ksg .harvard.edu/research/working_papers/dershowitzreply/pdf (accessed April 19, 2006); Alex Safian, "Study Decrying 'Israel Lobby' Marred by Numerous Errors," March 20, 2006, updated April 6, 2006, http://www.camera.org (accessed April 21, 2006). Harvey Sicherman, "The Flaws in the Noisome Paper about the Israel Lobby," *Foreign Policy Research*, March 28, 2006, http://hns.us/roundup/entries/23364.html (accessed April 21, 2006). Richard Baehr and Ed Lasky, "Stephen Walt's War with Israel," *The American Thinker*, March 20, 2006, http://www.americanthinker.com/articles .php?article_id=5342 (accessed April 21, 2006).

105. The disorientation had culminated in another media frenzy when in late October 2005 I. Lewis "Scooter" Libby, Vice President Cheney's chief of staff, was indicted on charges of leaking information to the press that had led to the identification of Valerie Plame as a covert CIA agent. The leak story, which also involved Watergate reporter

Bob Woodward and thus connected the lying Bush administration to the lying Nixon administration, intensified the public vilification of the cabal around Richard Cheney. In September 2006, however, the leaker was revealed, without much fanfare, to have been Richard L. Armitage. Cf. David Johnston, "Source in C.I.A. Leak Case Voices Remorse and Chagrin," *New York Times*, September 8, 2006, p. A22; Victoria Toensing, "What a Load of Armitage," *Wall Street Journal*, September 15, 2006, p. A12.

106. Judt, "A Lobby, Not a Conspiracy," p. A23. For a shorter rebuttal see Bret Stephens, "'The Israel Conspiracy," *Wall Street Journal*, March 25–26, 2006, p. A7.

107. "'Now it is finally revealed by some of the top academic sources in the country,' Duke said. 'It is not just David Duke anymore. None other than researchers at Harvard and the University of Chicago' have said that 'the Israel lobby controls US foreign policy and is responsible for this war' in Iraq." Quoted in Charles A. Radin, "'Israel Lobby' Critique Roils Academe," *Boston Globe*, March 29, 2006, p. A7.

108. Meghan Clyne, "A Harvard School Distances Itself from Dean's Paper," *New York Sun*, March 23, 2006, posted at http://www.nysun.com/article/29638 (accessed April 21, 2006). Charles A. Radin, "Harvard Dean Opens Faculty Papers to Rebuttal," *Boston Globe*, March 31, 2006, p. A7.

109. David Duke, "A Real Breakthrough in the Battle for Truth!" March 20, 2006, DavidDuke.com, http://www.davidduke.com/?p=501 (accessed April 20, 2006).

110. Rosen, "Bush and the Realists," pp. 32, 33.

111. Ibid., p. 33.

112. Cf. Alex Safian, "Will the Real John Mearsheimer Please Stand Up?" March 30, 2006, http://www.camera.org (accessed April 17, 2006).

113. Ori Nir, "Scholars Use Arab Forum to Slam 'Lobby,'" *Forward*, September 1, 2006. This point of view is severely challenged by the complaints of Israeli reservist generals that the Israeli army had been ill-equipped and understaffed. Cf. Peter Waldman, "View on the Ground: Israeli Reservists See Disarray in Lebanon," *Wall Street Journal*, September 1, 2006, pp. A1, A10. After the war Israeli reservists charged that the civilian political leadership had mismanaged the war and demanded that Prime Minister Ehud Olmert, Foreign Minister Tziporah Livni, and Defense Minister Amir Peretz resign. Cf. Ken Ellingwood, "Olmert, Israeli Defense Minister Clash over War Inquiry," *Los Angeles Times*, September 2, 2006, http://www.latimes.com/news/nationworld/world/la-fg-peretz2sep02,1,3506014.story?coll=la-headlines-world (accessed September 19, 2006).

114. Nir, "Scholars Use Arab Forum," p. 4.

115. John J. Mearsheimer and Stephen M. Walt, "Unrestricted Access: What the Israel Lobby Wants, It Too Often Gets," *Foreign Policy*, July/August 2006, p. 58.

116. See, for example, Arnaud de Borchgrave, "Touching the Third Rail," *Washington Times*, April 29, 2006, http://washtimes.com/commentary/20060428-083819-7632r.htm (accessed September 19, 2006). Borchgrave is editor at large at United Press International.

117. Ori Nir, "Groups to Bush: Drop Iran-Israel Linkage," *Forward*, May 12, 2006, p. 3.

118. William Kristol, "Misunderestimated," *The Weekly Standard*, November 15, 2004, p. 7.

119. George W. Bush, "Inaugural Address," *New York Times*, January 21, 2005, p. A16. See also Todd S. Purdum, "Focus on Ideals, Not Details," *New York Times*, January 21, 2005, pp. A1, A14.

120. Tom Wolfe, "The Doctrine that Never Died," *New York Times*, January 30, 2005, section 4, p. 17 (op ed). For a comment on Wolfe's op-ed piece, see "What We Hear

when Bush Speaks" (letters to the editor, commenting on Wolfe's op ed), *New York Times*, February 2, 2005, p. A22.

121. "Neocons See Bush Speech as Victory," posted January 21, 2005, http://www.news max.com/archives/ic/2005/1/23/103301.shtml (accessed September 19, 2006).

122. Terry Eastland, "Right from the Beginning," *Weekly Standard*, January 24, 2005, p. 15; George Melloan, "Bush's 'Freedom Speech' Had a Long Pedigree," *Wall Street Journal*, January 25, 2005, p. A17; Kiron K. Skinner, "Study the Words," *Wall Street Journal*, February 2, 2005, p. A14.

123. Joshua Muravchik, "The Democratic Ideal," *Wall Street Journal*, January 25, 2005, p. A16.

124. Eric Schmitt, "Senior Official Behind Many of Pentagon's Most Contentious Policies Is Stepping Down," *New York Times*, January 27, 2005, p. A13.

125. John D. McKinnon and Christopher Cooper, "President Provides New Detail of Plans for Private Accounts," *Wall Street Journal*, February 3, 2005, pp. A1, A12; Todd S. Purdum, "Bold Goal Risky Path," *New York Times*, February 3, 2005, pp. A1, A16.

126. James Mann, "Bush's Team Has Only a Spent Vision," *Financial Times*, July 7, 2004, p. A10; Philip Stephen, "The Preemption Doctrine Is Dead," *Financial Times*, July 16, 2004, p. A10; Moisés Naím, "Casualties of War: The Ideas that Died in Iraq," *Foreign Policy*, September–October 2004 http://www.foreignpolic   n/story/cms .php?story_id=2661 (accessed September 19, 2006).

127. Steven R. Weisman, "Rice Is Said to Pick Trade Negotiator as Deputy," *New York Times*, January 7, 2005, pp. A1, A10.

128. Steven R. Weisman, "World Bank Chief to Become a Special Mideast Envoy," *New York Times*, April 5, 2005, p. A6. For a portrait of Wolfensohn, World Bank president from 1995 to 2005, see Sebastian Mallaby, *The World's Banker: A Story of Failed Sto   s, Financial Crises, and the Wealth and Poverty of Nations* (New York: Penguin, 2004)

129. Jay Solomon and Neil King, Jr., "As 'Neocons' Leave, Bush Foreign Policy Takes Softer Line," *Wall Street Journal*, February 6, 2006, pp. A1, A17.

130. Richard Bernstein, "Is Europe Trying to Restore the Old Trans-Atlantic Club," *New York Times*, April 3, 2005, p. A11. For a positive assessment of Wolfowitz's career see Stephen F. Hayes, "The Visionary," *Weekly Standard*, May 9, 2005, pp. 20–27.

131. Sebastian Mallaby, "Loan Ranger: Wolfowitz, World Banker," *New Republic*, April 18, 2005, pp. 12–14. Stephen F. Hayes, "Crying Wolfowitz," *Weekly Standard*, March 28, 2005, pp. 9–10; Elizabeth Becker, "Similar Résumé, Different Decade," *New York Times*, March 22, 2005, pp. C1, C9.

132. Steven R. Weisman, "Wolfowitz Corruption Drive Rattles World Bankers," *New York Times*, September 14, 2006, pp. C1, C4.

133. James P. Rubin, "Lending the Good Loan," *New York Times*, March 22, 2005, p. A23.

134. Maureen Dowd, "More Con than Neo," *New York Times*, April 14, 2007, p. A27.

135. Steven R. Weisman, "At World Bank Meeting Frustrations Boil Over," *New York Times*, April 25, 2007, p. A10. A report by an internal committee of seven board members actually found that "Wolfowitz broke the bank's code of conduct and criticized him for 'questionable judgment and preoccupation with self-interest over institutional best interest,'" John Donnelly, "Wolfowitz Resigns from World Bank," *The Boston Globe*, May 18, 2007, pp. A1, A4. See also Steven R. Weisman, "Europeans Push U.S. to Force Wolfowitz from World Bank," *New York Times*, May 11, 2007, p. A14; David E. Sanger, "Between Bush and the World: Turmoil at Bank Goes Beyond Wolfowitz Fight," *New York Times*, April 14, 2007, pp. A1, A6; Steven R. Weisman, "Wolfowitz Resigns, End-

ing Long Fight at World Bank," *New York Times*, May 18, 2007, pp. A1, A12; Steven R. Weisman, "How Battle at World Bank Ended 'Second Chance' at a Career," *New York Times*, May 18, 2007, p. A12.

136. Steven R. Weisman, "Ex-Trade Envoy Is Bush's Choice for World Bank," *New York Times*, May 30, 2007, pp. A1, A13. "Zoellick's Clean-Up Duty," editorial, *Wall Street Journal*, May 31, 2007, p. A14.

137. Franklin Foer, "Identity Crisis: Neocon v. Neocon on Iran," *New Republic*, December 20, 2004, pp. 22, 27. On the cover of the magazine, this article was billed as "Identity Crisis: Iran and the End of Neoconservatism."

138. Nicholas D. Kristof, "Starting Another War," *New York Times*, September 12, 2006, p. A25; Seymour Hersh, "Watching Lebanon," *New Yorker*, August 21, 2006, p. 31; Seymour Hersh, "The Iran Plans," *New Yorker*, April 17, 2006, pp. 30–37; William Kristol, "Iran Is Not Iraq," *Weekly Standard*, May 8, 2006, p. 7; Jeffrey Bell, "Iran or Bust," *Weekly Standard*, February 6, 2006, p. 8.

139. Heilbrunn, *They Knew They Were Right*, p. 273.

140. Thalia Assuras, "Buckley: Bush Not a True Conservative" posted July 22, 2006, http://www.cbsnews.com/stories/2006/07/22/eveningnews/main182683.shtml (accessed September 11, 2006).

141. Heilbrunn, *They Knew They Were Right*, p. 275. Heilbrunn considers the "professionalization of the neoconservative movement . . . its undoing as both an intellectual and a moral force." He concedes, however, that as a result, "it will remain an institutional [force]" (p. 274).

142. Frederick W. Kagan, "Choosing Victory: A Plan for Success in Iraq," January 5, 2007, http://www.aei.org/publications/pubID.25396/pub_detail.asp (accessed March 15, 2008).

Nostalgia and Recognition

Ilan Stavans and Morris Dickstein in Conversation

Ilan Stavans and Morris Dickstein

The setting for the following conversation was the Eldridge Street Synagogue in Lower Manhattan, the first great house of worship built by Eastern European Jews in the United States. This National Historic Landmark has become a cornerstone of Jewish renewal. As Jews moved out to the suburbs and beyond, Asians and Latinos settled into the Lower East Side neighborhood. The synagogue was forgotten for years. But now this beautiful but decrepit structure is under renovation as the site is turned into a meeting place where the descendants of Jewish immigrants gather to encounter the ghosts of the past and to confront the challenges of the present and future. These reflections—intellectual, artistic, religious, and educational—often take a global twist. The fate of American Jews today is linked to international events, not only in the Middle East but in places as far away as Johannesburg and Buenos Aires.

This dialogue took place on Sunday, September 30, 2001, more than two weeks after the tragic events in the World Trade Center. Although they were still in deep shock, New Yorkers seemed eager to show that no terrorist act would stand in the way of affirming the continuity of their lives. The event was advertised as the launching of Ilan Stavans's memoir On Borrowed Words, *about his coming of age as a Jew in Mexico and his immigration to the United States. It took place in the neighborhood where the other speaker, Morris Dickstein, had spent some of his formative years. Yet the two discovered a great deal of common ground. As the exchange progressed its themes expanded, covering the role of language and culture in the shaping of identity, the place of intellectuals and books in the modern*

312

world, as well as American Jewish literature and the quest for a past that is veiled in nostalgia.

MORRIS DICKSTEIN: As I read your book *On Borrowed Words: A Memoir of Language*, I had no idea that some of your experience of growing up as a Jew in Mexico would be so similar to mine in New York. At times I found that I was reading another version of my own story. I too grew up in a Jewish subculture within a larger culture that was very different, and I too was trying to find my way in both. Your wonderful story of you trying to learn English by reading Melville's *Moby-Dick*—which has of course one of the most baroque styles of any book ever written in English—reminds me a little of my memorizing words for the college boards when I was a senior in high school, trying to expand my vocabulary through a forced march. It is peculiar because you, Ilan, could have come out sounding like a nineteenth- or sixteenth-century writer; instead, though you are modest about describing the difficulty you had in acquiring English, those of us who have read your other works, or who read *On Borrowed Words*, know what a wonderful writer that boy became and how the experience turned you into a public intellectual. This isn't easy; quite the contrary, it's a very difficult thing. We can only count, perhaps on the fingers of two hands, the number of writers who grew up in one language and not only learned to speak another language well, to live in that language, but became fine writers in their new language. It is rare. . . . In the second half of the twentieth century, a number of those writers spent their early years in a Yiddish-speaking home. Saul Bellow and Bernard Malamud come to mind. That transition from living in a domestic world of Yiddish to mastering a literary and professional English was something only a few people achieved, and you, Ilan, are only the most recent. This experience really fertilized and enriched the way these transplanted authors wrote English. It also added an element to the English language that really had not been there before.

While working on an essay of mine on Jewish writers in America for *The Nation*, I came upon a eulogy that Saul Bellow wrote for Bernard Malamud when he died in 1986. He focuses on the very point that is so important to your book, the whole question of language and the transition from one language to another. This is perhaps the most interesting theme in *On Borrowed Words*, what you call *hybridity*; that is, when someone becomes a hybrid of identities and makes use of a hybrid of languages. This is what Bellow said in tribute to Malamud, when Malamud died. You know that Bellow and Malamud and Roth all got tired of being described as the holy trinity of Jewish American literature. Bellow used to joke that they were the Hart, Schafner, and Marx of Jewish American literature. Shortly after Malamud died, Bellow was in London, and he was very grim and downcast about Malamud's death. In the cab from the airport he turned to Roth, who was then living in London, and said, "Well, Schafner's gone." (I guess he thought *he* was Hart—heart!—the premier member of the trinity.) Anyway, this is what he said about Malamud in his public tribute, talking about himself as well: "Well, we were here, first generation Americans. Our language was English. And a language is a spiritual mansion from which no one can evict us. Malamud, in his novels and stories discovered a sort of communicative genius in the impoverished harsh jargon of immigrant New York." I was fascinated when I read this remark by Bellow. Interestingly, you use the same metaphor, the metaphor of real estate, the idea that for a Jew a language often feels like a borrowed home. We use words that were never really ours, words we somehow have to take possession of. This is true perhaps for most writers, but especially for an immigrant or a child of immigrants. One of the elements of the Diaspora, as far as language is concerned, is that we're always working in someone else's language. We're always using words that are already inflected by people whose experience is far from our own. The other side of this coin, however, is that when we come to master those languages, we bring to them our own inflections, and if we somehow succeed we can really alter that language, the way the King's English has in fact been altered—at least as far as American literature is concerned—by the many varieties of immigrant English. (Unexpectedly, this has now begun to happen in Britain as well, as writers from the former colonies have energized and transformed the English novel.)

But Bellow's point is even stronger than that. In the first sentence Bellow seems to be saying that Jews can be kicked out, Jews can be exiled, Jews can be evicted from almost any place they live—and this, indeed, has happened to us often—but language, he says, is a *mansion* from which we can't be thrown out, a place that is secure; when we inhabit it, we know where we are; we know we belong. Bellow is describing English as a transition to assimilation, a way of becoming American, even becoming English, becoming Anglo-Saxon. And yet, Bellow's second sentence is quite different. Bellow says that Malamud discovered a sort of communicative genius in the harsh jargon of immigrant New York. He's arguing that Malamud had invented another kind of English that no one had dreamed could be so eloquent.

This is certainly true, for this new language was once the barbarous immigrant English that horrified Henry James when he visited the Lower East Side in 1904. James was upset with its cacophonous sounds. He describes the sounds around him as one of the torture chambers of the living language. He was tortured by what was happening to English right here in this neighborhood, around the corner from where we are and from where I grew up, on Henry Street, not too far from Eldridge Street. That world and that language were the province of Abraham Cahan, who for half a century was the editor of the *Daily Forward* yet wrote remarkable fiction in English. He became famous for his big novel *The Rise of David Levinsky*, which came out in 1917, but Cahan's first book was called *Yekl: A Tale of the Ghetto*. People know it better in the cinematic form that it took in the seventies, in a movie called *Hester Street*, directed by Joan Micklin Silver. In that book and several subsequent books by Cahan and Anzia Yezierska, and again in the thirties in the work of Clifford Odets, especially in the play *Awake and Sing*, or in *Call It Sleep* by Henry Roth, which must have been an inspiration to you, Ilan, English is used in a way that turns it virtually into a new language. Odets achieves an amazing eloquence with the rhythms and syntax of a Yiddish-inflected English, while Roth contrasts the lyrical glow of his speakers' Yiddish, which becomes so vivid in his translation, with their awkward efforts to express themselves in English, which makes them sound ignorant and uncouth. All of these are different forms of the immigrants' language, a hybrid eloquence that indeed led in the 1940s to the kind of language we hear in a play like *Death of a Salesman* or in the early stories and early novels of Bernard Malamud.

My point is simply that in *On Borrowed Words*, language figures in a number of interesting ways. It figures, for example, as something to aspire to, like a tall mountain that challenges you and seems at times insuperably difficult. It also figures, as in Bellow's statement, as a kind of portable homeland. Also, English is a place that you, Ilan, want to come to. English represents New York. English represents America.

There is an overlap between my own experience and what you describe in *On Borrowed Words*. Your growing up in a Yiddish-speaking enclave in Mexico City was certainly unusual. In fact, it's marvelous: I have not read any other book that describes this particular corner of the Jewish world, the Hispanic corner and all the various tensions within it. One of the intriguing qualities of your portrayal is that you feel no nostalgia for it. Many writers, writers of my generation or older, have typically written about their early experiences on the Lower East Side through a scrim of sentimentality and nostalgia. I've sat down to write about this a few times, and if I ever write a longer memoir, I think there will be no way I can avoid the Proustian or Wordsworthian feeling that people develop about their early lives—even about times and places when they were not particularly happy. My wife once pointed out that I tend to get nostalgic even for places where I was miserable simply because they had somehow woven themselves into the fabric of my experience and become part of the person I was. You, Ilan, do this wonderfully in this book about the people you grew up with, the people that most influenced you. You do this about your paternal grandmother, Bobbe Bela; you do it about your father, the Mexican actor; and you do it about your brother, the stutterer. You give extraordinary portraits of these people, but what animates these accounts, what gives them their emotional spark, is that these people helped form you. They helped make you the person who is writing this description of them, the person you became. Now they help you unravel the enigma of who you are. In your memory you quarrel with these people, yet you give a very complex and balanced portrait of them. This is not an approach that in any way flatters them, any more than you flatter the Jewish community of Mexico City.

Why do you have such mixed feelings about the world from which you spring? I know the answer, for it is obvious. You felt that you were someone who, especially in Jewish terms, but also to a degree in Mexican terms, was living in the provinces, living in a small world. Whatever was happening that was important to you in the world of ideas, of literature, and especially of Jewishness, seemed to be happening elsewhere. In many ways, New York seemed to you the center of the universe. In the light of what happened on September 11, *On Borrowed Words* takes on an interesting overto. e to me, one that I wouldn't have anticipated, for it is a kind of valentine to New York. It's not hostile to the world that you came from, but it's beautifully lyrical about the potential represented by New York. That potential is twofold. It's an opportunity to enter the mainstream of a world literature that fascinates and attracts you. But also, it seems to me as I read the bo   it represents the potential to be Jewish in a richer and freer way than you found yc could be in a Hispanic Catholic culture, interesting as that hybrid world had become to you. New York comes off as a rich, complicated, diverse city, but also, as I see it now, a place I never really understood or appreciated when I was growing up. I didn't know when I lived in this neighborhood that I was growing up in a Jewish city. Only years later, when I went to college, when I went off to other parts of America, I realized that in many ways I had not grown up in the United States. I'd grown up in a country that was *Jewish New York*. Anything that would happen to me for the r t of my life would be influenced by that experience of growing up in this neighbor-hood, which makes it so exciting for me to come back here for this discussion.

Finally, there was one other revealing feature of your memoir that struck me repeatedly. There are many small fragments of other languages that appear in *On Borrowed Words* that are not translated, though they are perfectly clear from their context. They represent the linguistic richness of the book as they represent the linguistic diversity of the writer's experience and his identity. What do those poles of experience represent to you, Ilan? I'm also curious about the role of public intellectuals in the Hispanic world. By becoming an immigrant without cutting the ties to your original home, by moving from south to north keeping a leg on both sides of the divide, your experience is not only in two languages but in two cultures, two *living* cultures.

ILAN STAVANS: You've developed a number of insightful ideas, Morris. Let me begin with language. It is true that for me, it's easier to think that I was born into Spanish than to think I was born in Mexico. I feel that the fact that my grandparents arrived in Mexico is sheer coincidence. They could have arrived in Puerto Rico; they could have arrived in Cuba; and some of them, indeed, settled just for a few months there. But, the fact that I was born into the Spanish language is for me a factor that determined the way I looked at the world dramatically, and immediately inserted me in a chain, in a tradition, and it forced me to see the world through the lens of that tradition. I might feel ambivalence and even rejection of Mexico, but, for as complicated as my feelings are for Spanish, I feel that the Spanish will always be there. It will always be mine, even if I sometimes feel I no longer have a *fresh* Spanish at the tip of my tongue. And I will have nostalgia for Spanish that I will not have for Mexico. Whenever I feel that my Spanish is becoming too bookish, or too academic, I sense the need to spend some time in a Spanish-speaking country just to make it come back. But, it doesn't have to be Mexico, and in fact, if it's not Mexico, I feel all the better. In the end, there is a struggle between the polar opposites, Mexico and the United States, and Spanish and English, is for me less about nationality than about something I refer to in the book as *translationality*—the fact that you are born into various tongues and you are their carrier and conduit. It is your responsibility to look back at what those tongues have done and feel how rich they are, and to continue to perpetuate them. Probably for that reason, the only city in the world that feels like a true Jerusalem (even though Jerusalem is the most beautiful city) is New York—it is for me the center of the world, the belly button, the navel, the origin, and the place I aspire to. And it is for a number of different things I try to convey in the book. Among them the fact that language is so alive in this city in so many different ways that I never experienced in Mexico and never experienced in Europe and the Middle East. It is a place that because of the history that it has, of its immigrations and clashes of cultures, where English is the pattern, is the vehicle that all of us use to communicate, and yet you walk just one block, enter a subway car, and so many different accents, so many different tongues, clash with one another. None of them disappear and none of them go away. They are all enriching in and enriched by New York. That English is becoming the global language, or has become the global language, the *lingua franca* of today, the Latin of the present time, and as America promotes, willingly or not, the sense that English is the way to go for business and politics and culture, we give others the sense that it is one English, that America produces one English, the English of Hollywood, the English of television, the English of certain best-selling novels. It only takes ten minutes to walk in New York City to realize the many Englishes, let alone the other languages that exist here, the many Englishes that collide all the time. I'm particularly attracted to one of these: Spanglish. Spanglish, in my eyes, is the encounter, the in-between of Spanish and English. It is to Hispanics what Yiddish was to thirteenth- and fourteenth-century Eastern European Jews. It is a mixture of two languages that is neither one nor the other. It is the announcement of a new identity, the announcement of a new Hispanic way of perceiving the world. And yet, it is, particularly in academic circles, or by politicians, it is looked down [upon] as the language of the illiterate, the language of those that are not part of society yet. Or the language that one should give up in order to become full-fledged Americans or full-fledged English-language Americans. If that Spanglish is alive and well, it is in New York City. Even within that Spanglish, there are so many possibilities. There is the Spanglish spoken by Puerto Ricans that is so different from the Spanglish spoken by Cuban Americans. The inflections are different. The words, the vocabulary is different. Terms like *kennedito*, which Cubans use to refer to a traitor because of the word *Kennedy* and the Bay of Pigs, *kennedito*, is something that a Puerto Rican Spanglish speaker would not understand. Certain words that a Spanglish-speaking Puerto Rican would use, in the same city, in the same bars, would not be understood by the Cuban American or the Mexican counterpart. And this happens in New York City, where all universes are synchronized in one, like a Borgesian aleph, either reduced or expanded into this undestroyable bubble, no matter how many planes crash against skyscrapers. This is where all begins and ends: *ground zero* in the history of Modernity.

Nostalgia . . . You put it perfectly, Morris: I have never felt nostalgia for Mexico City. It is a place I always wanted to leave behind, a place that my memory keeps alive in artificial fashion. But it is a place I often return to because my parents and siblings are there. When I do so, I am constantly amazed by the transformation that the country has undergone in the past twenty years and, in several respects, the Jewish community too. I'm struck by the fact that recently there has been an effort at developing a kind of tourism connected with the historical foundation of the Jewish community. A friend of mine (we studied in the same school) has organized an agency that takes visitors, mostly Americans, to the first mikvah built by the Ashkenazim in downtown Mexico City, the first synagogue, etc. She talks to them about the past, and also, in partnership with the central committee, there's talk of a museum. Last time I saw her, she told me about boxes being made ready for the museum. And about one of the works I had written early on being in one of those boxes, which was to be displayed behind glass: a Yiddish play I had written, and so on. The shock I felt I can't explain it to you. The fact that I have become a museum artifact and that somebody was nostalgic about that past but it wasn't me and it wasn't a Jewish community; it was American Jews.

MORRIS DICKSTEIN: Is there a paradox in the fact that other people look for the roots that we ourselves are trying to get away from?

ILAN STAVANS: The Mexican-Jewish experience is colored by being so close to the U.S. A dictum attributed to dictator Porfirio Díaz states, "Poor Mexico, so far from God and so close to the United States." Mexico Jews especially are too infatuated by *El Monstruo*. Do I feel nostalgia for Mexico? Not really, not fully. It was home while it lasted, but Mexican Jews never felt at home in it. Plus, I've always been wary about the nostalgia for the shtetl of American Jews. This genealogical search on the Internet, of looking for the place where your great-great-great-grandparent was born. Even traveling to it. And kind of celebrating the shtetl as a kind of place of companionship and in closeness. When the shtetl must have been a grim, uninviting place. A place people wanted to run away from. And it's thanks to Sholem Aleichem, to Tevye and his daughters, to other writers of his generation, that we look to it with a dose of *shmalz*. That *shmalz* wasn't an ingredient originally. Or was it? It is the shtetl in our mind, a figment of our imagination, the one we long for . . .

MORRIS DICKSTEIN: Eric Hobsbawm, in his book *The Invention of Tradition*, reflects on how many things we associate with old national traditions are really recent modern creations. I take a more sympathetic attitude towards it: people don't like the idea that their family came into existence three generations ago. They don't like the idea that they only have family names because Napoleon forced the Jews to take family names. They have a kind of envy for the British or the French who can trace their ancestry back to the twelfth or fourteenth century. Even if the shtetl is a mythical creation, it is I think a creation a psychological necessity for them. You might say that the mental shtetl they created, the Marc Chagall vision, is something separate from what historical research would reveal as the authentic shtetl. It has been *recreated* by artists and intellectuals, and promoted by the media and the academy.

ILAN STAVANS: A movie set—what in the critical jargon of today is known as a *representation*.

MORRIS DICKSTEIN: This, I hasten to add, is not an indictment of intellectuals and artists. Representations are everywhere—we use them to feed memory.

ILAN STAVANS: You yourself are an intellectual, and so am I. And an academic too . . . Let me take the opportunity to ask you a question I always wanted to ask, one that touches me deeply. It might push us in another direction, but it doesn't matter: a conversation such as this is ruled by chance. Anyway, the question is: is there a tension in you between the two identities, Morris Dickstein the academic and Morris Dickstein the intellectual? Or are they one and the same?

MORRIS DICKSTEIN: I have almost never written for academic journals. Most of my reviewing in the last thirty years has been for journals like the *New York Times Book Review*. More serious essays have mostly been for quarterlies like *Partisan Review*. Some of the publications I write for don't reach a very large audience, but they do reach an audience larger than my fellow academics. Some of the subjects I've dealt [with] over the years have been academic in the sense that poetry today, indeed, the whole literature of the past, largely rests in the hands of the academy. What I like to do, what I do in teaching as well, . . . is to try to tackle difficult subjects, to clarify them for myself in a way that might also clarify them for other people. So it is essentially a learning process. When I take on a writer that I've never written about, like the Israeli master Shmuel Yosef Agnon, my implicit goal is [to] further my own education. I've discovered that what drives me to teach a new course, and I rarely do a course more than twice, is the nostalgia I have for being a student.

ILAN STAVANS: *Academic* is a noun I feel uncomfortable with. In my mind academics are ostriches: they bury their head underground . . .

MORRIS DICKSTEIN: I trust *public intellectual* doesn't trouble you, right?

ILAN STAVANS: No, it doesn't. I see in it a parade of talent that goes from Matthew Arnold to Edmund Wilson and Malcolm Cowley. I fear it is an endangered species, though. How do you define the difference between an academic and a public intellectual, Morris?

MORRIS DICKSTEIN: Once there were academics able to cover broad intellectual areas. Their knowledge was wide. But academic life has become professionalized. The result is that the field of the generalist has become the domain of the intellectual. Academics, instead, become specialists. Yet academics who are really successful break out of their narrow field, leaping over its conventional boundaries; they go against the current and somehow get away with it. They might be condemned initially, but eventually they get respect. But there's plenty of good work by academics doing specialized research that I need and occasionally rely on. And there's plenty of bad work out there by public intellectuals, shallow, shoddy, merely opinionated, and painfully glib. Here I'd include many of the talking heads on TV. But in some ways the general level of public work has gone up; the *Times*, for example, has better critics than it had in the past, when they were strictly middlebrow, even philistine. Now a strong intellectual influence has seeped into it. Unfortunately, the *Times* is almost unique, and many papers have folded.

ILAN STAVANS: Had Edmund Wilson been born after World War II, his chances of developing a career like the one he had would not have been available, don't you think? The patience and dedication of mainstream magazines to intellectual debates has diminished. Or has it?

MORRIS DICKSTEIN: Intellectuals in the twentieth century were the product of a culture no longer in existence. Modernism incited intellectuals to be recondite, difficult, contemptuous of a mass audience, but it also nurtured a strong literary and a political culture of its own. It was a minority culture that depended on the narrowness of the culture at large, which had no interest in what the intellectual had to offer. The *New Yorker* didn't publish intellectuals early on; only much later did it open its pages to them. Edmund Wilson was unusual in that he didn't start out in the little magazines that flowered alongside the modern movement. He got started in *Vanity Fair* and then the *New Republic*, two outlets still available today. In the *New Republic*, intellectuals like Wilson and Malcolm Cowley could write weekly leader articles on a tremendous variety of subjects over a period of years. When politics and economics came to the fore during the Depression, they could also write about politics and society instead of simply reviewing literary works.

Wilson and others ultimately collected their pieces into books that became chronicles of their era. That was the type of intellectual whose judgment people learned to trust, even if they sometimes disagreed with them. They became the audience's reliable guides to the elusive twists and turns of modernist culture and radical politics. That kind of steady flow of criticism and commentary from a single mind, whether in a little magazine or in the *Nation*, doesn't exist anymore. Can intellectual debate be seriously pursued by way of rock culture or TV coverage? National Public Radio certainly makes a valiant try, but it's far better at informing people in depth—no small matter—than analyzing deep-seated assumptions and far-reaching consequences.

ILAN STAVANS: In principle, there is no reason why it shouldn't.

MORRIS DICKSTEIN: But literature is no longer at the center. The literary intellectual was defined by his relation to avant-garde movements and particularly to Modernism. Intellectuals depended on the obtuseness of the larger culture and developed by rejecting that culture. Now the new is rapidly ingested and turned into the old. This, by the way, is part of David Brooks's argument in *Bobos in Paradise*. He points out that intellectuals used to be dead set against consumer culture. They exercised their superior taste by looking down on middle-class greed and acquisitiveness, the love of possessions. They made strong claims to being spiritual and even unworldly, a sort of clerisy, focused on higher things, but in most cases their near-poverty was imposed on them since few were willing to pay well for what they had to offer. Now, of course, they welcome consumer culture. Also, intellectuals used to mask their worldly ambitions, but now they flaunt them. To me this means that the transformation of mainstream culture also entails a change of heart in intellectuals. And you, how do you see this transformation, Ilan? In the sixth chapter of *On Borrowed Words* you state your admiration for figures like Octavio Paz and Irving Howe. In fact, about Paz you have actually published a full-fledged meditation on his reach and shortcomings as an intellectual.

ILAN STAVANS: Coming as I do from Latin America, where the role of the intellectual is different from that in the United States and Europe, I have learned to perceive the intellectual—and particularly the critic, the cultural, literary critic—as an interpreter, or an in-between: the manifestation, the various manifestations of the imagination and talent, human talent in general, and the way those sit in society at large. Obviously a novel can always be written and always be read without any intermediary. But it is left to the critic to explain why we are the way we are *vis-à-vis* the expressions that we bring out. In Mexico and other places in Latin America the intellectual was always, by definition, at least up until the eighties, a leftist who functioned as an enemy of the state. The arrival of consumerism and the neoliberalism of the eighties and nineties changed the ideological spectrum significantly. Today intellectuals south of the Rio Grande are commodities of a society hypnotized by leisure. Is there still a need for the old-fashioned thinker? I am sure there is. The symptoms are clear: Latin America has ceased to reflect about itself, to ponder its place in history, to investigate its crossroads. . . . This, in my eyes, suggests a state of somnambulism, one that has frightening qualities. The intellectual is the conduit of a collective "stream of consciousness" that any group of people need[s] to remain spiritually, emotionally healthy.

MORRIS DICKSTEIN: I don't know that much about Latin America, bu I can detect a similar landscape in the United States. By public intellectuals I mean someone able to speak to a broader public, which is to some extent true. Mostly intellectuals are speaking to other intellectuals. And the conclusions they come to or the buzz about their debates filters down to a broader public, usually in a journalistic w y. But in response to you: the intellectual as a medium between the public and the world of art and politics is a modern development. It comes about with Modern-ism, when you have difficult forms of artistic expression which are really meant to be inaccessible to the masses. Criticism is really a creation of a mass culture as it collides with a difficult set of artistic or intellectual discourses. When the intel-lectual begins to merge more seamlessly with that culture, then you don't need criticism to interpret the arts as much as you did before. So the more intransigent intellectuals end up simply talking to each other. They become a separable profes-sional caste, sometimes spilling over and creating a buzz around certain issues. I don't see intellectuals play the mediating role today they did fifteen years ago, partly because the well-named "media" have taken their place, partly because their disturbing reflections are unwelcome, but also because they themselves leaped off a cliff called Theory and lost much of their public voice along with their relevance. They also became as predictable politically as the Latin American intellectuals you describe. But this has begun to change in the last few years, as the cocksure certainties of the seventies and eighties lost ground.

ILAN STAVANS: Let me pursue your idea of Modernism as the trigger that brought about the public role of intellectuals as we know it, then give it a twist. Clement Greenberg, Walter Benjamin, and Susan Sontag wrote about kitsch and pop cul-ture. Certain types of intellectuals embraced pop culture, either against, instead of, or together with high culture. Does this embrace of a middlebrow in con-sumer society necessarily mean the end of intellectual life? How about using the Internet to expand it? Or is it that the www, by virtue of its transient, volatile nature, [is] inherently allergic to intellectual debate? Have we simply not been able to cope as intellectuals with the rapid changes of our time?

MORRIS DICKSTEIN: Even intellectuals who specialize in the study of visual cul-ture are themselves often not very well adapted to that culture. They have no creative relationship to it. Meyer Shapiro was not a bad painter, though he never considered himself a real painter. And certain critics of poetry have certainly not been bad poets. Intellectuals are people who translate the arts into discourse. There is no reason why this can't still be done today. One problem, of course, is that new cultural forms succeed each other so rapidly. Film studios, for instance, have developed promotional methods to make reviews obsolete and unneces-sary. So that you'll read ten things about a movie before you actually read a re-view of a movie, which will tell you for the first time that it might not be the most wonderful thing you've ever seen. But by that point the power of the review [has] effectively been nullified. A consumer culture has increasingly invaded the arts, while clever marketing has seriously limited the role of the intellectual and neutralized the critical judgment that once provided a standard for the public. As I said before, the critics are better, but their influence has diminished. This doesn't mean that there is no longer a role for critics to play. The critics may be the only ones who can still keep people honest, maintaining standards and making a case for works that are worthwhile. They're great validators, as well as articulate witnesses to new trends. In a scene that changes so rapidly, they help the audience keep its bearings, and to a small degree they put to shame those who produce trashy and exploitative work—that is, if any shame is still possible.

On the issue of the assimilation of intellectuals to pop culture, I believe it was inevitable. The enforced hierarchy separating high culture, middlebrow culture, and mass culture was always artificial, always a pure construction. I don't think there's all that much difference between a Clement Greenberg, who talks about mass culture and kitsch from the viewpoint of an intransigent modernism, and Susan Sontag, who embraces certain forms of pop culture as simply another turn of the avant-garde. Sontag embraced mass culture at the same moment that she was embracing the French *nouveau roman*. Both situate mass culture on the same spectrum, using almost the same spectacles.

ILAN STAVANS: I remember that you talk about this in *Gates of Eden: American Culture in the Sixties*.

MORRIS DICKSTEIN: I think the sixties created a different kind of cultural mix. In part this was because mass culture in the sixties (starting with rock music) was so wonderful, so complex and resonant, that the old arguments about popular culture being simply kitsch and trash were no longer tenable. The magnificent new movies and new music of the sixties eventually filtered over into a transformation of a whole attitude towards mass culture and popular culture. But that in itself did not destroy or eliminate the old intellectual since most sixties intellectuals loved the new culture, enjoyed it personally, and even wrote sterling commentaries on it, in which the critical function was very much on display. Pop culture was a major incentive to criticism in the sixties, especially movies and music but also politics as theatre.

ILAN STAVANS: There is intellectual debate on the value of serious stories that take place in the form of comic strips. Think of Art Spiegelman's *Maus I* and *II*. It is an extraordinary marriage between highbrow and pop culture, and Spiegelman includes, in his introductions, an argument on how through comic strips he is able to reach deep into the horrors of history—a self-reflecting argument. Likewise, there is intellectual debate on the Internet about the Internet. Jonathan Rosen published a couple of years ago his book-long essay *The Talmud and the Internet*: two "infinite" channels, portable, self-referential, and intensely "intellectual."

MORRIS DICKSTEIN: The Internet is just information. It's a medium, not an art form.

ILAN STAVANS: Might we conceive of the Internet today as the equivalent of journals such as *Crisis* or *Partisan Review*?

MORRIS DICKSTEIN: I will answer with a question: could you have written *On Borrowed Words* not as a book but as a Web site? I doubt it. The style you use, your meditation on language, is scarcely appropriate for so mercurial a medium. You might carry your language with you as a homeland, but the Internet makes that homeland almost intangible. Some people write e-mails as if they were carefully polished letters, but it's artificial for writers to try maintaining that level of prose; it's a carryover from the typewriter, just as online magazines like *Slate* and *Salon* have some remnant from printed magazines. But they don't really represent the Internet. It's hard to produce good writing for the Internet because the Internet is so much an instant form of communication. So far I've never joined the "conversation" in a chat room, but it's like the letters column of a newspaper or a magazine, not like the featured contents. In other words, letters columns or chat rooms are good for keeping an issue afloat, for keeping the buzz going. They're not making any kind of definitive or important statement about an issue, though this may be changing with the Web-logs of intellectuals like Christopher Hitchens, Andrew Sullivan, or Mickey Kaus. Blogging is more like a series of diary entries than like an essay. Like the chat rooms, they're part of the phenomenon that the Internet is, in general, a completely unfiltered system of communication. Magazines in history have been hierarchical to the degree that some people had access to them, that there were editors who would decide what would go in and what wouldn't go in, and some people did not have access to them. That's not true about the Internet, and the technology has grown much easier to learn. Everyone has access, but not everyone's Web site is going to be looked at by many people. It's a wonderful research tool, and great for catalogue shopping. But those who spend much time browsing the Internet know how much of it is complete garbage. It is a matter of finding that 1 or 2 percent that is really worth spending your time reading.

ILAN STAVANS: The same goes for bookstores nowadays—that is, unless you stumble on the shelf of Penguin Classics.

MORRIS DICKSTEIN: Yes, but the bookstore is itself already heavily filtered. There are forty thousand books that come out a year. How many of these are there in the bookstores: 500, 1,000, 2,000? The Internet, on the other hand, is unfiltered.

ILAN STAVANS: By the way, how can you explain to me the popularity of Harold Bloom?

MORRIS DICKSTEIN: Bloom is a public intellectual in the sense that he has moved out of his initial field, Romantic and modern poetry, to take on large themes and a broad range of literature from the Bible to Shakespeare. From the ground up, he has tried to recreate the myth or the useful fiction of the general reader. His books *Shakespeare: The Invention of the Human* and *The Western Canon* reflect the assumption that general readers still exist or can be resuscitated, something that many academics long denied— though recently some of the best of them have also been reaching out to a general audience. Since Bloom's style is unique, initially he didn't gain access to this larger readership, but starting with his commentary on *The Book of J* he found great, ambitious subjects by developing a voice that could engage ordinary readers. He is a great phrase-maker, quick with the wicked one-liner, as interviewers have discovered. His opinions sometimes border on the outrageous, but they are always challenging. He developed a literary personality, as good writers usually do. He can be quite self-dramatizing, but his love of literature is enormous, omnivorous, and always deeply personal. Almost single-handedly, he has fashioned a role for the critic as generalist that many academics had long since conceded to journalism. Of course there were stalwarts like Frank Kermode and Alfred Kazin who were doing this all along.

ILAN STAVANS: But why does the audience turn so obscure a topic like Shakespeare into a bestseller?

MORRIS DICKSTEIN: The more distant the feeling for history and literature become, the more people develop a nostalgia for what was lost. Bloom's books are also a response to the academic attacks on the canon. Of course, I don't want to look too closely at how many readers have actually read *Shakespeare* and *The Western Canon*.

ILAN STAVANS: So you think nostalgia makes people buy books.

MORRIS DICKSTEIN: Yes, nostalgia and the sense of a common inheritance. This is especially clear these days when there's a multiplicity of competing canons shaped by multiculturalists for the consumption of ethnically defined readerships. Perhaps there is the feeling that maybe one ought to not bury European or Western literature so quickly; perhaps that helps make Harold Bloom successful. This is not, by the way, an empty nostalgia but an authentic one, which attests to the desire to recover something that we feel has become a gap in our own national identity, perhaps in our individual identity as well.

ILAN STAVANS: In your book *Double Agent: The Critic and Society*, you are the one that writes with a sense of nostalgia—nostalgia for a past that is no more. I feel as if the suggestion is made that previous generations had a depth that is inaccessible to us.

MORRIS DICKSTEIN: Though the kinds of critics I wrote about there are rare to-day, the critical impulse persists, as does the need for critical discussion. The whole culture is geared up to enforce passive acceptance, to let things simply wash over us. It's a strategy borrowed from marketing and advertising. It's meant to disarm resistance and to separate us from our cash. Criticism is stubborn resistance joined to articulate appreciation. Today, when I go to the movies with friends, we rarely get into the kind of heated conversation I remember so well from the past. You learn whether they liked it or didn't like it but not much more. Is it that we as a society have become apathetic? Or have the movies simply grown too banal, too predictable to discuss? Twenty years ago, my students were exercising wonderful critical judgment when they responded to music, which really meant a great deal in their lives. Subtle discriminations were required. I'm afraid the exercise of critical judgment has seriously eroded. People seem to think it's impolite, or futile. The question is: is judgment instinctive? Might we return to old times? Or does it decrease and vanish? Today our critical judgments come mainly in the act of grunting thumbs up and down. I think the Internet is likely to create a tremendous horizontal awareness of what's happening everywhere in the world, but it's not likely to heighten analysis in-depth.

ILAN STAVANS: Is ours a generation with skin an inch deep?

MORRIS DICKSTEIN: No, people don't live their lives an inch deep. Their pains, joys, and perceptions cut as deeply as ever. Look at *On Borrowed Words*: you take stock of your whole life, of the cultures in which you lived, the people that helped shape you, in a really prismatic way. The book shows, if nothing else, that our life today can be explored in all its complexities, not just in terms of the fashions of the moment. This is why I have no problem with the spate of memoirs that have been appearing in recent years. There's always something to be discovered by way of genuine introspection, and in being exposed to other people's experiences.

One can never tell how technology will evolve. Few would disagree that for twenty, thirty, or forty years, what we saw on television was relatively shallow compared to literature. That is no longer true today. Some of the most creative work is being done in this medium. There are always a few ongoing series that have the complication and fascination of *romans fleuves*, and the acting is often superb. It's hard to imagine better comedy than *Seinfeld*, thanks to the Jewish genius of Larry David, or better drama than the HBO series *The Sopranos* and *Six Feet Under*, both of them edgy, explosive, unpredictable. Cable has made it possible to direct television at smaller audiences, niche audiences, as good literature has often done. Serious creative thinking has always been a minority enterprise. Two hundred years ago, there was a sensational form of Gothic literature that was really a disposable form of pop culture. Wordsworth, for example, hated it, though some serious writers played off of it. There will always be people who will be impelled to think more deeply, in more telling detail, about what they're observing and experiencing. Memoir as a genre (which Rousseau and Wordsworth helped originate) enables a society to explore both the typical and the idiosyncratic. Of course, a memoir might also turn out to be self-serving and egotistical. America now stimulates such ventures. But when done with care, an honest, searching memoir can become a mirror of identity, perhaps even a piece of social history. It satisfies some of the same curiosity that draws us to read novels. For you, Ilan, identity and language seem to go together. That, I think, is what your memoir is about, and why it is so powerful.

ILAN STAVANS: I do believe that language and identity are intertwined.

MORRIS DICKSTEIN: Let's return to the point we discussed earlier about "the shtetl of the mind." It makes me think of what you said at the beginning of our conversation, about how you try to keep Spanish as a living part of you, and when you feel it is becoming too bookish, too academic, you find ways to refresh it. This is an almost . . . archeological metaphor, layers of language in you, which are also layers of your own identity. And it's in the nature of writing a memoir to do a kind of auto-archeology, an excavation of the layers upon layers of your own self, especially those that have long been covered over and are hidden from view. The point in writing a memoir is not in saying what you already know but trying to discover, in the course of writing it, just what went into making you the enigmatic person you are, a puzzle even to yourself. For someone who has moved between languages and cultures, as you have, this must be crucial. There's a wonderful passage in your book in which you describe the nature of acting and the actor. You describe your father as an actor who shifts into a different persona, and you tell us about your fear as a child that he would disappear into one of the roles you saw him playing on the stage or on television. You were afraid the father you knew would never come back to you. Later in the book you pick up this theme when you describe the feeling of speaking another language, not as becoming a different person—you are still the person that you were—but as adopting another persona, another part of you. And a persona, as we know, is a mask, the kind of mask that was used by actors in the ancient theater. In short, you're playing another role when you speak another language. I have had some experience with perhaps six languages. But I never went from really living in one language to living in another, as you have.

When I grew up, I heard Yiddish all around me. My parents did not speak Yiddish on a daily basis as their older brothers and sisters did, but my parents did the classic thing of speaking Yiddish when they didn't want the children (or strangers) to understand. So the children of course learned Yiddish perfectly by listening to their parents trying to conceal things from them. Perhaps even more importantly, in moments of crisis, in moments of emotional urgency, my parents would fall back on the language of their own childhood. So Yiddish for me had strong emotional associations. For you at the *Yiddishe Shule in Mexique*, your day school, Yiddish was something of an ideological language. It was a language of militant Yiddishism, I gather, a Bundist ideology. For me, Yiddish was two things. Yiddish was an intimate domestic language; it was the language of the home, a kind of feminine language. The prayer book would sometimes translate into Yiddish at the bottom of the page for the sake of the women who were assumed not to have a major Hebrew education. The other difference between us is that where you went to a secular Yiddish school committed to this Yiddishist ideology, I went to a Yiddish-speaking yeshiva, a religious school, just a few blocks from where we are now, where Yiddish was almost an act of cultural resistance—as it has become once again in Jerusalem and in parts of Brooklyn. So for me, Yiddish, besides having the domestic association, had that other, strongly religious association. When my parents enrolled me in kindergarten in 1945, the yeshiva had actually begun a Hebrew track, a Hebrew-speaking track known as *Ivrit b'Ivrit*. My parents had no idea what possible use speaking Hebrew could have, and so they enrolled me in what was familiar to them, which was the Yiddish track. So for four hours in the morning we studied Hebrew and Aramaic texts and translated and discussed them in Yiddish. For four hours in the afternoon, we got a complete secular English education in reading and science, history, and literature.

When you're a child, there's nothing strange about this. You go along with the choices your parents have made; you make do with the environment in which you happen to find yourself. Besides, children have a great facility with language. How wonderful it is when they learn several languages at one time! My wife grew up in a German-speaking family, but her parents foolishly stopped speaking German when she was quite young. They were afraid that it would damage her English, though a child can easily assimilate four languages at one time. Children take in languages even better than they learn to handle computers, which is really another language. I didn't have the experience of moving from one language to another, as you did, but I had a good deal of exposure to other languages. When I learned some Italian in my thirties, or learned French in high school, or studied German in college with the help of the Yiddish I had as a child, I found not so much that a different personality came out in me—my experience was too superficial—but I had access to a whole other cast of mind. I discovered that a language represented a complex, highly nuanced way of thinking, a culture, a tradition, constructed from the many layers of what people in the past have contributed to it. Learning languages became something akin to travel; it expanded my mental horizon without my making the very difficult leap into fully living in another language, as you did.

ILAN STAVANS: What do you make of the death of Yiddish?

MORRIS DICKSTEIN: Languages die, whole cultures die, just as people die. In literary terms, in terms of a spoken culture, Yiddish is dead. It is unfortunate that the growing populations of Orthodox Jews, who are committed to maintaining

Yiddish, have no interest in the rich secular traditions of Yiddish, including literature and the theater. That culture is inimical to them. They're not at all sentimental about it. Instead they wish to preserve a *way of life* that developed in
Eastern Europe, which they see not only as pious and just but as the key to Jewish
survival. They're actively hostile to the secular Yiddish culture that, in the end,
lasted only about a hundred years.

ILAN STAVANS: It is impossible to have access to a culture without having access
to its language.

MORRIS DICKSTEIN: Cultures wax and wane, but few are assassinated the way
Yiddish was—with a single blow. Even without the Nazis, Yiddish was on its way
out, certainly in America, in an inexorable process of assimilation. I find the academic obsession with the revival of Yiddish heartening but artificial. . . . Perhaps
this is an inevitable feature of American Jewish culture: trying to make an impossible connection with a past that is buried, and largely inaccessible.

ILAN STAVANS: Growing up in Mexico, I always felt that American Jews were
the mighty ones. They were the center of culture, they knew who they were. The
country respected them. Many of us wanted to be like American Jews. We envied
them. We would come to the United States to travel or to visit uncles or friends,
and there was always the sense that we were coming to them and that they were
the place to come to. When they visited us down there, it was a tourist vacation. For us it was a kind of coming home. It wasn't until I immigrated to the
United States that I was able to see from the inside a different side of what American Jews are all about—fragmented, shrieking at the same time about different
things, and fighting about religion and about culture in a very lively way, in a very
admirable way, but without the sense of concentrated univocal approach that we
from afar thought they had. Uncle Stanley in Long Island would say, "Oh, you're
learning English; that's good, that's very good." I would answer: "Why don't you
do some Spanish?" His response was sharp: "Why should I learn Spanish if you're
learning English?" Looking back, there must not be many powerful, potent Jewish communities in history that have been so frighteningly monolingual as the
American Jews are. Nostalgic about different languages, passionate about different languages and yet, imprisoned in their own unique sole language with everything that that entails. And in some ways I think that the refurnishing of Yiddish,
or the status of Yiddish today, is not that different from the synagogue where we
are, or the efforts of rebuilding it, of keeping it an academic space or a cultural
space, of putting money and showing that the past is there and that it's alive and
with all of the struggles that it entails. Why did I learn Yiddish in kindergarten in
school and high school? I was always uncomfortable with my parents. Am I not
wasting my time? Shouldn't I be learning French or English, languages in touch
with the rest of the world?

MORRIS DICKSTEIN: I take it from the book that you felt angry?

ILAN STAVANS: Angry and wrongheaded. . . . Morris, I want tell you something about the shaping of *On Borrowed Words*. I have written a bunch of books before, perhaps too many. A friend of mine always says, "When are you going to have a writer's block, Ilan? We readers need to have time to catch up with your writing." This book, though, was the hardest I've ever done. I knew the type of memoir I wanted to write, about language and identity. I committed myself to do so with the publisher. But immediately when I made the agreement, I felt paralyzed—with a frozen pen.

MORRIS DICKSTEIN: Your friend must have been delighted.

ILAN STAVANS: The freeze had to do with the thought that any memoir as such is an act of betrayal: betrayal of my own memory, and betrayal of the people that shaped me. That feeling of betrayal has never altogether disappeared. But there is another kind of betrayal: betrayal of myself. When I see the book finished in front of me, I feel I've engaged in a voluntary form of censorship. Is this who I *really* am, I ask myself? How much did I leave, have left out? Is this the book I should have become? Were there other routes I could have taken but didn't? At one point, before I started to write the first word, I felt that the authentic book I was meant to write needed to be drafted in four different languages. The first part, dealing with my Mexican days, should have been in Yiddish. The second third of the book should have been in Hebrew; this section would have been about my time in Israel. The third part should have been in Spanish; this portion would have addressed my return to Mexico—to a non-Jewish Mexico. Finally, the last part of the book would have been written in English, but as if written by a nonnative speaker. Indeed, every one of the four parts would have needed this nonnative ingredient to allow the reader to feel, like I do, never quite at home anywhere. Of course, as you mentioned earlier on, my inspirations were *Call It Sleep*, as well as Joyce's *Finnegans Wake*.

MORRIS DICKSTEIN: Nobody but you would have been able to read the book.

ILAN STAVANS: Precisely. And no publisher in a right sense of mind would dare to embark on such a fanciful project. And then the idea was to shape a book about the issue of translation with the sense that other languages aren't living in it and struggling to emerge and have a say, but it is in English because English is the language that will color the way I'm presenting myself to the audience. It is the language also in which I feel most comfortable writing nonfiction. But the thought has come recently about translating this book into Spanish. And I feel that betrayal is a down-going staircase, in that the lower I go, the more distant I will be from my original intention. Having gone beyond that point, I couldn't just write. I knew what I wanted to write, and I couldn't write it. And I spent six months to a year just going around ideas and never finding the right first sentence or first word. And the editor at Viking would suggest all sorts of questions and propositions, and nothing felt comfortable. I felt that becoming a page was something that I was forcing myself to do. I showed that editor a few pages, and he was as unhappy with it as I was, with the result. At one point he suggested, "I think the problem is, Ilan, that you're writing in the past tense. And thus you're *the* past. How about just trying to write it in the present tense . . . without exception, begin in the present tense; then there are detours to the past, and you come back to the present." And it was the only way I was able to cope with the past as an unclosed chamber. During the period of writing, I was visited by ghosts—images of long-forgotten people—I haven't seen in a long time. Ghosts gave me chests that had a padlock saying, "here, this is for you," and disappearing. Or people that have been dead for a long time, coming back and mentioning things in a language that I couldn't understand in those dreams. It was a time of intense transformation within my subconscious that I have never experienced writing anything else. And I did not like being visited by those dreams for six months. Obviously, I'm happy that the book is finished. Some of those dreams made it into the book; others didn't and are in notes. But it was a very rich period of dream-life that I have not had with other books.

Morris Dickstein: You probably were undergoing something like psychoanalysis, examining your experience in a way that you had never been pressed to do before. The term that you use, *betrayal*, is a very strong one. That word has often been used for another element of your book, not for writing a memoir but for the process of translation. There is a famous Italian saying, *traditore, traduttore*, any translation is a betrayal. The reason is that, as any translator knows, you're not only taking one set of words or ideas and putting them into another language, but you're putting them through a funnel or grille in a way that necessarily winnows out some elements. Language is not simply what it says, but all the undertones and overtones that color it. Language has almost a tactile texture, something very hard to carry over. When you translate, you find that some of what you convey comes through at the expense of other things that you simply can't then carry over. It's never crossed my mind before, but writing a memoir can feel like a similar act of betrayal. Your description of not wanting to become a book reminds me of what I heard a writer say recently: that once you write about an experience, what you've written replaces your memory of that experience. If you were to tell that story again, what you'd be remembering, most likely, is not what happened but what you wrote about it. In other words, you've turned it into something hard and fast, shaped into a story, narrated, and hence no longer fluid, as most memories are. You've bound yourself to that story, that version of the flux of recollection. I understand why the present tense was liberating and the past tense frightening to you. . . .

ILAN STAVANS: Why?

MORRIS DICKSTEIN: In recent years, some people have written memoirs at a tender age—even younger than your forty years, Ilan. Generally the tradition was for writers to write their autobiography not only late in life, when their social stature and literary position were assured, but when the rest of their work was complete. A favorite writer of mine, Joseph Heller, who wrote *Catch-22*, wrote a memoir a year or two before he died, telling us who some of the real people were behind his characters in *Catch-22*. That's like the ending of *The Wizard of Oz*, where you lift the curtain and see some of the machinery behind the illusion. To do that, in a way, is a kind of dying. It suggests that your real work is complete, and now you can reveal some of the secrets, the actual experiences, behind the more vibrant imaginary ones you've already written down. In your book you quote the opening of Mary Antin's once-famous autobiography, *The Promised Land,* which recounts her immigrant experience. Though she is still a relatively young woman, she describes her earlier European self as a different person, saying "I can write about that person because she was no longer who I am. That person really was dead." This is frightening, and we don't want it to happen to our own experience. We don't want to entomb it in a book so that it's fixed and dead and no longer ours. I suspect that feeling evoked this feverish dream-life that descended on you. What intrigues me, though, is the intersection of Hispanic and Jewish life in *On Borrowed Words*, and how each of these cultures I'm sure takes a different approach to the struggle against the "dead person" in us. This intersection of selves, I think, is crucial to the multicultural spirit in America today.

ILAN STAVANS: You asked a while ago if *On Borrowed Words* could have been released on the Internet first. By way of response, what crossed my mind is that its audience would have been defined by the ethnicity of the majority of Web browsers. Proportionally, Latinos have a limited access to the Internet, whereas Jews have, in a short span of time, turned this medium into a home turf. Democratic medium? Yes, but filtered through the prism of class and education. Anyway, *On Borrowed Words* exists as a book. And to the question, "Who is its audience?" the answer is easy: whoever is compelled by it and feels like reading it.

MORRIS DICKSTEIN: A good answer, and one that doesn't change with time. Literature is by definition elitist. Many novelists of the last two generations, including Malamud and Updike, survived thanks to a loyal but relatively small readership. Eventually, they managed to break through to a larger audience with a book that was not usually the best work they had done: Malamud's *The Fixer* and Updike's *Couples* are good examples. Often this more popular volume dealt with a sensational subject or focused on a major change in the culture. These writers thus found an audience for reasons that weren't strictly literary—for their explicit treatment of sex, for example, or their portrayal of history. But then readers went back to their earlier, more difficult, perhaps more intransigent work with admiration. Take Bellow's immensely popular *Herzog*, which *was* one of his best books. It's fundamentally a novel of ideas. Perhaps its closest predecessor is *The Magic Mountain* by Thomas Mann, a book in which ideas actually function almost like characters. When *Herzog* came out, I was a graduate student, working on a thesis on Keats. Bellow's protagonist was trying to write a book on Romanticism and Christianity. I remember some of Herzog's ideas about Romanticism helping me think through the problems that I was having with a particular Romantic poet. It isn't that the book included any kind of dissertation on Romanticism or that Bellow was a discursive thinker. Herzog as a character was always going off the rails, losing his mind, breaking down, and the Big Ideas were a function of what was happening to Herzog psychologically. The fact that the novel was built around an adulterous triangle and the story seemed to be autobiographical didn't do the book any harm. But it was well received and widely read because, first of all, a writer who was good with ideas—and whose characters *had* ideas—certainly had found his own subject in a way that he never had quite done before. Also, there was an audience, a new college-trained readership, prepared to digest the plot and style, with its many high-cultural references, but also with a high gossip quotient. Bellow showed that you could write a novel about an intellectual, reshaping parts of your own life, and reach quite a lot of people.

ILAN STAVANS: It was George Santayana that said, "I don't know what I mean until I say what I say." As you put it, Morris, once you write about the past, that past is no longer the past. It becomes a past that is fixed, deformed, reshaped. It is the same effect produced by family albums. Does one have a data bank of the past that the photographs help recover? Or are the photographs the memories themselves? Language too deforms and conforms. I remember thinking while drafting the chapter on Bobbe Bela: was she really like I'm describing her, or is language leading me in an act of creation of lost memories? This pushed me to wonder: how do we remember? And *what* do we remember? Do we remember in images? Do we remember in sensations? Do we remember with a certain approach to the language, the language of the body? Sometimes, Morris, I see myself moving my hands, making facial gestures, and instantaneously realizing that my father moves the hands and face in the same way.

MORRIS DICKSTEIN: The last scene of *On Borrowed Words* is beautiful—it remains in my mind in a haunting way. It describes an anonymous woman waiting alone in an airport. The reader soon finds out that she has forgotten who she is. It brings the whole question of memory, identity, and language home to us.

ILAN STAVANS: Having been perfectly normal, she no longer knows her name, her address, who she is. . . . It is a scene à la Oliver Sacks about memory and identity that I actually witnessed in Houston. I used it because I wanted to convey the message that memory is a data bank that at any point is capable of malfunctions.

MORRIS DICKSTEIN: Is that why you wrote your autobiography, to make sure the data bank doesn't disappear?

ILAN STAVANS: I'm often overwhelmed by a sense of uncertainty. What if I were to suffer an accident that would erase my memory? What would my children receive from the memory that is my self? But there is another reason, one you'll understand, Morris. Languages are universes in transition: fluid, ever-changing. . . . I have Spanish and English and Hebrew and Yiddish, but my acquaintance with them, my involvement with them is likely to change as I grow older. I wanted to write *On Borrowed Words* just as I was feeling more comfortable with English and less so in Spanish.

MORRIS DICKSTEIN: What you've just described helps me understand what I took to be a thread of sadness in your book. It isn't only the sadness of memoir and its relation to death, or the fear that all memory is perishable, as life is, as we are, or even the recognition that when we die all that's left is the memory of us. The title would feel different, for example, if you said, *IN Borrowed Words*; that, I think, would touch on the theme that I mentioned before. You feel, as I do, that a Jew is always to some degree alienated. A Diaspora Jew is always using other people's languages, trying to possess them, to make them one's own. It strikes me just now, though, that, as I look at the title of your book, I tend to misread it as *On Borrowed Wings,* for if language is like a rented house in which we're never fully at home, it can also be like wings that enable us to fly. Maybe like Icarus, our flight will always eventually be interrupted, and we'll fall to earth, but for a time, at least, we get the impression that we can go to wonderful places, that there are no limits placed on us. In that respect, the sadness of your book also has an exhilarating element to it. The very thing that was so difficult for you, you may in the end have found liberating. Your memoir is sad, in my view at least, because it establishes that that impression of freedom is something of an illusion. To take possession of other people's tongues might feel liberating, but it doesn't allay our sense of being eternal outsiders.

Afterword

The New York Intellectuals were one institution emblematic of what we can call the modern public intellectual. Not quite global, their diasporic, urban status certainly made them cosmopolitan and international in outlook. As Percival Goodman put it, "the Jew is *not* somebody from Judea, not anymore. Two thousand years have made the Jew an international being. That's what he must realize."[1] The New York Intellectuals may have realized that, but only in a kind of provisional way; seeing a stable historical identity as an obstacle, they chose a new, universal one. Since that time, the word *diaspora* has become commonplace, and numerous peoples have come to recognize themselves as international, or at least hyphenated, beings. Feeling freer to choose Jewish and American identities, at least some Jewish intellectuals have become, arguably, less global in outlook. The figure of the public intellectual—never as unitary as some posited—has become more diffuse, scattered among numerous groups and institutions. And the public intellectual mission has also become more complex and decentered, lacking a central ideology. A simple rubric or opposition, such as *socialism* or *capitalism*, will no longer do.

With history and complexity discrediting a pure form of socialism, is there a unifying philosophy for today's public intellectuals? Is such a philosophy even desirable? I would suggest that extreme relativism leaves little for the public intellectual because one system of governance then becomes as good as any other. And the fact is that the global community has been evolving toward a set of widely accepted beliefs that merges liberal democracy with an extended role for human rights. Although still evolving and contested, these core rights include the rule of law; the right to an education; freedom of speech; suffrage; the right to a fair trial; freedom from torture; private ownership; transparency; and access to food, shelter, and health care. Going deeper than the liberal democracy of Francis Fukuyama, these derive from, and extend, classic liberalism, for which the United States was at one time, and despite its many shortcomings, the global exemplar.

In this new world, the role of the United States has turned extremely sour. Fukuyama's thesis about the end of history may not be dead, but it is in critical condition. Perhaps the majority of the world's people do yearn to breathe free, yet the U.S. is no longer the primary role model. It is proving simply impossible to impose our will to force others to be free; the move toward liberal democracy needs to be more, well, democratic, with a deeper conception of rights. Perhaps the U.S. model will be replaced by the European one, with its international outlook, loose confederation of states, and guarantees of basic security to its people. Perhaps some other country, such as India, will step into the breach. Perhaps, frighteningly, the Chinese model, with its fusion of capitalism and authoritarianism, will spread farther. It seems likely, however, that we will simply move to a decentered world of great powers and smaller powers all jostling for power, in some ways a replay of nineteenth-century international politics. What has made this transition period so disjointed and uncertain?

Being the sole superpower appears to have damaged the United States, which has felt zero competition, no reason to become better. The old truism that empires perish from within seems apt here, at least so far as one considers the U.S. an empire. Complaining about the adversary culture of academia, in 1979 Irving Kristol asked, "has there ever been, in all of recorded history, a civilization whose culture was at odds with the values and ideals of that civilization itself?"[2] I would suggest that we have fallen victim to the opposite phenomenon, that earlier periods of self-reflectivity and allowance for dissent made our society stronger, made it flexible, able to bend without breaking. Contrarily, as victors in the cold war, we have encouraged a rigid version of triumphal capitalism for much of the planet. Indeed, because the actors were far from equal, the markets were not as free as our rhetoric pretended. An extreme version of this occurred when Halliburton received huge no-bid contracts to reconstruct Iraq following the war. This is capitalism without competition, capitalism that denies a people the right to help rebuild their own societies, capitalism divorced from the ideals of liberalism. In this new United States, the neoconservatives appear to have achieved a political influence denied most public intellectuals. They have also gravitated away from an original movement motivated by a backlash against the excesses of the New Left, together with a profound skepticism about the ability of government to solve all problems. Today's neocons are far more outward looking. How can a group skeptical of government support a grand global quest to spread American-style democracy, often through military means?

The idea that the neoconservatives are the central actors behind the Iraq invasion is, nevertheless, highly exaggerated. It is Bush and Cheney who made the decision. Susanne Klingenstein shows in the greatly updated and expanded version of her *Shofar* article how the backlash against the neoconservatives has taken on elements of classical antisemitism. During their second great period of influence, the neoconservatives have once again prompted a paleoconservative backlash, most prominently in the person of Pat Buchanan. His complaint on the eve of the first gulf war about "the Israeli Defense Ministry and its amen corner in the United States" draws upon, as Klingenstein shows, a deeper history of antisemitism, one that echoes in current attacks that reverberate in today's harping upon the Jewish supporters of the second gulf war. Similar critiques from the left point to the danger of confusing a small but influential Jewish group with the majority of American Jews, who opposed the current war. Nevertheless, the conspiratorial theory of a small group of Jews plotting world domination lingers in today's rhetoric of both the far right and far left.

Furthermore the neocons' insistence that people everywhere yearn for democracy may very well be right, as the overwhelming public participation in both the Afghan and the Iraq elections indicates. Perhaps the direction of history really is toward liberal democracy. Paradoxically, as the agent making these elections possible, the Bush administration has often neglected processes of democracy and the rule of law. Democracy, that is, must be deep and persistent, a way of life, of dialogue and civic participation, of which elections are only one validating moment. A country must spread them by example and by diplomacy; despite some serious lapses, this is how the United States was able to win the cold war. Classic definitions of conservatism (and neoconservatism) are profoundly pessimistic about human nature. To square this with a belief in the ultimate victory of liberal democracy takes extreme patience and long-term institution building. This is the opposite of the belief that the United States can impose democracy through military conquest and that corporations can be the singular edge of a globalization bringing peace and justice to the planet.

As the founding fathers knew, referring back to the Greek and Roman classics, all institutions become corrupt—a series of scandals, from such corporations as Enron and Worldcom, to the United States government, to the United Nations, continues to prove this. That is why American democracy began with a system of checks and balances so that when one branch of government lapsed the others would correct it. Among some, however, there seems to be a blind faith that a single kind of institution—corporations—is impervious to the need for such mechanisms. If the communists made the fatal mistake of believing that government could control business, making of the two a single institution, what happens when business impinges upon government, when the two become less and less distinct? Corporations, like all other institutions, must stay within the parameters of transparency, democracy, and a system of checks and balances. Neglecting these processes, globalization has been distorted so that the wealthy elite decides, behind closed doors, policies that affect the lives of millions. As Joseph Stiglitz describes his experiences with the International Monetary Fund, "Rarely did I see thoughtful discussions and analyses of the consequences of alternative policies. There was a single prescription. Alternative opinions were not sought. . . . Ideology guided policy prescription and countries were expected to follow the IMF guidelines without debate."[3] If yesterday's public intellectuals believed that a single system of thought—socialism—could solve all human problems, today's and tomorrow's must not make the same mistake with capitalism. Guided by a set of ideals, they must also understand complexity, a multiplicity of voices, and politics as process.

The move toward a global society cannot be stopped. More than economic interests, more than technology, demands this. Given a globalizing economy, instantaneous communication, and the fact that the environment knows no boundaries, the future will be international. Yet globalization also entails a powerful reaction, a growing defense of local ways of life often characterized by nationalist, ethnic, or religious identity. An international jet-setter class deeply involved in business, politics, and research and generally possessing advanced degrees contrasts with a more locally bound way of life. And if left out, ancient ways of life are indeed threatened and will fight back, often peacefully but in a variety of ways. In the eyes of the Arab fundamentalist movement, for instance, the United States has come to simultaneously represent the new globalist threat and the ancient Christian one. However brutal the fundamentalist response—however illegitimate its means and questionable its ends—there is legitimacy to its complaints about the ways the United States has manipulated the Middle East. It is incumbent upon public intellectuals to critique their own societies, and the voice for international economic and social justice has simply been too weak.

The intertwining of social, economic, and nationalist issues may be thorny, but at least public intellectuals have had a great number of years to study them. Yet the problems of the twenty-first century require a sophisticated understanding of another element, one less understood: the complexities of our global ecosystems. Our planet simply cannot survive the philosophy of unlimited growth that drove both capitalism and socialism. Although public intellectuals can draw on a centuries-old tradition of translating and debating economic systems before a broader public, the debate regarding ecosystems and sustainability has been of far shorter duration. Quality of life rather than quantity of goods must drive tomorrow's economic development. Global warming is the most prominent ecological worry, yet far from the only one. There is also desertification, the shrinking and polluting of water supplies, the impoverishment of soil, deforestation, the loss of biodiversity, a growing human population, the dwindling of basic resources, and more. If environmental movements have achieved local success, notably in the United States, they now face an even larger problem in strengthening a system of international treaties and organizations protecting a sustainable environment. Balancing this with the idiosyncrasies of local conditions and with the problem of unintended consequences in a complex, intricately linked global ecosystem adds to the difficulty.

It will be incumbent upon public intellectuals to translate technical knowledge into successful social programs globally, locally, and at levels between. The National Research Council states in *Our Common Journey*, "a successful transition toward sustainability is possible over the next two generations" even "without miraculous technologies or drastic transformations of human societies."[4] Clearly we are not making this transition, as the denial of the scientific consensus behind global warming in the United States demonstrates, as does the movement toward a car-based society with a dense highway system in China.

Although socialism, Keynesianism, and free market orthodoxy all assume continuing economic growth, that assumption is no longer valid, at least as relates to harvesting of biomass and the primary production of solar energy that it represents. Certainly, qualitative economic development is necessary, but endless quantitative growth must become a thing of the past.

Tomorrow's public intellectuals must be able to think on global, local, regional, and national scales all at once, must be able to consider economic, environmental, and governmental factors simultaneously. To help guide such a complex world, they must communicate, between each other and to the wider public from a vast array of specialties. A good guideline would be the opposite of what much of television and talk radio has become—a breaking down into hostile camps that care more about obliterating their opponent than about any kind of search for truth or a just society. Much of today's public discourse might be better referred to as the realm of public demagogues than public intellectuals.

The university, meanwhile, has become an isolated institution containing the largely lifeless remnants of an earlier tradition of dissent. In the decades since the 1960s, as the country has turned rightward, neo-Marxist social critique persists in academia. Much of this has been merely professed radicalism or paper radicalism, compartmentalized and domesticated by the search for academic status. So in 1987 Russell Jacoby described the university as an institution that "neutralizes the freedom it guarantees,"[5] while in a book published fourteen years later, the far more conservative Richard Posner makes a similar critique: "Today . . . the typical public intellectual is a safe specialist, which is not the type of person well suited to play [the role of] critical commentator."[6] While a stream of post-Marxist work continues to circulate throughout the university, this exists only among a small, intellectually inbred group employing esoteric and alienating language, a recipe that has effectively discouraged actual political action.

Both Jacoby and Posner describe a current atmosphere of public intellectual failure, not only regarding action but also analysis. Both blame the isolation of the academy. They fail to discuss, however, how this world is increasingly threatened as the privileges of tenure give way to armies of underpaid teaching assistants, adjunct instructors, and post-docs, all designed to give the university maximum quantitative output at minimum cost. The role of intellectuals in a university system that once seemed a safe haven is now threatened with contraction and perhaps extinction. The comfortable university into which American Jewish intellectuals integrated may be a thing of the past. Technical changes and corporate interests now overshadow the old ideal of the liberal arts. A liberal society marked by a balance between capitalism and state institutions is being swept aside, and with it the privileged role of the university.

If the university is no longer the safe, isolated home for the free play of intellectuals, in our increasingly complex and dangerous world good public intellectuals may be more necessary than ever. The new millenium is off to a shaky start, with 9/11 only the most obvious alarm. Terrorism, nuclear proliferation, the breakdown of peace initiatives, a widening gap between rich and poor, a burgeoning environmental crisis, all indicate the need for stronger analysis and articulation regarding global issues. Intellectuals today face a situation characterized by two opposite tendencies: a reality of fragmentation and a desperate need for integration. The fragmentation results from the proliferation of a vast array of specialties and subspecialties that use mutually unintelligible technical languages. Integration remains, if at all, as a lost ideal barely uttered, a unity of knowledge that seems simply impossible, that needs to go beyond the limited economic connections of today's globalization to include human rights, workers' rights, deep democracy, and environmental integrity. The cross-currents, the ways in which issues reach out and affect each other with increasing speed and scope, are staggering. Coping with such a world requires highly trained technical people who adopt complex language not as an ostentatious display of learning but out of need. It also requires generalists with broad visions who can untangle interconnected strands of knowledge. Yet high-quality analysis is useless unless it influences actual policies by actual politicians. And actual politicians always arrive encumbered with their own backgrounds, problems, and agendas. To influence such an international babble requires skilled rhetoricians who are committed to democracy and social opportunity and are able to convey these complexities to larger publics. As much as possible, it requires individuals capable of balancing multiple levels of analysis and discourse. This is the current challenge for public intellectuals, who must be postdiasporic and post-nation-state. One wonders if those intellectuals forced out of the university system will succumb to passivity and quietude or will return to the public arena with a sharpened edge. If the latter, perhaps there will be a new burgeoning of the public intellectual, not as aloof social commentator with little real influence but reviving and extending the best traditions of the New York Intellectual.

Ethan Goffman
Rockville, Maryland
August 2007

Notes

1.   Percival Goodman, "The Architect from New York," in *Creators and Disturbers: Reminiscences by Jewish Intellectuals of New York*, ed. Bernard Rosenberg and Ernest Goldstein, pp. 311–329 (New York: Columbia University Press, 1982), p. 322.

2.   Irving Kristol, "The Adversary Culture of Intellectuals," in *Reflections of a Neoconservative: Looking Back, Looking Ahead*, pp. 27–42 (New York: Basic Books, 1983), p. 27.

3.   Joseph E. Stiglitz, *Globalization and Its Discontents* (New York: W.W. Norton, 2002), p. xiv.

4.   National Research Council, *Our Common Journey: A Transition toward Sustainability* (1999; repr., Washington: National Capital Press, 2002), p. 160.

5.   Russell Jacoby, *The Last Intellectuals: American Culture in the Age of Academe* (New York: Basic Books, 1987), p. 190.

6.   Richard Posner, *Public Intellectuals: A Study of Decline* (Cambridge: Harvard University Press, 2001), p. 5.

Questions for Discussion

What distinguishes a public intellectual from other kinds of intellectuals?

What distinguishes a public intellectual from a journalist or pundit?

Who are some of today's public intellectuals? Who are merely television and/or radio personalities? What distinguishes the two groups?

What are some different kinds of public intellectuals? What social and political functions do they perform?

Why were the New York Intellectuals a predominantly Jewish group? Is it something inherent in the Jewish religion or traditions? How much is it due to the Jewish minority position? What other factors might play a role?

What were the primary reasons that the New York Intellectuals began as communists and socialists? What caused them to move away from these positions?

Traditionally most public intellectuals have been associated with leftist and/or liberal positions. Although there are currently some influential conservative public intellectuals, the majority still lean toward the left. Why do you think this is so?

Has the role of the New York Intellectuals in American life been exaggerated? Have other intellectuals been overlooked? Who and why?

Are there specific ethnic or religious groups with a special role as public intellectuals today? Why or why not?

How did the role of public intellectuals change throughout the twentieth century? Do you see/foresee a new role as the twenty-first century unfolds? What characterizes this role?

Bibliography

Memoirs

Abel, Lionel. *The Intellectual Follies: A Memoir of the Literary Venture in New York and Paris.* New York: W.W. Norton, 1984.

Barrett, William. *The Truants: Adventures among the Intellectuals.* New York: Doubleday, 1983.

Hook, Sidney. *Out of Step: An Unquiet Life in the Twentieth Century.* New York: Harper and Row, 1987.

Howe, Irving. *A Margin of Hope: An Intellectual Autobiography.* San Diego: Harcourt, 1982.

Kazin, Alfred. *A Walker in the City.* San Diego: Harcourt, 1969.

Phillips, William. *A Partisan View: Five Decades of the Literary Life.* New York: Henry Holt, 1991.

Podhoretz, Norman. *Making It.* New York: Random House, 1967.

Rosenberg, Bernard, and Ernest Goldstein, eds. *Reminiscences by Jewish Intellectuals of New York.* New York: Columbia University Press, 1982.

Trilling, Diana. *The Beginning of the Journey: The Marriage of Diana and Lionel Trilling.* San Diego: Harcourt, 1993.

Essays by the New York Intellectuals

Howe, Irving. *Selected Writings, 1950–1990.* New York: Harcourt, Brace, Jovanovich, 1990.

———. *World of Our Fathers.* San Diego: Harcourt, 1989.

Kristol, Irving. *Neoconservatism: The Autobiography of an Idea.* Chicago: Ivan R. Dee, 1999.

Macdonald, Dwight. *Memoirs of a Revolutionist: Essays in Political Criticism.* New York: Farrar, Straus & Cudahy, 1957.

Sontag, Susan. *Against Interpretation and Other Essays.* New York: Farrar, Strauss & Giroux, 1966.

Trilling, Lionel. *The Liberal Imagination: Essays on Literature and Society.* New York: Viking, 1950.

———. *The Moral Obligation to be Intelligent: Selected Essays.* New York: Farrar, Straus & Giroux, 2000.

Standard Histories

Bloom, Alexander. *Prodigal Sons*. New York: Oxford University Press, 1986.

Cooney, Terry. *The Rise of the New York Intellectual: Partisan Review and its Circle*. Madison: University of Wisconsin Press, 1986.

Dickstein, Morris. *Double Agent: The Critic And Society*. New York: Oxford University Press, 1992.

———. "The New York Intellectuals: Some Personal History." *Dissent*, Vol. 44, Issue 2, p. 83, Spring 1997.

Dorman, Joseph. *Arguing the World: The New York Intellectuals*. New York: Free Press, 1999.

Gilbert, James. *Writers and Partisans*. New York: Columbia University Press, 1993.

Jacoby, Russell. *The Last Intellectuals: American Culture in the Age of Academe*. New York: Basic Books, 2000.

Jumonville, Neil. *The New York Intellectuals in Postwar America*. Berkeley: University of California Press, 1990.

Klingenstein, Susanne. *Enlarging America: The Cultural Work of Jewish Literary Scholars, 1940–1990*. Syracuse: Syracuse University Press, 1998.

———. *Jews in the American Academy, 1900–1940: The Dynamics of Intellectual Assimilation*. Syracuse: Syracuse University Press, 1998.

McCarthy, Mary. *Intellectual Memoirs*. San Diego: Harcourt Trade, 1992.

PBS. *Arguing the World: The New York Intellectuals*, film and website. http://www .pbs.org/arguing/.

Posner, Richard. *Public Intellectuals: A Study of Decline*. Cambridge: Harvard University Press, 2002.

Rodden, John. *Irving Howe And The Critics: Celebrations and Attacks*. Lincoln: University of Nebraska Press, 2005.

———. *Lionel Trilling And The Critics*. Lincoln: University of Nebraska Press, 1999.

Sokol, Neal. *Ilan Stavans: Eight Conversations*. Madison: University of Wisconsin Press, 2004.

Teres, Harvey. *Renewing the Left: Politics, Imagination, and the New York Intellectuals*. New York: Oxford University Press, 1996.

Wald, Alan. *New York Intellectuals: The Rise and Fall of the Anti-Stalinist Left from the 1930s to the 1980s*. Chapel Hill: University of North Carolina Press, 1987.

Beyond

Appiah, Kwame Anthony. *Cosmopolitanism: Ethics in a World of Strangers*. New York: W.W. Norton, 2006.

Bloom, Allan. *The Closing of the American Mind.* New York: Simon & Schuster, 1987.

Du Bois, W.E.B. *The Souls of Black Folks.* Chicago: A.C. McClurg, 1903.

Friedan, Betty. *The Feminine Mystique.* New York: W.W. Norton, 1974.

Fukuyama, Francis. *The End of History and the Last Man.* New York: Simon & Schuster, 1992.

Gates, Henry Louis, Jr., *Loose Canons: Notes on the Culture Wars.* New York: Oxford University Press, 1992.

Glazer, Nathan, and Daniel Patrick Moynihan. *Beyond the Melting Pot: The Negroes, Puerto Ricans, Jews, Italians, and Irish of New York City.* Boston: MIT Press, 1970.

Rodriguez, Richard. *Hunger of Memory: The Education of Richard Rodriguez.* Boston: David R. Godine, 1982.

Said, Edward. *Orientalism.* New York: Routledge, 1979.

———. *Representations of the Intellectual.* New York: Knopf, 1994.

Stavans, Ilan. *The Hispanic Condition: The Power of a People.* New York: Harper-Trade, 2001.

Walker, Alice. *In Search of Our Mothers' Gardens: Womanist Prose.* New York: Harcourt Brace Jovanovich, 1983.

West, Cornel. *Race Matters.* New York: Knopf, 1993.

Index

Davis, Angela, 200
Davis, Miles, 208
Day, Dorothy, 102
Death of a Salesman (Miller), 315
Debray, Régis, 238
deconstruction, 195, 196
Decter, Midge, 21, 123
Democracy Matters (C. West), 205–206
Democratic Socialist Organizing Committee (DSOC), 140n57
Derrida, Jacques, 55, 68, 146, 149n8, 196
Dewey, John, 91, 97, 178
diaspora, polarities imposed by, 79
Diawara, Manthia, 264
Dickstein, Morris, 17, 55, 133, 190;
Double Agent: The Critic and Society, 325; *Gates of Eden*, 323
Dirie, Waris, 259
Disraeli, Benjamin, 48
Dissent, 6, 28–29, 72, 120n48, 122;
dropping of its masthead motto
("a socialist quarterly"), 132
Dorkenoo, Efua, 262, 264, 265
Dorman, Joseph, 125, 176
Dostoevsky, Fyodor, 41
Douglass, Frederick, 200, 201
Dowd, Maureen, 299
Dreiser, Theodore, 60
Drury, Shadia B., 305n68, 307n84
Du Bois, W.E.B., 2, 9, 167, 172–174, 200, 202
Duke, David, 295
Dupee, Fred, 118n39, 221
Duplessis, Rachel, 47
Dworkin, Andrea, 244
Dynamics of African Feminism, The (Arndt), 263
Dyson, Michael Eric, 201, 208

Eastman, Max, 230
Eddy, Fanny Ann, 264
Edward Said and the Politics of the Limit (Marrouchi), 220

Eldridge Street Synagogue, 312
"Elevation and Education of Our People, The" (Harper), 170
Elfriede Jelinek in the Gender Wars (Meyer), 266
Eliot, T. S., 4, 64, 136n9, 280; *After Strange Gods*, 282; "The Wasteland," 63–64
Ellington, Duke, 208
Ellison, Ralph, 123, 196, 202
Emecheta, Buchi, 264
Emerson, Ralph Waldo, 2, 167, 168–169, 206
Encounter, 29, 231
Enzensberger, Hans Magnus, 244
Epstein, Jason, 54
Epstein, Joseph, 123, 125
ethnic studies, 208

Fadiman, Clifton, 190n2
Fanon, Franz, 236, 237
Fast, Howard, 156
Favazza, Armando R., 269n20
Feffer, Itzhik, 35–36, 37
Feith, Douglas J., 287, 291–292, 298
Female Circumcision: Multicultural Perspectives (ed. Abusharaf), 258
Female Circumcision and the Politics of Knowledge (ed. Nnaemeka), 258
female genital mutilation (FGM), 258, 259, 269n21; African films against FGM, 259; criticism of Walker and Jelinek for speaking out against FGM, 246; as a custom in Africa and Egypt, 252; etiology of the term, 271n74; German Bundestag ruling on, 261; in Jelinek's *The Piano Teacher*, 248–249, 250–256; long-term effects of, 269n21; role of homophobia in, 263–264; use of the term in the international community, 272n75; Walker on, 256–260
"Female Genital Mutilation and Obstetric Outcome: WHO Collaborative